PENGUIN BOO

JOHN MAJOR

Penny Junor's previous books have included well-received biographies of Margaret Thatcher, Richard Burton and both the Prince and Princess of Wales. She began her career as a journalist, writing regularly for a number of national newspapers and magazines, including for a time a column in *Private Eye*. For the last fifteen years she has appeared regularly on television, presenting, among others, Channel 4's consumer programme *4 What It's Worth* (1982–9) and BBC2's *The Travel Show*.

Penny Junor is married to author James Leith and they have four children.

To Mummy

Happy Birthday

Love from

Richard

PENNY JUNOR

JOHN MAJOR

FROM BRIXTON
TO DOWNING STREET

PENGUIN BOOKS

PENGUIN BOOKS

Published by the Penguin Group
Penguin Books Ltd, 27 Wrights Lane, London w8 5tz, England
Penguin Books USA Inc., 375 Hudson Street, New York, New York 10014, USA
Penguin Books Australia Ltd, Ringwood, Victoria, Australia
Penguin Books Canada Ltd, 10 Alcorn Avenue, Toronto, Ontario, Canada m4v 3b2
Penguin Books (NZ) Ltd, 182–190 Wairau Road, Auckland 10, New Zealand

Penguin Books Ltd, Registered Offices: Harmondsworth, Middlesex, England

First published, under the title *The Major Enigma*, by Michael Joseph 1993
Published, with revisions, under the present title in Penguin Books 1996
1 3 5 7 9 10 8 6 4 2

Printed in England by Clays Ltd, St Ives plc

For the HW

CONTENTS

Illustrations ix
Acknowledgements xi
Author's Note xii
Preface 1
1. Longfellow Road 7
2. Brixton 22
3. Banking and Local Government 42
4. Marriage, Family and the Hunt for a Seat 61
5. Huntingdon 80
6. Early Years in Parliament 96
7. Senior Whip and Social Security 117
8. Chief Secretary 133
9. Foreign Secretary 156
10. Chancellor 175
11. Leadership Contest 192
12. Prime Minister 208
13. Election 233
14. Black Wednesday 253
15. Autumn of Problems 267
16. Paying the Price 285
Epilogue 299
Bibliography 315
Index 317

ILLUSTRATIONS

1. John Major aged five months (*Pat Dessoy*).
2. John Major aged five years (*Pat Dessoy*).
3. The Rutlish Boys school cricket team (*Number Ten Downing Street*).
4. His parents, Tom and Gwen (*Terry Major-Ball*).
5. John and Norma and the children at a WRVS Luncheon Club (*Number Ten Downing Street*).
6. The Majors with President and Mrs Bush in the presidential launch (*The White House*).
7. Prospective candidate in St Pancras North with his agent, Sue Winter (*Hulton Deutsch*).
8. Minister for Social Security (*Press Association*).
9. Chancellor of the Exchequer on Budget day (*Syndication International*).
10. Meeting President Gorbachev in Moscow (*Hulton Deutsch*).
11. An audience with King Fahd in Saudi Arabia (*Hulton Deutsch*).
12. Addressing the troops in the Gulf (*Hulton Deutsch*).
13. On the Great Wall of China (*Hulton Deutsch*).
14. A charity cricket match in Zimbabwe (*Hulton Deutsch*).
15. Hosting the G7 Economic Summit (*Press Association*).
16. With Margaret and Denis Thatcher (*Press Association*).
17. The launch of the Conservative manifesto (*Press Association*).
18. The famous soapbox (*Press Association*).
19. At Massey Ferguson Tractors (*Press Association*).
20. The Edinburgh Council, with Jacques Delors (*Camera Press*).
21. Welcoming Chancellor Kohl to the Birmingham Summit (*Press Association*).

22. Putting on a brave face at the Party Conference in Brighton (*Camera Press*).

23. With Sir Ranulph Fiennes and Dr Michael Stroud.

24. On board the Queen's Flight on the way to Rome (*Eve Arnold/Magnum Photos*).

25. With Sarah Hogg and Alex Allan at Number Ten (*Eve Arnold/Magnum Photos*).

26. Preparing for Prime Minister's Question Time (*Eve Arnold/Magnum Photos*).

27. A visit to the Mission Hi-Fi factory in Huntingdon (*Eve Arnold/Magnum Photos*).

28. Seated at the Cabinet table with John Wakeham (*Eve Arnold/Magnum Photos*).

29. John and Norma (*Eve Arnold/Magnum Photos*).

Copyright holders are indicated in italics.

ACKNOWLEDGEMENTS

ANY biography is dependent upon the people who contribute to it, and this one is entirely made by the dozens of people who very generously gave up their time to talk to me about John Major, including the Prime Minister himself. It has been a fascinating fourteen months, I have met some very interesting people and I am enormously grateful to them all.

I would also like to thank Jane Turnbull, my agent, without whom I might still be languishing over an unwritten novel, and Susan Watt at Michael Joseph. Working with her and everone else at Michael Joseph on this book has been a real pleasure and I look forward to the next. I must also thank Alexander Stilwell for some expert editing and for finding so many good photographs. My thanks also to Terry Major-Ball and Pat Dessoy for the early family photographs of their brother; and to Norma for others.

And last, but by no means least, many many thanks to everyone at Number Ten who has been involved in one way or another. I am extremely grateful for all their time and help.

AUTHOR'S NOTE

THIS is not a political critique; it is the story of John Major's life and an attempt to understand the man who has so divided opinion in Britain in the last five years. By and large, those people who have met the Prime Minister, come away impressed. Those who haven't tend to sneer. He looks a nice enough man, they say, but not up to the job. Most political pundits writing in national newspapers fall into the latter category, and their influence over public opinion has been considerable.

The account of particular crises which I detail in the latter half of the book is John Major's account of events. Others may disagree with his interpretation or memory, but it stands here as just that, his interpretation and memory, and I make no apology for allowing him a fair hearing.

April 1996

PREFACE

WHEN John Major was about nine years old he came second in an English exam. Thrilled, he came running home to the small suburban bungalow where the family lived, and told his father.

'I've done it,' he said. 'I've come second in the English exam. I knew I could do it.'

His father was sitting with a friend of the family named Aunty Flo. He listened to his excited son – he didn't hug him or congratulate him. He said two things which John has never forgotten.

'If you had worked a bit harder, you would have come first.' His second piece of advice was, 'Never tell people what you've done. It's much more effective. Never boast. Let others see what you've done and let them comment upon it. It cheapens you if you bang your chest and say "I have done it."'

The result was a little boy who grew up keeping things to himself, who was modest and restrained and well-mannered, but who nursed a fierce ambition to come first.

Alas, the old man wasn't alive to see his youngest son walk into Number Ten Downing Street as Prime Minister, thirty-eight years later. He would have been proud of him. And proud not just because of his achievement but because he had remained true to his principles. He is probably the most courteous man in the House of Commons. He has not climbed up on the backs of others. He has a high and rare regard for the truth. And he cares about making the world a better place.

But because he still can't bring himself to bang his chest, no one knows him. He is in many ways as much of an enigma today as he was when he stepped into Mrs Thatcher's shoes in November 1990, and yet there can hardly be a man, woman or child living in this country who would fail to recognize him. Most have strong views about him – views that come from newspapers written by people who also don't know him. One, who wrote authoritatively about his behaviour on Black Wednesday (wobbling in a nervous way – a charge he bitterly resents), also said he dyed his hair. 'Are they mad?' said the Prime Minister when he read it. 'If I was going to dye my hair would I really dye it this colour?'

Norma, who has been married to him for twenty-six years, is not even certain she knows him so much better than anybody else. 'I know what he's like to live with and what he is like as a husband and a father, and some of what his work entails, but I'm not sure that I entirely understand what makes him tick.'

This is no simple tale of a boy made good; although by any standards moving from a Brixton slum, where the family lived after their fortunes plummeted in 1955, to the best address in the land, is a remarkable achievement. To have done it with no real education, no influence and no money is extraordinary; and to have done it within the Conservative Party is little short of miraculous.

He is not the first person to have made it from humble beginnings to the top within the Tory Party. Ted Heath was a grammar-school boy. Mrs Thatcher was a grocer's daughter, but the difference is that they both shone at school and they both went on to university – they were both high achievers. John Major wasn't. He left school as soon as he was legally able, he hadn't even taken O levels. He had hated school and did nothing but play cricket. He flitted from job to job. He even spent a period on the dole.

Yet many of the high-flying Double First brains in Whitehall say John Major has a Rolls-Royce mind, a grasp of detail second to none and negotiating skills of quite extraordinary brilliance.

How did he do it? How did this Brixton boy come to be adopted as parliamentary candidate by the safest shire seat in the country, chosen out of more than two hundred applicants, including some of the most respected names in the Tory Party? How did he catch Mrs Thatcher's eye over the thrusting, brilliant and ambitious bunch he came into the House with, and become Prime Minister after just three years and five months in the Cabinet – the youngest this century? And how did he win an election in April 1992 when everyone said it was impossible? And how, having been one of the most unpopular Prime Ministers for most of the last five years, did he manage to confound his critics, challenge his party to 'put up or shut up', and romp home in a leadership election with a greater share of the votes than any leader of any party has had at any time?

For someone whose position has so often been described as tenuous, he has survived longer than most of his post-war predecessors. It has not been an easy life, however.

Until he took on the critics within the Conservative Party in July 1995 and was able to establish his authority once and for all, his life was a nightmare. No Prime Minister can have lived through anything like it. The catastrophes came fast and furiously and the personal attacks were remorseless. Stuck with the 'grey' label, given him originally as a joke because of the colour of his hair by his friend Robert Atkins, he was accused of being weak, of having no ideas, no vision, no direction, of being obsessed by what the newspapers wrote about him and afraid to sack friends from his Cabinet. And while Britain has remained gripped in the teeth of recession, with sky-high unemployment, a stagnant house market, an urban under-class and runaway expenditure, he has been obsessed by Europe and the length of queues – or so the newspapers would have us believe.

I first met John Major at Chequers, four days after Black Wednesday in September 1992. For someone who had been on the verge of nervous collapse, as some of the papers reported, he had made an excellent recovery. He looked and behaved that Sunday like a man whose only concern was to give the fifty or so guests he had invited to Chequers a good time. Any ordinary man would have cancelled the lunch. Everyone there had expected a call from Number Ten. This was not the time for social niceties. It had been a week of crisis, the most traumatic of his political career, and it was not yet over. That Sunday was the day of the French referendum. A No vote could have entirely scuppered the Maastricht Treaty, on which he had staked his parliamentary reputation. It is a measure of the man that he didn't disappoint his guests – that he didn't seize the opportunity to rest, or catch up on some of the work that had been piling up while his attention was on sterling. This was not the action of a man who couldn't cope, who was weak and reactive and who panicked under stress.

It was a mixed bunch – some famous, some not. The guest he chose to have on his left-hand side at lunch was not. She was no grand or glamorous figure, no one who would give great fortunes to the Tory Party, or be influential or useful in any way. It was

Gladys Simpson, the elderly widow of a man he had worked closely with on Lambeth Borough Council in the late 1960s.

He and Norma were so relaxed and friendly that we very soon forgot our apprehension. Forgot the security post at the gate, and the abundance of policemen in bullet-proof vests with automatic rifles under their arms. We forgot that this was the great Chequers of fame, and John Major the Prime Minister. And had he not joked about the irony of having found himself in church that morning singing a hymn to the tune of the German national anthem, we would have forgotten Black Wednesday too.

He is a much bigger man than you imagine, over six feet tall, and broad, and the first thing that strikes you is the handshake. His handshake is real, up and down, not a means of propelling you rapidly to the other side of the room, a technique that both Lady Thatcher and Douglas Hurd use to perfection. The smile is very winning, and when he talks to you it's a conversation not a monologue, and he looks at you, not over your shoulder to see who else is in the room, or who might be more interesting. His voice may betray his origins, but his manners put many an aristocrat to shame.

He is much more humorous than you might expect. Scenes of him wrangling with his opposite number in the House of Commons twice a week during Question Time, and snippets of formal speeches on the news, give the wrong impression. He is an engaging character, with no pretensions, no pomposity and no arrogance.

During the writing of this book I saw him repeatedly throughout much of 1993, and I went back to see him again recently to bring his story up to date for this paperback edition. By this time he had forced and won the leadership election and was a very different man from the one I had seen before: more confident, more relaxed and looked very much more in command. He admits he is a different man. Having lived through five cycles he has seen everything before and can see the pitfalls before he trips headlong into them. He now knows how the system works, he says, knows who he can and cannot trust, and can spot what might happen six months down the road in a way he couldn't at the beginning.

Don't forget how much of a novice I was when I first came here. I had been Foreign Secretary for three months, Chancellor for a year, before that two years as Chief Secretary, one year as Minister of State, one year as a parliamentary secretary, two years as a whip and before that I was a backbencher. Nobody has moved faster from the back benches to be Prime Minister, and except for Chief Secretary, I'd only had each job for twelve months. That is a very sharp learning curve. From time to time it felt like climbing up the north face of the Eiger with hob-nailed boots. And all the time you're living on your wits, you're learning from experience. For the first time in my political career I've got an experience advantage.

If I'd had five more years before I became Prime Minister I dare say I would have handled some things differently. I am sure I would have spotted the dangers down the road. I would have been more streetwise.

This new-found confidence, however, has not made any difference to his workload. Most nights he is busy on boxes until at least 1 o'clock in the morning and he is up again at 6.30. He has a cup of tea in bed, when he reads the newspapers or starts on his boxes all over again, and his first meeting of the day is often over breakfast – of a poached egg on white toast.

He works a seventeen- or eighteen-hour day almost every day of the year, makes decisions that can affect the lives of millions and takes ultimate responsibility for anything done in Government; and while the captains of industry, living with a fraction of the pressure, take home salaries approaching £1,000,000 a year, John Major gets £82,003.

As a child it would have been riches beyond his wildest dreams, but money has never been the thing that motivated John Major. His ambitions were more radical.

Smart writers have sneered at him for being ordinary, saying that what is needed in a leader is somebody extraordinary. They are right, the Prime Minister does need to be extraordinary. The office is quite unlike any other job in the land. It takes a character of enormous strength to prevent the power, the pressure, the lack of privacy, and the constant attentions of the media destroying them. Prime Ministers live life at one remove from reality. If they sneeze, three people are on hand to offer them a tissue. Every hour of their day is planned and written out with briefing notes, every journey effortless, every need taken care of, every request answered in triplicate. Ted Heath became arrogant and insensitive, Margaret Thatcher became a bully and thought she could ignore everyone, including her own Cabinet. Despite their roots, both entirely lost touch with ordinary people. Five years on John Major has lost none of his humour, his courtesy, nor his desire to take his Cabinet with him. In his taste and his habits he has remained steadfastly ordinary. But John Major is no ordinary man. This is his story – it is as extraordinary as he is.

1

LONGFELLOW ROAD

JOHN MAJOR's earliest memory of his father is very vague, like much of his childhood. He remembers being in the garden at the front of the family bungalow in Worcester Park, when his father, who must have been nearly seventy by then, came home from delivering garden ornaments.

> I think he had been to Gamages. He was wearing an old jacket and a Fair Isle sweater, and he was carrying a great hand of bananas. He always used to bring something back when he had been out.

Tom Major cut a dashing figure in Worcester Park. He had spent nearly thirty years of his life as an actor, and although he had given up the stage and gone into business when his children were born, he had lost none of his theatricality. He was still a grand and stylish Edwardian actor, over six feet tall, athletic in build and expansive in his gestures. Larger than life – 'A breed,' as his daughter, Pat, says, 'that no longer exists today.'

He was born in May 1879 with the surname Ball – Abraham Thomas Ball. Major was a name which he adopted for the stage, when he took up variety in 1901 at the age of twenty-two, and throughout his professional career he was known as Tom Major. Off-stage, he was officially Tom Major-Ball, but seldom used the Ball. His elder son, Terry, is officially Terry Major-Ball, but John was named plain John Major. That is the name on his birth certificate; it is also the name he was registered under at primary school. The only time he has ever been called Major-Ball was at grammar school, where his parents registered him under the double-barrelled name, which he found profoundly upsetting.

Tom spent most of his childhood in America; his own father had emigrated from the Midlands to work in the foundries making rails for the railways going west. They lived in the foothills of the Allegheny Mountains in Pennsylvania. It was the 1880s, an exciting time for a small boy. He went barefoot to school, and saw real cowboys gallop over the dusty plains. He dug genuine Indian arrow heads out of the bark of the trees, where they had been embedded not so very long ago, and saw legends like Chief Sitting Bull at the end of his life. It was a childhood that was to provide a wealth of stories for his own children as they sat on his knee or the arm of his chair by the fireside in Worcester Park; and Tom Major-Ball was a master of the art of storytelling. He would talk or he would sing and they would listen, enraptured, to wild and wonderful tales, no doubt richly embroidered for his audience.

By the age of ten Pat was an expert on the Wild West. She had read every book she could find on the subject and was just itching to get her hands on a Colt 45. When her father's friend, Uncle Mac, a sergeant-major in the military police, came to the house and left a Colt 45 on the bed with his coat, the temptation was more than she could bear. She picked it up and took aim, and when Tom and Mac appeared she was holding the gun to her little brother's head, looking puzzled. She couldn't understand why it wouldn't fire. There were no safety catches in the books.

Tom's family had come back to England shortly before the turn of the century and settled in Walsall, near Birmingham. He then went into the building trade for a couple of years, before running off, much against his father's wishes, to join a circus. His red clown's costume, with long feet, a bald head and ginger wig, was found in the roof space in the bungalow in Worcester Park years later by the present owners, when they had the building re-roofed in 1979.

His circus life was short-lived. By 1902 he was in variety, the medium he enjoyed most – singing, dancing, performing conjuring tricks and doing comic sketches – and it was there he met his first wife, Kitty Drum. She was the leading lady in the first show he joined. When the show closed he and Kitty, a very beautiful woman by all accounts, formed a double act together and later, in 1910, married. They made their home near Bromsgrove, but spent many of their years together on the road, working the theatres and music halls.

During the First World War, which Tom took no part in because of a weak heart, diagnosed when he was a teenager, they moved to a bungalow near Whitchurch in Shropshire, where he proved to be an excellent shot, so good that local landowners invited him to shoot their land. He would often tell stories about poachers and laugh at people who went shooting rabbits with a shotgun, which was like taking a mallet to crack a nut.

In 1921 he and Kitty became founder members of the Variety Artists Benevolent Fund. They were never big stars, but they were well-known and well-respected in the business. Tom Major had his own company of artists and dancers by this time, a thoroughly professional and respectable troupe which he ran with a rod of iron, and to which in 1921, sixteen-year-old Gwendoline Coates, who was to be his second wife, came to audition as a dancer.

Gwen was an intelligent grammar school girl, for whom her father had high hopes, but her heart was set on becoming a dancer. Her mother supported her ambitions, and unknown to her father, stole her out of the house one day to attend an audition for Tom Major's show. To his dying day her father never knew the truth, he always believed she had run away of her own accord.

Tom took her on, and because of her age, he and Kitty all but fostered the child, as was the custom with minors on the stage in those days. Tom and Kitty had never had children of their own, and Gwen virtually became one of the family.

She also turned out to be an exceptionally talented speciality dancer. She was spirited and vivacious, slim, small and dark with long hair, and for some time did a double act on stage with a large buxom lass called Gladys. Their act was called Glade and Glen, and involved Gladys, dressed somewhat like a caveman, swinging Gwen around by her hair. It came to an abrupt end, however, the day Gwen decided to have her hair cut in the new fashionable bob. She arrived for the evening's performance with no hair to swing, an irate manager in the shape of Tom Major, and an act that needed to be very quickly re-thought.

Tom and Kitty toured all over the country with their shows. There was scarcely a theatre in the whole of the British Isles they had not played in. They went to the United States and South America too, and became embroiled in a local uprising, which provided more fanciful tales for Tom's declining years.

But in 1927 tragedy struck. Kitty was involved in a terrible accident on stage when part of the scenery collapsed on top of her.

She was left severely injured and never recovered. A year later she was dead. Tom was overcome with grief, and had little heart for work now that their double act was at an end. Gwen was there to help pick up the pieces. She had probably always loved Tom from afar. He was twenty-seven years older than she was, a grand figure, a man of authority and stature, a hero, and he remained as much until the day he died. As Pat says, right to the end 'she ran after him as though he was the next thing to God'.

A year after Kitty's death, Gwen and Tom were married, and immediately began a family, although sadly their first child, a boy named Thomas Ashton, died at birth. It was a new beginning in every sense of the word. They gave up the theatre, settled down at number 260 Longfellow Road in Worcester Park, and went into business making garden ornaments. All that remained of their past life were theatrical books, piles of sheet music, and their props which lived in a large trunk in the bathroom. The children would dip into it and try on Tom's collapsible top hat and other bits and pieces.

Gwen was quite undomesticated when she married Tom. She was twenty-three and, having left home at sixteen and spent the intervening years living either with Tom and Kitty or in theatrical digs, she had never had to look after herself at all. She hated housework and couldn't cook. Tom would say that when he married her she was the only woman he knew who could burn water.

Tom taught her to cook, and she became very good, particularly at making pastry, which she always did by feel, never measuring anything. In fact she could do just about anything she put her mind to, and she settled into her new role with enthusiasm. But she was no conventional housewife, and quite unlike anyone the suburban inhabitants of Longfellow Road had encountered before. She gave dancing classes in the front room, did aerobics in the garden, swung Indian clubs on the lawn, and ran the ornament business on a par with her husband, taking charge of the men he employed and getting stuck into the sand and cement with the best of them.

She was very much her own woman, she knew her own mind and was quite prepared to speak it. She was broad-minded, well-travelled, well-read and had seen a lot of life during her years in the theatre. She had no time for the narrow-minded social niceties of her neighbours, and her Midlands candour shocked them. Her habit, for instance, of letting the milkman come into the kitchen to take his money at the end of the week, was beyond the pale.

But then Tom must have been quite a novelty too – a colourful theatrical raconteur in a street peopled with butchers, builders, plumbers, post office workers and civil servants. He was educated and cultured, and his horizons were broader than most. He was also an astute businessman. The 1930s were a period of rapid growth in the suburbs around London, particularly in neighbouring Stoneleigh and Ewell, and new houses with new gardens needed furnishings. Major's Garden Ornaments provided them, and the little business which he had started in the back garden grew quickly and was soon employing a work force.

It was hard work, both the making and the selling. Tom didn't drive because his eyesight was too poor, but he and his driver would set off with his van laden down with ornaments and not come home until they had sold the lot. Sometimes he would be away for days at a time, but he always telephoned Gwen at the same time every night for a chat – and always came home with a gift of some sort for the family. She played an equal part in the running of the business, she gave orders to the men if Tom was not around, and would even make the models – especially if it was an alternative to housework. Laura West, the grown-up daughter of a neighbour, was technically employed to work in the workshops, but as often as not, Gwen did a deal with her, and got Laura to do the housework and look after the children, Pat and Terry, while she spent the day in the workshop. Tom didn't entirely approve, but he didn't like to argue with his wife.

Holidays were rare, and non-existent for Tom. Gwen would take the children away for short spells from time to time, but Tom was always too busy working to accompany them.

As the business grew so too did the activity in the back garden, and it was not long before someone complained to the council that he was running a business from private premises. He didn't give up the garden entirely, but he was forced to take a workshop in Surbiton, which, perversely, turned out to be something of a blessing, because it enabled him to expand. By 1939 he employed a sizeable work force, and had diversified. He was doing crazy paving, turf, and landscape gardening, as well as supplying ornaments to a number of large retailers including Bentalls in Kingston and Carters Seeds in Raynes Park. The business was providing the household with a very comfortable lifestyle.

Having at first rented the little bungalow in Longfellow Road, they were now able to buy it. Furthermore, although the garden was only forty feet by twelve, they had a full-time gardener, Mr Weller, who Gwen would always joke was paid full-time, but worked part-time. After an active morning, he spent his afternoons sound asleep in the potting shed, but he kept the little garden so nicely that no one seemed to mind. His domain comprised a rockery, two ornamental ponds, a greenhouse, shrubs, flowers and an expanse of lawn leading down to a few apple and pear trees at the bottom. A collection of sheds, which lined the right-hand side of the garden, were used as workshops for the business, and any ornament that failed to pass Tom's strict quality requirements found its way to a graveyard of concrete squirrels, hedgehogs and herons at the bottom of the garden.

Tom would never accept second best in anything. 'Good enough' was not a concept he understood. If one of his children came home boasting that they had attained 97 per cent in an exam and come second, he would want to know who had come first. They were difficult standards for a small child to live up to at times.

Education was of vital importance in his reckoning. He would never play physical games with his children. He had been a sportsman in his youth, and a strong swimmer, but in middle age sport was of no interest to him; but he never tired of playing mental games with his children – memory games, such as remembering objects on a tray, or inventing limericks. Their schooling was a priority, and before the outbreak of war in 1939, he ensured they had the best that money could buy. Pat and Terry went to Kingsley High School, a private girls school which took boys in the junior department.

War changed everything. Demand for garden ornaments evaporated, and the men who had been employed in the business downed tools and went off to enlist in the armed forces. Major's Garden Ornaments, the family's only source of income, closed down and Tom, whose sight was deteriorating, and who was too old to fight, became a senior air raid warden. Pat and Terry were taken away from their fee-paying school and enrolled at Cheam Infants and Junior School at the top of the hill, about half a mile from their home.

A couple of years later Pat won a scholarship to Nonsuch Grammar School for girls, where she went on to do exceptionally well. Terry, when the time came, failed the eleven-plus exam and went instead to the local secondary modern school at Stoneleigh. The two were very different. As Pat says, she was and still is a dabbler. 'I know a little about a lot of things, most of them useless, but they intrigue me. So in exams I did well because I had a good memory and knew enough about enough subjects to get me through.' Terry was and still is a stickler for detail. 'That takes a long time, and is no use in an exam.' John, she says, has something of both of them in him. Plus an added ingredient. 'He has the one thing that comes from Father that both Terry and I are too lazy to have – the drive. He has my ability to pick the bones out of something; if he needs to know something for the job, he can absorb it with Terry's detail; but he's got my father's determination to do something with that knowledge.'

John was born on 29 March 1943. Pat was thirteen, Terry was eleven, and everyone assumed he must have been a mistake. Even he thought as much. He would tell the story of how his mother had been to see the doctor with indigestion, and come home with the news that she was seven months pregnant.

In fact John Major was no accident. Gwen wanted him very much indeed. She was thirty-eight, old in those days to be setting out to have a baby, but it was wartime, and with so much death around, she found herself with a powerful urge to create life. Tom was not so sure about starting again. He was much older than his wife, and at sixty-five felt he was too old to have another baby, but he was persuaded. Gwen won the day, as she usually did; John was conceived and safely delivered nine months later – his mother's precious, special, last baby.

His arrival however was a dramatic affair. Gwen was seriously ill at the time of his birth. She had collapsed in the kitchen at Longfellow Road and was taken to St Helier Hospital in Carshalton with double pneumonia and pleurisy. Her life was in the balance for some time. Then by a curious twist of fate, as she began her recovery, John, who was perfectly healthy when he was born, caught an infection from one of the nursing sisters and came very close to death himself.

Shortly after their return home he escaped death a second time. A stray bomb landed in the road outside and blew out the windows in the front of the house. John, still just a tiny baby, slept in his parents' bedroom, one of the two front rooms; his cot was installed beneath the window. Great shards of glass fell into the cot, and would no doubt have killed a sleeping baby, but by some miracle John was out of the cot at the time. Terry in the meantime had contracted scarlet fever and been taken away in a green fever ambulance to Banstead Isolation Hospital. And Tom, while out on duty in the blackout one night, had lost his footing and fallen heavily on his tin helmet. It apparently damaged his heart.

Gwen decided enough was enough and determined to take her family away to somewhere safer. Their neighbours on one side, the Cowleys, had already been evacuated to Norfolk to stay with relatives. Gwen and Bertha Cowley were good friends, and so it was agreed that the Majors should go and join them in the comparative safety of the countryside. They stayed initially with the Cowleys' relatives, near Wotton, but then found accommodation in a local mansion nearby, half of which had been taken over by the Government to provide temporary homes for evacuee families.

It was a delightful interlude. Tom found a job at the local aerodrome, but it all seemed a very long way away from the war. He was back in his element, and the family have a photograph of him still, looking every bit the country gentleman: tweed cap, wellington boots with his trousers tucked in, Fair Isle sweater, gun tucked under his arm, and cigarette in hand. He was back to his Shropshire days, and the locals immediately took to him. Other Londoners were treated with suspicion – the locals thought them wide boys – and the pubs fell silent when one of them came in through the door, but Tom Major was greeted in the Norfolk pubs as one of their own.

The mansion they were housed in had obviously been magnificent in its time, but had been neglected; part had become derelict and was shut off. Nevertheless the grounds were extensive, with a walled garden, a large orchard, and meadows with horses and pigs grazing, and the children loved it. German Prisoners of War came to work the land from a camp nearby, but everyone was very friendly to one another. As the guards would say, 'I don't know what the bloody hell we've got rifles for, we've got no bullets.'

The Majors stayed in Norfolk until just before the end of the war, when the danger from flying bombs was over, and they were back home in Longfellow Road in time for the VE celebrations.

With the war over, Tom endeavoured to get the business going again, but the climate was very different post-war and it was tough going. There was no question of employing labour, or even hiring premises. Everything was done in the sheds in the garden as it had been at the outset, and it became very much a family business once more, with everyone mucking in fashioning the models, making the moulds, mixing the sand and cement, and getting the orders out.

To bring in a little extra money Gwen went to work as manageress of a Chain Library, just around the corner in Worcester Park. After school Pat would go and join them and sit reading while she looked after John for her mother. But after a time Tom's health began to deteriorate at quite a rapid rate, and Gwen was needed at home to deal with the business. Tom was into his seventies, his sight was failing fast, his heart was weak, and he simply didn't have the strength to do the manual work, nor the eyesight for the detail. So Gwen stepped in.

Gwen is an unsung hero of the Major family history. She was a remarkable woman, small and slender but utterly determined, and it was she who held the family together and brought them with such equanimity through the difficulties that beset them. Tom issued the orders, and he was always allowed to feel that he was master of the household; but Gwen, in fact, was the linchpin. She was quite content to get dusty and dirty out in the workshop, then come in and cook the family meals, see to their welfare, listen to their problems and run after her ailing husband. Her family and her privacy were the most important things in her life, and she fought like a tiger to protect them.

Yet at the same time, she was concerned about the welfare of everyone else around her, and felt it incumbent on her to give a helping hand to anyone and everyone who was worse off than she. She was a refuge for anyone in need. Even when she had nothing herself, she found time, a cup of tea and a sympathetic ear for locals who were down on their luck.

To the children of the household, their mother's philanthropy was a source of some irritation. It was a very small bungalow, with no room to spare, and they didn't appreciate having a kitchen perpetually over-run with strangers. John remembers sitting at the kitchen table one afternoon when someone came to the door.

My mother whipped up my plate with crumpets and jam, and gave it to them, and that was the end of it. Whoever it was ate it. I had obviously eaten that day, or at least that week, and off went my crumpets! I was a bit puzzled by that.

Puzzled or not, her abhorrence of social injustice rubbed off.

Gwen's enthusiasm for lame ducks was matched by her love of animals, which John also shared. There have been only two occasions in his life when he has lost sleep. The second was when he was Chief Secretary to the Treasury. On the first occasion he was no more than five or six years old, and his father told him he could not have the pet mice he wanted. Mortified, he remembers going to bed, and with his dog Butch curled up beside him, lying awake fretting. John shared a bedroom with his brother, Terry.

Tom was not a stern man, by any means. He was a kindly man, but he had been brought up in the Victorian age, and he was not the sort of father a small boy argued with or contradicted in any way. They were not afraid of him. On the contrary, they adored him, and loved listening to the stories he told. But his word was law in the house, and his children were expected to do as he said and abide by the rules. Honesty, modesty, good manners and doing the best you could were of utmost importance.

In the matter of the mice, old Tom Major was eventually persuaded, possibly with a little cajoling from Gwen, and John had the pets he wanted. He also had a white Angoran rabbit that he kept in the back garden, and of course there was his sleeping companion, Butch, a cross between a scottie and a bull terrier, which had come from a lady up the road.

When Terry left school he began to work full-time in the business. He was so badly needed that his national service was deferred, and he didn't go into the army until he was eighteen-and-a-half. He remembers his mother seeing him off at the door of the house, with dire warnings against going with any German girls. Such was Gwen's strength of personality, when he returned eighteen months later he had no difficulty in meeting his mother's gaze.

Pat in the meantime, having turned down the opportunity to go to university because she didn't want to go away from home, was installed at art school in Wimbledon, studying dress design. Her father was delighted. He was keen for his children to be artistic, and once wanted to buy a kiln for Pat and Terry. He thought there would be good money to be made in handmade pottery.

John was only seven when Terry went off to do his national service in 1950. By then he was at Cheam Common County Infants and Junior School, and was taken with a party of thirty boys and two teachers to the Oval to watch his first cricket match. Surrey were playing Northants, and he watched Peter May, who was later to captain the England team, score 169 runs for Surrey.

John's passion for cricket was already well established by then. He doesn't know where it came from. It was certainly from no one in the family, none of whom was interested in sport. Yet almost as soon as he could walk he remembers running up and down in the tiny front garden in Longfellow Road, bowling a ball at the garage; and, in the back garden, putting a single stick into the lawn and bowling at it, then fishing the ball out of the pond.

He played football at school, and that became another abiding interest; but at that time he was also a very keen runner. He would run round and round the block for hours on end. It was a distance of a quarter to half a mile, and he would run races with a friend. They would each run in opposite directions, that way they had to pace themselves, instead of running side by side and sprinting at the end to win. It was an extra challenge he enjoyed, and although he would go race after race with different people, he didn't often lose.

Some interfering busybody of a neighbour put an end to it, however. They told his parents that he would do himself an injury running so much, and they evidently believed them. He was forbidden to run any more.

His memories of his childhood in Worcester Park are very sketchy. They were not the happiest times, therefore not times he likes thinking back to. He comes up with odd snatches here and there.

He remembers sitting on the back doorstep, upset because he had tried to walk to school by himself for the first time, and had lost his way and had to give up and come home.

He remembers sitting in the kitchen one night watching his father standing on a stool to change a light bulb. The light bulb flashed and he fell off. 'And I somehow thought him falling off the chair was the result of me misbehaving.'

He remembers the birthday when everyone pretended it wasn't his birthday because they didn't have any money to buy him a present.

He remembers play-fighting on the lawn with his brother. Playing around the brook at the end of the road, jumping across it onto the built-up bank on the other side. He remembers climbing a tree nearby and falling out of it when he was quite high up and cutting himself very badly. And he remembers going to Saturday morning pictures at the cinema in Worcester Park. They showed series: films like Dick Barton, Tarzan and Tom Mix, which always ended on a spine-chilling note so you were kept in suspense until next week's instalment.

Sundays were special, not for religious reasons – although

essentially Christian, the Majors were not a church-going family – but Sunday lunch with a roast joint of meat was sacrosanct. Everyone had to be there, on time, at 1 or 1.30, and there could be no excuses.

He had friends living round and about, who all went to the same school. They would kick balls around in the road, play cricket together. Opposite the Majors' house there was an alleyway, which lined up perfectly with one of the stone gate posts at 260, built by Tom. They drew stumps and bails on it and used the gate post as the wicket, drew a crease on the pavement, and bowled from down the alleyway, which gave them a bit of a run.

And they dabbled in capitalism. One of his friends, who lived round the corner in Green Lane, and whose mother was the local cat rescuer, had a black Bevan buck rabbit. They put him with John's Angoran doe, and sold the ensuing babies for 6d each, plus a slice of Mrs Major's home-made cake. He bred from his mice too, and put up a notice outside 260 Longfellow Road, announcing 'Mice for Sale'.

But it was essentially a lonely childhood. There was no shortage of affection in the family, and there were plenty of cuddles and hugs, but there was neither money nor time to devote to John. His parents didn't take him out, he never went to the circus or to football or cricket matches, or to visit relatives. There were no relatives. Pat has a memory of meeting her grandfather, Gwen's father, and there was an Aunty Minnie and Aunty Daisy – Gwen's cousin, now in her eighties – but Terry's memory is slight, and John never knew any of them. Visitors to the house would be called Aunty or Uncle, but it was just a convention of the time, they were not relatives.

John did have a godmother called Miss Fink. She was responsible for the middle name Roy, that has erroneously crept into his name at various times. All he knows about her is that she had long pink fingernails. And at the font, when asked the name, Miss Fink threw in a Roy. His father was furious. It crept into school certificates and his marriage certificate, but it is not on his birth certificate and he wants no part of the name. He never saw Miss Fink again.

There were no holidays away from home during John's child-hood. Those were a thing of the past, a luxury of more affluent times, pre-war. His brother and sister were almost a different generation. By the time John was five, Terry had left school and was working in the business, Pat was eighteen. They were too busy with their own lives to spend time playing with John. So his amusement was self-made. He became self-reliant and self-contained. He read a lot, and had plenty of books. Birthday presents would generally be books, classics like *Little Women, Black Beauty, Kidnapped*, Robin Hood and *The Count of Monte Cristo*.

He spent much of his time with the family next door, the Swains, who always gave him a warm welcome. He was particularly fond of Mr Swain, who would often help him with his homework in the evenings. He was doing well at Cheam Common Infants and Junior School, well enough to pass the eleven-plus exam and win a scholarship to one of the two grammar schools in the area, Rutlish Boys School in Merton, which was indisputably the best. His parents were delighted.

John has drawn a veil over Rutlish. He was never happy there, but it was not, he insists, the fault of the school. Part of the blame must lie with his parents who for some obscure reason put him into the school under the name Major-Ball. He hated it. It was ludicrous, he says, it wasn't him, he didn't like it, didn't understand it. He deeply resented it, and played up and made a fuss because of it. So much so that in later years he sought out his birth certificate to look at it and see what his real name was. There were other reasons why he got off to such a bad start at Rutlish, and it certainly did coincide with a particularly difficult time at home, which can't have helped.

The business was ailing. Tom was rapidly declining into old age and was able to do virtually nothing. The work was being done by Gwen and Terry, who returned to it when he finished his military service. But by this stage Gwen's health was beginning to go too. Like her husband, she had always been a heavy smoker, and every winter suffered a bout of bronchitis. Her chest was now becoming a problem all year round, so increasingly the business fell to Terry. It was too much for one man, but, more importantly, it was badly in need of capital. They had a serious cash-flow problem – the classic small businessman's dilemma of clients not paying quickly enough to cover the cost of materials that have to be bought to fill the orders.

Suddenly, as if in answer to their prayers, a woman approached Tom, looking for a business to invest in. She was a widow with a boyfriend, and her plan was to fix her boyfriend up in a business of some sort. Needless to say, she was welcomed with open arms, and the £3,000 she injected into Major's Garden Ornaments was the lifeline they needed. They at once moved into a big workshop near Worcester Park Station and Terry took the boyfriend under his wing and contrived to teach him the art of making ornaments.

It was in this climate of new-found confidence, no doubt, that the Majors splashed out on a black and white television set for the Queen's coronation in June 1953. They were one of the first families in the road to have a television, and as many neighbours as could fit crowded into the small living room at the back of the house to watch and celebrate.

Like most homes of the period, the focus of attention prior to that had been the wireless, which sat on top of a corner cabinet in the living room. Inside the cabinet was the whisky, Tom's favourite tipple, and his football coupon equipment. Pat also recalls it was Tom Major's remedy for toothache, even for little John. 'If he had a sore tooth a large whisky would be poured, and off he would go to bed – not with a toothache, but with a thumping headache instead!' Every Saturday afternoon during the season, Tom would sit down next to the inter-oven, the old black coal-fired range, and listen to the football results; and woe betide anyone who spoke while they were on. He filled in coupons religiously for years, and was rewarded but once, shortly before his sight entirely failed him, with a win of £1.50. Yet John was the only member of the family who was interested in the actual game.

Everything happened in the living room. Before John was born they had a best room at the front of the house, but after his arrival, that room became Pat's bedroom, and John moved in with Terry, leaving just the family room next to the kitchen for entertaining. There was no central heating, of course, at that time, each room had a coal fire, but there was this large inter-oven in the living room. Gwen had once tried to keep a litter of puppies, which had been rejected by their mother, alive in the side ovens. It was to no avail. As soon as she tried to reunite them with Jip, the mother, she took each and every one of them outside into the garden and left them to die.

It was seated in Gwen's chair by the inter-oven one evening in 1954 that Tom Major had his first heart attack. Because he was in his wife's chair rather than the one he usually sat in, he had his back to the door and didn't see his old friend, Uncle Mac, come into the room. He had evidently arrived unexpectedly, and on suddenly hearing the familiar voice, Tom dropped the glass of whisky he was drinking, which smashed on to the hearth, and collapsed.

It didn't affect his brain in any way but it did leave him with a seriously damaged heart, and greatly reduced his mobility. As a man who had always led a very active life, he found the restriction deeply frustrating. It was depressing for them all, and they were all well aware that another heart attack could kill him.

At this point disaster struck. The widow and her boyfriend broke up. He had never been a very enthusiastic apprentice in any event, but without him, she no longer wanted a share in the business, and announced that she wanted her money back. This was impossible. The money had long been spent, ploughed into the business. But there was worse to come. Tom, they discovered, had never drawn up any official contract with the widow. Their negotiations had been very largely word of mouth, and it was a moot point as to whether she was legally bound to the agreement.

Pat and Terry took the matter up on behalf of their father and consulted a solicitor. It was his opinion that the agreement was binding, but he pointed out that, if it came before a jury, she would be presented as a poor, defenceless widow, and he a cold and calculating businessman who had done his best to swindle her out of her savings. Although he felt that Tom would probably win at the end of the day, it might be a bloody battle. Tom's doctor clinched the debate. He doubted whether Tom's heart would stand the stress of a legal fight.

As soon as they heard that, there was no more argument. Nothing was more important than their father's health, and they would do nothing that might put it in jeopardy. And so Pat and Terry took the decision that was to change all of their lives. The widow would get her money. The rights and wrongs of it were irrelevant, the suffering that was inflicted on the Major household had to be tolerated. It became a debt of honour, for a family that was, above all else, deeply honourable.

2

BRIXTON

THE Majors had no money. The business brought in little, and took up all Terry's time and energy. Pat, now twenty-four, had a job which helped to provide for the family, and Tom had a small pension from the Variety Artists Benevolent Fund, but they had no savings, nothing to fall back on. Yet they had undertaken to pay back the widow the £3,000 she had invested in the business.

There was only one thing to do: sell the house. It was their only capital asset, and even then it was not enough. So 260 Longfellow Road was sold in 1955 for £2,150, but they did not see that much from the sale. Before the widow came into their lives, Tom had raised capital for the business by mortgaging the house, and notion-ally selling it to Terry. So first the mortgage had to be repaid. The remainder went to the widow, and it was another four years before the outstanding amount was finally paid off. Terry and Pat both worked themselves into the ground. Terry to keep the business afloat and feed the family; Pat, to pay off the debt; and it all but wrecked their lives.

Tom Major took no part in the sale of his home. When prospec-tive buyers came to look round he sat silent in his chair by the fire, and it was left to Gwen and Terry to do the talking. He was registered blind by this time, and was thoroughly demoralized. It was bought by Thomas Canter, a civil servant with the Ministry of Agriculture, and his wife Yvonne, who moved in during May 1955.

The Majors moved to Brixton where they knew someone who was prepared to let them have two rooms in an end of terrace house at 144 Coldharbour Lane. In comparison with the neat and ordered home they had come from, it was a slum. They took over two seedy rooms on the top floor. The only heat was a small electric fire, water poured in through the roof when it rained, there was a gas cooker on the landing, and a bathroom two floors down that they shared with all the other lodgers in the house.

The other lodgers were a motley crew. They included a cat-burglar who was sent to jail, a man who tried to knife a policeman, and another who tried to push the woman he was living with – not his wife – under a bus. He also spent some time at Her Majesty's pleasure.

They were not out of the ordinary for the district. Brixton by that time was a rough, tough part of south London, and its fine terraces, neat villas and handsome town houses were rapidly turn-ing into slums, as West Indian immigrants with young families, who had come over to Britain to work on the buses and in the hospitals, struggled to live on next to no money.

It was a long long way from the calm and normality of Worcester Park, and a rude shock to each and every one of them. Yet largely thanks to Gwen, they survived it. With extraordinary fortitude she set the mood for the whole family. She refused to let their circum-stances get her down. There was regret, but no recrimination and no despair. Things could have been worse. They may not have had any money, but they had a roof over their heads – albeit a leaking one – they were still a family, with the same feelings they always had for one another – why should she worry about what people thought? Instead, she busied herself dealing with the practicalities of life, which had to go on, wherever they were. If there was nothing to eat in the house but a couple of eggs, for instance, she would scramble them to make them go further, and if someone brought a friend, she would just make it stretch further still. Whatever the problem there was a positive way of looking at it, and she was not going to be defeated by a situation for which none of them was responsible.

In many ways Tom must have suffered most. Though no one ever apportioned blame, he must have felt he had let his family down. He had always been an immensely proud man, he had been quite wealthy at times in his life, he was expansive, he had travelled, he had lived, and he had talked about it. To find himself in a decaying room in Brixton, in debt up to his ears and unable to do anything to change things, must have been practically unbearable.

Each member of the family dealt with the trauma in a different way. Pat had nightmares for six months after the move. In her dream, which was the same night after night, she would go back to the bungalow in Longfellow Road and find it empty. She would go inside and wait and watch. When nobody came, she would move all the family belongings back into the house.

Terry hid in his work. Immediately after the move he still had the workshop in Worcester Park, so he spent most of his time there, working all round the clock, much of it, since there was no electricity in the building, by candle-light. A neighbour in Longfellow Road offered him a bed in her house, where Gwen believed he was staying, but in practice he frequently curled up and slept on the bench in the workshop. Later he moved to a workshop nearer to home, in Camberwell.

His problem was that the moulds for all the garden ornaments he made were so worn that the detail was being lost. They needed to be replaced, but Terry was in a Catch 22 situation. When he delivered an order, he was paid and the family ate. He was working on his own. If he was to take the time off that he needed to make new moulds, he would have no money coming in to buy the materials to do the work. He couldn't afford to stop, he had to keep up production. His father still insisted on perfection. So to get round the problem of worn moulds, Terry carved in the detail by hand with a penknife, immediately after he turned them out, while they were still 'green' or soft. It was an agonizingly time-consuming process. The heron, for example, one of the most popular ornaments, stood four or five feet high and all the feathers down his back had to be done by hand, as well as the reeds and the rocks on which he stood. Terry spent increasing hours doing this, and was trapped in a vicious circle, because, of course, the worse the moulds became, the more work needed to be done by hand. A new heron would have taken him half a week to make.

Sometimes he was so desperate to get an order completed, he would work all day, come home at about 10 p.m. for something to eat, fall asleep in a chair for half an hour, then go back to the workshop and carry on all night. Occasionally he would be stopped by the police on his way back, suspicious that he should be walking about the streets so late at night with a bag of tools. He once worked solidly like this for five days, and was so exhausted when the order was finished, he slept for three days.

John retreated further into himself. On the surface he remained stoic. He confided in no one – no friend, no member of his family, so no one knew just how badly he was hurting inside. His friends at school scarcely knew he had moved. They certainly had no idea that his world had been turned upside down; but then John had always kept himself at one remove from other people. He never allowed anyone to get close enough to know what he felt about anything. There was never any special friend. He was liked by everyone, because there was nothing about him to dislike. He was pleasant and he had a good sense of humour, but he never projected himself in the way that wins admirers or sets boys apart as a leader of the pack. John was no leader. He was contained and unassuming, and sank very successfully into the quiet anonymity he sought.

Rutlish Boys was a grammar school, so there were no fees to pay. But there were extras that inevitably cost parents dear. There was the uniform, for instance, which was regulation and, as well as normal day wear, there was kit to be bought for the various sports the school played. Pre-war, it had been a public school, and some of the customs lingered from those days. They wore extravagant blazers in summer, for example – blue, white and gold striped, with a boater hat; prefects wore mortar-boards, there was a cadet corps, they had school on Saturday mornings, and they played rugby instead of football.

All the uniform came from Elys, a specialist outfitter in Wimbledon. The boys wore dark-grey flannel trousers, black shoes, dark socks, with a white shirt, the school tie, and a blue blazer. But like many school uniforms, some small detail made the regulation item subtly different from a similar garment you could buy far more cheaply elsewhere.

So it was with the blazer. It was like any other blue blazer in every particular, except for the buttons. The buttons were gilt with a special design on them. Little realizing the significance these buttons were going to take on in her younger son's mind, Gwen sent John off to school in the autumn of 1953 wearing a second-hand blazer she had picked up cheaply, unaware that the buttons were different from everyone else's.

Like so many boys of that age, particularly starting out in a new school, John was anxious that everything should be just right, that he should be no different from anybody else, and have all the equipment that he was supposed to have. He didn't yet have the confidence that comes with familiarity, and was acutely aware of the difference between his and everyone else's buttons, and the humiliation that attached. He felt quite miserable as a result but the situation could not be easily remedied. New buttons were very expensive – he forgets now whether they were half a crown or seven and sixpence each from Elys. Whichever it was, it was way beyond what his mother could possibly afford. Finally Gwen solved the problem by buying a dilapidated blazer in a school jumble sale, cutting off the buttons, and sewing them on to John's blazer.

Despite the public school pretensions, it was not a snobbish school. Its pupils were drawn from a wide range of backgrounds, some were extremely poor, and John certainly had no reason to feel uncomfortable among the 650 boys. Several were unable to afford cricket whites and had to play in grey flannels instead. John had whites, but he did wear a normal white shirt, rather than a special cricket shirt, and white plimsolls for cricket instead of proper boots.

The boys divided neatly into those who were academic and those who were sporting. John fell firmly into the latter category and his only happy memories of Rutlish are on the cricket field. Cricket was played in the summer term only. It was compulsory on Wednesday afternoons when lessons finished at 1 p.m., there was net practice on Tuesdays and Thursdays after school between 3.30 and 5.30, and those who were keen managed to play at other times during the week as well. Saturday afternoons were match days, which usually involved John. He was not an exceptional player but he was good enough to be useful in a team. He played in the Under-fourteens, the Under-fifteens and the Under-sixteens, and had he stayed at the school longer, would almost certainly have made the First Eleven. Boys liked having him on their side because he never argued, as most players did, about whether he should bat number five or three or seven; he was always happy to play wherever anyone wanted him, he always played well, and he was always enormously keen.

During the other two terms they played rugby. John liked rugby, and played both for the school and for his house – Argonauts – and, being something of a natural sportsman, he played well. However, he was trying hard the while to start a football team at Rutlish. He had little success: rugby fans are notorious for scorning football. So, although he had support from some of the boys, the staff were unmoved, and appeals to Mr Blenkinsop, the headmaster, were a waste of breath. Blenkinsop disliked all sport, with the possible exception of cricket. However, John did manage to organize a Saturday side, played out of school.

Rutlish was not actually such a good school by the time John went there. The excellent reputation it had once had, under the previous headmaster, had been eroded by more than ten years of Blenkinsop, his replacement. The boys called him Champion the Wonder Horse, because of his big teeth. He had come in during the war as a purely temporary appointment, and had stayed; but he was a weak man, an academic at heart, ill-suited to controlling such an assortment of active boisterous boys, or harnessing their talents and enthusiasms.

He was a pacifist, so he did not like the Combined Cadet Force. Because he had no interest in sport, he would never announce team results, not even those of the first team. His subject was divinity, although he seldom took his classes and he very seldom administered any discipline. When the cricket team, with John in it, was reported for smoking in the changing rooms at Queen Elizabeth Barnett school after a match, Blenkinsop did nothing. Boys felt he had dreams of making Rutlish the Manchester Grammar School of the south, renowned for its brilliant academic success. Instead he presided over a school that repeatedly let down bright pupils like John Major.

After two years at Rutlish, the opportunity arose for John to sit a scholarship exam for Charterhouse, the famous boys' public school in Godalming. As well as having a good all-round reputation, they had a wonderful cricket field, and John was very keen to try for a place. He was going through a difficult period at school, and wanted to try for this place very badly. The school, however, thwarted him. Looking back, he suspects that they knew his parents could never have afforded to send him to Charterhouse. Even boys on scholarships have a host of extras to pay for, and the school would have wanted to spare his parents any unnecessary distress. This charitable explanation he places on the school's motives today, doesn't sound entirely sincere. He was certainly very disappointed not to have been allowed to sit the exam, and there was no second chance to escape.

Once the family had moved to Brixton, John's journey to Rutlish was tortuous. Even when they were living at Worcester Park, he had lived further away than most boys, but from Brixton it took a good one-and-a-half hours each way; tiring for a young boy at the beginning and end of every day. He would take a train from Loughborough Junction station to Wimbledon Chase, then walk to school from there. It was not a difficult journey, but for a while he regularly had to walk past a group of non-grammar school boys who taunted him, and he would come home very distressed.

There was corporal punishment at Rutlish. Only two masters administered beatings – Mr Walker, the geography master, and Mr Blenkinsop – but if any parent objected to their son being caned, they could do so at the beginning of his school career. Mr Walker would stand up in front of a parents' meeting when boys first arrived, with cane in hand, and say that he intended to use it on boys if they deserved it, but if any parent didn't want their boy caned, they should come forward now so he could make a note of their wishes. If they didn't, he would take it as read that their sons could be beaten should the need arise.

John was beaten just once. Walker had set the class some homework, which only one boy in the class had done. It involved going to an industrial estate, some mile-and-a-half's walk away, and making a note of all the companies that worked there. It was a nuisance, they decided; a long way to go for what seemed a very pointless exercise. The result was a class beating, and twenty-four sore bottoms. Yet no one resented Walker. He was the most popular and most respected teacher in the school and the only one without a nickname.

School hours were from 8.30 a.m. to 3.30 p.m., except on Saturdays when lessons finished at 12.30 p.m. Lunch was in the canteen, food cooked on the premises, and the younger boys waited on the older ones. And at the end of the day there would be about two hours' homework to be done. So even if he had wanted to socialize with the other boys after school, John would never have had either the money or the time. While they met up with girls from Wimbledon County school and hung around the local coffee bars, John began the journey home to two crumbling rooms in Coldharbour Lane.

But he never complained to anyone. No one realized how deeply unhappy he was. They were the worst days of his life. Indeed, when he went back to Rutlish in 1991, as Prime Minister, for a special anniversary, he said he had no memory of the school at all – so deeply had he buried that period of his life, he didn't even recognize the building.

The school had actually moved during John's time there, into a brand-new building in Watery Lane. The sight had formerly been the headquarters of Carter's Seeds. Acres of glass houses had been demolished to provide a playing field, but the handsome old buildings, the laboratory, and the original manor house were left intact. They sat uneasily alongside an architectural abomination, with no character and no atmosphere, which all the boys hated. The walls were painted in pastel shades and couldn't be leant on or scuffed, the floors were white maple, and couldn't be trodden on by shoes with black soles. It might have been light and airy with up to date technology, but they hankered after the rambling Victoriana they knew.

John never allowed himself to stand out in any way that would make him noticed. He survived school by blending into the crowd and being largely invisible. He was never very good nor very bad, either in the classroom or on the sports field. He was neither very smart nor very scruffy. He never played any great pranks, but he was no great respecter of authority. He didn't drink and he didn't smoke – despite stories that have been told to the contrary. He was neither one of a gang, nor was he a loner. He was quiet, affable and self-contained, and many of his contemporaries scarcely remember he was there at all.

There were one or two exceptions, people who knew him and remember him because of cricket, and who played in teams with him. Tony Waymouth was one. Tony lived near the school in Griffiths Road, and he would sometimes sneak off home at lunchtime, often taking John and one or two others with him. He and John arrived at the school in the same year, they played in the same cricket teams all the way up the school, and they sat through the same classes. Tony reckons he must have been as close a friend as anyone, and yet he readily admits he scarcely knew him. He never saw him out of school, never went to John's home, never met any of his family, and never even knew he had a brother and sister.

He had a few friends at home, boys with whom he would kick a football about or play cricket in the street. There are still the stumps they painted on the wall in Eastlake Road, just opposite the house on the corner of Coldharbour Lane. They played Knock Down Ginger – knocking on doors after dark and running off. Knocking a second time was better still; although he had the wrath of his parents to face if there were any complaints. There were not many children living around Coldharbour Lane. Families with children tended to live in the council flats, while the houses round and about had a few remaining owner-occupiers who were mostly elderly, or they were multiple lets taken by working people. But three Irish boys lived on the floor below at 144 for six months of the year. They came and went regularly – it was some tax dodge – and when they were there, John played with the younger ones. They were very keen on football, and took him to his first match, at Chelsea Football Club, Stamford Bridge, soon after Christmas in 1955. He can't remember that match, but does vividly remember the next one he went to, Chelsea versus Wolves, when Chelsea won one-nil, the game that effectively won them the Championship, with penalty scored by Peter Sillett, who, when he celebrated his sixty-fifth birthday, received among the cards wishing him many happy returns was one from Number Ten Downing Street.

The Oval became a favourite haunt too. Test ground and home of the Surrey County Cricket Club, it was only a short walk from Coldharbour Lane to Kennington, and he spent many a happy afternoon watching some of the greatest cricket in Surrey's history. Between 1952 and 1958 the side were county champions for a record seven years in succession. He saw stars like Peter May, Jim Laker, Ken Barrington and Alec Bedser; and occasionally, along with other young dreamers, went along to Wandsworth during the holidays to the cricket school run by the coach and former Surrey and England player, Alf Gover.

Brixton had a very unsettled population in those days and could be rough at times. From his bedroom he could hear trouble sometimes as people spilled out onto the streets at closing time from the Enterprise, the pub across the road. An illegal bookie lurked underneath the station at Loughborough Junction. John was once sent along to place a bet with him by the cat-burglar who lived at 144; but only once. Tom Major got wind of the arrangement, and he quickly put a stop to it.

Although Brixton was very rapidly being populated with immigrants, there was still a huge theatrical community living in the area, so Tom was not entirely isolated in his blindness. His pride was hurt because of the change in circumstance, but he was not unhappy in Coldharbour Lane, and in some ways he felt quite at home. Actors and performers he had not seen for thirty or forty years would track him down and come and visit, and they would talk about the good old days when they played together at all the old theatres and playhouses.

He had visits also from a lady whose mission in life must have been to rehabilitate the blind. She came to teach Tom basket work and would start him off on a sea-grass basket, and leave him to it, promising to return at a later date. Tom had no intention whatever of making baskets, but he didn't want to disappoint the lady, so the task fell to everyone else in the house. When the lady returned she was always so delighted with the baskets he had made, she would leave more and more. No one ever had the heart to tell her.

Academically John stagnated at school. He might have been invisible for all the contribution he made in the classroom. Science bored him. Maths was not much better. He quite enjoyed English, but the only subject he really found any pleasure in was history, and that was no thanks to the school. His history master was named Blenchly, a young man, whom he remembers as perfectly competent, but his interest in history predated anything he was taught there. It originated with the early books he had read, and perhaps family influence – his father's vivid tales about his life were possibly the best modern history lessons a boy could have. So it was something he enjoyed despite Rutlish.

He and Rutlish were doing one another no good, and so John decided to leave at the first opportunity he legally could, at the age of sixteen in 1959. He retracts the word 'hate' when describing how he felt about the school as being too strong a word. I rather doubt it is. He says:

> Anyone who thinks schooldays are the happiest days of your life should have their bumps felt. In my experience school had to be endured before life could be enjoyed.

He turned sixteen on 29 March, at the end of the Spring term, but there is some confusion about when he actually left. John cannot remember himself. He cannot remember whether he left before or after his birthday. He has always said he left at Easter, and went back to the school to take his O level exams in the summer. However, there is a photograph of him in the Second Eleven cricket team in 1959. It seems unlikely that he would have played in the team if he were no longer on the school register. None of his contemporaries seems to be able to remember any better than he can. Since the school records from that period were put into the Surrey county archives in 1988, and specific instructions went out a year later to keep his secret, unless John Major agrees for their contents to be known, the date he actually left school will remain a mystery.

The number of O level exams John passed also appeared to be a mystery for some time. The matter was resolved with a statement issued by Downing Street in April 1991, in order to put an end to the 'silly speculation' about the Prime Minister's O levels. He passed in English Language, English Literature, History, Maths, British Constitution and Economics.

Given that John definitely played in the Second Eleven during the summer of 1959, the most likely explanation about the termination of his school career is that, nominally, he did stay on at Rutlish that last term so he could take his O levels with the rest of his year. But most of the work, in the weeks between the beginning of the summer term and the examinations, would have been revision, and John might well have done that at home and not gone into school on a daily basis. He passed three O levels that term and subsequently took three more by correspondence course.

Three was as many as any of his friends passed. They all came away from the school with poor results, but no one was in the least surprised or upset. They had no interest in school work, there had never been any discussion about A levels or further education, and it was assumed that this bunch at the bottom of the academic heap would leave at the age of sixteen with what qualifications they had been lucky enough to scrape together. Having always regarded John as one of them, a no-hoper in class and a quiet, down-beat sort of character, with no evident fire in his belly, his friends were utterly incredulous when he became Chief Secretary to the Treasury in 1987, the man being tipped most likely to succeed Margaret Thatcher. No one could believe that Jack Major-Ball as he was known at school, could be one and the same person as John Major.

They had not even known John was interested in politics. He had shown no interest in anything in particular, except perhaps cricket. There was certainly no encouragement at school. Rutlish was not in the slightest bit political – the most political gesture it ever made was to invite Lord Burleigh to Speech Day one year. Yet by the age of thirteen John had begun to take a real interest in politics. It was when he was taken round the House of Commons for the first time and he decided then and there that this was the place where he wanted to work one day. An extraordinary ambition for a thirteen-year-old, and it must have been a tremendously exciting day out, and yet he told no one.

John had met the Labour MP for Brixton, Marcus Lipton, at a fête in St James's Church, Knatchbull Road, and they had started talking. Obviously intrigued to find someone so young with such a strong interest in politics, Lipton invited him along to see what went on at Westminster. John went alone, and remembers above all how much at home he felt in the Commons. Nothing particularly exciting was going on that day; it was one of the days of the Budget debate. He looked into the gallery and remembers seeing various people he recognized sitting on the benches below. Macmillan was there briefly, also Iain Macleod, and he was struck by the intimacy of the debate, and the relaxed air in which people delivered their speeches. Having only ever seen the Commons before in portraits in the history books, depicting great occasions, like Disraeli reporting on the Congress of Vienna, he was surprised to discover how small the Chamber was, and surprised to find it so empty. But the atmosphere excited him, and that curious sensation of feeling so much at home. He determined that one day he would return to sit on one of the green leather benches himself. He knew it was possible, but also knew it would be very difficult.

His interest in politics was already established by the time he met Marcus Lipton, although where it originated he has no idea, except in as much as it came from what he saw around him, living in Brixton. His love of history would have contributed too, of course.

It was certainly not something he picked up at home. His parents were not political; he cannot even say for certain how they voted, although Pat and Terry feel they would have been Conservative by instinct. John never remembers the family having a political discussion, but he does remember squabbling on two or three occasions with his father about race. Brixton had a very large and condensed black population, and Tom, it would appear, had absorbed some of the early American bigotry about colour when he was living in America as a young man in the 1880s. John challenged his father, in as much as a twelve or thirteen-year-old can take on a man in his late seventies. He remembers thinking it odd, and no doubt disappointing, that a man whose outlook was basically tolerant should be so intolerant over the colour of a person's skin.

John wouldn't pretend to have been very knowledgeable or sophisticated in his political outlook at that age, but he knew it was Conservative politics that interested him. He accepts there was no rationale behind his choice at that age, just instinct, and he probably didn't know the distinctions between the two main parties very well, but the instinct was strong, and he has rationalized it since, but he has never wavered from it. As he says:

Right from the start politics fascinated me. Seeing Westminster in action was very frustrating and I instinctively wanted to be part of it. I can't easily explain why, but I do recall that right from the outset the pull was very strong.

He knew he would need qualifications to become a Member of Parliament, but he also knew that Rutlish was not the place where he was going to get them, which is why, rightly or wrongly, he closed the door on formal education at the age of sixteen. Looking back, thirty years on, he says it might have been a silly judgement, but at the time he was certain it was the right one.

He felt uncomfortable being at school when he could have been out in the world earning money which would help towards the family grocery bill. The situation at home was grim. They were literally living from hand to mouth. The widow was still being paid off. Most of Pat's salary, from BP in the City, had been going towards the debt. The business had to provide everything else. If Terry completed an order of garden ornaments before the week was out, there would be food for the weekend. If not, they would survive on what was left over in the cupboard. All five of them were still sleeping, eating and living in two rooms. Tom was quite blind and almost completely bedridden. Gwen was looking after him and trying to hold the family together and maintain some semblance of normality under the most difficult circumstances, and in poor health herself. Yet on top of everything she was still finding lame ducks – she had a whole new brood in Brixton – who filled an even smaller space. In this climate, wanting to acquire qualifications must have seemed faintly obscene. It is not surprising John told no one he hoped to be a Member of Parliament one day.

He left school without consulting anybody, neither his parents nor his brother and sister. He knew they would be vehemently opposed to it because, although they needed the money he might be able to bring in to the family if he had a job, they believed education was more important. He had been clever enough to go to a grammar school, he had an opportunity to make something of himself, and he ought to seize that opportunity. But, under the circumstances, John didn't have the appetite for it. Pat, he knew, was delaying her wedding because of him. She had met the man she wanted to marry several years before, but had felt she must settle the widow's debt and see John through his education before she married. So John knew he had to present his decision to them

34

as a *fait accompli*; and, as he expected, they were far from happy when he told them.

However, his education did not stop there; he spent several years studying on his own, getting up early in the morning to do so. But the first imperative upon leaving school was to find himself a job. He wrote to several companies asking for an interview and before the end of the year found himself working as a clerk for Price Forbes, an insurance broking firm in the City. He had no particular interest in insurance, what he wanted was a job with prospects, and this seemed to him to fit the bill. It was not a success. He earned £5 per week, £2 of which he gave to Gwen, but he felt like a fish out of water in the smart offices, awkward in the cheap ill-fitting suit he bought himself. He was not sophisticated or worldly-wise, and the office environment was quite alien. No one treated him badly, he insists, he simply didn't feel at home, and so he left.

By this time there had been major changes in the business, and in turn to the family's finances. Terry had reached the end of his tether. He was physically and mentally exhausted. He had been working all the hours God sent, desperately aware that the family relied upon him, that if he failed them there was no money for the weekly groceries, but it was to no avail. It was too much for one man. The business was in debt, the equipment was desperately in need of renewal, he couldn't keep pace with the orders and he could see no way out.

He wasn't helped by his father. Although he was a virtual invalid, Tom continued to issue orders, continued to demand the best, and although Terry had been running the business, on and off, for more than six years, he refused to hand over anything. He wouldn't let go. He could never accept that his son, so much younger than him, and with so much less experience, could ever be better equipped or better qualified to make a sound judgement.

Terry failed to see that he was so handicapped. The task was Herculean, and yet he blames himself for having been unable to keep the business going, and the failure to do so seriously undermined his self-confidence, and in many ways upset the course of his life. He tried his damnedest to keep Major's Garden Ornaments afloat, but no one could have done so, under those circumstances, single-handed.

In 1959, just when he was on the point of despair, Terry was approached by one of his customers, Commander David, who ran a company Terry supplied called David's Rural Industries. He was a retired naval commander, one of life's real gentlemen, as Terry says, wealthy in his own right, and in business more for the fun of it than as a livelihood. He liked Terry, and knew he was in trouble, so he offered to buy the company for the price of its debts and employ Terry to work for him on a salary of £20 per week.

It was a godsend. Suddenly out of a maelstrom of uncertainty there was a measure of security in their lives once more, a regular income and no more worries about mounting debts from the business. The other debt, the widow's due, could finally be paid off, and they were free at last of the perpetual blood-letting that had debilitated them all for more than four years. At long last they could keep the money they earned, and at long last the Majors could afford to find themselves a more respectable home.

Thus in the autumn of 1959 they moved into part of a house at 80 Burton Road, a stone's throw from Coldharbour Lane, which was owned by the Minet Estate. It was a vast improvement on Coldharbour Lane. They still shared a bathroom, on the first floor of the house, but they had the bulk of the house – three bedrooms, a kitchen and a dining room. They had the ground floor, plus one room halfway up the stairs, which John and Terry initially shared. To have a proper kitchen, and a room to sit in, somewhere to entertain friends was a luxury after the squalor they had put up with for so long.

Shortly after the move Pat married her long-standing boyfriend, Peter Dessoy, and they went to live in Wimbledon. But within six weeks Pat was back home. Her mother was having her annual attack of bronchitis, more severely than usual because of the general deterioration in her health, and someone had to be there, not only to look after her, but to look after Tom. After a while Peter suggested they both move into Burton Road and take over Tom and Gwen's lease. The Majors, he reasoned, were living in a three-bedroom flat that they could scarcely afford, he and Pat were renting a two-bedroom flat in Wimbledon which was costing the earth, and they were never seeing each other because if Pat wasn't at work she was at her parents' house. It seemed a sensible solution, and so they moved into Burton Road. Everyone still treated it as Tom and Gwen's flat, but the Dessoys paid the bills.

In the meantime Terry had met his prospective wife, Shirley Wilson, who worked in the offices at Woolworths in Brixton. Sometimes when the business had been going really badly he had taken temporary jobs elsewhere, and one had been on the counters at Woolworths. When they had met Terry was in no position to marry, but by 1960 his fortunes were looking up. He was being employed by Commander David, who decently let him have a week off to go on honeymoon to the Isle of Sheppey.

Commander David was a charming man and a generous employer and Terry remembers him with a great deal of affection. He left Terry to his own devices, installed electric lighting in the workshop in Camberwell, replacing the gaslight, let him build all the shelves he needed and paid for everything. Given this new lease of life, the business began to flourish, and Terry needed to take on an extra pair of hands. So when John abandoned his job at Price Forbes, he was employed by Commander David and went to work with Terry for £8 per week.

It could not have been more different from shuffling paper at Price Forbes. Dressed in wellington boots, with giant plastic sheets wrapped around their waists, to try and keep the worst of the cement off their clothes, this was manual labour. They would start at about 7 o'clock in the morning, summer and winter alike, sometimes in freezing temperatures, work for a couple of hours, then break for some of the best breakfasts John says he has ever eaten in his entire life at a greasy-spoon café round the corner.

They worked according to Tom Major's stringent specifications, ensuring that only first-class ornaments left the workshop. The first job was to mix dry sand and cement together, then to make sure there were no little stones in the mix – a small stone on the tip of a nose, for example, could break off the finished article and the thing would have to be scrapped – the sand and cement had to be riddled through a large perforated-zinc sieve. Then it had to be watered until the consistency was just right for packing into the moulds and tamping down tight. When the cement was set, and the moulds came off, the selvages would be filed smooth and any broken bits made good, then the ornaments were coated with Portland stone and Venetian marble, and finally 'antiqued' with a mineral dye, to make them look weathered.

It was hard work; the ornaments were heavy, particularly the larger ones, like the bird baths. The dust went into their mouths and noses and the dye took hours to scrub off their hands. But they had fun together. They had a little electric ring to make tea on, and if they had a few pennies in their pockets, John, being the youngest, would be dispatched to the cake shop around the corner, for a couple of buns at teatime.

By this time John had joined the Young Conservatives, and a whole new social life had opened up for him. Quite by chance, there had been a knock at the door shortly after his sixteenth birthday, and there had stood a Young Conservative, canvassing for new members. His name was Neville Wallace, a shortish boy, slightly older than John, and he had the thankless task of seeking out new recruits from the unlikely youth of Brixton. But at 144 he struck gold, and John, just eligible, had signed up immediately.

Suddenly he found himself among people with similar interests and enthusiasms, and some of the friends he made there have lasted to this day. Brixton Young Conservatives socialized with Young Conservatives from other London boroughs, and an entire network opened up before him. It was quite a lively branch, surprisingly. There was an average attendance of thirty people for most functions, although at one point the number rose dramatically. A guitarist called Ernie Richardson joined and suddenly huge numbers of people started turning up, until someone discovered that Ernie Richardson was actually Ernie Tubb, a Young Socialist, who had signed up because he thought the Young Conservatives had a better social life.

Apart from the social life there was the more serious business of politics and John was swiftly thrown into a crash course on public speaking, on abstruse subjects such as the life cycle of the money-spider. These were games they played among themselves; they would each be given a subject, then have to stand up in front of everyone and speak for one minute. Never having had so much as a line in a school play to perform before, John found the exercise nerve-racking. Then there were days spent on a soapbox in Brixton market and along Brixton Road, addressing people as they came past, and being heckled and harangued in return – another vital part of the aspiring politician's training. There were not many sympathizers to be found in Brixton, but it was a great training ground. They developed the ability to speak for a long time on a wide range of subjects, and, even if they did take themselves too seriously, they had a great deal of fun in the process.

They went out into the streets and did some canvassing too, and John was particularly active during the run up to the London County Council elections in April 1961. The Conservative candidate was Ken Payne, who was unsuccessful, and unsuccessful again when he went on to stand as the parliamentary candidate for Brixton at the next general election, in 1964; but he did remember that of all the YCs canvassing on his behalf in both campaigns, John Major had inexhaustible energy. These days Ken Payne is a regular visitor to Downing Street. 'He helps to keep me in touch,' says John.

John stayed with Commander David and Terry in the ornament business for about two years. Although he had fun working with his brother, he knew that manual work was not going to further his ambitions. He doesn't remember the precise time of his departure, or what he did immediately afterwards. Neither does his brother. But what is certain is that at some time between his leaving David's Rural Industries and beginning work as a clerk at the London Electricity Board, between nine and sixteen months later, he was unemployed and, despite applying for a multitude of jobs, he was unable to find work and forced to go through the humiliating ritual each week of 'signing on' at the local labour exchange. He was nevertheless determined not to give up, and was studying the while, by correspondence, to take three more O levels and improve the look of his CV.

Tom was in a very poor state of health by this time, blind and completely bedridden. He had lost none of his authority, however. He would lie in his bed and call down for his tea in an imperious voice and in no time at all Gwen would be there, ready as always to do his bidding. She would put the cup down on the bedside table, guide his hand to it, so he would know where it was – thoughtful to the last. Then she would go, and just as she had reached the bottom of the stairs, he would call her again, 'Gwen, Gwen,' and she would run back up. When she had reached the top a second time, he would say, 'Have you stirred it?'

Gwen was not so well herself, and there was a period when the bronchitis was at its worst, and she had developed emphysema, when she could not cope with Tom on her own, and so while John was unemployed he undertook the task of caring for them both.

On 27 March, two days before John's nineteenth birthday, Tom died at the grand age of eighty-three, at home in his bed, surrounded by a family who adored him. It was no sudden event, and although painful, it had been painful to watch the progressive degeneration of someone who had once been so vigorous. The mercy was that he was mentally alert until the day he died. He never lost his memory or his mind, or his capacity to talk about anything under the sun. At the end he had lain half awake and half asleep, in no great distress, until he gradually slipped away. It was, remembers John, the most peaceful thing you can imagine. He went for a walk around the streets, the tears stinging his eyes, and remembers thinking 'I'll never see him again'. He leaned against a wall in floods of tears and then went home to comfort Gwen.

After a service in the Variety Players Benevolent Fund chapel at Streatham Vale, Tom was buried in the cemetery there, honoured and remembered by the profession he loved.

Having been turned down by a number of employers, including London Transport, where he was passed over for the job of a bus conductor, John finally struck lucky with the London Electricity Board. He has no precise memory when he began working there. He has never kept a diary; the only records he ever made were details like his National Insurance number, to avoid inconvenience; and he made a note of where he went on holiday each year.

Holidays began at the age of sixteen when he joined the Young Conservatives. There had been none before that. Thereafter they would be three or four days at the seaside during the Conservative Party Conference, which would alternate between Blackpool and Brighton. He would go and stay in a small boarding house with YC friends, but it was not the conventional sort of holiday. The only holiday he remembers of that sort was the year he went with an early girlfriend and her family to Grado on the Italian–Yugoslav border. He was eighteen or nineteen and it was the first time he had been abroad.

Life with the LEB at the Elephant and Castle was a vast improvement on being unemployed, which he hated, but the work was indescribably dull, and clearly going to lead nowhere. He stuck it out for about a year, but by then he had a much clearer idea of where he wanted to go. He was by now much more aware of the route to Parliament, as a result of his association with the YCs, and he knew that he needed some sort of professional qualifications before he could ever come close. Anyone who thinks that convincing the electorate of one's worth is the key to becoming an MP, doesn't begin to understand the workings of the Tory Party. That is the last and possibly the easiest task for a potential candidate. Getting on to the Candidates' List in the first place, at Conservative Central Office, is an infinitely more difficult task. Once on the list you have to be invited for interview by a constituency, and finally selected.

John's background hardly made him a natural for the Candidates' List. With six O levels and a shared house in Brixton for a home, no money and no profession, he was perfectly qualified for the Labour Party's list. But John had no inclination to go that way. He says he had seen what Labour rule in Brixton had done for the people, he had seen at first hand the bureaucracy it bred, the patronizing attitudes it dished out to the poor, and he wanted no part of it.

What he needed was a profession, and his researches at the local library told him there were two alternatives open to a boy in his situation. He could become a banker or an accountant. Both could have been done by starting at rock bottom and working his way through exams in his own time. If he was to become an accountant, he reasoned, he would ideally become a chartered accountant, which would have involved being articled on very low pay for a long period, and it would have shackled him too much to one particular firm. Banking, on the other hand, offered a whole range of opportunities to work at home or abroad. It could be done very easily by correspondence course, the exams could be taken externally, and they could be taken at a speed that was appropriate to his circumstances: rapidly, very slowly, all at once or one at a time. The course itself included a bit of everything: there was law, accountancy, banking, economics, and monetary theory. When he began, he thought he might take a Bachelor of Law degree afterwards, which he could also have taken externally. As it turned out, he had no need, but it was with all this in mind that, after a year at the LEB, he applied to the District Bank, which was the beginning of a long and remarkable climb to the top.

His stay at the District Bank was brief, no more than eighteen months, but it was an important step on the ladder. Not only did it provide him with a good understanding of the rudiments of banking, it gave him the opportunity to study for the crucial first stage of the Institute of Banking exams. This was the qualification which would start to open doors.

3

BANKING AND LOCAL GOVERNMENT

ASK John Major which period in his life has been the most difficult and he will say the early sixties: that time between the ages of eighteen and twenty-three. It is obviously a hard choice in a childhood that he looks back on with so little affection, but as a child he had no control over his situation. As a young adult he did, and it was a period of great uncertainty. He was in and out of work, in jobs he saw no future in, toying with politics, unsure whether anything would ever come of his ambitions or whether he was just fooling himself and wasting time. He was essentially unsure of where he was going or what his place was.

Yet he had ambition. He was determined to try to make something of his life, and he knew he had to do it alone, away from the encumbrances of the family. His mother was over-protective of her youngest child. With no Tom to look after any more, although she was unwell she transferred her attention to John, even though he was now in his twenties. He had to make a life of his own, but however he made the break it was going to be hurtful. None of Gwen's children had lived away from home before they were married, and she could not comprehend why any of them would want to, certainly not her special one.

The chance presented itself in 1965 when Pat and Peter decided to move away from Burton Road, taking Gwen with them, and asked John if he wanted to come. They had a baby by this time, Mandy, and new people had moved in upstairs, who also had a baby. Pat had said they could keep the pram down in the hall, but she hadn't meant with the baby in it. There it sat for much of the day, and whenever the baby cried, its mother would lean over the banisters and shout obscenities down the stairs. Peter came home from work one evening when the mother was in full flood and was horrified by what he heard. There was nothing to keep them in Brixton any more, and so they decided to move away.

Terry and his wife had moved to Thornton Heath, near Croydon, where they shared a house with Shirley's parents. It seemed natural to follow, so they could all be near one another, and early in 1966 they bought a house just across the road from Terry's. Fortuitously there was a doctor living next-door-but-one, whom they would dash to fetch when Gwen fought for breath in the night, as she increasingly did towards the end of her life. He would come over and give her an injection to help her through the night, as the asthma and emphysema took an ever greater hold.

John stayed in Brixton, and it very nearly broke his mother's heart. She could not believe he had chosen to live on his own without her. He moved out before they left Burton Road, as soon as he had made the decision not to move with the family, and found himself lodgings around the corner, in Templar Street. It is not surprising this is the period John would least like to live through again.

The move more or less coincided with another milestone in his life: joining the Standard Bank in September 1966. By this time he had passed Part 1 of the Institute of Bankers exams in all five subjects, which he had taken a few at a time over the course of a year. Based in Clements Lane in the City, Standard was one of the big international banks, later to become Standard Chartered in 1970, with branches all over Africa and the Far East. The District Bank had been small and parochial, and the opportunities limited, but here John could see a future that he might enjoy. He wanted to travel and a career with Standard could certainly provide that.

As it happened the opportunity arose almost immediately. Recently incorporated with the Bank of West Africa, Standard had a host of branches in Nigeria, which were suddenly acutely short of staff. Ninety per cent of their workforce, mostly Eastern Nigerians, had fled during the inter-tribal feud that preceded the Biafran war, and the bank was looking for volunteers to take their place. There was no stampede for this particular posting, and John immediately saw the advantage: a chance to travel, a chance to save money, and a chance to do an interesting job, at a level of seniority which he might have waited years in London to have achieved.

Thus in December 1966 he was dispatched to Jos, in Northern Nigeria, one of the bank's larger branches, as Assistant Accountant, two down in the pecking order from Manager. The Manager was Bert Butler, and his Assistant, Ron Altrincham.

Jos, he remembers, was heaven on earth, one of the most glorious parts of the world, even now, he says he has ever been to: on a plateau in the north, a long way from the bustle and squalor of Lagos, 3,000 feet up, with an idyllic climate. He was met at the little airport, having flown from Kano, by a young Nigerian boy called Moses Dewa who, because of John's name, was fully expecting a soldier. Moses was to be his steward for the duration of his stay, and was clearly astonished to find a white man who treated him with such consideration. 'You can't believe it,' he says, 'but sometimes he did some of the jobs for me. Anytime Mr Major came home ahead of Mr Cockram he would ask me to go home with the promise that he would serve Mr Cockram when he came home.'

Richard Cockram was another bank employee with whom John shared a comfortable two-bedroomed flat at 7 Club Road. But it was not just Moses; Nigerians working in menial roles in the bank were impressed by how well John treated them, and how unlike the manner in which they were accustomed to being treated by Europeans. Joctock Kilba, for example, who was a messenger, recalls, 'The young man was very hardworking, punctual, friendly to even people like us, and was never overbearing.' Victor Kofoworola Laniyi was the officer in charge of current accounts, and liked John most for 'his industry, humility and his non-racist tendencies. You won't believe it, but he called me one day and said, "Vicky, don't call me Mr Major, call me John."'

The day began early. John would always be up and about well before 6.30, when Moses arrived for work. The early mornings had a particular magic which he looks back on with obvious nostalgia. He remembers sitting on the balcony of the flat, and looking out over nothing for miles and miles and miles, with the highest skies he has ever seen anywhere in the world. He remembers the stillness at five or six in the morning, with wisps of smoke rising in the distance, the huge sky, and the beginnings of the heat that was going to come up later in the day. He loved Africa. He would jump at any opportunity to go back, and can well understand why so many people have never wanted to leave, but he is too English, he says, to have wanted to stay for ever himself.

The other high spot of the day was after work. Each afternoon he would rush home from the bank, change out of his suit into a pair of trousers and short-sleeved shirt, hang a towel round his neck and dash off to the Plateau Club to play a game of some sort, usually lawn tennis, and have a swim. There was no cricket at the club, but a handful of enthusiasts did get together a team and used the runway in Jos, which was little more than a field, as a cricket pitch. It was on this makeshift pitch that John scored 77, his best innings ever, and there's no doubt he would have scored a century had a plane not arrived and interrupted play. 'I would have done it,' he says ruefully. 'I was never batting better than that day.'

He would be home for dinner by 6.30 or 7 o'clock, usually preferring to stay in during the evenings. There was no shortage of social life to be had in Jos if he had wanted it. It had a booming tin mining industry, so there was a large European population, and life revolved around the expatriate clubs. It was a very seductive lifestyle. The expats lived high on the hog, in comfortable houses with servants to cook, clean, garden and attend to their every wish. They all had swimming pools, and there would be card games and dinner parties and dances on Saturday evenings – all the trappings of colonial life; and it was difficult not to be drawn into it.

But there was another side to Africa that John was shocked by. He was shocked by the poverty he saw around him, shocked by the standard of living that so many Nigerians endured, and shocked by how little was done to help them.

On the whole he shied away from the parties. According to Moses, apart from the Plateau Club, he seldom went out. He would rather eat a simple dinner – a favourite was potatoes, beans and carrots – then sit quietly in the living room reading novels and newspapers, or in his bedroom listening to foreign news on his radio.

There was one fateful night when he did go out, however. It was 8 May 1967, when he had been in Nigeria for five months. Richard Cockram had just bought a car, a bright red, two-door Ford Cortina, and they had driven to the Yelwa Club, in Bukaru, another club for whites in a suburb nine kilometres away. John's memory of the evening is sketchy. He remembers seeing a film, projected against the white wall of the club, and he remembers that they were both drinking Coca-Cola all evening. Then he climbed into the passenger seat of the car to come home. The next thing he remembers is lying on a grass verge by the side of the road, unable to move, his clothes torn to shreds, and thinking 'Oh, God, we've done it this time.' Richard was sitting beside him with his head in his hands.

He seems to remember that if you were white you didn't need to pass a driving test in Nigeria at that time. In any event, he says, the Cortina was bigger than Richard. They never found out exactly what happened, but the car left the road and ploughed into a ditch, and since the only piece worth saving was the rubber rim that had been round the windscreen, they must have been doing quite a speed.

They sat on the verge for a long time before help arrived. John could see that his left leg was quite clearly broken in a number of places and there wasn't much of a knee cap left. He thinks he must have been thrown through the windscreen and hit his knee cap on the way through. His right leg was cut, but he couldn't move either of them, and thought he might be paralysed. The pain was intense, but he thinks he was probably unconscious for much of the time.

The two of them were finally collected from the roadside and taken to the Our Lady of the Apostles Hospital, one of two missionary hospitals in Jos. Richard was treated for minor injuries and sent home, but John was in a very serious condition. Apart from the legs, he had head and facial injuries; and it seemed quite probable for some weeks afterwards that he might lose his left leg. The knee cap was shattered, and he had compound fractures of every bone in his leg.

Yet when Moses went to visit him in his private room the next day, he said cheerfully, 'Don't worry, Moses, I'm all right.'

Alas he wasn't, and his injuries needed more expertise than the OLA Hospital could provide, so as soon as he was stable enough to move, he was flown to a mission hospital in Lagos. He stayed there for several weeks, too ill to make the long flight home, still in considerable pain and still uncertain about whether his leg could be saved. Eventually he travelled home, accompanied by a boy from Barclays Bank, and was sent to the Mayday Hospital in Croydon.

He remembers arriving at the hospital after the journey, still seriously ill, and lying on his bed with a terrible noise going on around him, wishing it would all go away. Some young nurses were cleaning the ward, and larking about and making a frightful racket, oblivious of the effect it was having on the patients. Suddenly the Sister on duty arrived, and everything changed. She saw at once that there was a new patient on the ward in a critical condition who needed looking after; the cleaning stopped, the larking around stopped, the noise stopped, and the nurses were shooed away. He was never more relieved to see anyone in his life. It was a salutary lesson on the importance of discipline in certain situations. Over the weeks that he lay there, uncomfortable and sometimes pretty miserable, his leg strung up – in plaster from his foot to his thigh – she nursed him with the closest attention possible, helped him, encouraged him and kept his spirits up. The moment she saw he was getting better, she lost interest in him and moved on to other more urgent patients. Another salutary lesson on good nursing.

It had become apparent, soon after his return to Britain, that if he was to have any use of his leg in future it would have to be broken again and reset. So he was moved briefly to King's College Hospital in Dulwich for surgery, before returning to the Mayday which then became his home for months and months while his body healed. He had plenty of visitors during that time, but no one was encouraged to write on his plaster cast. Thornton Heath, where Gwen, Pat and Terry were all now living, was just around the corner, so the family looked in frequently and brought him whatever books or bits and pieces he needed, including long knitting needles with which to scratch itches under the plaster. Someone from the personnel department of the bank came to see him every single week too. The bank couldn't have done more for him, and he was enormously impressed. Considering he had only been with them for a few months when he had the accident, their behaviour was astonishing, and his affection for them remains to this day. They paid for everything, all the medication, the flights, the transport, and during the year or so that he was away from work, he was given not only his salary but his annual pay rise, and other increments due. And if ever he needed anything, they would provide it.

Books were what he needed most. He did a great deal of reading while he was in hospital – nothing too improving, because for most of the time he wasn't fit enough – but he devoured Agatha Christie detective novels at the rate of one a day and read the lot. He read most of Anthony Trollope, who became an enduring favourite, and everything Jane Austen ever wrote, as well as some history and political biography.

When he was finally discharged from hospital in the autumn of 1967 he went to stay with Pat and her family, to recuperate; but it didn't work out. Gwen was over-protective again. She fussed over

John and treated him like a child. She told him not to go climbing the stairs, or doing things which she thought would hurt his leg, she ran around after him and leapt up to get whatever it was he wanted, and chided him if he did something that she could have done for him. He couldn't stand it, and in no time at all had fled back to Brixton, to his old bedsit at 9 Templar Street. Once back on home territory, he plunged straight back into politics.

Other regular visitors to the Mayday Hospital had been friends from Brixton Conservatives, delighted to have him back in their midst and full of political gossip and plans for the forthcoming local council elections in May. Two who were particularly close were Clive Jones and Peter Golds. He had met Clive, who had been a member of Vauxhall YCs, in the early sixties. They both stood unsuccessfully for hopeless wards in the local elections in 1964, and had become firm friends. He was a giant of a man, outsize in figure, and with a heart to match, who, as John says, would give you his last sixpence, but has never had much luck in life. He adored Gwen and made a great fuss of her, which she loved, and had always been a favourite when he had come to Burton Road.

Peter Golds was younger than John and Clive, a colourful character with an encyclopaedic memory for politics, and an abiding passion for football and opera. They had met when he was a grammar school boy in the mid sixties. The Labour controlled Inner London Education Authority had plans to abolish grammar schools and Peter's school had drawn up a petition in protest, which he delivered to the Conservative Party in Lambeth. There he had met John and Clive; John was Chairman of the Lambeth Borough Young Conservatives at that time, and quite a hero to a fourteen-year-old with political aspirations, and they had become friends.

John had held offices in the Brixton YCs – he had been Treasurer, Vice Chairman, Political Officer and Chairman – but in the mid sixties the constituencies of Brixton, Vauxhall and Clapham merged for administrative purposes, to become the North Lambeth Conservative Group, and John became founder Chairman of the new group. Because they were such safe Labour seats, the Conservative Associations in each had very little money and were unable to afford a professional agent. But it created a Catch 22 situation: with no professional agent raising funds and rallying interest in the

Conservative Party, there was little chance of the Tories ever winning the seats from Labour. Under this new scheme the three constituencies shared the expense and each had a slice of the expertise, and the expert who organized it all was Jean Lucas. So in the Lambeth Borough Council elections in May 1968 she was agent to forty-five candidates.

John had fought the hopeless ward of Larkhall in the 1964 elections, when he was twenty-one and only just eligible, and was encouraged by Jean Lucas to have another go if only to get himself better known. She knew his real ambition lay in the House of Commons, and she had been a very positive voice in making him believe he could get there one day, but not without experience, and this was an ideal opportunity. Most of the seats had already selected their candidates by the time he returned to the fray, and the only one that still had a vacancy was Ferndale. It was a hopeless ward, where Labour votes tended to be weighed rather than counted, and everyone knew that John's chances of success were non-existent.

The results were incredible. Lambeth council had been controlled by Labour for years. Before the May elections, they had held fifty-one seats, compared with the Conservatives' nineteen. But a curious set of circumstances played against them. Harold Wilson's Labour Government had reached mid term and was deeply unpopular; and in April, just a month before the elections, Enoch Powell had made his highly emotive 'Rivers of Blood' speech in Birmingham in which he predicted racial atrocities if immigration was not controlled, and his rhetoric sent a significant number of Labour voters in Lambeth, which had the heaviest concentration of immigrants, running to the Tories in the mistaken belief that Powell spoke for the Party. A number of Tory candidates capitalized on the situation: they went around the borough sticking notices on cars saying 'We Back Enoch', and were elected on that ticket.

When the votes were announced, there had been a complete turnaround. The Conservatives had swept the board, and had fifty-seven seats on the new Council to Labour's three. Even Ferndale, the most unlikely of all, had changed hands, and John Major had his first political success. Clive Jones was also in. There was fantastic excitement when the results came through, and on his way home in the middle of the night, with some fellow revellers, John decided to stop off and break the good news to an elderly lady who had helped in the campaign but been unable to come to the count. She was obviously in bed and asleep because all the lights were out and there was no answer from the door. So John was hoisted up a lamppost outside the house by his friends and was throwing gravel at her bedroom window with as much force as he could muster, when a rather unamused policeman appeared. He didn't swallow the explanation, convinced that no Conservative would ever win a seat around these parts, and the newly elected councillor for Ferndale very nearly spent the first night of his political career in custody.

Exciting though it was, this startling landslide in Lambeth presented problems for Bernard Perkins who was Council Leader. Of the fifty-seven new councillors, only twelve had any experience at all. The rest were completely green, and completely unprepared, some more so than others. Sir George Young was elected, and so was his wife, Lady Aurelia, who had no desire to be a councillor at all. She had very young children at home and only agreed to stand because the ward was desperate for a candidate and everyone said she was certain to lose. Once in, however, she had enormous fun, as they all did. They were mostly very young and enthusiastic, and Lambeth became quite a vibrant council during their period of office, and in some respects quite a model. So the twelve who had any degree of experience were made chairmen of the committees irrespective of their suitability, and their vice-chairmen were chosen entirely at random from the remaining newcomers. Thus it was that, sight unseen, John was appointed Vice-Chairman of the Housing Committee.

It was a piece of extraordinary luck. John became fascinated by housing, and there was no place with more fascinating housing problems at that time than Lambeth. More significantly, he came under the tutelage of Harry Simpson, Director of Housing and Property Services, who was widely acknowledged as one of the most knowledgeable and experienced people in his field. He was also a most inspiring man, and, delighted to find such an intelligent and willing pupil, took John under his wing and taught him all he knew. He took him to look at houses and housing schemes, took him to housing conferences all over the world, gave him books and papers on housing to study, and taught him everything he knew. He taught him that bureaucracy can be used as a force for good rather than a force for interference, and he showed him how to overcome the barrier that naturally goes up between officials in suits and people who need their help, which so often prevents them from getting the help they need. John Major remembers:

> Harry Simpson had the great gift of bringing people into things instead of locking them out. He'd sit down before a meeting with a gin and tonic and explain what the questions were, what problems people had and what might be done to deal with them. He taught that you could achieve more by persuasion than by bludgeoning.
>
> He would take people who were totally opposed to his view, he would analyse their outlook, and the first thing he did was to understand their argument and why they made it. From that perspective you can dismantle it unless of course *you* get a better understanding and realize they may be right. If you operate from the other side of the wall without comprehending someone's thinking, you will never get through.

No one knew his politics to the day he died – quite suddenly of a heart attack in 1988. They were unimportant to him. What he cared about were people and the conditions they lived in, and he was convinced good housing for everyone, no matter what their status in the community, was the key to improving society. For three years he and John were very close. After meetings and committees in the Town Hall, Harry would drive John to his home in Purley for a meal. His wife, Gladys, would snatch a couple of hours' sleep in the afternoons so that she could stay up to give them something to eat when they arrived, which would never be before 11 o'clock or midnight. Then, while she went off to bed, they would settle down with a gin and tonic each and talk about housing until 3 or 4 o'clock in the morning. Harry would then drive John back to his flat. Having been blown up four times during the war, he was a poor sleeper, and John didn't drive.

John would be a regular visitor to the house at weekends too, often helping Harry in the garden. There was a great rapport between the two men. They came from similar backgrounds, and would compare notes about their humble beginnings – Harry was one of seven children, brought up by his mother in very poor circumstances, who had left school at sixteen, and started out as a rent collector. In many ways he became like a father to John during that period, and when he met Norma, one of the first places he took her was down to Purley to meet Harry and Gladys.

Late nights were inevitable. Council activities all took place in the evenings and at weekends, and during the daytime John was working at the bank once more. It must have been a punishing schedule, particularly after October when he became a trainee dealer in the Foreign Exchange Market. The dealing room was the sharp end of banking, nothing like as frenetic as it is today, but still at times a highly pressured job. They began at 8 o'clock in the morning and were there until the markets closed at 5.30, making snap decisions sometimes on alarming amounts of money. Chief dealer at the time was Alan Orsich, who was amazed that John had the stamina for his council work as well. But the council work was what he cared about. John did the job conscientiously, and he was well-liked by his colleagues – several of them are still friends, including Alan Orsich – but banking was never much more than a means to an end.

As Vice-Chairman of the Housing Committee his main concern was running the council estates, of which Lambeth had a vast number, and his main responsibility was for housing management; but John didn't stick to his own brief. Encouraged by Harry, he sat in on all sorts of other committee meetings, and read briefs on other aspects of housing, so that he saw and understood a broader picture. His enthusiasm and industry paid off. After the first year Bernard Perkins shuffled his councillors around and John became Chairman of Housing, where he stayed until the Conservatives were unceremoniously thrown out of office in 1971. He was the first member of the new intake to be given a chairmanship, and at twenty-six, the youngest ever Chairman of Housing.

Bernard Perkins was another extraordinary man, who was a considerable influence on John. He was Deputy Director of Housing in Wandsworth by day, and councillor by night; he had led the small Conservative group on Lambeth council the year before. Forty years old, he was a politician through and through, a pragmatist, autocratic, shrewd, with a healthy sense of humour, and a deep concern for the poor and disadvantaged in life. He also had a great intolerance, like John, of racism in any shape or form, which made them firm friends early on.

There was no Race Discrimination Act in 1968, and racism was endemic in Lambeth. People said and wrote the most offensive things. People with a room to let, for example, would put notices in the windows saying 'No Indians', 'No Jamaicans', or 'No blacks'. John hated it. If he heard anyone making pejorative remarks, telling racist jokes or referring to black people in a derogatory way, as many people did, he would have nothing whatever to do with them.

A number of racists, of course, were on the council, the group who had been elected on the We Back Enoch ticket, and who did their best when they first arrived to persuade their fellow councillors to follow the same line. Bernard wouldn't have it, and determined to smoke them out. A furious debate ensued, in which he found that John Major and Sir George Young were two of his strongest supporters. In the end he made a public statement, denouncing their views in the council chambers, which he had printed and circulated; and coped with the offending councillors by marginalizing them. They spent their time in office with the most uninteresting jobs, on the most boring committees where they could do the least damage. As a result of it all Bernard Perkins was appointed to the Community Relations Commission by Reginald Maudling, who became Home Secretary two years later.

It was a tremendously exciting period for John and enormously influential in the development of his political ideas. They had a mini parliament in Lambeth, a debating chamber in which what was said mattered because it led to decisions – they were able to change things. Peter Brown, now John's agent in Huntingdon, says he has never been better than in the Council chamber at Lambeth. He had a killer instinct, which has been sadly toned down since. His powers of rhetoric and debate, he says, were such that the opposition were demoralized.

John Major says,

If you wanted to boil down my political views to a single sentence, it would be that I don't believe anybody should know their place. Where people end up in life shouldn't depend on where they started out.

During most of his youth, in one form or another, there were people who wanted him to know his place, who wanted him to know what he could and couldn't do. He always found that deeply offensive. And nothing infuriates him more than people from modest backgrounds who say 'We can't do that, that's not for people like us.' It's deeply ingrained in him. Once you understand that you understand a great deal. You understand the Citizen's Charter, why he has a certain antipathy for the great and the good and why he doesn't want to be part of it. Those ideas were well honed during his time in Lambeth. Brixton was the scruffy end of Lambeth, Streatham was the smart end. Streatham returned Duncan Sandys to Parliament, Brixton had Marcus Lipton. Streatham rather looked down its collective nose and was rather sorry it was part of the same borough as grotty old Brixton. Brixton might have been at the other end of the world for all they knew and cared.

Some of the greatest changes they brought about during their three years in office were in housing policy, although most of the credit, he says, belonged to Bernard Perkins, Peter Carey, Bernard's deputy, and above all to Harry Simpson. He may have been an apt pupil but he wasn't the driving force behind that. He was able to carry out reasonably efficiently what Harry was able to lay before him.

The real cause of the problem in Lambeth was multiple occupation. West Indian immigrants who wanted a stake in the community had bought property, and to cover the cost, they had sub-let. Single houses might have forty or fifty people living in them, in indescribably squalid conditions, and because no maintenance was ever carried out, or decoration, and no one cared for the fabric of the buildings, they were literally falling down. The area is crowded today with a population of over 200,000, but in the 1960s there were many more people living in Lambeth – the figure was closer to 300,000. Whole streets were collapsing. Peter Walker, who became Conservative Minister for Housing in June 1970, came down to look at one of the houses in Lambeth, and left ashen faced and in tears.

Under the guidance of Harry Simpson, John introduced a registration scheme for these houses and Lambeth became the first of the London boroughs to do so. The aim was to restrict the number of people living in a house by ensuring that, as people left, no one else took their place. It was no easy undertaking. The landlords were hostile because they resented interference and the tenants were suspicious because they thought they were going to be evicted. Much of the housing was already so far gone it had to be demolished, which was a great tragedy and entirely changed the face of Lambeth architecturally. Two streets which were particularly notorious were Geneva and Somerleyton Roads, and it was the demolition of areas like these which led to extensive and ugly redevelopment, particularly the high-rise blocks built at that time which proved to be such a disaster in later years. John says:

At the time they simply seemed a good use of scarce space, but we were all wrong about that, as events proved.

They set up a Housing Aid Centre, the first of its kind in the world, which Peter Walker opened in 1970. It was Harry Simpson's brainchild, but it seemed to John that it was only one half of what needed to be done. People could come in and get advice, but the Council was still shielded in anonymity. People couldn't get at the people who made decisions, so he took the Housing Aid Centre out on tour and they held a series of large public meetings at which he spoke, which were also attended by the Planning Chairman, the Director of Housing, the Director of Planning and the Lettings Officer – the people who had the biggest impact on how people lived in Lambeth. If you couldn't get a council house it was because the Lettings Officer didn't give you one, and they were out at those public meetings telling people what was going on. Hundreds and hundreds of people came to those meetings. John remembers one at Saint Anselm's Church, Kennington, when someone threw a dead rat at him. He asked where the man came from, and his address was in Southwark, not Lambeth, so he suggested he collect his rat and throw it at Alderman Ron Brown who was the Southwark Housing Chairman, and not at him.

At another meeting a woman stood up. She was wearing a black leather hat, a black leather jacket, a black leather mini skirt and black leather thigh-length Dick Whittington style boots, and was really rather lovely. She stood up in the middle of this audience and said, 'I am the wife of the local vicar,' and the place fell apart.

The meetings were great events which went on for two or three hours where you really saw the sharp end of the need, he says, and the thing that struck him most about it was the anonymity of the people who made the decisions. It was the Town Hall who made the decisions. People are frightened of those in authority, afraid that if you upset them you won't get anywhere. By going out he began to feel how they felt and to see the problem from their perspective. It was a very early version of the Citizen's Charter.

Housing was of paramount importance during the Conservatives' brief reign at the Town Hall. Under Bernard Perkins' leadership the system was turned upside down and made more businesslike. He formed a Policy Committee, made up of the chairmen of all the committees, which he chaired. The Housing Department was reorganized to embrace valuers, environmental health, and parts of the legal and financial departments to provide a complete service.

But it was an expensive decision and one which they paid for three years on when the bills started coming in. In addition to their own programme to provide a thousand units a year over the five-year period – with the price of land at £250,000 an acre – they also decided to fund housing associations to provide a further thousand new and improved units per year – a scheme which ironically was scrapped by the left-wing Labour council which replaced them in 1971, in which Ken Livingstone was Vice-Chairman of Housing.

Bernard Perkins was not unduly surprised. He recalls the cynicism of Anthony Crosland, Labour Minister for Local Government, who came to Lambeth to see what the borough was doing for homeless families. At the end of the day, he said, 'You're making too much provision. If you didn't make so much you wouldn't have the problem.'

At the same time as John was serving on the council, he was still active with the Brixton Conservative Association, which in the late 1960s acquired a reputation for some rumbustious politics. It went through three chairmen in as many years. John had been Treasurer, and Deputy Chairman, and in 1970 he became Chairman. They were interesting times, particularly leading up to the general election in June. In neighbouring Norwood the Conservatives had selected a parliamentary candidate by the name of Bernard Black, who was Leader of Gravesend Borough Council, and admirably active in the community. It turned out, however, that his activities were not so admirable after all, and shortly before the election he was fingered by the boys in blue and invited to spend some time at Her Majesty's pleasure. He resigned from Gravesend council, resigned as a Justice of the Peace, and Norwood were left to find a substitute at the eleventh hour.

Marcus Lipton was just a few months short of his seventieth birthday, a rather courtly figure who campaigned from the back of a large vintage car. Bernard Perkins says he was an old fraud, but John liked and admired him, although he lost no opportunity to score a political point. Lipton introduced a bill in the House of Commons at one time to abolish fox hunting. John was swiftly on to his soapbox the next Saturday morning with an extensive and lurid catalogue of all that was wrong in Brixton before delivering his denouement. 'Yet our Member of Parliament,' he boomed, gesticulating towards Brixton Hill, 'horrified by the sight of the hare and the hounds and the continuous fox hunts up and down Brixton Hill, wants to abolish fox hunting.'

Clive Jones stood as a candidate for Vauxhall in those elections and, despite John and Peter Golds' best efforts in his campaign, he lost to the Labour MP George Strauss, who had held the seat for twenty years. Several of their fellow councillors had parliamentary ambitions: Bernard Perkins, who was thwarted by ill health, developed multiple sclerosis; Peter Carey his deputy, who died of a heart attack; Laurie Kennedy, who never stood; Barbara Wallis, who stood unsuccessfully in Feltham and became secretary to an MP instead – and from 1979 to 1992 that MP was John Major. The only one who had any luck in finding a seat apart from John Major was Sir George Young, who was elected for Ealing Acton in 1974. He was on the Housing Committee with John, and twenty-odd years later became Minister for Housing in John Major's Government.

John did not even look for a seat in 1970. He felt that it was too early, and he was worried about being turned down, afraid that if he failed once it would be more difficult to find a seat the second time round. He was also very uncertain about his ability to get even so far as the candidates list. Beside Sir George Young, a baronet, educated at Eton and Oxford, and the stuff of which Tories were traditionally made, he felt woefully inadequate. He was not brimming with confidence. When he was first elected to Lambeth council he was so nervous he would be physically sick every time he had to make a speech in the chamber. He was quiet, efficient and hard-working, and he sought and took the advice of his officers, but he was not an inspiring figure. He was at his best in committees. Several friends from the past claim to have seen a leader in John from an early age. Bernard Perkins didn't; he saw an excellent manager, although, to be fair, at that stage there was no call for him to be anything else.

His various offices in the Brixton Conservative Party at the time inevitably brought him into close contact with Jean Lucas, the agent who had set up the Lambeth Conservative Group. She was fifteen years older than John, a bright, efficient, smartly-dressed, no-nonsense sort of woman, with acute political antennae, who has put many a young Conservative on the road to Parliament in her time. John liked and admired her enormously, respected her judgement and found her ruthlessly clear-minded. He calls her one of the shrewdest judges of political horseflesh he has ever encountered; and she is still a close friend and confidante. She came into John's life at a crucial time and gave him encouragement that was not forthcoming from anyone else: not the sort that people give when they want to be kind, but genuine encouragement. She made him believe that Parliament was not a hopeless dream, and she told him precisely what he needed to do to turn it into a reality. After late-night meetings she would frequently drive him home and they would sit in the car outside his new flat in Streatham, and talk, sometimes long into the night, and often long after Jean would have liked to have gone home to bed. One night he finally came out with the question he had obviously been plucking up courage to ask: did Jean think he could become an MP? She told him he was capable of doing anything he wanted to do. But he must have money, a good job and a decent curriculum vitae.

One of the advantages of his sojourn in Africa, and all those months spent lying prone on a hospital bed in Croydon, was that John had managed to save money, and by the end of 1968 had enough for a mortgage on a flat. It was the first time he had lived in a property that was not rented. It was a little two-bedroomed flat at 24 Primrose Court, Hydethorpe Road, in Streatham, which he furnished with the bare necessities: a bed, a chair, a record player and a carpet.

He was reliant on friends with cars in those days. Clive also had a car, and after meetings at the Town Hall, they would often get fish and chips or a curry from an Indian take-away in Brixton Road, which served enormous portions, then jump into Clive's car, with Peter Golds in the back carrying the food, and drive to Primrose Court, where they all made an unseemly dash for the one and only chair, and settled down with a couple of beers each and talked politics into the night. It was a popular address for Lambeth councillors. No less than three lived there and for some time there was graffiti on the wall of the gents in the Town Hall, which read, 'I live in Primrose Court and don't want to be a councillor'.

Among John Major's political heroes he lists Gladstone, 'who was like a volcano that erupted from time to time'. It was his powers of oratory that impressed him most; he was one of the greatest orators Westminster has ever seen, addressing three or four thousand people in the open air, often for an hour or more, without a microphone, simply by sheer force of personality and moral conviction. He also cites the darling of his generation, Iain Macleod, another great orator, who inspired dozens of John's contemporaries in the House, whom he first heard at a Young Conservative meeting in the early 1960s.

Macleod was on a small platform, sitting behind a table with the usual cloth draped over it, and from where John was sitting he could see his hands under the table. He was only addressing fifty to a hundred people, all Young Conservatives, yet before he stood up to speak, Macleod's hands were clenched and shaking with nerves. When he got to his feet all trace of it was gone, and he was superb. John was very struck by him on that occasion, and admired the way he made himself so readily available to the YCs. He heard him many times at party conferences subsequently, and in 1970 Macleod came to Lambeth to a pre-election rally in the Town Hall.

These were the elections for the old Greater London Council which took place in April, a couple of months before the general election. Lambeth had four votes *en bloc*, which they had won convincingly three years earlier. They knew 1970 would be tougher, but they lost one seat out of sheer bad luck. Three candidates, all women, had names which all began with G, so they were lumped together on the voting slip in alphabetical order: Diana Geddes (Con), Anna Greaves (Lab) and Muriel Gumbel (Con). Voters put a cross beside the first two, and Muriel Gumbel lost.

As Chairman of the Association, John was involved in looking after Iain Macleod during the rally, and there was a private dinner for him afterwards at Muriel Gumbel's house. Macleod was then Shadow Chancellor, and although a relatively young man, in his fifties, very severely crippled with arthritis. It was not many months before his death, and he was hunched and misshapen with the disease. Yet he gave a performance that no one watching will ever forget. As he began speaking he seemed to grow before their eyes, and he stood on the rostrum with an aura about him that had his audience riveted. 'Mr Wilson promised us government with guts,' he roared, his gnarled hands gripping the lectern. 'His Government, your guts.' John watched him transfixed. He says today:

> The great point about Macleod was his capacity to leave you feeling better at the end of a speech than you did at the beginning, in a way that I've not heard equalled by anyone.

He made formidable speeches, particularly at the Party Conference. His voice carried like a great bell, he had a domed head, and because his disabilities made it impossible for him to turn his head, his head would remain rigid and he would turn his whole body to look at his audience in a way that was quite compelling.

But it wasn't just his oratory that attracted so many young Tory politicians to Macleod. He was a romantic figure, a liberal Tory, who would probably never have been a Conservative in the 1930s; and that's what made him such a hero to so many of the young meritocrats who were forging their way in the Party in the 1960s. Iain Macleod represented the new, reborn, post-war Party that believed in equality of opportunity and social responsibility, that was not just a party for the Establishment to protect the interests of the Establishment. Iain Macleod made the Tory Party respectable for people who came from humble backgrounds and who might once have been accused of betraying their roots.

4

MARRIAGE, FAMILY AND THE HUNT FOR A SEAT

POLITICS have been John Major's life. Most of his waking hours since his early teens have gone into politics. When he worked for the bank he spent evenings and weekends in committees and meetings or campaigning out on the streets on his own or someone else's behalf. He has spent holidays and other bits of spare time poring over briefs and latterly Red Boxes. His conversation has been very largely politics, and much of his reading too. Yet ask him when he is happiest and the answer is not standing at the Dispatch Box at Prime Minister's Question Time bettering the Leader of the Opposition. It is not coming away from Maastricht with a deal no one thought was possible. It is not even watching the results come in for the general election everyone said he would lose.

His happiest moments have nothing to do with politics at all. They are snatched minutes of tranquillity, sitting in the garden he has made in Huntingdon, with the forsythia in bloom and a thousand daffodils in flower, surrounded by his family, watching cricket maybe, or immersed in a good book. Politics have been his life, but they are by no means all he lives for, and he will have no difficulty leaving them when the time comes. His first priority is home. A secure homelife is the bedrock upon which his entire parliamentary career has been built. And Norma has been pivotal.

They met on 9 April 1970, the day of the GLC elections, in the hallway of the Brixton Conservative Association at 332 Brixton Road – he says the hallway, she says the committee room, and they will happily argue for hours about who was standing where and when who first saw whom. Three weeks later they were engaged, and five months after that they were married. Norma was a friend of Peter

Golds. Like him she was an opera devotee, a fan of Joan Sutherland in particular, and had met him at Covent Garden some years before. Sutherland had been doing a season at the Royal Opera House, and Norma and Peter, like many an opera fan, would save every last penny for the occasion, and watch her sing night after night from 'the gods' (the cheapest seats in the house, which they might have spent all night out in the street queuing for) then wait outside the stage door for her to come out after the performance. Discovering that they both lived in a similar part of London, they became friends. They had met many friends this way. But their friendship was confined to opera. Norma knew nothing about politics and had no interest.

Norma was a very independent woman, with whom all John's friends immediately fell in love. She was twenty-eight, a year older than John, disarmingly pretty, and with, as John remembers, the biggest brown eyes he had ever seen. She had been a domestic science teacher at a school in Camberwell for six years, but by the time she met John she was working for Simplicity Patterns as a dressmaker, making the clothes which they took on tour to school fashion shows. One such travelling show had come to her school in Camberwell, and she had applied to Simplicity for a job. At the same time she was doing freelance dressmaking, and one of her clients was Diana Geddes, one of the Conservative candidates in the GLC elections.

So when Peter Golds asked whether she might come along to Brixton on polling day to answer the phone, and help ferry voters to the polling station, so that every other available body could go out knocking on doors, she had a particular interest. She was wearing a beige, brown and white-checked two-piece suit with a short skirt that day, which she had made herself, with a pale coffee-coloured blouse and high white leather boots. John remembers the outfit in detail. Over the top she wore a black rabbit-fur coat, which she loved and wore until it fell apart. They disagree over what he was wearing. She swears he was wearing a brown suit, he denies it. It may have been green but he swears he has never possessed a brown suit. What neither of them deny is that they both felt enormously attracted to each other. John said, 'Who's the girl with the big brown eyes?' and immediately asked Peter to introduce him. They shook hands, chatted briefly, then John turned to Peter and said they must get Norma into the count.

The count took place that night at the Town Hall. Tickets were allocated by name, and by that time they were all gone, so once John and Peter and everyone else had got in to the count themselves, they had to smuggle one of their tickets out of the building for Norma to come in with. At the end of the evening she drove John home, and their relationship grew from there.

Norma had a crash course in politics. Two months later she was back at the Town Hall for the general election count. Again she had no ticket, but candidates were allowed to take their wives, and since Clive Jones, who was the candidate for Vauxhall, had no wife and no girlfriend at the time, he took Norma. Since John had already asked him to be his best man, it caused much hilarity among their friends.

Norma was greatly impressed by John's position as Chairman of Housing on Lambeth Council. She discovered early on that politics interfered with normal life, but the life he introduced her to was very grand. The Town Hall itself was a splendid building, and he took her to glittering functions, introduced her to important people, and life was exciting, not least because they were in love. She had no idea during those few whirlwind weeks that John's ambitions went any further. She rather imagined that Chairman of Housing was the pinnacle.

His decision to marry Norma was, he says without hesitation, the best decision he has ever made in his life, but there is no doubt it was 'something of a spec buy'. On the face of it, they had almost nothing in common – John loved politics, cricket and football and knew nothing of opera; Norma hated sport, knew nothing about politics and lived for opera. But in fact they came from similar backgrounds, and life had not been easy for either of them. If anything, Norma's family circumstances had been even more difficult than John's, and certainly more tragic. Her father, Norman Wagstaff, who was in the Royal Artillery, had died two days after the end of the war in 1945 when Norma was three. He had been posted for much of the war at All Stretton, in Shropshire, where Norma was born, but towards the end he was sent to Western Europe. His young wife, Edith, was terrified for his safety, but when Victory in Europe was declared she thought he had survived, until a telegram arrived telling her that her husband had been killed in a motorcycle accident. It was the second tragedy to hit her in a matter of months, and her grief must have been hard to bear. Just the year before she had lost a baby. Her second child, Colin, born on New Year's Day in 1944, had lived for only six days; he died of broncho-pneumonia.

Edith had been staying with her husband's aunt in Bourn, near Cambridge, while he was abroad, but when the news of his death arrived, she took Norma back home to Bermondsey in south east London, where she and Norman both came from, and where they had married. The area had been badly damaged by bombs during the war, and was even more neglected than it had been before. They moved back to Norman's old flat in a run-down block with very basic amenities, where Edith, known as Dee to her friends, courageously set to work to improve life for herself and her daughter.

Edith was only twenty-two when she was widowed. She had had a very difficult childhood herself – her father died when she was a child, and her mother struggled to bring her up alone – and was determined to improve her lot. She worked hard. She was a book-keeper, and later trained as an accountant, and at one time was doing three jobs at once: one by day, another in the evening and one she did from home. Her industry paid off, and in time she and Norma moved out of London to Beckenham in Kent. But financial success came at a price. Edith decided that, if she was going to work all hours, Norma would be better taken care of in a boarding school, so at the age of four Norma was sent off to a school in Bexhill-on-Sea, paid for by Royal Artillery charities.

Horrific as it sounds, it was by no means traumatic, and Norma was perfectly happy. Her mother came to visit her every weekend, and stayed in a guest house in the town. In many ways it was the ideal training for her future life with John. She grew up as a very self-sufficient and independent little girl, and one who always cherished close family bonds, although she has never been tremendously confident. She has always had a very close relationship with her mother – their voices are strikingly similar – but friends say they were always more like sisters than mother and daughter.

In time Edith fell out with her in-laws to such an extent that she reverted to her maiden name, Johnson, and Norma too was known thereafter as Norma Johnson. At the age of seven, Norma was moved from Bexhill to a private school in Dulwich, called Oakfield, where she was a weekly boarder, going home at weekends. At eleven, when financial support from the Royal Artillery ran out, she moved yet again, to Peckham School for Girls in Camberwell. She came away with seven O levels, two A levels and a place on a teacher training course at Battersea College.

Opera had not been part of her childhood. Her father had been a talented pianist, and clearly passed on some of his talent to Norma, but she had grown up with a love of popular classical music. It wasn't until she was twenty-three and met the singer June Bronhill that she seriously listened to opera for the first time. She was introduced to it in a round-about way by a boyfriend with theatrical connections. He was a fellow teacher in the school at Camberwell, and was a great friend of the stage manager of the Lyric Theatre. Ronald Millar's musical comedy, *Robert and Elizabeth*, was playing at the time, with June Bronhill and Keith Michell in the title roles. The boyfriend took Norma to see the show, and she went backstage with him and met the cast. Years later Ronnie Millar was to become a valued friend and speech writer for John Major.

Norma saw from the programme that June's past performances had been in opera. She had succeeded Joan Sutherland as Lucia di Lammamoor at Covent Garden and sung Gilda in *Rigoletto*. Norma had always loved the theatre, but opera was something she had never explored. She decided she ought to give it a try, and find out what all the fuss was about, so she started borrowing records. By chance the particular recordings of the Lucia and the *Rigoletto* that she took out of the library were sung by Joan Sutherland. They were pure magic, and Norma was hooked.

By the time she met John opera had become a way of life. She had made a lot of friends who were the same way inclined, and they had enormous fun together, as they queued in the freezing cold outside Covent Garden, or bedded down at the Albert Hall for the last night of the Proms, when they would stand at the front waving flags. Sometimes they went further afield. One weekend Norma packed three friends into her white Mini and drove to Hamburg to see Joan Sutherland sing Handel's *Julius Caesar*; and there were a couple of trips to Holland on a similar mission. 'Crazy,' she says looking back. 'With your foot on the floor we couldn't do more than forty miles per hour.'

So while Norma endeavoured to learn about the workings of the council during those early days of her relationship with John, he began to take a serious look at opera, but it was slow work. He fell asleep during the first performance Norma took him to, and although he professes to enjoy it now, and has seen a great deal of opera and can talk knowledgeably about it, Norma says she is still not certain to this day whether he genuinely does enjoy it.

Their success lay in their ability to tolerate each other's passions, and to give each other the freedom to go away and indulge in their own activities without interference.

Harry Simpson was a great lover of classical music, so he and Norma hit it off from the start. He had a large collection of records, and was delighted to have someone to share his enthusiasm with. Gladys, like John, was a philistine, so he and Norma would sit and listen to music together. But Norma and Gladys became very close too, and in the early days Gladys used to warn her what life with a councillor would be like. 'You stay with him,' she would say, speaking from years of experience, 'and you'll never know where he is. He'll be out every night at meetings.' But Norma was undeterred. 'Oh, I'll put up with that,' she would say. It didn't take long to discover that Gladys was right. Shortly after they became engaged, she realized it was not just evenings either. John went off on a housing trip to Finland, he also went to Leningrad, where he saw the Bolshoi Ballet, and there was another housing conference in Poland. He and Harry went to that one together, and Norma would go over to Purley to speak to John when Harry phoned home.

John and Norma spent a lot of time together during those weeks before they became engaged – their day jobs and his council work permitting. They met one another's family too. Gwen Major was seriously ill by this time, and was in and out of hospital so much she said she ought to have a season ticket. John had taken her on holiday to Spain with him the year before, just the two of them, which she had loved. It was the first time she had ever been out of the country. Pat made her some clothes to go away in, and she was enormously excited by the whole adventure, especially at being able to stay up almost all night and have a nap in the afternoon. But she had gone downhill since then. For some time she had been using an inhaler pump to help her breathing, which had increased in strength over the years, until the doctors said they couldn't give her anything stronger. She had been on steroids too, which had made her very overweight, but she was still smoking furiously. It didn't help, but the specialist said she was going to die anyway, why make her last years unhappy?

She died on 17 September in the Mayday Hospital in Croydon at the age of sixty-five. On the day of the funeral the little tobacconist shop around the corner from Pat's house, where she had lived, closed its doors as a mark of respect while the cortege was in the street, and a queue of puzzled customers built up outside. She had been a gregarious woman to the end, and much loved by everyone who knew her. Clive Jones, who had always had a particularly soft spot for Gwen, was one of the few outsiders in the family group at her funeral. It was a simple ceremony and she was finally laid to rest in Streatham Vale next to Tom.

Sad as it was, her death had not been a surprise to anyone, and in many ways, having watched helpless as she fought for breath, it was a release. Everyone who knew her missed her, but of all the family, Terry was the most affected. He had always had a particularly close bond to his mother and he became seriously depressed by her loss. He and Shirley had two children by this time, Fiona and Mark. Pat was pregnant with her son, Christopher, born in October. Her husband, Peter Dessoy, sadly died of cancer two years later, and she was left to bring up two small children on her own. She was very like Gwen and has become increasingly so over the years, and like her mother, has a great capacity for collecting lame ducks and devoting herself to others.

By the time of Gwen's death, John and Norma had fixed the date for their wedding, for 3 October, and at once thought they should delay it, but Pat was adamant that they should go ahead with their plans. She insisted it was what Gwen would have wanted, and so the preparations continued. John had always consulted Pat in times of uncertainty, and talks to her in moments of stress to this day. 'He was under the impression as a younger man', she says, 'that I was cleverer than him. As a result he would sometimes listen to what I had to say.' Because of the thirteen-year age gap between them, she has always felt and behaved as much like a mother to him as a sister, and so as the mother rather than the sister, when his marriage was looming, she took a conscious decision to back off and let her 'son' go. She has never pursued him or interfered in his family life since but has always been there when he has needed her. 'I used to think sometimes he was looking for his mother's approval. If I said, "No I don't agree," he would defend himself and we would end up having a shouting match at one another over the phone.'

The wedding was glorious, if slightly unusual. John chose the Battle Hymn of the Republic, not noted as a favourite for nuptials, but the ceremony was lifted on to another plane by June Bronhill's offer to sing *Ave Maria*. She stood in the gallery and her voice filled every last corner of St Matthew's Church, Brixton, sending tingles down the spines of everyone there. She was to have sung while the newlyweds signed the register, but Norma put her foot down because she wanted to listen, so a couple of chairs had to be found for John and Norma to sit on while June sang, and they signed the register to some mundane organ music instead.

June Bronhill and Norma had become friends after that first meeting at the Lyric Theatre, and Norma had worked for her for a while, and kept in touch in the intervening years. June had a young daughter called Caroline, whom everyone called Biddy, and Norma would babysit for her sometimes when June was at the theatre. Norma was still teaching at the time, so it was by no means a full-time job, but during the school holidays she would stay in June's house in Harriet Walk in Knightsbridge and look after the house and Biddy while June was working.

The church was packed for the wedding. John had particularly wanted to be married in St Matthew's, and because he didn't actually live in the parish, gave his address as the Housing Department, which was two hundred yards down the road. That is his address on the wedding certificate. Built in the 1820s, it was one of the Waterloo churches. The inside has been mucked about with since, but at the time it had the original layout and fittings and was very handsome.

As well as their family and personal friends, John and Norma had invited almost everyone on Lambeth Council, thinking it was the thing to do. Looking back on the group photograph today, there is scarcely anyone there that they still know. Everyone was dressed in morning suits – not John's favourite dress. He is no great lover of ceremonies even today, and dislikes having to put on formal clothing. He refers to his dinner jacket as 'that barmy outfit'. But the occasion demanded it. Norma wore a dazzling white dress she had made herself, and was given away by her uncle John. He and his wife, Beryl, had come down from Wilmslow, and their daughter Clare was principal bridesmaid.

What also made the wedding slightly out of the ordinary was that the bridegroom very nearly had to be carried down the aisle. Ever since the accident, John's knee had given him trouble from time to time. The problem was that after all the operations tiny bits of bone were left floating around behind the shattered knee cap and every now and again, quite without warning, one of these little pieces would hit a ligament and his leg would give way under him.

On one occasion he and Clive were walking up Brixton Hill from the Town Hall to the Housing Department, when Clive suddenly realized John wasn't there any more. He looked back and there was his friend lying on the ground in a great deal of pain. He happened to fall right outside the old ABC cinema, now a nightspot called the Fridge, and had been spotted by the commissionaire who rushed out, and between them they helped John into the foyer and onto a chair. The first aid officer came to look at him and said he should go to hospital, but John refused. They had a Tenants' Association Committee waiting to see them and he didn't want to let them down. So they telephoned the Housing Department to explain why they were delayed, and Clive and the commissionaire half carried John the remaining hundred yards. John sat through the meeting, in considerable pain, and it was only when the meeting was concluded that he let Clive drive him to King's College Hospital, where he was told in no uncertain terms that he should have come immediately.

It happened again on the night before the wedding. He had had his stag night several days before. It had been no great event, just a few friends going out and having a few pints. On the eve of his wedding he and Clive spent the evening with Geoff Murray, a fellow councillor, and his wife, Joy, who also lived in Primrose Court. At the end of the evening Clive went back to John's flat with him, intending to drive home, when suddenly the leg gave way. He managed to manoeuvre him into bed, then, lest he should be unable to get out of it again in the morning, went home to collect his clothes for the next day, then came back and spent the night on the sofa. John had accumulated a little more furniture by then.

By morning the leg had fortunately eased up a little, and Clive didn't, as he had feared, have to lift him into the bath. However, the wedding was in the afternoon, and they had a visit to a housing estate lined up for the morning. Every six weeks or so they would go out and visit an estate with three or four councillors. It was obviously more effective to see any problems first hand than to have them explained, and one such visit had been planned for 3 October. When the Housing Department realized this was John's wedding day, they said they would change it, but John would have none of it. It could be good publicity, and besides, they had to do something with their morning. So Clive rang a reporter friend, who was invited to the wedding anyway, and he sent along a photographer, and a picture of Councillors Major and Jones in their top hats and tails duly appeared in the *South London Press* the following Tuesday.

The leg was exceedingly painful, and he spent most of the morning sitting on a bollard, while the rest of the party inspected the housing estate. It didn't improve during the day, and Clive imagined he would have to carry John up the aisle. However, the leg held up. They went back to Primrose Court for some sandwiches with the Murrays at lunchtime, and when they arrived at the church at 2.30 p.m. he walked up the aisle alone and unaided. During the reception afterwards, however, instead of the bride and groom circulating among the guests, the guests did the circulating and the bride and groom sat down and stayed where they were.

The reception was held in the Town Hall across the road from the church, in Room 119. Afterwards John and Norma left for their honeymoon in Ibiza, while a great party, which included Norma's mother, who had paid for the wedding, John and Beryl, Terry and Shirley, Clive and Peter Golds, who had been an usher, all went out and had dinner in a Chinese restaurant in Beckenham.

Some of the party had come close to a Chinese meal the night before. Although Norma was living in a little flat of her own by the time she met John, she spent the night before her wedding at her mother's first-floor maisonette in Anerley Park and invited some close friends round, including Peter Golds and Alicia Gains. Alicia, another opera fan, eccentric at the best of times, was late, and thinking that there would be nothing to eat, arrived wielding the most enormous bag of Chinese food which she had bought on the way. Alicia was somewhat accident prone – prompting Peter once to say, 'Pull up a chair and plug it in for Alicia' – and past experience had taught Norma's mother to treat her with caution. On this occasion no one was disappointed. As she came through the front door, she tripped and lost her grip, the bottom fell out of the bag, and generous quantities of chicken chow-mein fell ankle-deep all over the step.

When John and Norma returned from honeymoon they lived at Primrose Court. John was seeking re-election to Lambeth Council in 1971, and needed his address to be within the borough. Norma transformed the flat. She redecorated and brought furniture from her own flat, and turned what had been a very basic bachelor pad into a home. She didn't have much assistance from her husband in all this. Norma is the practical one of the partnership. Having had no man about the house as a child, like her mother, she is very capable. John was hopeless before they married and is hopeless to this day – he doesn't even know where the fuse wire is kept, and has no doubt made an effort never to find out. But Norma already knew as much. He had telephoned one night before they were married and said, 'The lights have gone out, what do I do?'

Norma has always had a great gift for home-making, attested by everyone who has been into any of her houses. As Barbara Wallis, who has known all her houses, says, 'When you walk into Norma's house you immediately feel a sense of warmth enveloping you. You feel totally relaxed, even when you go for the first time; you feel this is a home. It's a great talent.' It was a talent she exercised on very little money. When they first married they had £8 a week for food and general housekeeping expenses, and they just about managed on that, but it didn't cover the big bills like electricity and telephone. John was not earning very much at the bank. He left the dealing room the month they were married, and moved into the business development department at the bank, but he was still quite a junior figure. Norma began doing some supply teaching, to supplement what she earned from dressmaking, but that didn't last long, and their income was very modest.

Those early days of married life established the pattern that Gladys Simpson had warned about. John would come home from the bank and go straight on to council work, and invariably be late home for dinner. Norma was an enthusiastic cook, it had been one of the subjects she taught, but time after time John would ring to say he was going to be an hour late; then the hour would pass, and he would phone again and say, he was sorry he still couldn't get away. Even when he was at home, he was still studying for his banking exams, so much of his time was spent working.

But they had a lot of fun together, and much of the time was spent out anyway. There were functions which John always took Norma to, often very dressy occasions, and as Chairman of Housing he was an important figure in Lambeth. It was on the way to one such glittering evening, in full evening dress, that Norma suddenly had an irresistible urge for some stewed eels in green liquor, and there was nothing for it but to stop at a stall and buy some. It was the first inkling she had that she was pregnant.

Nights out with the Chairman of Housing came to an abrupt end in the spring of 1971, however, when all the Conservative councillors elected in 1968 were bounced off in the local elections. A left-wing Labour group swept the board, returned to Lambeth with a thundering majority, and the revolutionary five-year plan died a death. Norma was very upset, and there was great despondency all round, but John seemed remarkably unperturbed. The council had been a stepping stone. His sights were set not in local politics, but in Westminster, where the previous June a Conservative Government had been returned under the premiership of Edward Heath, and he felt it was time to start in earnest.

But first they had a holiday. John and Norma, plus Norma's mother, Dee, and Peter Golds all went off to Slapton Sands in Devon, where they rented an old priory. It was a lively combination. Dee had taken to John from their first meeting, and he has always been very fond of her, but there have inevitably been tensions at times and neither is beyond the odd waspish remark. They repeated the exercise the following year, taking a cottage instead of the priory, when John and Peter sat riveted to the men's finals at Wimbledon between Stan Smith and Ilie Nastase, one of the most exciting finals ever. Norma wanted to watch Prince Richard of Gloucester's wedding and was allowed the occasional flick.

John knew getting his name on to the Candidates' List at Conservative Party Central Office would be a tough job. In order to apply he needed to be sponsored by a Conservative Member of Parliament and he didn't know any. There were precious few in Lambeth. Brixton, Vauxhall and Norwood were all Labour. The closest was Streatham, the other end of the political world from Brixton, where Duncan Sandys was MP, a rather grand old-style colonialist Tory, who would have been quite unapproachable. However, he had once met Jill Knight, now Dame, the MP for Birmingham Edgbaston who lived in Vauxhall. She had attended a meeting at which John spoke and had been very kind afterwards. Prompted by Jean Lucas, John wrote to her and asked whether she would sponsor him if he were to apply for the Candidates' List, and she agreed.

As it happened he found his first seat without ever applying. It was, he says, pure fluke. Peter Golds, who had become deputy to Jean Lucas, was very friendly with the agent at St Pancras North, Tony Dey, and knew he was in the process of selecting a new candidate. He told John to apply. John said he couldn't, his name wasn't on the Candidates' List, but Peter insisted he should just apply and let St Pancras decide whether they wanted to see him. After several interviews they decided they did, and John was officially selected, although still not approved by Central Office. It was only once he was prospective parliamentary candidate that he sent in an application.

Exciting as it was, the timing could scarcely have been worse. At much the same time as he became candidate for St Pancras, he became the proud father of a bouncing little girl. Elizabeth was born in hospital on 13 November 1971, and was a complete joy to them both. Norma had not been very well with the pregnancy in the early months and had had to stop teaching, but there were no problems with the birth, and everyone was thrilled to bits. She was born on a Saturday and the bush telegraph worked quickly; in no time everyone knew the news and mother and baby had a stream of visitors.

John knew from the start that, given the boundaries it had at that time, St Pancras was a hopeless seat. It encompassed Camden Town, Chalk Farm, Kentish Town and lower Highgate, none of which had yet been taken over by the chattering classes, and was held by the Scots Labour MP Jock Stallard, now Lord. Nevertheless, although it was a small Conservative Association, it was filled with optimistic and enthusiastic people, and before the year was out all his spare time was being channelled north of the river, while Norma was left holding the baby.

Now that she had Elizabeth to look after, Norma's activities as a political helpmate were severely limited. She couldn't go to meetings, as she had done previously, and she couldn't go to functions in St Pancras with the regularity that she had done in Lambeth. Yet the pressure didn't ease off John. He knew that if he was to make any impression on the electorate at the next general election he had to be in the constituency, getting to know the people there, and understanding their problems. Inevitably it meant there was less time at home, little time with the baby and less time with Norma.

As Elizabeth began to grow bigger and more active, it became apparent they were going to need more space. Primrose Court, which John had bought for himself, was on the second floor, and although it had two bedrooms, they wanted a garden. Besides, since he was no longer on Lambeth Council and had no intention of standing again, there was no need to be living within the borough any more. They decided to look for somewhere in Bromley where they would be close to Dee, and found the perfect little house in a pretty rural development called West Oak. They had three small bedrooms, a little terrace, a tiny kitchen with an open hatch through to the sitting room, and another small room that could be opened up to form a larger living area. There was a manageable little garden, and the whole area was surrounded by trees, mostly oaks.

It was ideal, and Norma, in particular, was very happy there. There were about thirty houses on the estate, most of them filled with people in the same situation as John and Norma, with young children, and wives who were at home all day. There was a great sense of community, and a good social life. The husbands all went off to work in the mornings, and the wives and children would get together and, if they organized it properly, they could have lunch in a different house each day. So Norma was never lonely, and although John was often away, she knew she was surrounded by friends.

She had other interests to keep her occupied as well. She was still dressmaking, for instance, even when Elizabeth was quite small. The layout of the house couldn't have been better. She would put Elizabeth in the sitting room with the hatch to the kitchen open, and she would sew in the kitchen, with a breadboard across the sink, then the sewing machine on top of that, so there was no danger of Elizabeth getting under her feet, and yet it was as if they were in the same room. She still went to the opera whenever possible – Dee would babysit – and she wrote letters. Norma has always written remarkably long and newsy letters to friends, and it is a very important part of her life. Even now she keeps in touch with dozens of people all over the world; some of whom she has never even met, but they correspond because they are Joan Sutherland fans.

For all the nights and weekends spent on her own, a widow to politics, Norma never resented John's craving. She realized from the start that he and politics were inseparable and has never tried to come between them. Equally, she has been quite firm about her desire to remain in the background, and get on with her own life. She accepted his absences, and although he has always been the focal point in her life, she was never lost or bereft when he wasn't there. She had been capable and self-sufficient before she married him, and she remained so. In fact, looking back, she doesn't think she could ever have coped with a 9.00 to 5.00 husband, who came home, put his feet up, and sat in front of the television all night. She is far too active, it would have driven her crazy.

There was no danger of that with John. Even during holidays

from the bank John would be off pursuing his politics. The Party Conference came around every October, and in 1972 it was in Blackpool. He went up with Clive and Peter and they all stayed in a little bed and breakfast called the Mount Hotel, on the North Promenade. 'Ah, Clive,' said John one morning as his outsize friend appeared for breakfast. 'Come and pull up a couple of chairs.' John had put his name down to speak in every debate that conference, and day after day sat at the back doggedly drafting speeches. At the end of each debate he would tear up the one he had just written and start on the next, but he was never called. Clive was; a bachelor to this day, he was called to speak in a debate on family planning, and was immediately descended upon by John and Peter with ideas. The conference was fun in those days, far less structured than today, and of course there was none of the security.

His sister, Pat, had been against John going into politics, and she had told him so. The council she had been happy with: council work is voluntary, it is something you do for your community, and you carry on with your career. But politics she knew was like the theatre or anything else intensely competitive. You spend a long time and give your life getting there, and for what? The public are very fickle. You ruin your family life, your health, your entire life, then they kick you out, and there is never another good word said about you. He was doing well in his career, she reasoned, why did he need the hassle?

And so he was, but John was bored at the bank, and he was never going to set the place on fire. Standard Chartered was as interesting as any bank could be, and it was international and multi-racial, which he liked, but it was still a hierarchical institution, in which he was still on a relatively low rung of the ladder, and he knew it would be a long hard slog to get anywhere. He wasn't even convinced that, at the end of the slog, banking was where he wanted to be anyway. Politics had far more scope, and was very much more interesting. His colleagues at the bank were well aware of the situation. They knew that John's heart wasn't in it, and that it was only a matter of time before he found a seat. They had seen his enthusiasm when he talked about politics, and heard him on the phone. They knew when he had the seat he wanted he would be off. However, as Alan Orsich, his boss in the dealing room, says, 'He knew who was paying his salary.' He did not skimp the work.

In February 1974 Edward Heath called an election to determine who ran Britain, the Government or the unions. The country was in chaos. Ambulance drivers had begun selective strikes. Miners had been on an overtime ban since November, rail drivers since December, and coal stocks were so low that, to conserve fuel, Britain was put on to a three-day working week. In February 81 per cent of miners voted for an all-out strike, and three days later Heath called an election. The outcome was no clear majority for Heath and he resigned. Harold Wilson headed a minority Labour Government, and the miners called off their strike.

In St Pancras John put up a brave fight, and Norma put a brave face on electioneering. They moved into the constituency for the duration of the campaign, staying in a house that belonged to a friend. Norma was very much in evidence, attending all the rallies and functions, making tea in the committee rooms and providing the support that the Party expects wives to provide. The constituents adored her. It was to no avail, as they had all expected, but it hadn't stopped them trying. What was clear almost immediately was that with no majority Wilson was stymied and would be forced to call another election very soon.

The second election was eight months later, in October, but in the meantime St Pancras had given John a roving license, which allowed him to find a safer seat if he could, but to return to them if he had no luck. He had no luck. He was turned down by Portsmouth North, Norwood, and Paddington, and so for the October election he was back in St Pancras. Tony Dey, on the other hand, had found himself a more promising constituency, so he had moved on, and John had a new agent for the second election – a pretty, intelligent, but totally inexperienced twenty-year-old called Susan Winter. Central Office were short of agents for that second election and had had to put her straight into a constituency with no qualifications. They had chosen St Pancras because it was such a safe Labour seat; if she made a mistake, it wouldn't matter. It was no very great compliment to the candidate, who believed, like everyone that fights a hopeless seat, he might be able to effect a turn-around, but John showed no irritation whatsoever, and Sue remembers him as being nothing but kind and courteous and endlessly patient.

She was no innocent, however, and knew enough about politics to know that John Major was like no Conservative she had ever met.

He would bang on about homelessness, social injustice, racial discrimination, and the underdog. He always championed the underdog. All the things he would get really upset about weren't normal Conservative Party things. I do remember thinking this wasn't the normal sort of candidate. He was a Conservative with a socialist conscience.

It was a pretty unpleasant campaign. Jock Stallard has denied it since, but he was very personal in his attacks on John. The Labour Party in St Pancras didn't like him and ran a nasty campaign against him. Hecklers in Brixton Market, even hecklers, like Ken Livingstone, shouting from the gallery in the council chamber at Lambeth had not prepared him for this vitriol, and John took it to heart. He was particularly upset when everyone arrived for work at the campaign headquarters one morning, a corner house in Leighton Road, with a large expanse of newly painted white wall, to find written across the wall, in letters six feet high, 'NOT A MAJOR SUCCESS'. Everyone else thought it was very funny.

He worked extraordinarily hard in that second election, and took the campaign very seriously. What he needed, he knew, was publicity, but the local newspapers were very left-wing and very seldom wrote about the Tories. Sue came up with a series of schemes which all backfired, in one way or another. On one occasion she managed to interest the *Evening Standard* in some story and a reporter duly turned up, but when the story subsequently appeared, it was nothing to do with the campaign, it was about Susan Winter being the youngest agent in the country. John was not amused. 'This is totally ridiculous,' he said. 'Either they don't mention me, or they mention me in passing. That's not what it's meant to be about at all.'

One of her schemes did yield some excellent publicity, although John thought it a very silly idea. Sue arranged a press call on the day he handed in his deposit of £150 to the returning officer. He came out brandishing £150 in Monopoly money, making the point that this was what would happen to the pound if the Labour Party were re-elected – it would be as valuable as the money in a board game.

She tried repeatedly to encourage John to loosen up. She suggested more fashionable clothes, a more interesting hairstyle and some new glasses. He was only thirty-one, she reasoned, he was good looking and had a nice figure; he ought to make the most of it, instead of looking like a rather staid and serious banker. But her suggestions fell on stony ground and didn't endear her to her protégé. He would say:

If people want me, they can take me the way I am.

It was an attitude that pervaded his life. Sue was astonished to discover some years later, quite by chance, that John had been to the famous 1976 International Monetary Fund conference in Manila as personal assistant to the Chairman of Standard Chartered, Lord Barber. It had been a highly publicized affair. Chancellor of the Exchequer, Denis Healey, was going cap in hand to the IMF to negotiate a loan to ward off a collapse in the economy.

Tony Barber, who had been Chancellor himself before the Conservative election defeat in February 1974, came under a barrage of fire from the media in Manila about the economic situation at home, and John, as his assistant, handled the bulk of the questions and fielded a great many calls from journalists all over the world. Tony Barber was very impressed with the way he handled the situation. He had chosen John for the trip because he seemed reliable and agreeable, but otherwise knew little about him, but found him 'a good communicator, confident without being arrogant; quite prepared to talk on the bank's behalf to journalists, and never frightened of the press'. When they returned to London, he put John in charge of public relations at the bank in place of the existing incumbent, whom he says was not outstanding.

Inevitably Tony Barber discovered John had serious political ambitions during the course of their week or ten days together, and became more and more impressed by his ideas. 'I was impressed by the combination of economic realism and compassion. It was the right combination.' Normally when young men talked to Barber about the House of Commons he would say, if you have no capital and a good manager's job, forget it. But John was an exception. 'He was determined,' he says, 'and he was obviously a high-flyer. I encouraged him.'

Sue was exasperated when she heard the story. Why, she asked, did he never tell anyone about the IMF and what he did there? He could have made so much capital out of it by dropping it casually into the conversation. How was he ever going to get anywhere if he wouldn't promote himself a bit, push himself forward, and say 'Look at me', as other thrusting young candidates did? His answer was:

Oh, no. If people really want to know about me they will find that out.

The election in October went to Labour – both nationally, where Harold Wilson was returned with a majority of three, and in St Pancras North, where the majority was considerably greater. It was to be expected, but John was nevertheless very depressed. He was also determined to find a safe seat where he could win.

Norma had played a less active role in the October election. She was six months pregnant with James – and craving Jacob's Club biscuits this time around – and hadn't felt up to tramping the streets or standing for hours making small-talk at Party functions. Sue, like others in the constituency, felt she was just riding it out, waiting for John to get politics out of his system before he settled down. She was giving him support, but because she loved him, not in the hope that it would lead anywhere. It was obvious to them that she had no interest in politics whatsoever. One of the last pieces of advice Sue gave him, before going off to another constituency, was to give up politics if he wanted to keep his marriage happy. 'He ignored it,' she says, 'but I think he knew what I was talking about, he knew there was a problem, but not one he was going to let stand in his way.'

5

HUNTINGDON

TWO years later John and Norma were driving up the A1 for an interview in Huntingdon. John was feeling pretty despondent; the green fields of Huntingdonshire, one of the largest farming constituencies in Britain, where Sir David Renton, now Lord, was standing down as MP after thirty-one years, were a long long way from Brixton. This was by no means the first time they had set off on a similar quest. They had trekked all over the country, and for two years now there had been nothing but rejection. Norma had the impression during this journey that if Huntingdon turned him down that would be it. He would give up the search for a parliamentary seat. They had reached the end of the road.

Looking back now, she realizes nothing would have stopped him – he had far more ambition than she ever appreciated; but at the time she really thought he was about to give it all up. The previous two years had brought nothing but disappointment. After the 1974 election he had put his name forward to one constituency after another, and was never invited for so much as an interview, until one day his old friend Jean Lucas, his agent and mentor from Brixton days, telephoned. In 1971 she had moved to Putney, and early in 1976 the constituency was looking for a new prospective candidate. She suggested John apply, which he duly did, but nothing came of it. She rang again. Why hadn't he applied, she wanted to know? He had, he insisted, but he had heard nothing. She then did a little investigating and came up with his CV. She rang him back. Why on earth had he not put down any of his Lambeth Council experience, she asked? Why was there nothing about St Pancras? But he had, he protested. Suddenly the light dawned. There were two John Majors on the Candidates' List, and

Conservative Central Office had sent Putney the wrong CV – just as they had done to every other seat he had applied to in the last year. It was small wonder he had had no interviews. The other John Major was a GLC candidate.

As soon as the discovery was made, the picture changed, and John began to be invited to interviews. He was short-listed for Putney, from over eighty applicants, along with David Mellor, and stood a good chance of being selected. But at the eleventh hour he withdrew. The retirement of Robert Carr in Sutton Carshalton presented the opportunity, if he were selected, of a parliamentary by-election. John applied and was short-listed. It was a much safer bet, and after much agonizing, he plumped for Sutton Carshalton, leaving David Mellor to become the prospective candidate in Putney. He was unlucky. Carshalton chose Nigel Forman, and John was left with neither option.

There was another disappointment in Dorset South, then in June Sir David Renton announced his intention to retire at the next election, and Huntingdonshire (as it was officially called until a boundary change some years on) began to look for a successor. John put in an application and was invited for an interview.

'You're not going to get that, are you?' said Peter Golds, when he heard the news, certain that such a safe Tory stronghold as Huntingdon would go to a typical Tory of the old school. With a majority of nine thousand, it would attract dozens of good-quality applicants; they were unlikely to choose a grammar school boy from Brixton. But as Peter began to look more closely at Huntingdon, he began to change his tune. He had taken to doing a bit of research for John on the various constituencies he applied to, and he noticed that the electorate in Huntingdon had risen visibly between the two elections in 1974, and between 1970 and 1974 it had positively erupted. The tell-tale signs of London overspill.

He was absolutely right. People were pouring into Huntingdon from the very places John knew best, like Brixton and St Pancras, and in that short time the population had risen from around fifty thousand to somewhere in the eighty thousands. Although he was not to know this at the time, the local Association were determined to have a candidate who could relate to this vast London overspill. John was very much the right person, in the right place, at the right time.

It was a very interesting time in the constituency. It was changing rapidly, not just in terms of population, but in other ways. There was a massive building programme underway of houses and factories, new businesses were springing up, electronics companies growing at an alarming pace, and local people making good. It was ideally situated geographically, in the middle of the country, on the north, west, south, east axes; it had good communications; it was close to the east coast ports; close to the university city of Cambridge. To the north it had the new town of Peterborough, an industrial city once heavy-engineering based, now the model of a modern city. Surrounding it all were vast tracts of farmland. So the constituency had significance geographically, economically, politically and socially, and the Association wanted 'the new man' to take them forward. They also wanted a potential Cabinet Minister.

Sir David had been a good constituency MP, thorough, caring and conscientious, and had an excellent rapport with local people. He and his late wife, Paddy, were very popular figures in the area, and he had served them well, and had built up a very sound majority, but he had been there since 1945, when life was very different, and he belonged to the old school. Educated at Oundle and Oxford, he was sixty-eight, a QC, a member of Pratt's, and fitted very comfortably into the squirearchy. He had been perfect for his time, but the Party had changed. The squirearchy were not extinct in Huntingdon, but they were decreasing, and there was a growing feeling inside the Association that it was time the Association was dragged into the twentieth century. Women in particular were becoming restless. It was assumed their role was in making the sandwiches, for which they were rewarded with a pat on the head, but they were not expected to voice any opinions.

There were nearly three hundred applicants for the seat. It attracted some big names, including three former MPs who had lost their seats, Michael Howard, Chris Patten, Peter Lilley, two local men who were highly regarded, and Charles, Marquess of Douro, the son and heir to the eighth Duke of Wellington. The Chairman of the Association had asked David Renton for his help in choosing a successor, but feeling it was none of his business, he crossed the Atlantic while the selection process ground on, to be well out of the way. He returned to find that they had chosen not one of the illustrious names on the list, but an obscure banker from Brixton. Flabbergasted, he said, 'But has he ever been on a farm in his life?' To which the Chairman, Commander Archie Gray, replied, 'I don't suppose so, but wait until you've met him.'

The opportunity arose a week later when a full meeting of the Association convened in Huntingdon Town Hall to adopt John as David's successor and prospective candidate. His speech left a great impression. He spoke fluently for twenty minutes without a note; and the speech was, David remembers, 'modest, charming, well-informed and contained very shrewd comments on the current political situation.'

He had greatly impressed the selection committee too. Sixteen officers, split into three groups, waded through the applications. By the third week they had narrowed the list to twenty-five, plus five locals, whom they wanted to interview, so they threw a cocktail party for the thirty, to which they also invited their wives. The interviews took place over two days, and there was one crucial question: was the applicant willing to live in the constituency? They were also looking for someone with experience in local government, having recently swept the board in council elections. By the Sunday night they had four names to present to the local executive: Charles, Marquess of Douro; Jock Bruce-Gardyne; Alan Haselhurst; and John Major.

Different factions on the executive had their own favourites, but the two obvious front-runners were Charles Douro with his splendid title, although he was blighted in the eyes of some in Huntingdon for having married Kaiser Wilhelm II's grand-daughter, and Jock Bruce-Gardyne, an eccentric, outspoken, and highly intelligent man and much loved character within the Party, formerly MP for South Angus, but one of the hunting, shooting, fishing Tories. He died sadly in 1990, while only in his late fifties. Alan Haselhurst and John Major were the outsiders. Haselhurst was solidly middle-class, with a good education, liberal Tory views, but somewhat serious. Major was very much an unknown quantity, he was the wild card; but he had his supporters.

As the selection process ground on, he had secured support. He had done his homework on the constituency, found out about the issues that affected people, and had been up there, not just for the formal interviews, but so that he could meet people informally, and the people of Huntingdon were beginning to like him. In fact they were finding it hard to fault him. He was personable, young, appeared to have a grasp of every subject, and to be in tune with the way they felt the Party should be moving. There was a lot of talk: was this man someone rather special, as they were beginning to suspect, or was he just a good swot, too clever by half?

One of his champions was the Conservative Leader of the Council, Mary-Jo Elphick. Shortly before the final selection she telephoned him at home and said, 'You don't know me, but I think you would be the best candidate for us. There's a meeting of the Huntingdonshire District Council coming up, I think you might find it worth your while to come along.' John took the day off work at the bank and went. In the midst of the meeting, Mary-Jo pointed to John sitting in the gallery and said, 'There you are, that's the candidate I told you about. He's the only one that's had the interest to come along to a Council meeting.'

The Constitutional Hall in the High Street, where the final selection took place, was packed for the occasion. The four contestants were to speak and answer questions from the panel in alphabetical order, which made John the last to speak. Cups of tea were being made in the waiting room at the side of the hall, and there was quite a fever of excitement – it looked as though it was going to be a close-run thing. Andrew Thompson, the agent, anticipated there would be up to three ballots.

Jock Bruce-Gardyne didn't perform well, neither did the Marquess of Douro, who was obviously very nervous. Alan Haselhurst, witnesses say, gave the speech of his life. Then John Major stood up and gave the speech of many people's lives. Extravagant praise for someone whose oratory has never been dazzling, but John certainly did give a speech that was perfectly judged for the audience. He spoke about unity and reconciliation, on two levels: the need to heal the rifts that had grown up in the community locally, and the task before the next Conservative Government to heal the rifts in society nationally. Roger Juggins, a local farmer on the committee, fired some agricultural questions at John, which he floundered over. Juggins suggested he didn't know much about the subject. 'You're quite right,' he said. 'I don't know much about cows – but if you'll teach me, I'll learn.'

His reply won him great credit. As Roger Juggins says, 'David Renton when he came in 1945 knew nothing either, but within six months he knew the politics. We don't need him to know about rearing pigs, but he must know the politics.'

When his time was up, he and Norma left the hall, and while the voting was taking place, they went for a walk down the road. As they came back they could see a commotion in the hall. Suddenly there was a mighty roar, and through the open doors of the hall they could see Mary-Jo Elphick standing on a chair with her hands held triumphantly in the air. They had missed the announcement, but John knew when he went back into the room that he was to be the next MP for Huntingdon. Out of one hundred and eighty-six votes cast, he had a clear majority in the first ballot with one hundred and nine votes.

A burst of applause greeted them when he and Norma walked into the hall. Then he stood up on the platform and, looking rather emotional, said, 'It's a long way from the back streets of Brixton to the green fields of Huntingdon.' Whereupon a local character stood up at the back and said in a ringing voice, 'It may be a long way from the streets of Brixton to the green fields of Huntingdon, but let me tell you, many of us here tonight have followed that route.' The hall erupted in cheers and roars of approval.

There were a few sour faces. The Chairman's wife, for one, who had wanted the Marquess of Douro to win, couldn't bring herself to shake John's hand when he came down off the platform. There were no congratulations from some of the county set either, they were horrified by the result; the old guard couldn't understand how this great Tory shire could have selected a banker from Brixton with a South London accent.

The majority of people, of course, were thrilled and couldn't wait to express their enthusiasm as they filed out of the hall to shake hands with John and Norma. They felt they had selected a man of the people, an ordinary fellow they could relate to, who could understand ordinary people's aspirations. They felt he was sincere and genuine, and best of all, they liked him. There were three or four hundred people in the hall and it was quite an overwhelming experience, particularly for Norma. Very shy at that time, she looked as though she had been completely stunned by the day's proceedings. One of the last people out of the hall was Jo Johnson, a delightful Scots lady, a past Chairman, and stalwart of the Association, who has since become a close friend.

'You'll get a jolly good sleep tonight, dear,' she said to Norma.

'I shall never sleep again,' said Norma.

It was certainly a momentous day, and John and Norma couldn't believe their luck. They drove home to Beckenham that night with a whole new vista ahead of them.

For the first time I knew it was overwhelmingly likely that I would be elected to Parliament. We would have to move, we would need a new beginning, but it was something we looked forward to with huge anticipation.

'Apprenticeship over,' said Norma. 'Now you'll have to do some real work.'

It was the beginning of what, he says looking back, was probably the happiest period of his life. He was thirty-three, he had two children, a boy and a girl, who were bright, happy and fit, they had their own house, they were contemplating moving to the countryside, which would mean a bigger and better house for the same money, and he had a different career ahead of him, the career he had wanted since the age of thirteen.

Mike Harford, another past Chairman of the Association and county councillor, was intrigued by John's desire to be an MP. They were paid a pittance at that time, there was no job security, and not much home life, so why had he been so determined?

'I've always wanted to,' John had said simply. 'It's my life.'

Looking back he says it was a mistake. If he could have his life over again, he wouldn't have taken such an interest in politics when he was so young. He would have spent more time studying and reading and preparing himself for later life. His one regret is the conscious decision he took at school to stop working. On the other hand, if he had worked harder, if he had stayed on at school and taken A levels, and if he had been to Oxford or Cambridge, he questions whether he would ever have become Prime Minister. He might have discovered other interests, and, if so, would not have pursued politics with such a single-minded interest. As he says,

Just think, I might have been anonymous and rich, instead of public and poor.

The people of Huntingdon were immediately welcoming to their new candidate. Everyone now is slightly jealous of their initial contact with John, but they were not slow in issuing invitations to dinner, and friendships which were established then have remained solid to this day. Some of his closest friends are there in the constituency, and they are far closer than most of his colleagues in Westminster. Among the most friendly was David Renton, who took John under his wing, and put him in the picture about the local farming industry, and just about every other aspect of the constituency. He took him around the towns and villages – of which there were eighty – and introduced him to a great many people. John and Norma even stayed with the Rentons two or three times during that first winter, before they had a house in Huntingdon. Norma's mother would look after Elizabeth and James the while.

Norma and Paddy struck up a firm friendship, and David found John an increasing pleasure to know. He was always very quick on the uptake, never had to be told anything twice, had a marvellous memory and was very quick in understanding difficult situations and other people's problems. He also liked what he calls 'his friendly modest manners'. It was a great boon to find such patronage from the incumbent Member, and by no means customary. In the neighbouring constituency where Francis Pym, now Lord, was retiring after twenty-six years, many local people didn't even know who his successor was until the day the election campaign began. By the time the election was called in 1979, there was scarcely anyone in Huntingdonshire who hadn't met or seen or heard John Major.

His first public appearance was on the racecourse. Roger Juggins took him to the Huntingdon Super Chasers – which turned out to be the first time he had ever been to any racecourse, and with a day spent on Roger's farm already under his belt, his country education was well underway. Norma did know something about the countryside, and by coincidence, this was the very area she knew. She had spent several school holidays with her great aunt in Bourn, and played with children on a farm nearby, which made his success here all the more auspicious. For John it was all quite new, but he took to it immediately, almost from the first day he visited Huntingdon he felt at ease there, and at home. It was never just a constituency for him, as parts of the country are for so many MPs. If and when he decides to give up politics, there is no doubt John will carry on living where he does today. He has always had a very strong sense of belonging there. The whole family have made it their life.

So there was no doubt about moving to Huntingdon. There had been a time in her life when Norma could never have envisaged living out of London, but the advent of children had changed her attitude, and when John was selected they didn't even need to sit down and discuss the move. It seemed the natural thing to do; and Huntingdon was close enough to London so that John could commute to the bank without too much difficulty. In fact it was a terrible journey; with no high-speed inter-city trains, it took a long time and was very expensive, but it was a small price to pay.

At this time John was running the Public Relations Department at Standard Chartered, put there by Lord Barber after their trip to Manila. It was a job with status that was not matched by the reality. He had the ear of all the directors and the general manager of the bank, and ate smart lunches most days with clients, bankers, or financial journalists from the national press, but there was no real substance to the job, not much enjoyment, and still not a great deal of money. He spent much of the time working on a joint venture with the Economics Department to launch a booklet on Foreign Exchange Forecasting. It was a service for clients and other banks which came out six times a year, and John's department liaised with the printers and designers.

The smart lunches were not usually much of a treat. John has never taken much interest in food. He has always had a very healthy appetite, although he maintains Norma can eat twice as much, but he has never wanted to experiment or explore new tastes. He likes plain food. He doesn't like sauces or fricassees or anything that could remotely be called *haute cuisine*, which over the years, with ever more glamorous feasts to attend, has made life difficult. Many is the time he has come away from a sumptuous dinner grumbling about the food, which others have thought out of this world. His love of curry is a curious exception. His preference is English and unadulterated. He used to enjoy Gladys Simpson's meat puddings, and he likes a greasy-spoon type of fry-up every now and again, but his favourite meal is plain roast meat with vegetables.

One of the perks of the job was tickets every now and again for the opera. The bank had a box at the Coliseum and regular seats at Covent Garden, and when they were not being used by the directors, they would be offered to bank employees. A notice would appear on a board outside the canteen, on the top floor next to his office, and John would often sign up. Colleagues used to tease him about his interest in opera, which they always took with a pinch of salt. They didn't think it married up with all his talk about Chelsea. They were all Arsenal supporters, so there was a lot of office banter during the football season. His other preoccupation, apart from politics, which some shared, others endured, was of course cricket. He talked tirelessly about it, knew every last wicket, and if a Test match was on he would always have a radio in his desk so he could listen to the match.

He hadn't been able to play himself since his accident, but he had high hopes, in the excitement after his selection for Huntingdon, of taking a City team to play cricket there, but it never happened. Friends who were awaiting the call, like Clifford German, former deputy City Editor on the *Daily Telegraph*, are still waiting. He and Clifford lunched regularly for some years, but although the talk was ostensibly about Standard Chartered, they invariably talked about cricket. He was certainly never in any danger of giving away anything indiscreet about the bank.

Another welcome distraction was John's involvement with the Warden Housing Association, which took him to board meetings in Harrow about five times a year, and back to a subject he thoroughly enjoyed. Warden was a charity that provided housing for low-income families, and he worked for them on a voluntary basis. He was one of several professionals – solicitors, bankers, quantity surveyors and the like, some of them retired – on the committee of management. At thirty-two, he was younger than most, but was invited to join principally because of his housing record in Lambeth. Yet, despite his age, he exerted considerable influence over the board. He was quiet but determined: he always arrived at a meeting knowing what he wanted, and by the end of the day had usually extracted it. In this same low-key way he persuaded the board not to set up a sub-committee structure, which most organizations had. He hated bureaucracy.

'I don't want to come to a board meeting and just be a rubber stamp because everyone's discussed everything at sub-committee level,' he would say.

And the board went along with him. All the decisions were made at board level.

John Drew, the Chief Executive of Warden, remembers going to the opera with John and Norma one night after John's selection, while they were still living in Beckenham, and John spent the performance either sleeping, or scribbling down notes for some speech he had to make. David Renton would take him to branch meetings around the constituency, and business forums, make a short speech himself, and then leave the floor to John. So one way and another he was working long hours, and the fact that he still didn't drive meant that every trip to Huntingdon from Beckenham involved a series of trains, and was twice as long as it might have been.

They didn't move into the constituency until 8 December 1977. The buying and selling of property has never gone smoothly for the Majors. They have only ever moved house three times during their married life, and yet they have experienced every kind of housebuyer's nightmare, including being gazumped, and being caught with a crippling bridging loan. This move was no exception. It took eighteen months to sell their house in Beckenham and find a suitable house to buy in the constituency, and even then it was a house that none of them liked particularly. It was one of a pair in a little close of detached houses in the village of Hemingford Grey. The houses all looked bigger and grander than they were. There were three reception rooms, one of which was very big, and three substantial bedrooms. It was empty when they bought it; the previous owner had obviously had trouble selling the house, and they in turn found it difficult to sell five years later. It was the wrong one of the pair, as far as the garden and the sun were concerned. Nevertheless the family settled into the house. Norma began making curtains, as she has done for every house they have lived in, as well as doing the decorating, and transformed it swiftly into a comfortable home. In no time they were part of the local community. Elizabeth, just six, and James, who was nearly three, enrolled at the little village school and playgroup respectively and they were all very happy with their new life in the country.

Although they were installed in Huntingdon, and it was as safe a seat as they could possibly have found, John and Norma were both nervous about John's prospects. Well-intentioned people kept telling them not to worry if John didn't poll as well as David, he was such a popular figure in the constituency, so many of the votes were personal, and it was only to be expected if they fell away with a new man. So when a general election date of 3 May was finally announced at the end of March, John swung into action with all the vigour he had put into St Pancras. He was taking nothing for granted.

There had been colossal ructions within the Conservative Party in between times. Tory leaders have to win elections. In the eyes of the Party nothing is more important, and after leading the Tories to two defeats in 1974, Edward Heath was ousted. A leadership election was held in February 1975, and to his eternal rage, his successor was Margaret Thatcher. He would have been bitter whoever had taken his place, but to have been passed over for a woman was beyond the pale, not least a woman whom he had never much liked.

Margaret Thatcher had stepped into the contest as an outsider.

In the second ballot she was standing alongside Willie Whitelaw, Geoffrey Howe, James Prior and John Peyton. Whitelaw was the clear favourite, but she had two influential sponsors: Airey Neave, a highly respected back bencher, and Gordon Reece, a media guru; and with their help and guidance she had led an extraordinary campaign against all the odds. It is hard to believe now, but when she emerged the victor in February 1975, she was virtually unknown by the general public. She had had a stormy time at the Department of Education, and achieved brief notoriety when she was branded 'Mrs Thatcher, Milk Snatcher' for the decision to cut free milk in schools for seven to eleven-year-olds. But to the average man in the street she was unknown.

There had been major changes in the Labour Government too. In the spring of 1976 Harold Wilson stunned both country and colleagues by announcing his resignation as Prime Minister. Jim Callaghan, who had been Foreign Secretary, took over, and remained at the helm for three more stormy years, during which he lost his majority in the House of Commons, the economy collapsed, and he faced a revolt over spending cuts. Twice Margaret Thatcher introduced a vote of no confidence, which he managed to stave off by making a pact with the Liberals, but the economy was not so easy to fix. Chancellor Denis Healey had no option but to borrow several billion pounds from the IMF – the occasion on which John Major accompanied Tony Barber.

Each year there had seemed to be some possibility of an election, but none more so than in the autumn of 1978. On the recommendation of Gordon Reece, Saatchi and Saatchi had been brought in to advertise the Conservative Party, and eye-catching posters were to be seen all over the country, such as the one depicting a long queue of people on the dole with the slogan, 'Labour Still Isn't Working'. The agency's Chairman, Tim Bell, handled the account personally, and with Gordon Reece was responsible for grooming Mrs Thatcher for the electorate. He became a crucial part of her regime for years to come and was always a trusted and influential adviser.

John was quietly preparing himself for the campaign in Huntingdon, but it was a false alarm. In September Callaghan summoned his Cabinet to Number Ten and asked the BBC for five minutes of air-time the next day. It seemed inevitable he was going to announce the date of the election. He didn't. Instead he said that there would be no election just yet, the problems of the country required continuity of policies.

At Brighton the next month, John heard Margaret Thatcher deliver a diatribe against Socialism and the Labour Party, which met a rapturous reception, and which articulated his own views, having experienced years of life under Labour in Brixton.

Many of us remember the Labour Party as it used to be. In the old days it was at least a party of ideals. You didn't have to agree with Labour to understand its appeal and respect its concern for the underdog. Among those who lead the Labour movement something has gone seriously wrong. Socialism has gone sour. Object to merit and distinction, and you're setting your face against quality, independence, originality, genius, against all the richness and variety of life. When you hold back the successful, you penalize those who need help.

The wizard behind that, and all of Mrs Thatcher's best speeches, was the playwright Ronald Millar (since knighted), whom Norma had met at the Lyric Theatre at the same time as she met June Bronhill, back in the mid sixties. It had been his production of *Robert and Elizabeth* that June was in. He had first offered his services to the Tory Party when Ted Heath was Leader because he was so fed up with life under Wilson that he decided, if he was going to carry on living in this country, he had better do something to get Wilson out of office. He subsequently also wrote speeches for John Major after he became Prime Minister.

That winter Britain was plunged into chaos, which by the New Year was being likened to the General Strike of 1926. Hospitals and schools closed, Underground trains ceased to run, grave diggers refused to dig, and the refuse workers refused to collect the rubbish. Mountains of garbage littered every street and rats ran riot. When the Prime Minister arrived home after a summit away from it all in sunny Guadeloupe, reporters asked him what he thought of the crisis. 'Crisis?' he said. 'What crisis?'

At the end of March Margaret Thatcher introduced another vote of no confidence, after a referendum on devolution for Scotland and Wales. She won by one vote, Parliament was dissolved and a general election was called for 3 May after which Callaghan resigned. It was a great triumph, the first time a Prime Minister had been forced out of office and into a general election since Ramsay MacDonald was defeated by Stanley Baldwin in 1924. Everyone was greatly excited, but the excitement was shortlived. Two days later a bomb exploded in the House of Commons car park critically injuring Airey Neave, who had been Shadow Northern Ireland Secretary. He died during surgery in Westminster Hospital. Having lived through Colditz, and won the MC, the DSO and an OBE for his bravery, he died at the cowardly hands of the INLA, who fixed a remote control device to the underside of his car. The nation was stunned. It was the first murder of its kind on the mainland and security for politicians immediately became an issue.

Nationally it was an election of personalities: 'Sunny Jim' versus 'The Iron Lady', a label the Russians had given Mrs Thatcher after a particularly eloquent speech in 1976 against Harold Wilson's commitment to an East–West détente. The Labour Party smeared Thatcher as a right-wing extremist. The Tory manifesto countered: 'This election is about the future of Britain – a great country which seems to have lost its way.'

In Huntingdon it was an election of personalities to some extent too. The Labour Party imported a candidate who had been a Camden councillor, called Julian Fullbrook. He was never going to be a serious threat, yet John fought a tough election, as though his life depended upon it. He was obsessed with the need to poll higher than David Renton's nine thousand majority, and if possible to get into double figures. He canvassed far and wide, going to every last little gathering to which he was bid, out into all the villages, meeting as many individuals as·possible, eliciting their worries and problems, and listening to what ordinary people had to say. The atmosphere in any room immediately became relaxed when he arrived. He put on no airs, and pretended to be nothing that he wasn't, and people opened up to him.

This is one of his greatest skills. He makes people feel good. He shakes their hand as though he is aware of what he is doing, instead of a man on auto-pilot; he puts his arm around people, or touches an elbow or a shoulder; he looks at them when he is talking to them, listens to them when they answer a question he has asked, and gives an honest answer to whatever they might ask. It goes beyond common courtesy, and is extremely rare in anyone, let alone a politician. This is John Major. This is what makes people who meet him, whatever their political stance, like him.

The magic has certainly worked over the years on the people of Huntingdonshire, and not just the voters. Everyone involved in the Party has enjoyed working for John. The women of the constituency were delighted to be brought out from behind the sandwiches at last, and, although everyone has worked harder than they did before, they obviously all have fun.

John hung around the count that night in May with Norma, both anxiously waiting for the result, still afraid to hope for too much. It was held in the St Ivo's Centre in St Ives, a few miles south of Huntingdon. While the counting was still underway, John called up to Andrew Thompson, the agent, to see where they stood. 'Twenty thousand,' he called back. 'We've got our first twenty thousand votes,' said John to Norma, entirely misunderstanding the figure Andrew had given him. 'We're OK.' Andrew had not given him the number of votes – he had given him his majority. By the end of the night, that figure had risen to twenty-one thousand five hundred and sixty-three. Everyone was in raptures. It was better than anyone could ever have expected. It was worth all the hand-shaking, the foot-slogging, and the knocking on doors. Worth all the frustrating years of driving round the countryside to be rejected by one constituency after another. John's dream had finally come true – in spades. He was not just a Member of Parliament, he had more than doubled the majority of a very popular predecessor, confirming Huntingdon as one of the safest seats in the country. Barring any unforeseen problems, it would be a job for life.

He has never quite believed it, though. He and Norma have never taken anything for granted, nor felt wholly confident. In that first election Norma was secretly afraid that, although everything they had worked for had come right, it could suddenly be snatched away at the eleventh hour, and they might be the ones who would lose this safer than safe seat. Every election John Major has fought since, he has fought as though he were in danger of losing, even when he fought it as Prime Minister in 1992, when he polled not just the largest majority in the country, but the largest majority of any Conservative MP ever.

He has nursed the constituency since 1979 with extraordinary care. Even David Renton has been impressed. When David was the MP he held surgeries (one-to-one meetings when anyone in the constituency can come and talk to their MP) more often in the course of a year than many of his colleagues, but he never held them when Parliament was sitting. John Major holds more surgeries when the House is sitting than not. Even now he sets aside one day a month to the constituency when he runs an advice bureau, and opens a factory maybe, visits a school or hospital, and does a couple of Party engagements. The weekend before he flew to Maastricht to negotiate arguably the trickiest and most complex treaty he has yet had to deal with, he held a two-hour surgery, taking notes himself, and he didn't leave until the last person who had wanted to see him had been seen.

The rapport he has with his constituents is quite remarkable. Given there is an electorate of nearly ninety-four thousand, he is on first-name terms with a surprising number, and whenever he attends functions where there is an opportunity to meet people and talk, he will talk way beyond the allotted time. His time-keepers tear their hair trying to keep the Prime Minister on schedule. It is the same whenever he has an opportunity to talk to people, but he feels contact with people who live in the real world is vitally important. The House of Commons is a very closed community where issues can take on an importance out of all proportion to their true significance. John Major recognized this, and realized that it was only by coming home and mixing with ordinary people that he could adjust his perspective.

When he first became a Whip he would criticize colleagues who neither lived in their constituencies nor visited more than once a month. He would say to Roger Juggins when he used to drive him to constituency meetings:

You keep me sane. I go up there from Monday to Friday and everything gets out of proportion. I come down here and you pick me up, I listen to you, and what was terrible to me is just an everyday matter to you, and by the time I've left the cheese and wine, other people have said the same thing, and I'm back on an even keel. If I didn't do this my view would be completely distorted.

6

EARLY YEARS IN PARLIAMENT

JOHN had just arrived in the House of Commons on his first day. He was standing in the Members' lobby, outside the Whips' office, feeling slightly unreal. He had been shown his hanger, and his locker and key, but he didn't know his way around, he didn't know many MPs and he knew scarcely any of the new intake. He was like a new boy on the first day of school, when suddenly someone tapped him on the shoulder. He turned round and there was Barbara Wallis, one of his old friends from Lambeth Council. They had had a standing joke all those years before, that when John became an MP, she would be his secretary.

'Well,' she said, 'now that you're here, I am working for you, and these are my terms and conditions.'

She was no longer joking. She told him what she had been earning working for other MPs in the intervening years, and the deal was struck. It was the start of a great working relationship that only came to an end when Barbara retired last year.

John had been into the House since his first visit at the age of thirteen, but not frequently. Before 1976 he found it quite painful to visit, not knowing whether he would ever get there. After 1976 he didn't like to come because of the frustration of not knowing how long it would be before there was an election and he would be able to take up his seat. Now the sense of history that had swamped him as a teenager washed over him again, and a feeling of awe as he walked into the Chamber for the first time. He wondered if he would ever be ordered out of it.

It was quite an historic Parliament in itself. Britain had its first ever woman Prime Minister in Margaret Thatcher. The Conservative Party were home with a majority of fifty-four seats in the

House of Commons. It was the beginning of an extraordinary era of government and an extraordinary career for one of its least likely newcomers. There was an exceptionally brilliant intake of new Tory MPs in 1979, of which John was not at first recognizably one. The most obvious high-flyers were probably Chris Patten and William Waldegrave, both of whom had been tipped as future Prime Ministers before they even came into the House. Both were career politicians who had come via Oxford and the prestigious Conservative Research Department. William had gone on to head Ted Heath's political office. Chris had become Director of the Research Department, and at the same time worked in the Cabinet Office and the Home Office.

William Waldegrave and Chris Patten found themselves sharing an office in Dean's Yard with John Patten, Tristan Garel-Jones and Richard Needham. They were of a like mind, and all enjoyed shouting the odds and setting the world to rights. After a while they formed a dining club. The Tory Party is famous for its dining clubs. This one actually had no name, but it was referred to by those outside it as the Dirty Dozen, or more commonly, the Blue Chips, because of the preponderance of aristocrats and Old Etonians among its members. They were joined by Ian Lang, Peter Fraser, Lord Cranborne, Sir Nicholas Lyall, Matthew Parris, and Robert Atkins. Atkins, known by the rest of them as *Rattus Vulgaris*, the Rat, because of the first letters of his name, was the odd one out, both socially and intellectually, but he was good company and brought in as cellarmaster. Their first meeting was held at William's house in Notting Hill, but thereafter they moved to within the Division Bell area, to Tristan Garel-Jones' home in Catherine Place, where his Spanish wife, Catarina, played host. They ate good food, drank good wine and engaged in good conversation, interspersed with a fair amount of passionate political argument – all traditional Tory pastimes.

The other common factor among the Blue Chips was a tendency to think Mrs Thatcher and her policies too harsh. She was a strict monetarist, believed in non intervention at any cost in either pay disputes or management of the economy, and took her reforms forward with a zeal not seen since Joan of Arc. Within a month of taking office, her Chancellor, Geoffrey Howe, had produced a budget so stringent that it shocked most of his own Cabinet and rooted the Opposition to their benches. One back bencher even shouted 'Treason!'

The Opposition and the unions were predictably outraged, but so were some of her own side, and when it came to the crunch, some of Mrs Thatcher's own Cabinet blanched, particularly when it came to implementing such radical cuts in public expenditure. They were mostly the more moderate Heath supporters, whom she had been obliged to keep in the Cabinet. Mrs Thatcher branded those who, to her mind, lacked guts, 'the wets'. Those who had the courage to administer the medicine, albeit unpalatable, which she thought essential for Britain's recovery, became known as 'the drys', and over the years the distinction became increasingly acute.

John supported Geoffrey Howe's Budget, and making his maiden speech in the House of Commons on 13 June, during the Budget debate, revealed himself financially 'dry'. Public opinion, he said, required the Government to cut taxes, to curb inflation, to create new jobs, and to maintain, as far as possible, satisfactory public services. However,

> With all the best will in the world the Chancellor and his colleagues cannot possibly achieve them all at the same time. In order to create jobs and to maintain public services, it is necessary first to cut taxes and to curb inflation.

Of the spending cuts he said,

> Whenever we talk about spending cuts there is bound to be a certain amount of uproar. It is never popular to cut services. But it seems that much of the uproar which is currently being engendered is to a large extent synthetic. I think that the spending cuts are desirable.

It was not a very remarkable speech, as he is the first to admit, but then maiden speeches seldom are. They are an opportunity for the new member to pay tribute to their predecessor, which in this case was not difficult, praise his constituency, and make a few uncontroversial remarks about the issues of the day. On the subject of Huntingdon, he reminded the House that it was where Oliver Cromwell came from.

> He caused your predecessors, Mr Deputy Speaker, more trouble than I anticipate causing, at least in my early days.

He liked the habit, he said, of Huntingdon re-electing its members, although as one eighteenth-century voter explained,

> Of course we re-elect the member; how else could we be rid of him for six months at a time?

Norma wasn't in the gallery to hear him, nor was any member of his family. It was late in the day and he could virtually count the number of people in the Chamber on his fingers and toes, but there was one supporter to witness his performance. Looking up he saw the familiar face of Canon Jennings, the Canon of St Ives, sitting up in the gallery; he was very keen on politics, and he had come down to London to support his new MP.

John Major was allocated a room in the House with John Butcher, John Carlisle and Tom Benyon, and he was not among those invited to join the Blue Chips. He knew none of its members and he was not the sort of character to have caught anyone's eye as a likely candidate. Like most ambitious young politicians, they were mostly loud and opinionated, eager to make an impression. They also had the fundamental confidence of either a privileged background, an outstanding education, or both – the confidence that allows people to be eccentric or unconventional, and quite unconcerned by what others think of them. John had none of this confidence. His life has always been circumscribed by convention. He has never made an exhibition of himself in any way, never shouted the odds, or pushed himself forward, and it is not surprising he didn't stand out among the new arrivals as dynamic. He has never wanted to stand out in a crowd; in fact quite the reverse. The crowd is protective camouflage. It allows him to observe others without being noticed, to establish the lie of the land, so that he never goes into anything unprepared, never risks making a fool of himself.

He once made a fool of himself at the age of nine when he mistook two words. He was with his family but there were others there as well, and he wished the earth would open up and swallow him. It wasn't a sensation he has cared to repeat.

John was not alone among his peers at the start of that Parliament in having neither family nor education. The Tory Party had ceased to require good breeding as a prerequisite for becoming an MP long ago. The passport had become education instead, as people like Ted Heath and Margaret Thatcher bore witness. Heath's father was a builder, Thatcher's a family grocer; but both had graduated from Oxford. Margaret Thatcher had the additional bonus of having qualified at the Bar, and married a man of some substance. There were already a growing number of Tories in the House who had come a similar route, from grammar schools, via university and a good job, or marriage into an established family. But the 1979 entry saw a new breed of Tory altogether. John was not the only one to have no A levels. Graham Bright didn't even go to a grammar school. Elected MP for Luton, he became the first Tory MP to have been to a comprehensive, and like John he left school at sixteen with a few O levels and went straight into a job in industry and marketing.

Graham was one of the few people John knew when he arrived in the House. Their paths had first crossed in the late sixties when Graham had been on the Housing Committee on Thurrock Council, while John was at Lambeth, and they were thrown together over housing matters. Being from similar backgrounds, and with similar interests, they had become friends. They would meet each year at the Party Conference, and kept in touch as their careers ran parallel; when John was fighting St Pancras, Graham was battling in Thurrock, then Dartford, before moving to Luton at much the same time as John was adopted by Huntingdon.

They joined a rival club to the Blue Chips called the Guy Fawkes, so named because they held their first meeting on 5 November. It was set up by John Watson, who has since left the House, and its membership was not nearly as exclusive as the competition. There were about eighteen members, including David Mellor, John Lee, Peter Lloyd, John Butcher, Stephen Dorrell, and Robin Squire. There was much chat about which of the two dining clubs would produce a minister first. It was the Blue Chips – John Patten was the first – but overall both groups produced an equal number of ministers.

The Guy Fawkes met every month in one of the dining rooms downstairs in the House of Commons, and every month they had a speaker, who would be a guest one month, followed by one of their own members the next. For a bit of fun at their first meeting, everyone said what jobs they would most like to do in government. By no means everyone wanted to do senior jobs. John Major said he would like to be Chancellor. Graham Bright said he would like to be the Prime Minister's Parliamentary Private Secretary. He reminded John of this conversation, almost exactly eleven years later, when John, newly elected Prime Minister, appointed Graham to be his PPS.

John was popular among his new colleagues. He became someone whom friends would confide in, someone who always had time for his friends. He wasn't pushy, he didn't dominate conversations, but they immediately recognized a quiet authority in him, and a sense of commitment, but above all they were impressed by his ability to get on with everyone without merely agreeing with them, or making himself acceptable by saying the things they wanted to hear. He was entirely unpretentious, didn't try to deny his past, or seek to re-invent himself, neither did he trade on his background. It came out easily and naturally. His sense of humour made him good company, and because he was so genuinely benign, he could say things that others might not have got away with.

Fifteen months or so after the election, the MP for Southend fell down the steps at Westminster underground station and died. Teddy Taylor, now knighted, who after fifteen years had lost his seat in Glasgow Cathcart at the 1979 election, won the by-election and became the new MP for Southend. Shortly afterwards he and John and a bunch of others were having a cup of tea in the tearoom in the House. Teddy was discussing the move. 'I've had so many letters from people saying they wish I was still the MP in Glasgow,' he said. 'And did they all have Southend postmarks?' said John.

As soon as he became an MP John gave up his marketing job at Standard Chartered Bank. If you ask him whether he ever considered going back to banking at any time during his parliamentary career, he says, never, he could never be that desperate, ever. He says it tongue-in-cheek, but clearly the idea appals him, and no longer having to work in the bank was a tremendous release, although he did go back during the summer recesses on occasion to help out in the Advances Department and do a little public relations. Nevertheless, he still feels a debt of gratitude. They looked after him when he had his accident, and they allowed him to pursue his political ambitions, while still employing him on a full-time basis, neither of which he has forgotten. He was fortunate in that the Managing Director at the time, Sir Peter Graham, was sympathetic. Now Chairman of the Equatorial Bank, he firmly believes that the City has a lot of talent and would like to see more of it go into Parliament. He allowed John to take time off to secure a seat, as he has done for other aspiring politicians in the bank. But he had made it quite clear to him long beforehand that if he was successful in becoming an MP he would have to terminate his employment. He also wanted to be sure John had considered all the pros and cons of a parliamentary career. Had he thought what would happen if he lost his seat?

John and Norma had indeed thought about what would happen if he lost his seat. It is a thought that has never entirely disappeared from the back of their minds, even to this day. Money has always been a worry, which is why they have always fought each election as though Huntingdon were a marginal seat. However, his income didn't stop entirely. When John took up his seat in the House, the bank allowed him to carry on, working on a part-time basis. They moved him out of Public Relations into an analysis job and they paid him the difference between his parliamentary salary and the amount he had previously been earning from the bank. He also carried on studying for his Banking Diploma Part II exams. As with the Part Is he took the five exams in ones and twos over several years, and completed the last of them in September 1971.

The part-time job brought diminished status. Gone were the smart lunches and the spacious office on the fifth floor. He was called rather grandly, Adviser to Lord Barber on Parliamentary Affairs, but there was clearly no prestige attached. A desk was found for him in the temporary offices of the Economics Department in Clements Lane. It was in the basement, which was dark and dismal, he had no secretary and had great difficulties every time he needed something typed. He had to rely on kindness from other people, or would go and see his old secretary. He relied on the people sharing his office; he would always be asking them to take calls for him or phone Norma with some message. They liked to help because they were fond of him, but they did feel he was being treated shabbily by the bank.

Before he was elected John always went back to Huntingdon at night, but as soon as he was in the House commuting was impossible. From the start he had no pair, the custom whereby MPs are paired with their opposite number on the Labour benches, and therefore excused from registering their votes. With no pair John had to be in the Chamber late every night in order to vote, and so he established a routine at the very beginning of his parliamentary career, which he has maintained since. He would take the train to London on Monday, stay in London all week, and go home on Friday.

For the first couple of years he stayed in a series of rather unprepossessing bed-sits and little flats, moving from one to another as he found something better. One was in the basement of an interesting building in Kennington Park Road, which was set behind a shop front. Norma came down and tiled the bathroom for him. Then John came across an old friend whom he had worked with at Standard Chartered who let him the top part of his flat in a house in Durand Gardens in Stockwell.

Norma and the children carried on living in Huntingdon. They both decided instinctively when John moved down to London that she and the children should stay put. They never even discussed any other arrangement; there was no question of getting a flat and all moving to London during the weekdays. The expense, apart from anything else, would have been beyond their means, and they both felt the children would be far better off in the country, settled in one place. And Norma wasn't keen. She knew she would never see John. It would be like Lambeth days all over again. He would be busy working, all hours of the day and night, and she would be left on her own, trying to second-guess what time, if at all, he would be home for a meal. She knew it would have driven her mad, and she knew she would have been very lonely. They had now made a home for themselves in Huntingdon, she and the children had made friends, they were established in their schools, and her own interests were there. Far better, she reasoned, to let John work during the week, without worrying that he had forgotten to ring and say he would be late; and for her to know he would never be there from Monday to Friday, so she would never feel cross or resentful, but to know that he would always be home for the weekend, when they could enjoy life as a family.

The fact that Norma was practical obviously made life easier. If there were problems with the plumbing or the electrics she would have been the one to fix it in any event, so it was no loss not having a man around the house. And Norma was resourceful. She was always busy at something. She had become involved in Meals on Wheels since her arrival in the constituency, which she delivered regularly once every three weeks, and she has continued to do so ever since. She had her sewing and her letter writing, she looked after the house and garden, and the children; and in addition, just for fun, she had started compiling a catalogue of every performance Joan Sutherland had ever given.

Joan Sutherland had become an abiding passion. For years, whenever she had been about to take on a new role, Norma would make a little doll dressed in the costume of the part, and had a large collection of these miniatures. And because all her friends knew Norma was a great fan, she would constantly find herself being asked questions about when Joan Sutherland sang such and such an opera or where. Her knowledge only extended to the years she had been following the diva, so to give herself something to do during the weekdays when John was away, she began researching backwards. It was an extraordinary project. She listed every performance, live and broadcast, with the dates, places, and names of the conductors, designers, and pianists, going back to her first student performance in Sydney Town Hall on 12 December 1946.

It was a mammoth task, but Norma became engrossed. She knew Joan Sutherland slightly. Joan was very good to her fans. She knew all of the regulars who stood outside the stage door for autographs. She would ask their names and stand and chat for a while. And Norma, having the same name as one of her great roles – Bellini's Norma – was someone she always remembered especially well. One thing led to another. The more Norma discovered about Joan's singing career, the more interested she became in her life, and finally approached Joan Sutherland with the idea of writing a biography.

It was more of a document than a book for several years, and Norma had no publisher for the work, but Joan Sutherland was happy with the idea, and so at the beginning of 1981 Norma flew out to Australia for three weeks to see members of Joan's family, and do some research in her native land.

John took some time to come to terms with Norma's plans to disappear to the other side of the world on her own, but she is a very determined lady. However, she says that if John had really objected she wouldn't have gone. In typical style, she organized everything for her absence, found somebody to look after Elizabeth and James, a lady who had looked after them quite frequently in the past, and when she was happy that everyone was going to be all right without her, she set off. It was a marvellous trip. She felt homesick, as she always does when she is away, but she met some of the family, learnt about the Australian opera scene, and spent a night of magic in the Sydney Opera House when she heard Joan Sutherland sing Desdemona in Verdi's *Otello*, conducted by Carlo Felice Cillario.

Soon after Norma's home-coming, John was offered his first job in Government. He was walking through the Division Lobby when

Patrick Mayhew, now knighted, newly appointed Minister of State at the Home Office, tapped him on the shoulder and said he would like a word. Outside he asked whether John would like to be PPS to both him and Timothy Raison, also a newly appointed Minister of State. A minister chooses his own PPS either from his own knowledge of the person or in consultation with the Whips. Mayhew didn't seem to be very sure that John would want to do the job, but he leapt at it, and it turned out to be an enjoyable period.

He remembers going to his first meeting the following Monday morning at the Home Office. Willie Whitelaw, now Lord, was Home Secretary and held regular meetings for his ministers and PPSs.

> I wandered into Willie's room on that first morning. It was a vast room, and there was the Home Secretary sitting down. Willie jumped up at once and made a great fuss of me, as though my arriving at the Home Office was the most important thing that had ever happened there. It wasn't, of course, but that was Willie and that's why he inspired such affection with the people who worked for him.

It was not just the greeting. Throughout every meeting, he was meticulous about bringing the junior members of his team into the discussion. John Major was in the job for two years and learned a great deal from Willie Whitelaw.

The job of PPS is not very glorious. It is essentially that of bag-carrier to the minister, and being his eyes and ears in the House. He attends all the meetings and briefings and gets involved to the extent his minister allows it. John was fortunate in his, they encouraged him to get involved. He has to sell the department's line on any given issue to the back benchers, and feed back general feeling among MPs to the minister. If anyone is particularly unhappy, it is up to the PPS to arrange a meeting so that the policy can be explained.

The Home Office is a thankless ministry at the best of times. It covers a vast area of responsibility and is fraught with potential embarrassment for the Government. These were particularly difficult times, and the Government was in serious trouble during the early years of the Thatcher reign. The economy was in a mess, businesses were collapsing on a daily basis, there were crippling strikes, unemployment rose to over two-and-a-half million for the first time since 1935, and there was rioting in the worst of the inner city areas, in Bristol and Brixton, then erupting in Toxteth, London, Birmingham, Hull, Preston, Reading and Wolverhampton. In the autumn of 1981 Mrs Thatcher was rated the most unpopular Prime Minister ever in the opinion polls – a record John Major has since surpassed. The Conservatives trailed third behind the newly formed Liberal-SDP Alliance and Labour.

There were leaks from Cabinet meetings, some sackings and some resignations, and two former Prime Ministers openly criticized their successor. It was in this climate that the Blue Chips produced a pamphlet, written largely by William Waldegrave and Chris Patten, called *Changing Gear*, which decried Mrs Thatcher's monetarist economic dogma, and called for more capital investment by government, 'partnership' in industry, the uprating of child benefit and entry into the European Monetary System. They also wanted an elected House of Lords, and toyed with proportional representation.

Margaret Thatcher sat tight throughout. It was a situation strikingly similar to the one her successor suffered a decade later. She despaired at times, but she had no doubt that her policies were the right ones, and she refused to change them. As she had said to the Party Conference in Blackpool, echoing Christopher Fry's play, *The Lady's Not For Burning*:

> To those waiting with bated breath for that favourite media catchphrase, the U-turn, I have only one thing to say. You turn if you want to; the lady's not for turning. I will not change just to court popularity ... If ever a Conservative Government starts to do what it knows is wrong because it is afraid to do what is right, that is the time for Tories to cry 'Stop'. But you will never need to do that while I am Prime Minister.

John Major admired her courage, and agreed with her sentiments. He was still in broad agreement with Mrs Thatcher economically, but he was extremely worried about the social repercussions. Angela Rumbold, now Dame, came into the House at a by-election the following year, and shared an office with John in Norman Shaw North, a barn of a building across the road in Whitehall. Their other room-mates were John Carlisle, who seemed to spend most of his time in South Africa, and Tom Benyon, who ran into difficulties with his business and was thrown out by his local Association. He was in tears the afternoon he heard, and John and Angela comforted him. John was convinced Angela must have won the by-election on Mrs Thatcher's right-wing ticket, and assumed she was 'drier' than their Leaderene. She was not at all, but she teased him about it, and they often laughed about their degree of moistness. John would say of himself,

> I'm a bit wet on home affairs, but I'm quite dry on economics.

John had met Angela before she came into the House. She had been a local councillor in Kingston, and John had come to speak at a conference she had organized on Conservative Housing Policy. Shortly after that they had met a second time at a reception at Number Ten. Angela had been invited as chairman of the Local Education Authorities, and she and her husband arrived, thrilled to be there, but knowing no one. John was there too, and immediately introduced them to people. He was very kind again, in those early days in the House, when she didn't know her way around, didn't have an office or a secretary, and no one else took much notice.

John scarcely remembers his first visit to Number Ten, except that it was after a Royal Garden Party and he walked in with Robert Cranborne, heir to the Marquess of Salisbury, who described it as a 'nice little town house.' It was in 1979. MPs are invited to the Queen's Garden Party every year, followed by a reception in Downing Street. They had bumped into Harry and Gladys Simpson at Buckingham Palace. Harry had spent four years in Northern Ireland since leaving Lambeth, as Director General of the Housing Executive, and was now Controller of Housing to the Greater London Council. John and Harry had seen one another in London quite frequently, but Gladys and Norma hadn't seen each other for years. They had kept in touch, Norma writing great long newsy letters, and, of course, Gladys was Elizabeth's godmother, so they had a lot to talk about. They were both thrilled to be at Buckingham Palace, and stood on chairs so they could get a better view of the Royal Family walking into the tea tent. Little did Norma dream that one day she would be inside the tea tent herself.

Norma felt quite over-awed by Number Ten. She was petrified, not just by the house and its significance, but by the people they were going to meet. She has always been very happy to listen to political conversations, and swears blind she is not bored by them, but she hates being asked to contribute. And that was always the terror with Mrs Thatcher; that one day she would ask Norma her opinion on some political matter – but it never happened. On the way out Robert Cranborne asked what she had thought of Number Ten. 'Oh, it's smashing, a wonderful place,' she said enthusiastically. 'Yes,' he said, 'it's not a bad little pad, is it?'

Their first visit to Chequers, the Prime Minister's official country residence in Buckinghamshire, was no less scary for Norma, although she was intrigued to see the house. Like most people arriving for their first visit, they allowed more time for the journey than they needed, and stopped to freshen up in Great Missenden, where they bumped into Sydney Chapman, the new MP for Chipping Barnet, and his wife Claire, doing much the same. By sheer good luck the Majors' car was British, and after that first visit to Chequers, British it remained. One of her guests, a newspaper baron, turned up in a large Mercedes and Mrs Thatcher left him in no doubt about her views on the matter.

In April 1982 the Argentinian forces invaded the Falkland Islands, and Britain went to war to reclaim them. Eight thousand miles from Britain, and three hundred miles from Argentina, they had belonged to Britain for the last one hundred and fifty years, and Argentina had disputed Britain's claim for as long. Logically they should have been handed back long ago, but the eighteen hundred residents were of British origin, spoke English and had no desire to become part of a foreign culture. Margaret Thatcher became their champion, and determined to prove to General Leopoldo Galtieri, and his new fascist military regime in Buenos Aires, that no one snatches land from Britain by force and gets away with it. There was a principle at stake.

Margaret Thatcher was lucky. On 15 June the Argentinians surrendered. Fourteen ships from the Task Force were either damaged or sunk, but miraculously no more than two hundred and fifty men died. Events could so easily have gone the other way, and destroyed her. Twenty-seven thousand British lives were at stake. As it was, the Falklands War was her salvation. She grew in stature as the crisis unfolded. Having never experienced a war, she wobbled at first when the early casualties started coming in, but after a kindly lecture from Willie Whitelaw on the need for leaders to appear strong, she quickly pulled herself together and never looked back. She became a leader of extraordinary distinction, and the British people, who had been so disillusioned in her before the war, now greeted her as a heroine. She had given them national pride, she had brought the striking factions together and given Britain a sense of unity once more.

Although the Opposition soon went on to the attack in the House of Commons, the public sense of euphoria lasted well into the autumn as each returning ship was given a fêted welcome. At the Tory Party Conference in Brighton she was given a six-minute standing ovation.

By the following January John had become dejected. His colleagues were being promoted all around him and he felt he was being passed over. He was even beginning to mutter that banking might have been preferable – he was truly glum. Then one Friday afternoon the phone rang in his room and it was the Chief Whip, Michael Jopling, inviting him to be a Junior Whip. It was the call he had been waiting for, and he was tremendously excited. Nevertheless, his immediate thought was Norma. 'What shall I do?' he asked Angela Rumbold. 'The children are very young; shall I risk it, is it fair to Norma?'

'Of course you're going to risk it,' said Angela. 'It's the first step on the ladder – off you go.'

He called Norma from King's Cross station on his way home and told her he was going to be a Junior Whip. She was thrilled. She didn't quite know what it meant, but she realized it was good news, knew that John was pleased, and was therefore very pleased too. What it meant was more work and longer hours, but it was an opportunity to shine.

John had always worried about the effect his politics was having on Norma, but particularly so now that he was in the House and living away from home during the week. He would talk about her, especially to women colleagues, saying how worried he was that she was left on her own so much with the children, living in some ways like a one-parent family. He had also been dismayed by the effect his politics had on his friends. He once said to Angela Rumbold, 'Since you've come into politics, Angela, have you lost all your friends – the friends you had outside politics?'

'Oh, yes,' said Angela, 'they all went when I was on the local council.'

'Yes,' said John, 'that's the bit we find most difficult, that they are no longer able to see us as ordinary beings. They regard us in a slightly different light. I find that quite hard.'

He had plenty of friends inside politics, however, and all those friends from Brixton and Lambeth days he has never lost touch with. He made more friends within the House during his two-and-a-half years as a Whip. In order to become a Whip in the first place you have to be popular. Whips are appointed from within the Whips' office, with the Prime Minister's blessing, but everyone within that office has to agree the nominee – one blackball and it goes no further. They are a secretive and closely-knit clique whose job is to know everything that is going on in the House, who is thinking what, and who is plotting with whom, so that one way or another they make sure that the Government's business gets through, and whenever there is a vote, the Government has a majority. It requires skilful man-management: it means befriending, cajoling, explaining, flattering, bargaining and, if absolutely pushed, threatening back benchers to lend their support and toe the Party line. Each Whip looks after a group of MPs, and has responsibility for a department, which usually changes with each session. So the Whips not only have to know all about the MPs in their group, they also have to know enough about the Bills they are responsible for, so they can explain the finer points to their MPs, and iron out their worries. John left his spacious room in Norman Shaw North, and moved into a cramped office in the bowels of the House of Commons, with the four other Junior Whips. Shortly after his arrival, Michael Jopling was shuffled to the Ministry of Agriculture, and John Wakeham replaced him as Chief Whip.

Once again it was hard work that made John such a good Whip and brought him to the attention of ministers and back benchers alike. He worked hard at mastering the detail of the Bills he whipped, and hard at gaining the confidence of his colleagues, and persuading them to his way of thinking. He made good deals, and he was tough, but never discourteous. Some say he was the best-mannered Whip there was. It was an effective combination, which brought him to the attention of a number of people, including William Waldegrave. He was then a junior minister, and was so impressed with the way John handled his Paving Bill for the abolition of the GLC, that he remembers going to the Whips' office – in a 'wonderfully patronizing way', he happily admits – and writing a note saying, 'There's a fellow called Major who's just done my Bill, and he's absolutely bloody good; you ought to do something with him.'

What had so impressed him was the speed with which John managed to get this Bill through the House. It was a highly contentious, very complicated Bill which involved a lot of late-night and all-night sittings.

> He was incredibly competent. We were getting through things extraordinarily fast. At first one thinks that's one's own eloquence, but of course it isn't, it's because the Whip is making deals with the Whip on the other side and making them stick, and is running things properly – he is the sort of business manager for the Bill. He was wonderfully courteous, but extremely tough. It just wasn't worth the other side reneging on a deal because there would be serious trouble; he would keep us up all night for a week to demonstrate that it wasn't worth breaking a deal. There's a lot of tungsten carbide in him.

He helped Angela Rumbold get a Bill through too. She was PPS to Nick Ridley at the Department of the Environment at the time, who said if she wanted to get on she should do a Ten Minute Rule Bill, and suggested one about the GLC and the advertising campaign that Ken Livingstone was running. So she queued up all night, got her name on the list, but she was not very hopeful. That day she went into the tearoom and spotted John, so she went and sat down opposite him and pinched his crisps. He always had crisps and she always pinched them. He noticed she was looking a bit glum and asked why. She explained that she had this Ten Minute Rule Bill, which she knew would be defeated because Tony Banks (the Labour MP who was a member of the GLC, and became its last chairman) would oppose it and there would be a vote, 'and the Government doesn't care enough about any of this stuff to do anything about it.'

'Why do you say that?' asked John. 'It's quite an important little Bill in my opinion; it might get somewhere.'

'Rubbish,' said Angela, 'nobody cares,' and went off in her gloom to write her speech. She duly delivered it, there was a division, and, much to her astonishment, the payroll was in and she won. 'I am absolutely certain that was John,' she says. 'He got the government ministers to come in and support me, so they all voted for it and I had a majority.'

Angela was already a friend, but one by one other colleagues were beginning to notice John Major and discover that there was more to him than met the eye. Tristan Garel-Jones was another. They sat next to each other in the Whips' office for two years – Tristan had arrived ahead of John – and they became friends; but it was a friendship based entirely on politics.

> I hate all the things he's interested in, like football and cricket. He really likes it, seriously likes it, and knows a lot about it. If you asked how many left-arm bowlers opened the bowling for England and took a hundred Test wickets before tea, he would tell you. He knows the answer to all those sorts of questions. He watches it obsessively on television in the office – and football matches. Even now, wherever you go in the world, you're followed by cricket scores.

They had nothing in common socially either. Tristan is a confident, public-school Tory, a linguist, married to a wealthy Spaniard, clever, witty, charming, and some say unscrupulous. John was never rough as a Whip, they say, because he had Tristan to do the dirty work – he was the bully boy.

He is also a masterful tease, and he found John an irresistible target. He delights in finding the weak spot in anyone's armour and inserting the knife. In John's it was his appearance, his suits, his physique. 'He is rather charmingly sensitive about all kinds of things that people like him are usually sensitive about,' he says. He describes John as the personification of Middle England with all the values, inhibitions, worries and aspirations that 95 per cent of the population have.

> When my constituents ask what he's like, I say he's the sort of person I would expect to see with his car parked by the pavement on a Sunday, washing the car, eating some Polo mints and listening to the cricket match on the radio. He is extraordinarily ordinary.

So when the Blue Chips were next discussing whom, if anyone, they should bring into the group, he suggested John Major. Robert Atkins, who had a prior claim to John – they had been cricketing friends since the sixties – claims it was he who brought John into the Blue Chips. Either way, when his name was suggested at table everyone agreed and he was duly invited to join.

John's promotion to the Whips' office coincided with mounting speculation about the forthcoming election date. Mrs Thatcher finally opted for June, hoping to benefit from her Falklands success, so she could go into the winter with a fresh mandate, before the inevitable round of union wrangles. The Tory manifesto promised nothing new, just a continuation of the policies which, Mrs Thatcher boasted, in the previous four years had brought inflation down to less than 5 per cent, brought down interest rates, reduced the frequency and number of strikes, brought down tax rates, and slashed the National Insurance Surcharge – Labour's tax on jobs – giving £2,000 million back to industry.

The Labour Party offered no real threat. Nominally led by Michael Foot, it was in disarray, split by internal power play between the extreme left and the moderates. Their manifesto was derided by *The Times*: 'This party promises the moon; but it would have to borrow the moon. Somebody else, as always, would have to pay.'

More threatening, because it was an unknown quantity, was the Alliance, with a manifesto designed to appeal to malcontents from the other two parties, the cornerstone of which was electoral reform. They wanted proportional representation to replace the current first-past-the-post system – the need for it nicely demonstrated at the end of the day, when they won 25 per cent of the vote, and just twenty-three seats in Parliament to show for it.

John's position in Huntingdon was never in any danger, but there had been boundary changes since the last election, and a large part of Peterborough now fell within the constituency, which meant several thousand new voters who had yet to be charmed. Looking back they don't know why they were so nervous, but at the time the prospect of the election was something of a nightmare. Just as things were going right, it seemed as though yet another hurdle had been put in front of them to jump. For the three weeks of the campaign they worked round the clock, canvassing once again as though they were fighting a marginal seat, and once again it paid dividends. John was returned with a handsome majority, and Mrs Thatcher became one of the few Prime Ministers of the twentieth century to return to Downing Street for a second term without a break.

Roger Juggins and his son Stephen took three weeks away from the farm to drive John and Norma around, and between them they covered the length and breadth of Huntingdon. They became connoisseurs of cheap wine and indifferent cheese, with at least three cheese and wine parties in a weekend.

One day when Roger arrived to collect John for yet another cheese and wine do, he found him leaning over in the kitchen, fiddling uncomfortably with his eye. 'What's up, John?' he asked.

'Contact lenses,' John replied. 'I've been wearing them in London this week, and I don't like them.'

'Forget them,' said Roger. 'Make a feature of your glasses because you'll be known by them. If you wear contact lenses you become just another back-bencher.' It didn't take much persuasion. The contact lenses were never seen again.

John had brought about some fundamental changes in the constituency during his first four years. Not only had women come to the fore, the old order had been forced to beat a retreat. Soon after his election in 1979, he and Norma had been invited to dinner with two of his wealthier constituents. She was an heiress, he was an influential bigwig, and they lived in a palatial mansion in one of the outlying villages in Huntingdon, and liked to think that they ran the county. That evening they had gathered around the dining table a collection of their county friends. The only other guest who looked or felt as out of place as John and Norma was the local doctor. As the evening progressed, the wine flowed, and the braying of their hosts grew louder, John realized why he had been invited. They wanted to make sure he was not going to tamper with their cosy set-up in the constituency. They wanted to ensure he could be counted on as one of them, and to leave things as they were, a mutual back-scratching exercise to suit them both. John was appalled. He went straight to his agent, Andrew Thompson, and told him never to accept an invitation from those people for him again.

One of the most striking and unusual features of John Major is that he has never tried to ingratiate himself with the great and the good. Most people who make it to the top from humble beginnings adopt the taste, lifestyle and aspirations of their social betters, becoming, in many cases, more pukka than the Establishment. John has done none of it. While his contemporaries in the House would be busy in the social round, wheedling their way into the sight of those who could be useful to them, with dinner parties night after night and weekend country house parties, John simply declined. He doesn't much like the Establishment even now – although of course he likes individuals – and he is equally uncomfortable with the super-rich, and has never had any wish to emulate them or be one of them.

Andrew Thompson had left Huntingdon by the 1983 election, poached by Margaret Thatcher whose agent in Finchley had retired. There was a dearth of good agents at that time; Central Office had put out feelers and Mrs Thatcher had chosen Andrew Thompson. He had been popular during his time in Huntingdon; he was a lively character, good fun and excellent at public relations. Everyone had thought him a good agent. Some people had taken a dim view when his marriage broke up, but no one doubted his ability. None the less he was a controversial agent, so when the call came from Finchley, several people heaved a sigh of relief.

In his place the Association were offered a man and a woman. The man failed to turn up for his interview and so the job went to a lady called Sheila Murphy. Jo Johnson was president at the time, and waited for John to arrive to give him the news. They had never had a woman agent before. 'It makes no difference to me whether it's male or female,' he said without hesitation. Having grown up with strong, intelligent women, having worked with them and having married one, he has always had a very high regard for women and never questioned their ability to do a job as well as a man.

Sheila Murphy wasn't quite the right woman for this particular job, however. She was well liked, and she served John well, but members felt what the constituency needed was a good shake-up. It needed someone with energy and drive to bombard the villages where there was no Conservative organization or representation and get things moving, get subscriptions coming in and start making some money. Sheila wasn't the one to do it. So the job of galvanizing the constituency fell to Peter Brown, who took over as agent in 1985.

Peter Brown was an old friend from Lambeth days, although he swears there was no nepotism. He says a lot of people thought that a three-legged donkey had been put up against him, but he was actually one of five candidates and more than qualified. He had been the agent in Norwood when John was in Lambeth; from there he went to Kingston, where he was Norman Lamont's agent for twelve years. But there is no doubt John was delighted to see him in Huntingdon, and they have had a particularly close relationship ever since. He is a very direct, down-to-earth character, with a healthy sense of humour, and no affectations. He is a friend as much as an agent, and he has never doubted John's ability or his ambition, but little did he imagine he was going to preside over quite such a meteoric rise. When he arrived he was looking after a Whip. Five years later he was looking after a Prime Minister. Peter Brown says:

The interesting thing about John Major is that he hasn't put a foot wrong. You can't just put that down to luck. I thought Chancellor would be the pinnacle of his career. He's ambitious, yes, but not overtly so – you'd never think he was. This is part of the Major scene. The diffidence is entirely genuine. There are times when he'll say, 'What do you think I ought to say?', even now, and I'll say, 'Oh, for God's sake, we're not having this again, are we? You know very well you'll stand up in ten minutes' time and make a fabulous speech.' He likes a bit of guidance, but in a way I think it's a bit of an act. He likes people to think he's asking their views.

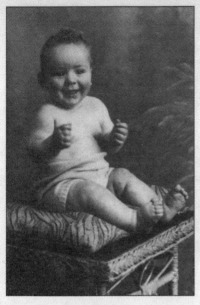

1. John Major aged five months.　　**2.** John Major aged five years.

3. John Major (*back row, 3rd from left*) in the
Rutlish Boys school cricket team.

4. His parents, Tom and Gwen.

5. John and Norma and the children with Jim Jackson and Mrs Lerner at a WRVS Luncheon Club in 1979.

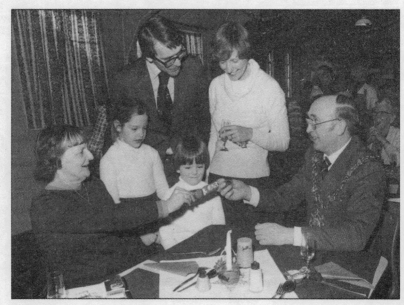

6. The Majors with President and Mrs Bush in the presidential launch, 1991.

7. Prospective candidate in St Pancras North with his new young agent, Sue Winter. She tried to get him to loosen up a bit, stop him looking like a banker, but he got very shirty.

8. Minister for Social Security, where he had his first taste of criticism in the outrage over cold-weather payments and his second, but by no means last, battle with Mrs Thatcher.

9. John Major as Chancellor of the Exchequer on Budget day, 21 March 1990.

10. Meeting President Gorbachev in Moscow, with their interpreters, in March 1991. Five months later the architect of *perestroika* had been removed. John saw Gorbachev in Moscow again on the day he surrendered power.

11. An audience with King Fahd during a second visit to the Gulf to thank the troops. Kuwait city was devastated. There was no water – even in the loos they were using Evian water.

12. John Major with Brigadier Sir Patrick Cordingley. He had been afraid the troops would be hostile when he went the first time, but they appreciated being told the truth. Afterwards all they wanted to know was when they could go home.

13. The Great Wall of China shrouded in mist, during a visit to Hong Kong and China in September 1991.

14. A charity match in Zimbabwe during a Commonwealth Heads of Government meeting. He was afraid his knee wouldn't stand up to it, but the chance to play with England Test cricketer Graham Hick was too good to pass up.

15. Hosting the G7 Economic Summit in July 1991. *Left to right*: the Dutch Prime Minister, Ruud Lubbers; George Bush; Helmut Kohl; the Italian Prime Minister, Giulio Andreotti; and François Mitterrand.

16. With Margaret and Denis Thatcher celebrating their 40th wedding anniversary in December 1991. Out of loyalty and good manners he put up with her attacks.

17. Surrounded by members of his Government at the launch of the Conservative manifesto for the election no one thought he could win. His own confidence was pure instinct.

18. The famous soapbox. At Cheltenham on the campaign trail, giving as good as he got from hecklers; but it wasn't all fun.

7

SENIOR WHIP AND SOCIAL SECURITY

MARGARET Thatcher could behave abominably. People laughingly referred to it as 'a hand-bagging' in later years, but it was no laughing matter. She could be quite vitriolic in her abuse, and reduce strong men to pulp. The late Lord Soames, who spared no one his tongue and was known as one of the rudest men in politics, once came out of a meeting with Mrs Thatcher reeling. 'I have never, ever, been spoken to by anyone like that in my life,' he said.

She could also, of course, be perfectly charming, and very thoughtful and caring. But she took careful handling. She liked people who stood up to her, but not everyone. Several people tried and ended up on the political slag heap as a result. Others prospered.

In July 1985 John was Lord Commissioner of the Treasury – a senior Whip – and Mrs Thatcher gave a black-tie dinner for the Whips from the Commons and the Lords to welcome John Wakeham back after months away. He had been badly injured in the Brighton bomb, which killed his wife. She was one of five people who had died in the explosion at the Grand Hotel during the Party conference the previous October. It had been planted by the IRA. Several others had been badly injured, including Norman Tebbit and his wife, Margaret, who has been confined to a wheelchair ever since the blast.

The dinner was primarily social, but after the first course Mrs Thatcher was bored so they moved on to business. Since business usually revolved around the Treasury, John Cope, who had been acting Chief Whip in John Wakeham's absence, suggested the Treasury Whip start.

So John Major began to give the Prime Minister the intelligence he had gleaned from the back benches about the Government's economic policy. It was not good news, and he talked in some detail and for quite some time about why MPs were not convinced by some of the arguments. They were loyal, he assured her, and supportive, but they were unconvinced.

Mrs Thatcher listened until John had finished, then she drew herself up to her most haughty and said, 'I am astonished.' She then launched into the most vitriolic attack on John as though the views he had passed on to her from the Party were his own views. He had not mentioned his own views, he had simply reported as a Whip, but she took it as a personal attack.

'I don't like what I'm hearing,' she said icily.

'I'm sorry about that,' said John, quite rattled by the injustice of the attack. 'But you asked for the truth and what I have told you is the truth.'

The argument continued for some time, becoming increasingly violent. The mild manners in John Major belie a tough street-fighter underneath, who can be every bit as devastating as Mrs Thatcher if he is pushed too far.

Bob Boscawen came to John's defence, and Mrs Thatcher turned on him, implying that he was cowardly in not standing up for the Party. She picked the wrong man. Robert Boscawen won the Military Cross in 1944, was blown up in tanks several times and was one of the 'Guinea Pigs' whose face was rebuilt by plastic surgery after the war. He is a very, very brave man; John has never, he says, met one braver.

The insult was not lost on Carol Mather, another holder of the MC, one of Montgomery's aides during the war, and close friend of Boscawen. Furious, he weighed in on his friend's behalf, and the whole thing disintegrated into a full-scale row.

And so it continued until suddenly the voice of Baroness Trumpington rang out above the mêlée, 'You're so right, Prime Minister.'

'What about?' said Mrs Thatcher.

'I've forgotten,' said the Baroness, and the tension was at once broken.

At the end of the evening Michael Alison, the Prime Minister's PPS, came across to John and said, 'Do you think you ought to make your peace with the Prime Minister?'

'No,' said John. 'I think she ought to make her peace with me. It's up to her.'

Denis Thatcher came over and slapped him on the back and said, 'She enjoyed that.'

John then went over to John Wakeham and said, 'I'm not taking this. She can find someone else to join the Whips' office.'

'No, no, don't worry,' said Wakeham, 'it'll all be perfectly all right.'

The next day John was sitting in the Chamber as the Whip on Duty, when Mrs Thatcher came and sat on the bench beside him, and ostentatiously asked his view about something of no importance. He expressed his view. 'I'm sure that's right,' she said, 'we'll have a meeting with the Whips straight away.' Whereupon the entire Whips' office was called together, and John's view publicly endorsed. There was never any apology, but it was clearly an attempt to make friends again, and admit she had been in the wrong the previous night, which he found very heart-warming. A little over a month later she made him a junior minister.

John evidently went up in Mrs Thatcher's estimation as a result of their fight, but it could easily have gone the other way, as John was very well aware when he took her on. He could have languished in the Whips' office indefinitely. He didn't care. He was wholly unrepentant and he had lost not a wink of sleep over it. As far as he was concerned she was wrong, and she had behaved very badly. Not only was it bad in man-management terms, it was downright rude, and if she hadn't made her peace with him he was quite prepared to resign from the Government. He was furious. What was the point in having a Whips' office to tell you the truth, if you behaved badly when they did tell you the truth?

There is no doubt John Major has worked phenomenally hard in every job he has had during his parliamentary career, and has impressed colleagues and officials alike, but there is equally no doubt that he has been lucky in his job. He has had the knack of being the right person in the right place at the right time. His promotion from junior Whip to Lord Commissioner was no exception. The job should by rights have gone to Tristan Garel-Jones, who was ahead of John in seniority in the Whips' office, but he didn't want the job; he wasn't interested in the finer workings of the Treasury, and knew that John was. So he suggested to the Chief Whip that John go in his place.

Not only did it result in this seminal confrontation with Mrs Thatcher, it brought him into contact with Nigel Lawson, the Chancellor of the Exchequer, who later proved an influential patron. Just how much he noticed John at this stage is debatable. In his autobiography, *The View From No. 11*, he says he 'had formed a high opinion of him . . . when he was responsible for assisting the passage of the 1985 Finance Bill through the House of Commons' after the Budget, but there is no further mention of John Major during that period. They met regularly three mornings a week at 'prayer meetings', when ministers, special advisers, and PPSs in the department met to discuss policy issues. It was a happy team at the time, which included John Moore, Barney Hayhoe, Peter Brooke, and Andrew Tyrie, head of the Economic Section of the Conservative Research Department.

John Moore says that Lawson was impressed by John Major at that time. His arrival among them, he says, was 'the most amazing breath of fresh air'. He and Nigel Lawson both prided themselves on having read ten official papers before breakfast. Suddenly at prayer meetings, they had a Whip – very much the outsider of the team – who also knew what was going on, and was very much in tune with their underlying attitudes. He understood the political nuances of the issues, and was quite ready to argue a point, undaunted by anyone's seniority. He was good at reporting back the news and views of the House, he knew exactly what was going on, and which policies were likely to cause trouble. Even at Monday's meetings he knew precisely what back benchers had been discussing over the weekend, and with whom.

Andrew Tyrie, on the other hand, who went on to work closely with Nigel Lawson after that period, isn't sure whether he talent-spotted John at that point. He wonders how well he remembered him. 'He used to look up from his papers and, it seemed to me sometimes, that he didn't always register some of the younger people there.'

However, John had one other thing going for him which ensured his popularity in that group: cricket. Nigel Lawson and Peter Brooke were both cricket fanatics, all knew the almanacs backwards, and during the cricketing season or the Test series there would be quite a different agenda at the Treasury. Cricket has provided a bond with a tremendous number of colleagues over the years, and it cuts across every social barrier. Kenneth Clarke is another fan. The first time they got to know one another socially was over cricket. Kenneth Clarke invited John to watch the Test match at Trent Bridge, and they've been watching cricket together on and off ever since. He says John is absolutely fanatical – far more interested in cricket than he is in politics! He likes to talk about it, but the acid test of someone who's interested is that he actually likes to watch it. A lot of people knock around cricket grounds just to socialize. He doesn't do that. He sits down for a few hours and watches the game. He knows most of the people in cricket; he's very knowledgeable. He's just a paid-up, classic cricket buff.

Much of John's life is landmarked by cricketing events. The day John was promoted from the Whips' office, Richard Ellison took five wickets to beat the Australians at the Oval. It was a Friday and he was watching it on television at home when a call came through from Number Ten saying that Mrs Thatcher would be telephoning later. She was in the midst of a reshuffle and he knew she would be ringing to offer him a job; everyone had been saying he would be promoted in the reshuffle. For two hours he waited in utter despair, thinking that she was going to offer him the job of Parliamentary Under Secretary for the Minister for Sport at the Department of the Environment. If she had he would have turned it down. He didn't want Sport, he didn't think it was a good way to start. He paced around the garden rehearsing what he would say to the Prime Minister when she rang; he would tell her that he didn't want to be responsible for Sport, he wanted to do something more substantive in terms of politics.

As Peter Brown says of John,

He comes from the grass roots, and his interest in politics has never been for personal aggrandizement, as many people's is. It is a genuine desire to help people. With his family background, struggling, living in Brixton, he saw how people had to live. He despised the way the Labour Party and local councillors looked down on everybody and tried to treat them like peasants. He was genuinely moved to come into politics to help people improve their way of life. That's been his aim all along.

When the phone call finally came she asked him to go to the Department of Health and Social Security, as Parliamentary Under Secretary to Norman Fowler. As he says, he must have been one of the few people in history to be relieved at the thought of learning about the social security system.

The garden he paced in his despair is the same garden he paces today when things are getting him down. It is at the Finings, the home he and Norma bought in 1983, the place he loves above all other. It is in the village of Great Stukeley. Norma found the house, and although she wasn't immediately taken with it – it was rather dark – she knew it would be exactly what he wanted. She was right. He fell in love with it and decided to buy it almost instantaneously, before he had even seen inside. He drove round the turning circle at the front, saw the garden and the little copse that shields it from view, three acres in all, and that was it. Emily Blatch was one of the first friends he took to see it. They had been at a meeting one Saturday morning, and he asked if she would like to come and see his new house. He was enormously excited, and keen to know if she liked it. It was quite empty, and he stood in the middle of a bare room and looked about him. 'Nobody, but nobody, will understand what this means to me,' he said, and seemed almost maudlin for a moment. 'Not only to have a detached house, but to have a house that doesn't have neighbours.'

It is a comparatively modest four-bedroom house, built in 1938, to which they have since added an extension with an extra bedroom, but financially it was a big leap from the house in Hemingford Grey, and came with a very hefty mortgage which John could ill afford. And in keeping with all their moves, disaster struck in the midst. They bought the Finings before the sale of their old house in Hemingford Grey was finalized, the sale of that fell through at the last minute, and they were left with a massive bridging loan. It practically ruined them. The house was on the market for months and months before they found a buyer, and John became increasingly desperate.

They had another drain on their resources by this time in the form of school fees. Elizabeth had been at the state primary school in Hemingford Grey, and when the time came for her to move, they agonized over what to do. Most children went on to the local comprehensive, but John and Norma were afraid that, as the daughter of the local MP, she might have had difficulty. Norma had run up against some hostile teachers and was very concerned on Elizabeth's behalf. The alternative was the private system, and after consulting with a number of friends, they decided on Kimbolton, a private co-educational school where she attended as a day-girl. James followed her there in due course.

John's colleagues in the Whips' office were well aware of his anguish as the weeks and months went past with still no offers on the house. After a while a couple of them could bear it no longer and approached John with the offer of help. Aware that he might be insulted by the suggestion, they offered to lend him the money that he had borrowed from the bank as a bridging loan, interest-free, for as long as it took to sell the house. John took their offer in the spirit in which it was extended, but refused. He said that, much as he appreciated their concern, at the end of the day, he had got himself into this situation and it was he who would have to get himself out of it. And in due course the matter resolved itself.

John arrived at the DHSS in September 1985 aware that Norman Fowler was profoundly suspicious of him. He suspected him of being a Thatcherite Whip's nark who had been moved into his department at exactly the moment when he was carrying out his social security reviews. Social security then, as now, was one of the most politically sensitive areas in Government, and represented by far the biggest item of Government spending – more than the total amount it recouped in income tax. These were the most ambitious and far-reaching reforms that had been effected in nearly forty years, and inevitably they aroused some fierce opposition from some of the pressure groups.

Norman Fowler had been appointed Secretary of State in 1981. He had studied the system for over two years, then in early 1984 set up four separate reviews of different parts of the system, all of them manned by interested outsiders as well as ministers and officials. They had produced their recommendations by the end of the year, and a specially convened Cabinet Committee, chaired by the Prime Minister, published the Government's conclusions in a Green Paper in June 1985, and a White Paper in December – legislation followed in 1986. It came into effect in April 1988. So John was in the DHSS during a crucial period.

Despite his early misgivings, he and Norman Fowler hit it off well together. Norman was a difficult man to work for. He was slow to trust people, and was sceptical about anyone else's political judgement. A skilled tactician himself, he liked to keep control of everything, and junior ministers in the past had been apt to feel left out. A number of careers had foundered under the weight of the job. It was arguably the toughest junior minister's job outside the Treasury, and, along with Immigration, the largest generator of letters – they count them in thousands at Social Security. John inherited quite a backlog when he first arrived. Norman Fowler remembers him going off one weekend with thirteen red boxes full of submissions and letters. But it was a job he was good at. It involved mastering a maze of complicated detail, understanding the intricacies of the benefit system and a mass of technicalities – and detail was his forte. As the reforms worked their way through the House, there were often late-night debates, which he would have to wind up, and there were committees to sit on too.

John won Norman Fowler's trust faster, colleagues say, than anyone else who came into the department. He won it for several reasons: partly because of his ability to master a complicated brief, and deal with it; partly because he was easy with colleagues – he showed no side or arrogance, which made for a happy team; and partly because he was canny in his judgement about the way colleagues in the House would react. He usually got it absolutely right, and, because he was so on top of his brief, he was able to withstand detailed attack from the Opposition benches.

Kenneth Clarke, who had been Minister of State for Health, remembers gossiping with Norman late one night after John had been at the DHSS a while.

'He told me to keep my eye on John Major, firstly because he was very good, but also because he was probably the most ambitious person he had ever met.'

There was just one small problem in this perfect working relationship. The DHSS office at that time was at Alexander Fleming House at the Elephant and Castle, and every Monday Norman Fowler held a meeting with all his ministers in the pizza restaurant opposite. Every Monday his Under Secretary failed to show, detained by some other engagement. Norman could never understand it, until the truth emerged, that the pizzas were full of garlic, which John couldn't bear. 'It's not the taste,' he says, 'it's the smell. Very unsocial.'

Norman didn't hold it against him. Twelve months later, when Tony Newton, who had been John's immediate boss, moved sideways to take over Health, leaving the position of Minister of State for Social Security and the Disabled vacant, Norman managed to persuade the Chief Whip to give the job to John. 'Normally,' he says, 'one wouldn't have considered someone so quickly for that, but he had star quality. I remember one of the ministers there saying that with John "you had a Rolls-Royce service".'

Margaret Thatcher, who had to approve the appointment, was

very much in favour; she felt Social Security was important ground-work, having been in Pensions herself, and she put people she liked into the job. She was a great one for favourites. Colleagues were neatly divided into 'them' and 'us', and she had decided by this stage that John Major was definitely 'one of us'. In fact, not long afterwards, in 1986, she confided in Angela Rumbold that John Major was the man she would like to see succeed her. 'There's only one person, now that Cecil's gone,' she said. 'John Major.'

Cecil Parkinson had gone from the Cabinet in 1983, disgraced by the Sara Keays affair. Margaret was still enormously fond of him. He had been called 'the son she wished she'd had' – strong, handsome and independent – and she had hoped, one far-off day, he would succeed her. But that hope was shattered when the news broke that his secretary, Sara Keays, was expecting a baby, and that he, a married man, was the father. Margaret had known of the affair and the baby at the time of the election, when Cecil was Party Chairman, but didn't believe it should force him from office. However, by the autumn Sara Keays had begun talking to the press, and Margaret was left with no option but to accept his resignation from his new post of Trade and Industry Secretary.

Another favourite had been Norman Tebbit, whom she made Chairman of the Party in 1985, but his star was definitely on the wane. She grew suspicious of him: he had begun to behave like the heir apparent, which she hated. It was always the end of the road for a favourite when they began to behave like one, particularly if they posed a serious threat, and Norman did. As time went by she became convinced that he was plotting against her, forming his own power base at Central Office. What appealed to her about John was that he was so young. He was only forty-three, while Norman Tebbit was fifty-five, so she felt she could earmark him as her successor, safe in the knowledge that it would be ten years at least before he would even want the job.

John was Minister of State for less than a year, but it was an eventful time, during which he was briefly elevated to the position of Public Enemy Number One, which brought him once again into confrontation with Margaret Thatcher. It was during the second week in January when exceptional weather conditions hit. Britain shivered under several feet of snow, with freezing temperatures, which as usual affected the elderly more severely than anyone else. The Government had a system for providing emergency cold weather payments to pensioners, which had been set up by John's predecessor, Tony Newton, but like so many welfare benefits it was immensely complicated, and essentially mean. As the frail began dying of hypothermia, it was evident that what money there was, was not reaching those who needed it most. As the Minister in charge of benefits, John was held responsible.

He realized, he says, within twenty-four hours of the big freeze that the scheme wasn't working and needed to be changed, and went to the Treasury to ask for more money. John MacGregor was Chief Secretary at the time, and he was completely unforthcoming, so he went to see the Prime Minister. He remembers looking out of Mrs Thatcher's window at Number Ten, over a landscape deep in snow, and saying, 'It's pretty cold out there in the snow.' He knew as soon as he said it that he had won, that John MacGregor would have to give him the money. That afternoon in the House of Commons he announced an extra £5 would be paid to all those on supplementary benefit while the cold weather lasted.

John was genuinely interested in social security, which made him quite a rarity within the Tory Party. Kenneth Clarke is another one who became quite a buff, and was the Party's expert on pensions for a time, but he admits that there is no one in the Cabinet today who understands the social security system better than John Major, with the exception of Tony Newton. He is a walking encyclopaedia on the subject, and knows as much if not more than his officials. Most Tory ministers regard social security as an academic exercise – benefits are important but expensive – but that is the extent of their interest. Mention details and their eyes begin to glaze, because it is not usually something they have had any personal experience of. Having grown up in Brixton, John had been surrounded by people living on the edge, and knew precisely how important the issues were. As the Fowler Review made its way through the House, he was just the right man in the right place at the right time to face an Opposition, briefed by the various pressure groups, waiting to trip the Government up at every turn.

Nicholas True, who is now in the political office at Number Ten, was special adviser to Norman Fowler during the time John was at Social Security, and remembers in particular the way John always brought insights into the discussion which clearly came from his own life experience and which were quite illuminating to the rest of his colleagues gathered around the table.

Those discussions were always better for having him there because he would often say 'we ought to look at this the other way round', and that is often as important as saying, like these Think Tank boffins, 'I've worked out this incredible idea'. He puts an original spin on things because he comes at it from a different direction.

Concerning the Disabled, for which he was also Minister, he frequently sought advice from Lord Renton, his predecessor in Huntingdon, who has a severely disabled daughter, named Davina. He was quite an authority on the subject, having been heavily involved with Mencap, the National Society for Mentally Handicapped Children, for much of his life. John had a little peripheral knowledge already. Shortly after they had moved to the constituency, the local Mencap branch had held its Annual General Meeting. David was then President, and John and Norma went along. Norma had subsequently become involved with the charity, becoming President herself after some years. She had been determined to be an active President, and every Christmas took it upon herself to sell Christmas cards. Every year she would go round the villages of Huntingdon knocking on doors with the Mencap catalogue, and much to David Renton's admiration, raised over £1,000 this way every year.

In May 1987 Mrs Thatcher named the date of the next election. It was not the most perfect timing for Norma. Her book on Joan Sutherland was about to be published. She had been working on it, on and off, for about ten years, and this was the culmination of a challenging, but at times disheartening, labour. So disheartened had she become in her gloomier moments that she considered giving the whole thing up. She was wasting her time, she told herself, she was never going to finish it, and nobody would ever publish it. 'All I needed was an excuse to abandon it,' she says, 'and I thought, well, an agent won't want it, that will be the excuse to abandon it.' But an agent did take it, and very soon they had a publisher, Queen Anne Press. The only problem was the book was not yet finished. So suddenly she had a deadline to meet, which after working at her own pace for so long, fitting her writing in between children, constituency commitments and John, was very difficult. The pressure was intense and she had so little time to call her own. It was a difficult period all round and everyone in the house felt it. In the list of acknowledgements at the front of the book she ends by expressing her gratitude 'last, but by no means least, to the tolerance of my family as a little indulgence became a viable proposition. I am sure they will not mind if they never see egg and chips or spaghetti bolognese again.'

The job was finally done, and Norma felt a real sense of achievement. Dame Joan had approved the manuscript and written an introduction in which she paid tribute to Norma:

> I shall always be grateful for the loving response of my public and of many wonderful colleagues and friends throughout the years and I hope they will all enjoy Norma Major's book. Norma's diligence and stamina in accomplishing such an enormous project have been admirable.

Having been nothing but a wife and mother for so many years, an appendage to the local MP, such praise was like oxygen. The book was an important monument to her self-esteem, and she was looking forward to the launch party with great excitement. It was set for 27 May in Huntingdon – she had wanted it in the constituency rather than London – and friends were coming from far and wide.

Then Mrs Thatcher announced the election, and Norma realized at once that everything she had worked so hard and so long for would be swept aside by politics; and it was. 'I remember now,' she says, 'John and Peter Brown sitting discussing the date of the adoption meeting and they were talking about the date of my book launch, 27 May. I said, "I don't believe I'm hearing this."' Norma won. The book had to be launched on that particular day and John's adoption meeting was moved to the next night. Norma says,

> Looking forward to things is tremendous, and there have been plenty of things to look forward to, but looking back is a great pleasure as well, in fact in some ways I think it is even more of a pleasure, and that's one of the things that I do regret, if I regret anything at all, that because of the pace everything's moving at, there's never any time to look forward or look back. We're always rushing on. And there was this wonderful party and friends that had come from everywhere to give birth to my 'baby' and the next day we were into an election campaign, three weeks of really hard work.

The election date was 11 June, and all the soundings indicated the Tories would be back for a third term. It was as well for them that they started so far ahead, because the campaign didn't go well, while Labour's got off to a brilliant start with a professionally filmed profile of Neil Kinnock that sent his ratings in the opinion polls up by 19 per cent overnight. The Tories' was a muddled campaign with two chiefs at Central Office – Norman Tebbit, and Lord Young, whom Mrs Thatcher had put in there because she didn't wholly trust Norman Tebbit. The result was what Nigel Lawson describes as 'in every way the most incompetent' campaign in which he had ever participated in twenty-three years. Two advertising agencies were brought in: Norman retained Saatchi & Saatchi, who had run the Party's campaigns in the past, and David Young brought in Tim Bell, late of Saatchi & Saatchi, Mrs Thatcher's favourite image-maker. The manifesto had three 'flag-ship' policies: the Poll Tax, education reform, and housing, but the latter two had been cobbled together so quickly that none of the people running the campaign were sufficiently familiar with the details to field questions, and there were a number of embarrassing moments at the morning press conferences. They were fortunate in the Poll Tax in that no one had yet realized its full horrors, and the Labour Party signally failed to spot them too.

John was involved in these televised briefings, which took place every day of the campaign at 10.00 in Central Office. This meant he had to be in Smith Square by 6.00 so that he could park his car and prepare for the cameras. But he also had his own campaign to run in the constituency, so the minute he was free from the briefing he would drive straight up to Huntingdon, arriving at about noon. He would meet his chairman, Roger Juggins, and they would go off to a luncheon meeting, followed by two meetings in the afternoon, then home, if he was lucky, for a quick cup of tea, then off to two evening engagements. Norma would drive out to meet them after the last engagement, to give John his car, so that he could then dash back to London for two or three hours' sleep, before the dawn start to Smith Square, while Roger delivered Norma home. It was worked out with military precision and this was the pattern day in, day out for most of the campaign.

In the end the Labour Party shot themselves in the foot over defence. In an interview with David Frost, Neil Kinnock said that if the Russians invaded a non-nuclear Britain they would be resisted by guerrilla bands who had taken to the hills. The Conservatives at once capitalized on the image with posters showing a soldier with his hands up in surrender, with the simple slogan 'Labour's Policy on Arms'. And they were bettered over tax. Nigel Lawson had organized an elaborate costing of Labour's spending plans. Among them was a raft of new and updated social security benefits, which his advisers worked out would cost £34 billion, implying the basic rate of tax could be no less than 56p in the pound, or VAT at almost 50 per cent. Andrew Tyrie was the special adviser put to the task of costing the social security pledges. He had all the factual information he needed from officials, but he needed a decision from one of the ministers and went to see John Major. He had last seen him at prayer meetings when John was Treasury Whip, when he had been impressed. He was enormously impressed again. These were very tricky issues and it was vital they got it exactly right, so they couldn't be accused of double-counting or being unfair to Labour. John went straight to the heart of the problem and decided what was required with no hesitation.

It was some time into the campaign before the hard work bore fruit. Labour stuck to the line that no one who earned less than £25,000 a year would be worse off under a Labour Government. In the final week, friendly journalists, well briefed by Andrew Tyrie, forced Neil Kinnock to admit that this was untrue in several instances. The most damaging was Labour's plan to increase child benefit. They had failed to mention in their manifesto that this would be financed by abolishing the married man's tax allowance, which meant that millions of married couples who had no children under the age of eighteen would effectively face a substantial tax increase.

The Alliance between the Liberals and the Social Democrats, led jointly by David Owen and David Steel, was not the potent force everyone had feared, and fell into disarray after the election, having failed to make much of an impact on either of the two main parties. So, despite the inadequacies of their campaign, the Conservative Party was returned for an historic third term with a majority in the House of Commons of one hundred and one. And in Huntingdon John Major had yet again increased his majority.

The next day Margaret Thatcher promoted him to the Cabinet as Chief Secretary to the Treasury. He had made it from Junior Whip to the Cabinet in just over two-and-a-half years, which was quite some feat. But once again there was no time to celebrate. As Norma says,

We won the election as a country, then we did our count in Huntingdon, and the next day he was in the Cabinet, but there was no time to celebrate anything really because everything had rolled on so fast. And by this time the book was old hat. I look at it and I still can't believe I did it. It sold out.

The move to Chief Secretary was entirely down to Nigel Lawson, and the ever-present element of luck. At the beginning of February Mrs Thatcher had made it clear to Nigel Lawson that she wanted him to continue as Chancellor after the election, and he had started to think about whom he should ask her for as Chief Secretary, knowing that the present incumbent, John MacGregor, would be certain to get a ministry in the next term. As he writes in his book,

I still have the diary card, for 4 February 1987, on which I scribbled my conclusion: John Wakeham, who had entered the House of Commons with me in 1974 . . . or – failing him – John Major, who had seemed to me the pick of the 1979 intake.

Just before the election he sounded John Wakeham out – he was then Chief Whip – but Wakeham turned it down.

He thanked me, but indicated that the job did not greatly appeal to him. He obviously hoped for something better.

And indeed he went on to become Leader of the House.

This left me with John Major, whom I had first come across during his time in the Whips' Office . . . and I had formed a high opinion of him. Subsequently, as Minister of State for Social Security, he had demonstrated an impressive grasp of the complexities of the Social Security rules and an ability to put the Government's case across in a firm, clear and agreeable way. This relatively unusual combination of mastery of detail and likeable manner would, I felt, make him an excellent Chief Secretary.

Mrs Thatcher had earmarked John for the job of Chief Whip, and needed some persuasion. Nigel Lawson argued that it was very hard to find a good Chief Secretary, and much less difficult to find a good Chief Whip. John Major, he insisted, was the only strong candidate for the job. David Waddington, he suggested, would make an admirable Chief Whip. Willie Whitelaw, the only other person present at this Cabinet-making discussion, concurred, and Mrs Thatcher gave Lawson the Chief Secretary he wanted. As Nigel Lawson points out,

> It is ironic that, had he instead become Chief Whip as Margaret had intended, he could never have been a candidate to succeed her when she stepped down in 1990.

8

CHIEF SECRETARY

IT was halfway through his first public expenditure round as
Chief Secretary that John Major suffered his second sleepless
night. He had a meeting with the Secretary of State for Education,
Kenneth Baker, the following morning and had a very complex
brief to master beforehand. It was the autumn of 1987 and he was
living on the top floor in Durand Gardens. He sat up until 2
o'clock in the morning reading a mass of detail on Higher and
Further Education. He was very tired and, as he says, couldn't get
it into his thick head. He went to bed and didn't sleep, and when
the light began to filter in through the window at 5.30 he got up
and had another look at it, working until 8.15 when he had to leave
for the Treasury. He went into the meeting, found he had
succeeded in getting it into his head, and discovered to his immense
relief that Kenneth Baker knew no more than he did.

Kenneth Baker acknowledges he was good.

I'd dealt with several Chief Secretaries. I think he was the
best. He knew his subject, he was in calm quiet control and at
the end of the day he was prepared to do a political deal. He
was very pleasant to deal with, he had done his homework,
knew his brief.

Angela Rumbold, who was Kenneth Baker's Minister of State in
those negotiations, and knew John better, was quite alarmed when
she saw him that morning.

That is the only time I have ever seen John look quite ill. It's
a ghastly job – you have to read everybody's papers and go

through all their budgets and I think he really had been sitting up all night trying to swot up all this stuff and it had really got to him. I think he found that first year quite tough in the Treasury. He was working tremendously hard. I remember him saying to me one night when we were eating crisps, 'My God, I'm not going to do this for ever – this is ridiculous – there must be other things in life besides this.'

Nevertheless, John's two years as Chief Secretary to the Treasury were two of the happiest years he has spent in politics. It was the hardest job he has ever had to do, including being Premier, but it allowed him to do what he loves, and what he knows he does best – negotiate – and what's more, to come out of those negotiations having achieved his objective without making enemies. He finds nothing more exhilarating than being given a Gordian knot to untie: he loves to go into a meeting filled with people who have sharply differing views and pull the strings together, get the best out of everyone, and bring them to an agreement that they can all live with. Acknowledging his own immodesty, he says he has never known anyone who did it better.

It is something he has always been able to do, but eighteen months in the Whips' office provided him with considerable experience. He had some of the most difficult Bills to get through Parliament, and didn't fail on one. As Chief Secretary the job is almost entirely negotiation. The trick, he says, is being able to give people an orange while lifting their wallet. It's a wonderful job, he says, absolutely marvellous, the best job in Government.

Only two people in the Cabinet see right the way across Government – the Prime Minister and the Chief Secretary. The Chancellor sees three-quarters. But it's the Chief Secretary who sees the detail. He's in the engine room oiling the machinery. The job was invented by Harold Macmillan in the early 1960s to relieve the Chancellor of what had become an unbearable load; and the specific task was to keep public expenditure under control. Technically it is the most junior position in Cabinet, but used properly that position has more influence than almost any other. The Chief Secretary can shift the Government's priorities in his public expenditure bilaterals without the rest of Government realizing it. He knows exactly what is going on, he learns a huge amount about his colleagues, he knows who knows their facts and who doesn't, who can negotiate and who can't, who has a clear idea of what he wants to do and who hasn't, who really cares and who just wants a presentational triumph. The Chief Secretary absorbs such a storehouse of knowledge about how the system works and how his colleagues work that he learns as much in a year at the Treasury as he would in three years in any other job. It is a job, he says, to put your best and your brightest into because if they pass through it successfully they are very well placed for almost any job. Michael Portillo, who held the job in John Major's first Government, has already been identified by commentators as a probable future Prime Minister.

It was not long after becoming Chief Secretary that John chanced to bump into Ken Livingstone, the newly elected Labour Member for Brent East, waiting for a cab outside the House of Commons. Although he had heckled John from the public gallery in Lambeth, before succeeding him in the Housing Department, he had quite admired some of the work John had done there.

'Given what you were doing in Lambeth,' said Ken, 'how on earth do you put up with all this reactionary crap?'

'You remember me, Ken,' said John. 'I haven't changed. And one day I'll be able to do what I want.'

Mrs Thatcher was apparently unaware of just how socially 'wet' John Major really was. His two years as Chief Secretary should have alerted her, but because he was so in tune economically, and so reliable and confident about his facts and figures, it passed her by. He wanted to bring about change in the way people at the bottom of the pile were treated. He wanted a fairer society, in which people who needed help were given it and allowed to maintain their dignity. Long before, he had said if he ever had the chance he was going to alter the attitude of the Civil Service towards members of the public. He once told Roger Juggins about the days when he had had to go cap in hand to the social security department in Brixton.

'I was embarrassed as a teenager drawing unemployment benefit,' he said. 'Perhaps I shouldn't have been, but I was and it did make me understand how others must feel in the same circumstances.'

As Chief Secretary he had greater power to help people at the bottom of the heap than anyone else in Government and he found it immensely satisfying. Ministers can come forward with ideas, he says, but ideas mean money, money means the Treasury and the Treasury means the Chief Secretary. And priorities are the key.

Spelling out the importance of priorities in a speech to the National Association of Conservative Graduates after his second public expenditure round, he said,

Just spending money is of itself no virtue, particularly if you take it in taxes from other people. What matters is getting it spent efficiently.

He went on to say that the public expenditure survey

can never be about more for everyone. It is about providing more by shifting resources into the most important areas. Aneurin Bevan once famously quoted Lenin by saying that socialism is the language of priorities – and the standard of political debate in this country would be immeasurably improved if the modern Labour Party had grasped this simple fact. To steal the phrase, I would say that the public expenditure survey is supremely about priorities.

There is a story faithfully recorded in several books that John plotted his future at this point in his career; that in August 1987 he and his old friend Robert Atkins were sitting on the back of a narrow boat meandering through the Staffordshire canals, with their two wives up front, discussing how best John should set about working his way to become Prime Minister. Having seen the rest of the Cabinet at work, he had realized that he was capable of doing the job, and they had worked out a plan of campaign together. Robert Atkins, subsequently a minister, is the source of the story and tells it again at the drop of a hat. 'John said, "I can run rings around these people. Do you know, I think I could be Prime Minister?"' But John denies it. Robert, he says, has a very fanciful memory.

The truth is more prosaic.

It's my fault. I was teasing Robert. He was enthusiastic on my behalf and I played up to him. It was over a drink at the end of a day on a long boat.

Robert was sure I would go all the way. 'OK,' I said, 'I'll do it. I'll run rings around them. Prime Minister next week.'

I was sending Robert up. He thought I was agreeing with him in an off beat way. Hence the story.

John is clearly very fond of Robert Atkins; he is an old friend, in a Laurel and Hardy capacity – he's the one that always gets the other into trouble. He's known Robert since he was only a minor menace, he jokes, but his telling of this particular story has not been very helpful.

When he became a member of the Cabinet he certainly did realize that the people in it were not possessed of extraordinary abilities way beyond those people who were just outside it. Time was when he had held Cabinet ministers in awe. John Drew, from Warden Housing, remembers going to have lunch with John in the House shortly after he became an MP, and him pointing out important figures and famous faces with all the excitement and adulation of a small boy. He had obviously lost the awe long ago, but watching them in Cabinet he realized that what they had over and above their junior colleagues was experience.

Nigel Lawson claims in his autobiography that for a time after the 1987 election he was concerned that he might have made the wrong choice of Chief Secretary,

> a view I suspect shared by John Major himself. He found the job far more difficult than anything he had ever done before, and had to work very hard to try and master it. He would come and see me at Number 11, ashen faced, to unburden himself of his worries and to seek my advice.

John regards this as another fanciful memory at work, although he doesn't deny it was very hard work.

Andrew Tyrie, who worked very closely with John on the 1987 spending round, says he certainly found his initial spell as Chief Secretary tough and thinks he may have relied on Lawson for moral support. It was an excellent team in the Treasury at that time. He says,

> We had every kind of character required. Lawson had, I think, the best mind in politics. But he wasn't a natural presenter, and his manner could occasionally be misinterpreted as rudeness. Major was not naturally an intellectual, but he was brilliant at the human side of politics. Perhaps the best of all at that.

All the more strange that the human side is what appears to have been lacking in John Major's performance as Prime Minister in his early years. The skill hadn't disappeared, but the sheer volume of work and the pressures of the job distorted his view. He had been too busy elsewhere and sometimes had not been able to see the wood for the trees. The same thing happened to Mrs Thatcher. As Norman Tebbit says,

> She allowed the Single European Act to get through the Cabinet. We were wrongly advised by the lawyers about some of the implications, but we all had our noses deeply into our own affairs, and if the Foreign Secretary said that's what it was, and if it didn't cut across what we were doing, we would accept that.

Andrew Tyrie says,

> Nigel Lawson and John Major were an excellent foil, one for another, in terms of their ability, and as a double-act, to send in to achieve something – immensely effective. And if you look at the rest of the team, there was a lot of talent. One of the crucial roles of the Financial Secretary is to get the Finance Bill through the Finance Committee and through the House – fending off the Opposition with detailed arguments, and also very much convincing and assuaging the concerns of one's own side, on a number of detailed points. That is absolutely Norman Lamont's bread and butter: he is brilliant in the House, and he is very good in committee. Then we had Peter Brooke. We didn't have a patriarch of the Party, a Whitelaw figure, in either Major or Lawson, but we did have something of that in him – he knew just how to handle the Party. And then we had an intellectual workhorse in Peter Lilley, who was the fifth minister, and of course they all went on to do greater things. So Major was an important player in a very strong team in 1987, and I think that that also helped him rise out and get noticed quickly. And that team worked very closely together; it had the confidence of the Prime Minister, and the Prime Minister's policies were very Treasury-oriented, and that boosted the morale of the whole building. It was a very exciting place to work, in the Treasury after the 1987 election, and Major was part of that, benefiting from it enormously and undoubtedly acquiring many of the skills and knowledge that would subsequently be required as Chancellor and then as Prime Minister.

John says of himself that he is neither as stupid as people say, nor is he brilliant; he has to work hard. Some people, he says, think from the top downwards. Douglas Hurd is an example: he starts with an idea and fills in the detail afterwards. John thinks from the bottom upwards; he starts with the foundations and the bricks, as it were, and keeps on building until the concept falls into place at the top. It takes him longer to get there, but it is a securer house, he says, when he's finished. Other people are secure if they have the end product in their mind and it doesn't matter to them that they know none of the details. John can't operate unless he is on top of every last detail. He needs to know how something works, why it works, what it will mean to people if it is implemented, and what it would mean to people if it wasn't. Details are to politicians what bullets are to soldiers, he says. They need them.

It was knowing the details that other European leaders didn't that enabled him to get such a favourable deal for Britain at Maastricht in 1991. His triumph went sour later, but at the time he returned to a hero's welcome. Again, at the Edinburgh Summit a year later, he came away with concessions no one thought he could get, simply, he says, because he knew the detail when other people didn't.

The details he had to master as Chief Secretary were no less than the individual budgets and the policies of every department in Whitehall – preferably better than its own Secretary of State – so that he could engage in hand-to-hand combat with each of the ministers responsible when they came to submit their bid for the next year's spending. That hand-to-hand combat could be very varied. In his first public expenditure round John spent nearly twenty-five hours, over a period of four or five days, locked in battle over the Defence budget with George Younger. George Younger was a skilled negotiator, but not always a total master of detail, and that was where he fell eventually, though he fell with honours. Another minister came into the fray with huge bids, but didn't know his facts and by the end of three hours' discussion he had had his bids halved and had left with his case in tatters.

The whole process is a bit of a game. The Chief Secretary starts out by arguing for an unrealistically low figure and the Secretary of State argues for one that is unrealistically high, and each side gives a bit until they have a figure that meets the genuine needs of the department, and is politically acceptable. The Chief Secretary is effectively on the side of the taxpayer, making sure taxpayers' money isn't squandered, but, of course, he is also a member of the Government, and if he is too successful in his argument, services become starved of money, and the Party becomes deeply unpopular.

John Moore, who became Secretary of State for the DHSS, taking over Norman Fowler's old job after the election, decided to abandon the normal bidding conventions. Having been a Treasury minister himself, he well understood the rules and thought them absurd. Far better, he thought, to be open and honest from the start, so that instead of 'going through the undergrowth for three months' while silly bids and counter bids went back and forth, everyone would be arguing on the same platform, from the same data, and the real debate would be about the political choices to be made. 'It seemed to me if you were serious about being one government and you really wanted to have rational debate, rational arguments, then one of the first things you did was open up properly.'

So open up he did, but he came away badly bloodied by the encounter. Not long before he had been promoted by the press as the man most likely to succeed Mrs Thatcher. He was her Golden Boy, and articles and profiles abounded. There is no doubt he was the sort of man she liked, smooth, good-looking, self-made, and politically dry, but he had never been a member of her 'kitchen cabinet' and doesn't know why the media seized on him in the way they did. He says he wasn't involved in any of it. He refused all interviews and didn't speak to a single journalist, but they wrote about him none the less. So having been a political pin-up he suddenly found himself under fierce attack and his future very much in doubt.

It has often been suggested that John Major deliberately put the boot into John Moore because he saw him as a rival for the crown; that here at last is evidence that 'nice Mr Major' is far more ruthless and ambitious than he has ever been given credit for. People who witnessed that public expenditure round, however, say that the effect of ousting a rival was incidental. John Major's prime concern was to impress Nigel Lawson and the Prime Minister, with whom the Chief Secretary has a lot of contact. He knew that, at the beginning of a new Parliament with a hundred-seat majority, there was some room for manoeuvre in public spending (unlike before an election) and he could afford to be tough in some negotiations; this would be a way to earn his spurs as someone Mrs Thatcher could trust.

The main area where the two Johns came to blows was over Child Benefit. John Moore wanted it to continue; John Major wanted to freeze it, and target the poor by increasing Family Credit. For years the Treasury had wanted to do this, John Major achieved it, and John Moore paid the price. The press at once described it as defeat at the hands of the Treasury.

Observers say the real cause of the problem was that John Moore had been promoted beyond his ability. The DHSS was the biggest-spending Department of all and quite the most unwieldy – the Department of Health alone was the third biggest employer and bureaucracy in the world, after the Indian railway system and the former Red Army, and John Moore wasn't experienced enough. In their negotiations John Major simply outwitted him. Social security was, after all, a subject he knew like the back of his hand.

And John Moore had antagonized him. He had made some rather inept speeches when he first arrived at the DHSS about the huge job ahead of him, and how he was really going to get to grips with the problems of social security, as though nothing had been done about it for years. As his immediate predecessor, Norman Fowler assumed the remarks were directed at him, but he thinks John Major took it rather personally as the outgoing Minister of State. He reckons John Major was not very amused by the presentation. As one minister says,

There should be little books of guidance for people taking over other people's jobs. You just don't do that. You try not to blame your predecessor. So he made a bit of an enemy there. When he started saying this social security system needs to change radically, and benefits are going out to people who don't need benefits, it's not surprising that the Treasury looked upon that with glee. Up to that point he'd been quite a cautious politician. I don't know what happened.

When the Government came under fire the following spring for not spending enough on the health service, as wards closed and operations were delayed, John Moore took the blame for having failed to secure enough money in the Autumn Statement. He took the blame again in April when the Fowler social security reforms started to bite. Having lauded him as the man most likely to succeed Margaret Thatcher, the press suddenly turned against him. As he says, the criticism at the time focused on the settlement in the autumn. He had been content with that settlement, but there had been another debate concealed within that public expenditure round, which had to do with long-term funding and restructuring of the health system, and that was where the real trouble lay and that was never understood at the time. Throwing more money at hospitals was no use unless that money was used more efficiently. What was needed was radical reform.

Shortly after his appointment he had suggested reform to Mrs Thatcher and she had warned him off it. But by January, he says, he had won the argument in Government and the Prime Minister had committed to a review. Nigel Lawson claims it was he who persuaded Mrs Thatcher to agree to a review. Kenneth Clarke says she set it up because Bernard Ingham, her Press Secretary, suggested it would be a good thing to say on a *Panorama* interview, where she was about to be slaughtered. Whatever the reason, she did set up a review of the Health Service – and did announce it during a *Panorama* programme. Mrs Thatcher presided, and other members were Nigel Lawson; John Moore; his Minister of Health, Tony Newton; and John Major, plus two others. Halfway through, Mrs Thatcher decided to cut the DHSS in two, and sent John Moore off to look after Social Security – widely perceived politically as the less important of the two ministries – and brought in Kenneth Clarke to take his place as Secretary of State for Health.

As a result, John Moore went into that autumn's public expenditure round fighting, and the issue once again was Child Benefit. John Major wanted to continue the freeze he had secured the year before, and increase Family Credit again. John Moore wanted an increase in Child Benefit, and threatened to resign if he didn't get what he wanted. Normally when the Chief Secretary and a spending minister reach an impasse the argument goes before a specially convened Star Chamber of senior ministers who adjudicate. In previous years it had been presided over by Willie Whitelaw, but in December 1987 he had collapsed with a minor stroke, and on doctor's advice, had retired from Government, where his voice of calm and wisdom was sorely missed. Cecil Parkinson became Chairman of Star Chamber in his place.

John had managed to settle all the budgets in the 1987 round without recourse to Star Chamber and it looked dangerously as though the matter of Child Benefit was going to spoil his record. However, in the end the two Johns brought their disagreement to the Prime Minister and Nigel Lawson instead. Nigel Lawson describes it in his book as

> a tense and difficult occasion. John Moore was quiet, but highly emotional. The arguments on both sides of the Child Benefit case were gone into in considerable detail. His case became no better as the argument developed, but at the end he said that he had not changed his mind about resignation. He simply couldn't carry on with his job unless Child Benefit were increased.

Margaret told him to sleep on it, and by the next day when Lawson saw him privately, 'his mood had changed. He was less emotional, and clearly did not wish to resign.' Lawson offered him a deal on pensioners as a way out, which he rejected. 'I then offered him what the official Treasury had had in mind all along: a freeze in Child Benefit, but extra money for Family Credit. This he accepted.' Nine months later he was out of his job.

It is widely thought that Mrs Thatcher sacked him, which Nigel Lawson describes as 'a sad, unnecessary, heartless and foolish act; for apart from that one aberration over Child Benefit, John had been loyal to a fault throughout his ministerial career.' John Moore says he was not sacked. He had decided to go as early as August 1987. 'That was prior to my being run up in the media and prior to being knocked down and prior to being very ill.' Not long after the Child Benefit showdown John Moore became seriously ill, so ill his wife was brought in to say goodbye to him.

> At that point I told the Prime Minister that I had decided to go but hadn't decided when. It was clear then that I had to for myself and my family.
> What is little understood outside politics is how key to some of us our families are. One of the worst things happened to me: my family were attacked, even my mother and father. If I even contemplated going back into politics I think my wife would leave. All the years she was begging me to call it a day, and you read about this aggressive wife who was pushing. I've talked to John [Major] about this. He, like I, feels very

strongly about the relationship he has with his wife and the privacy – it's impossible. It's an enormous strength in the ability for you to do your work, but it's a weakness because you care so passionately about your wife and children that to stay in office at a certain point, despite all sense of duty, isn't worth it. Everyone assumes we're all career mad, ambitious, but the modern senior politician is worked to death. It's not like thirty or forty years ago. I was picked up at 7 and never home before 11, there's no money, no holiday, you never see your family – you make a huge sacrifice.

John Moore says he harbours no bitterness, and certainly feels no ill will towards John Major. John has told him, he says, that he feels he was very unfairly treated. In fact John Moore has nothing but admiration for John Major and his ability:

There is a serious Rolls-Royce mind there. We had some extraordinary discussions in Cabinet committee and Cabinet, where Margaret legitimately challenged us. I've forgotten the issues – they were a lot to do with the interrelationship of housing benefit – really tortuously difficult issues, where John had not just a succinct ability to distil the essence of the issue, but also to leap through to what we do about the problem, as opposed to taking the standard negative route.

His performance inspired the confidence of Mrs Thatcher. When Kenneth Clarke was brought into the Health Service reviews in place of John Moore, he found that she was relying on John Major quite heavily:

He was very calm, very considered, very good in a small group, and she was obviously increasingly looking to his judgement. We had endless meetings, extremely lively, rather passionate debates – bloody great rows – and you came out exhausted at the end. John was very keen on all of that. He was there to keep an eye on the Treasury aspects and keep pointing out to us all that the options were expensive and to keep an eye on public expenditure. I found him, in terms of what I was trying to do, the most helpful colleague I had in the whole thing. One or two times, where Margaret sent John and me off to try and agree various things between ourselves, I reckoned if I could persuade John of something I was 90 per cent of the way to persuading Margaret to go along with it.

He was a genuinely useful bloke to talk things through with. I didn't feel as though I was dealing with a Treasury mandarin manqué and we agreed a surprising amount. He played quite a key role in that and helped a lot subsequently, and having been involved all the way through, he was one of the minority of my colleagues, and tiny minority of the public, who actually understood the Health Service reforms; what they were for and how they were supposed to work.

In the autumn, when they launched into the public spending round, their meetings were rather more confrontational. John's Private Secretary, Carys Evans, who witnessed his meetings with all the ministers that year, says these were the most entertaining. They were very well matched, there was a lot of banter and the meetings were very good value. She remembers Ken Clarke coming into one dressed in a double-breasted suit. John Major said he looked just like Aneurin Bevan (founder of the National Health Service) in it, and the tone was set, but they were tough meetings.

Kenneth Clarke says,

I was determined to go long and late and try and blackmail my colleagues against a background of crisis in the Health Service. A good settlement was one way of getting us out of the mire. Hence I remember we had one early meeting, classic for the silliness of the public expenditure round. We sat there for five hours surrounded by officials, none of whom said very much, just going over the whole field, testing the ground, at the end of which neither of us had conceded a single thing.

That year he brought the thing to a conclusion by losing his temper first, or purporting to, because I was almost filibustering. The two of us were enjoying exchanging our respective and incompatible arguments. John brought it to an end by insisting on seeing me on my own, sitting down together, and I don't know how he phrased it, but he said, 'Do let's stop messing about. Life's too short for this interminable thing to go on. You cut out all the rubbish and I'll make you an offer.' We then moved gear quite dramatically. He persuaded me; I did trust him – more than practically any of my colleagues. I eventually decided, just recklessly, to trust him completely and abandoned everything I was prepared to concede. I put all my cards just face up on the table, showed him my hand, whereupon he made an offer and we settled, the whole thing done. He made a generous offer, and we settled, I'm sure, far above what the Treasury base line was. We came to a political deal; sorted it all out in about ten minutes.

The only department which the Chief Secretary has no involvement in is Foreign Affairs. He knows the policies and the budget, but has no hand in any negotiations. Defence was a huge budget, and because of the constant updating in the technology and the exorbitant cost of military hardware, inherently difficult to control. It is practically impossible to argue with the Defence Secretary about the need for individual pieces of equipment, some of which cost billions of pounds to develop and operate, because he will be straying into the realms of strategy. Masterminded by Steve Robson, an official with specialist expertise, the Treasury's line of attack on Defence was efficiency. It was such a large budget that if you made small gains in efficiency you could finance these new technological developments without having to raid other budgets. John took the plan into battle with the Secretary of State, George Younger. The meetings were grindingly tedious. George Younger insisted on every point that they were already operating with maximum efficiency. John insisted there was room for improvement, and dredged up one area after another, prepared to keep going for hour after hour until the Secretary of State was worn down.

John was enthused by the benefits to be reaped from improved efficiency and value for money. It provided the key to so much more, and here once again were early stirrings of the Citizen's Charter. Of all the ideals and policies which he has pursued during his premiership, the Citizen's Charter is the one which most bears his personal stamp. Improving efficiency wasn't as glamorous and dramatic as finding funds for projects like the Channel tunnel, but the rewards were considerable. There was £1.25 billion a year saved in the Civil Service, for example, and cost improvement programmes in the NHS which would yield cumulative savings approaching £900 million – the cost of twenty District General Hospitals or 70,000 nurses' salaries. Cost efficiency was part and parcel with improving management and motivating workers – enabling them to provide a better service for the public.

As he said to the Adam Smith Institute in June 1989,

After two years as Chief Secretary it has become increasingly clear to me that anyone who seriously wants to improve the service to the consumer must give priority to pushing decisions down to the individuals who can best take them. For the quality of service depends ultimately on individuals working in the health service, in local authorities and in the local offices of central government departments and agencies.

The incentive and ability to provide a better service is a vital motivating force.

The public expenditure rounds were the busiest time for John and the staff in his private office at the Treasury. They worked hard and they worked long hours, but it was a happy office with plenty of humour and an up-to-the-minute score on any Test match. The officials who have worked with John over the years have all found him a pleasure to work for, from the most highly qualified Treasury economists to the messengers. This is partly because he is so genial around the office but also because he makes them feel he appreciates the work they do. He assumes people are competent, and gives them their head. He is also tolerant of mistakes, provided he is satisfied that people are doing their best, so his staff don't live in fear of putting a foot wrong.

His Private Secretary for the first year had been Jill Rutter (now a member of the Policy Unit at Number Ten) who shared his enthusiasm for cricket. She was also a member of Surrey and they would occasionally arrange their day around a quick trip to the Oval during the Test match, or more frequently watch it on television in the office, and much of the chat, when it wasn't work, was either cricket or soccer. He was always very relaxed among the staff in his private office; he enjoyed their company, and Terry, the clerk, was a Manchester United supporter, which provided plenty of sparring. Carys Evans, who took over from Jill during John's second year, knew nothing about either football or cricket, but the assistant she brought with her, Peter Wanless, did, and she once caused uproar in the office by asking, 'Who is this Don Bradman you are all talking about?' Whenever she was asked to get hold of someone on the telephone thereafter, somebody would say, 'You don't mean the famous cricketer?'

Jill Rutter was experienced when John came into the job – more experienced than he – and provided invaluable assistance in his early days. She had already done a year in the Chief Secretary's office working for John MacGregor. Carys was very junior when she took over, didn't know anything about most of the subjects and felt slightly nervous. John, she says, sensed it and was very encouraging, but very soon assumed that she was on top of the job. He involved the office in everything, confided in his officials and helped them understand the reasons for decisions he took, particularly the political ones. This was a huge advantage for them in that they felt well-informed and able to speak with authority to other officials about what the Chief Secretary really thought.

The day began at 8.00 with tea and toast, made by Dennis, an old Treasury character who was John's personal messenger. John loved white toast and Marmite and ate it at all hours of the day with endless cups of tea which Dennis made in a little room next to his office. Much of the day would be taken up with meetings with secretaries of state, particularly in September and October, which generated an enormous amount of paperwork for the office, typing and photocopying, and sending out notes of all the meetings. They all worked late at that time of year, and John would frequently send out for fish and chips for everyone, which he paid for out of his own pocket, and they would all go into his room and eat together.

Ministers don't often fraternize with their junior civil servants, but John often did. On one occasion Sheldon Kosky, his diary secretary and general office jester – he was a great mimic and did marvellous impressions of the Chief Secretary – was appearing in an amateur production of the Gilbert and Sullivan operetta *HMS Pinafore*. He invited John and Norma and Elizabeth. It was staged in a church hall near Harrow, and they all went off to see him.

Norma would occasionally come up to London for an evening at the opera with John and would come and collect him from the Treasury, but she would invariably drive home to Huntingdon again afterwards in order to be there for the children in the morning. The office staff came to know her quite well and were tremendously fond of her. As luck would have it, she always seemed to arrive in the midst of some kind of panic so she would sit and wait for him in the outer office and chat to everyone. They were struck by how entirely unassuming she was. Even when she phoned she would ask whether she could speak to John if it wasn't too much trouble. The children came up from time to time too. He would show them round and they were amused by how big his office was.

They were clearly quite unaware of the significance of their father's job. They were a world apart from politics; Elizabeth had been horse-mad for most of her teens and spent every spare moment down at the local stables; with James it was football. Politics was not a subject much talked about at home. Home was John's escape, and he wanted to talk about other things; the children's comings and goings, the garden, domestic matters. Even when political friends came to lunch or dinner they seldom discussed politics other than in the most peripheral way. Norma often wished he would talk about it, share some of his worries. One of the pleasures of his being Prime Minister is that she accompanies him to more dinners than she ever did before, and gets to hear what he thinks and feels about political issues from his conversations with other people.

His family were clearly important to him and he spoke about them a lot in the office. The garden was under siege by rabbits and Norma had taken to shooting at them. She always missed. James joked that she was such a lousy shot, if she aimed at the sky she would miss. John would report on progress, and talk about how Norma was being pressed by her publishers to write another book. He talked about Elizabeth's career plans – she wanted to be a veterinary nurse – and about their birthdays and illnesses, and arranged for Sheldon to send flowers on Elizabeth's birthday. Not many days passed without at least one telephone call to or from home.

At the Treasury sports day John was invited to present the prizes. Wandering around the ground he bumped into Sheldon's precedessor, Tony Dight, a West Indian who had been diary secretary during John's first year as Chief Secretary. He had his wife and very new baby with him, who was the immediate focus of attention. John said he remembered how complete it made him feel when Elizabeth was born. Norma and the children are his soft spot. What hurts him most is the effect that his career has had on them; the sacrifices they have had to make and the intrusion into their privacy. The only time in his life when he has ever been truly frightened was over one of the children. James, when just a few months old, developed croup and couldn't breathe. He was choking and coughing and John and Norma thought he was going to die. They were living in Beckenham at the time, and they spent the night walking him around the kitchen with steam billowing from every kettle and pan they possessed in an attempt to get moisture into his little lungs. There was so much steam that they had to redecorate the whole room. He just stopped breathing. It was the most terrifying, awful night, which John says he wouldn't go through again for a thousand pounds a second: terrifying because he didn't know what he could do. In the end the doctor came and gave James an injection, and the croup subsided.

John was interested in other people's families and home circumstances too. Carys seldom left the office before 10.00 or 11.00 at night, nor Jill Rutter before her, because by convention a civil servant always remains on duty while the minister is still around. John was almost always still around at that sort of time. He often had to be in the House to wind up a late-night debate, or there would be some financial drama, and he would be coerced into talking about it on *Newsnight*. And very often they would go and have some supper together and talk. Carys says she has him to thank for at least two pieces of advice which she heeded. When her two-year stint in the private office was over she was interested in going abroad for a year. John encouraged her to apply for the Harkness to study the welfare state in America, which she did and had a marvellous year. On another occasion she was contemplating selling her flat and buying a house in Clapham with her brother. John cautioned against it. 'You might regret being locked into a bigger mortgage, or he might, or one of you might want to get married.' She decided against the idea, and not much more than a couple of years afterwards did indeed get married.

These were the kind of common sense questions that he brought into political debate too – not remarkable in themselves, but the sort of questions that are very often lost sight of when talking about budget lines. The Health Service review was looking at two policy areas: the NHS and what has come to be called Care in the Community. During one of the discussions on the latter, talk turned to the elderly, and finding ways of enabling them to stay in the community by providing home-help backup. John said,

> What does this mean? A family, husband, wife and children would have to look after grandma even if she was very dependent and demanding. What about the effect that would have on adolescent children? Having an old person around can be very demanding and put a strain on the marriage. Is this what we are saying, that all families will have to look after their elderly relatives indefinitely, however difficult?

It was, and it is the situation that exists today as a result of Government policy, and John is as unhappy about it now as he was in 1989. But it is one of the problems facing society which he can't yet see the solution to. Hundreds of thousands of middle-aged women, in particular, are trapped for one reason or another looking after elderly parents. He knows the difficulties they face, but at the moment he has neither the money nor the solution.

On another occasion the debate was about the privatization of a council house estate. John wanted to hold back. Not everyone was a thrusting Thatcherite go-getter; people had different needs, some wouldn't want a change. He had an aunt, for example, who had always been a council tenant and enjoyed the security it gave her. She would have hated the responsibility of becoming a home owner, or having the tenancy bought up by some fly-by-night.

Carys was always amazed by John's stamina. All she had the energy for when she arrived home after an exhausting day of back-to-back meetings and mountains of paperwork, was sleep, but she knew he would still have to work on his boxes, and possibly have a speech to write too.

It was nothing new. John says he has put seventeen or eighteen hours into every job he has done since becoming a junior minister. Because he moved so quickly from one job to another, and with each move had to assimilate another mass of information, it was inevitable – particularly with his obsession about being in command of every detail. As Chief Secretary he not only wanted to be fluent with the detail, he liked to plot the way the debate would go beforehand. He had a feel for how the other protagonists would react, what the atmosphere was likely to be, who would rub along together, and what the most realistic outcome would be. Having considered the advice, he would call the officials in and say, 'Look, the way this meeting is going to go is like this. The Prime Minister will be concerned about Y, someone else about X, the points I have to make to sway the argument are these three. You have given me the ammunition for two, please can I have a note on the third?'

'His reading of how it would go was uncanny,' says Carys Evans. 'He was almost always right.'

Officials responded well to that. They felt it was worth putting in the work, because he appreciated it. Carys says,

> Meetings were a genuine discussion. You didn't have the feeling that he had made up his mind in advance. He had

always taken in every bit of detail in the advice. Some of the things you had to deal with as Chief Secretary were incredibly tortuous, but he had an enormous appetite for work and would take it all in, and he would marshal the arguments well in meetings. If he had a meeting with a minister at 10.00, say, and had been briefed by an official the night before, he would summon him up for tea and toast in the morning and go through it again. He didn't go for set meetings. He liked to find the person, whatever their rank, who actually knew about the subject under discussion, and say 'The problem I see is this. What do you think?' That's how he first met Gus O'Donnell who was later to follow him to Number Ten.

His appetite for work also infuriated Carys at times. Papers came into her office first. She would read them and write a summary, and maybe some comments of her own to help draw his attention to important areas, or to remind him that last year this particular department were arguing something quite different. As an official her job was to add a different perspective. They were mostly weighty documents, and it took time. John would get impatient. When he finished whatever he was doing he would wander through to her office and start ferreting through her In-tray looking for something to do, and it drove her mad.

John has never been able to sit still behind the increasingly grand desks in the increasingly grand offices that he has had. He has always hated being cut off from the activities of the outer office, and would invariably wander through for a chat. And if ever he wanted someone, he wouldn't press the buzzer on his desk like most ministers rather imperiously do. He would come out and find the person he wanted to talk to. He has never liked working alone. He much prefers to have someone to talk things through with, and that someone is usually a private secretary or a special adviser. In each department those are the people with whom he has always formed the closest attachment. They are the people he would chose to eat with in the canteen at lunchtime, or take out for some quick supper in the evenings if they were working late. From the Treasury they would often go to the Gandhi in Kennington for a curry, or to a pub near Waterloo called the Horse and Groom for a beer and a beefburger.

One of the joys of the job, as far as John was concerned, was the anonymity of it. Apart from the occasional appearance on

Newsnight, he attracted very little publicity, and that was the way he liked it. Sometimes, however, he was obliged to parade at City lunches, and this was the aspect of the job he liked least. It was standard fare for Chief Secretaries and Chancellors: elaborate lunches in the smart executive dining rooms of City banks and financial institutions, at which they would explain the Government's economic policy to small groups of senior directors. Treasury officials liked nothing better because the food was always delicious, and it was something of a treat to be wined and dined in such splendour; but John took no pleasure in the food at all, and would invariably come back grumbling about it. He was often interrogated during lunch about matters which were not in his field, such as arcane tax points, which made him uncomfortable. But most of all he took no pleasure in the company.

He has continued to resist the company of City fat-cats and the cosy camaraderie of the 'chattering classes'. He warms to people who come from a similar background to his own. He disguises any chips he may have on his shoulder with self-deprecating one-liners. 'Curious that two such colourful people should have produced such a grey son,' he will say of his parents, for example, or 'Not bad for a grammar school drop-out like me.' But deep down he seems to harbour a sort of inverted snobbery. It doesn't show. He handles the Establishment and the fat-cats superbly, and appears to be as comfortable in their company as with his own family. They have no inkling of his true feelings because he is such a consummate actor, and he is a wily enough politician to know that they are the backbone of the Tory Party and he needs to massage their egos. But the people he really likes are those he might have grown up alongside.

John's relationship with Mrs Thatcher went from strength to strength during his time in the Treasury. Partly because he was meticulous about keeping Number Ten informed so that problems were never bounced on her; and partly because she also had an obsession for detail and was pleased to discover that her Chief Secretary was every bit as capable of mastering every annex of a ten-annex brief as she was. He would always anticipate the sort of questions she would ask; she never caught him out and she came to realize that if he said something was so, it was.

But it was by no means an entirely smooth relationship, and at the end of 1988 they came to serious blows. It was over the privatization of Short Brothers, a large aircraft manufacturing company in Northern Ireland. The company had huge debts and was on the brink of collapse, but it was politically sensitive. It was a very important employer in the province, where there was generally massive unemployment, and the best hope of saving the company and thousands of jobs was to privatize. But it couldn't be done without giving the company a dowry, a large injection of public money to pay off the debts and help with the capital restructuring. John was in charge of working out the deal with Tom King, the Secretary of State for Northern Ireland, and they had negotiated long and hard over how much money should be put into the company, how it should be paid, and when, and came to an agreement. John was satisfied it was the best deal that could be achieved from the point of view of both the taxpayer and Shorts.

In such negotiations, if the Chief Secretary and a spending minister bring their case to the Prime Minister it is customary for the Prime Minister to side with the Chief Secretary, as guardian of the taxpayer. Mrs Thatcher on this occasion, however, said she thought John had been over generous; the implication being that far from guarding the taxpayers' money, he was squandering it. Had she tried to overrule him on political grounds, he would have been prepared to listen, but in attacking his figures she delivered a serious blow to his pride, which he was not prepared to take. He knew his figures were right and he was damned if she was going to get away with it.

The final confrontation took place in the Cabinet Room at Number Ten. There was John, Margaret and Andrew Turnbull, her PPS at the time, and for two hours they were locked in furious battle. She accused him of not caring about public expenditure. He pointed out that he had just completed a public expenditure round that stopped expenditure rising for the first time in a decade. She went on with what he calls her usual blustering bullying tactics and he left. He went straight back to the Treasury and wrote a letter of resignation. He told Carys Evans that if he didn't get his own way Mrs Thatcher could find herself another Chief Secretary. He was absolutely furious. He was also slightly anxious about what he had done. He telephoned his friend Baroness Blatch. 'Emily,' he said, 'I've blown it. This time I've really blown it.' He then explained the row he had just had and said she was really spitting tacks. 'She's wrong, and I just know I'm right. I couldn't compromise.'

The following day Mrs Thatcher called him into her office. 'I've thought about what you were saying,' she said, 'and I'd like you to give me two sides of A4, flesh it out.' He did, she agreed his figures and the matter was closed. She had an astonishing ability, which can only be marvelled at, to walk away from a disagreement without a single bruise. She liked argument for its own sake, and no matter how violent and vituperative it had been, once it was over she behaved as though it had never been.

John is quite capable of taking part in screaming matches, but would never do so under those set of circumstances. He believes they are counterproductive and lousy man-management. He says,

> You get the best out of people if you encourage them, not if you abuse them and undermine them. I prefer encouragement because it's more productive.

But if sufficiently provoked he has a temper and a tongue that those who have witnessed it say is utterly devastating. His formative years spent in the back streets of Brixton are no doubt partly responsible, but the temperament runs in the family. His sister, Pat, is the same: mild-mannered, benevolent, easy-going 99 per cent of the time until someone pushes her too far. 'John's temper is slow burning,' says Pat. 'It simmers and simmers and then it explodes. He goes to great lengths to control it.'

9

FOREIGN SECRETARY

IN June 1989 John would have been MP in Huntingdon for ten years and the local Association wanted to give him a small party to celebrate. He had group of close friends in the association, Olive Baddley among them, and as Chairman that year, the lot of organizing the event fell to her. The small party very rapidly grew. So many people wanted to take part that plans to hold the event indoors at Elton Hall had to be abandoned in favour of an increasingly large marquee in the garden. In the end they had to call a halt at over five hundred people. The invitations announced there would be a presentation and guests were invited to contribute if they wished, but not more than £5. Olive asked Norma what present they would like and the answer was some glasses. All they had, she said, were garage glasses – free from Shell filling stations.

Olive bought an entire suite of crystal glassware with the money she collected, eight of everything, and still had such an embarrassment of cash left over that she and Emily Blatch went down to London to Garrards in Regent Street, and bought a silver salver as well, which they had engraved. The evening was an enormous success and John and Norma were entirely overwhelmed, both by the warmth of feeling and the extraordinary generosity. Nigel Lawson, who came as guest of honour, was quite flabbergasted by the event. He said that when he had been MP for ten years his association didn't give him so much as a coffee party.

John had certainly earned it. Every weekend he would be home in the constituency and remorselessly turning up at events, no matter how tough and tiring a week he had had. There was one occasion in the middle of winter which was typical. It had been a crisis week. Roger Juggins was talking to Norma on the Thursday.

'God, John's had a week,' she said. 'He's had two hours' sleep a night.'

'Oh, dear,' said Roger, 'we're due to go to a little constituency do tomorrow night.'

'Well, he'll insist on going,' said Norma.

That night and the following day it snowed heavily. Early that evening he went to the Finings to see what the score was. John was home, and had his head down.

'Well, you tell him I'll pop along and give his excuses and explain,' said Roger.

Norma was hesitant. 'I don't know about that,' she said, where-upon a head appeared round the corner.

'Give me ten minutes, Roger,' said John. 'I'm coming.'

Once they were in the car, slipping and sliding all over the road, he explained.

'Look at it this way. People are going to turn up tonight. There may be only six or eight but they will have come through the snow and they expect to find me. The least I can do is to turn up.'

With that he fell fast asleep for the rest of the journey.

The centrepiece of the tenth anniversary dinner was a very large cake, which one of the constituents had made, in the shape of an open book with a ribbon marking the page. Written in icing was a list of all the jobs he had done up to and including Chief Secretary. Little did anyone guess – least of all John – the job that was coming next.

On Monday 24 July Mrs Thatcher reshuffled her Cabinet. The press were forecasting promotion for John Major, and made various suggestions such as Chairman of the Party, Northern Ireland Secretary, Transport Secretary. The sweepstake in the Treasury was Transport, but John himself felt ambivalent about moving. Indeed, he and Carys Evans had a bottle of Champagne in the office fridge which they were going to open if he didn't get a new job.

Reshuffles normally follow a pattern. Early in the morning senior ministers who are leaving go to see the Prime Minister, immediately followed by the ministers who are going to be taking over their jobs. So anyone hoping to be promoted to the Cabinet would expect to hear before lunchtime. The reshuffle started, people were going back and forth all morning, by lunchtime John had heard nothing, 2 o'clock nothing, 3 o'clock nothing. Norma was sitting by the phone in Huntingdon. Peter Brown, John's agent, was on holiday in Cornwall, and rang regularly throughout the day. Other friends rang too. Olive Baddley rang at 3 o'clock. Peter rang again just before 4 o'clock. Everyone was on tenterhooks. 'Nothing yet,' said Norma to every caller. 'And I don't know what's left. Maybe Transport.'

At 4 o'clock a call came through to John's private office from Charles Powell, Mrs Thatcher's Private Secretary, asking him to go and see the Prime Minister. It wasn't welcome news. As the day had progressed he had grown less keen on the idea of moving. He arrived at Number Ten to find Mrs Thatcher showing obvious signs of relief that the day was over. This was her final appointment, and she had saved it until last, she said, because the appointment was the cherry on the cake of the reshuffle. This was the move that would catch the eye. She had been planning it for some time, she said. She would like him to be Foreign Secretary.

John was flabbergasted. Of all the jobs in Government this was the very last he had ever expected. Whenever a reshuffle was looming and he and Norma would discuss the possibilities, Foreign Secretary became almost a joke job, so remote were the chances. He says,

> I was very apprehensive about becoming Foreign Secretary because I felt Douglas Hurd was the obvious choice. He was made for the job. I was not. His appointment would have been applauded. Mine was bound to be viewed suspiciously.
>
> I had thought I might be moved from the Treasury. I'd hoped to go to Northern Ireland, Social Security or Transport. I did not expect the Foreign Office, but then neither did anyone else. That said, I did know far more about foreign policy than I was credited with and I found most of the work thoroughly absorbing.

'Are you sure this is a good idea?' he said to Mrs Thatcher when she offered him the post.

'I am very sure it's a good idea,' she said. And with the benefit of hindsight, he now says it was indeed a very good idea – although it's quite possible Mrs Thatcher may have changed her mind given subsequent events. What he learned during the short period that he held the post was invaluable when he became Prime Minister; the Foreign Office was a huge gap in his knowledge of government, and it would have been disastrous, he says, if he hadn't had that experience.

The emotional ramifications of the appointment, however, were another matter. Before the day was out top-level protection descended on the Finings and normal life as the Major family had known it entirely disappeared. A security caravan became a permanent fixture in the driveway, the house was torn up and wired with alarms, an external lighting system was installed, and a stout perimeter fence went up round the property. John already had a ministerial car but he was assigned a personal bodyguard who accompanied him everywhere, and the children came under the spotlight for the first time in their lives. It was, John admits, disastrous from the point of view of the family; at a stroke their privacy was gone. The only benefit was that rabbits no longer had the run of the garden, and as John rather flippantly remarked, they would no longer have any problems parking.

Norma was thrown into the political arena in a way that she was neither prepared for nor wanted. She had always known that of all the jobs in the Government that he could have, this was the one she would hate. She had dreaded the possibility because she knew it would involve her, and while she had been happy enough to play the role of MP's wife in the constituency, her home, the diplomatic circuit was another matter. Of all the ministries, this was the most sociable, a round of high-powered official functions. Wives were expected to dress up in their finery and entertain, and to travel and work in partnership with their husband. The prospect filled Norma with horror.

It was no picnic for John either. For if it was a shock for John Major to find himself Foreign Secretary by supper time, it was an even greater shock to his predecessor, Sir Geoffrey Howe. He had thought he had been told he was going to stay on in the job. Instead he was sacked in a way which maximized his humiliation and left friends and colleagues both inside and outside the Foreign Office feeling very sad and angry about it. Some vented their wrath by attacking John's appointment. It was easy game. After all it was unprecedented. He had none of the diplomatic pedigree or Foreign Office experience that most Foreign Secretaries have when they come to the job; he had never even been in Defence. And in that most hidebound enclave of intellectual snobbery, people assumed that he was not the type to have travelled much either. One or two colleagues were disappointed not to have been given the job themselves, and snide comments made within quickly found their way out. There were suggestions that John Major had no passport, and didn't know where the Isle of Wight was. A typical cartoon at the time showed him learning the names of foreign cities. It was the first time the press had turned on him. He had hit the headlines during the big freeze in 1987, over severe weather payments to the poor, but that was political criticism. This was personal and offensive and it stung.

Mrs Thatcher had made him Foreign Secretary because she was in trouble and she needed someone whom she could trust, and who was untainted by the Foreign Office, to help get her out of it. Her two most senior colleagues had become rebellious over the question of Europe and she found herself increasingly isolated. Both Sir Geoffrey Howe and Nigel Lawson wanted greater involvement in the Community; Lawson had been urging her to join the ERM since 1985, which she had refused. And, although she had signed the Single European Act committing Britain to closer union, she was growing ever more sceptical.

The European Common Market was set up under the Treaty of Rome in 1957, with no structured plan for political or monetary union. The founding members, France, Germany, Italy and Benelux, committed themselves simply to 'ever closer union'. It was in 1972 at the Paris Summit, that specific goals were agreed, 'irrevocably to achieve economic and monetary union' by 1980. Britain joined just after that, in January 1973, along with Denmark and Ireland. Five years later, the European Monetary System was set up, and the Exchange Rate Mechanism was the means for stabilizing the various currencies. Nothing very much was done about it, however, until 1986 when, at a meeting of the European Council in Luxembourg, Margaret Thatcher among others agreed to the first substantial amendment to the Treaty of Rome, known as the Single European Act. Geoffrey Howe, as Foreign Secretary, introduced it into the House of Commons. This had three important provisions: a date for the completion of the Single Market, 1 January 1993, when capital and labour would be free to move across Community borders; a switch to majority voting on matters which previously had required unanimity, and which had been the cause of the hold up thus far; and a commitment to achieve Economic and Monetary Union.

The Single European Act caused no great fuss at the time, and indeed the Conservative manifesto the following year remained constant on Europe. However, by 1988 Mrs Thatcher had changed her mind. Some say it was because the nature of the Community had changed and was no longer the club we had originally joined. Others say she saw opposition to Europe as a populist cause which would revive her flagging fortune. Either way she began to backtrack, falling badly out of step with her Foreign Secretary and her Chancellor, and antagonizing her partners in Europe by her increasingly strident and confrontational manner at meetings. In the early days her table thumping had been remarkably effective in reducing Britain's financial commitment, but latterly it had become counter-productive. She was using the same confrontational style at home, and beginning to fall badly out of step with her Cabinet. They had had enough hectoring, and it was affecting her popularity in the country too.

She was particularly hostile to the plan put forward in the Delors Report in April 1989 for economic union, produced by Jacques Delors, President of the European Commission. She was against a single currency and against his proposed social charter governing workers' rights, and hostile to the ERM. In fact she was hostile to the man himself. He had boasted to the European Parliament that in ten years' time 80 per cent of all the key economic and social decisions would be taken in Brussels rather than in the member states. In September 1988 she met him square on in a famous speech in Bruges in which she said, 'We have not successfully rolled back the frontiers of the state in Britain only to see them reimposed at the Community level.' That was very much a turning point in her attitude to Europe.

Nigel Lawson was also against a single currency, but he did want to join the ERM, and with the Madrid Summit in June 1989 looming, he ganged up with Geoffrey Howe to force Mrs Thatcher's hand over a date for sterling's entry. It was a policy she was already committed to, in the Single European Act, and they wanted a firm deadline. They both threatened to resign if she continued to delay. Furious, but boxed in, she agreed at Madrid to join the ERM on the fulfilment of five conditions.

A month later she sacked Sir Geoffrey, and would no doubt have liked to sack Nigel Lawson too, but realized it would have had a destabilizing effect on the financial markets. But his days were numbered – and it was no accident that four months later he found his position untenable. Geoffrey Howe had been one of her loyalest supporters over the years, yet she had stamped on him time and time again, been rude to him in front of others, shouted at him and he never fought back. The chemistry between them was wrong, he irritated her, and she disliked his formidable wife, Elspeth – for whom the feeling was entirely mutual. When they had been neighbours in Downing Street, when Geoffrey was Chancellor and living at Number Eleven, nothing had irritated her more than the fact that 'that woman' as she venomously called Elspeth, should have such a large flat. 'Have you seen the flat at Number Eleven?' she would say to friends. 'It's huge. Why should that woman have a bigger home than me?'

She offered Geoffrey one of two jobs when she removed him from the Foreign Office: Home Secretary or Leader of the House. He chose the latter, plus the rather empty title of Deputy Prime Minister, saying afterwards that it was a mistake. He should have resigned. Douglas Hurd continued as Home Secretary, but knowing the job had already been offered to and turned down by Geoffrey Howe. All in all it was an unhappy series of appointments. Douglas Hurd was the obvious candidate for Foreign Secretary: he had been a career diplomat for most of his working life, he had also been an official at the Foreign Office, and worked in the Conservative Research Department. No one could have been better qualified, but Mrs Thatcher feared he would be too sympathetic to the Foreign Office and insufficiently sceptical about Europe. John Major fitted the bill. She thought he was a sound right-winger who would redress the balance of power between Number Ten and the Foreign Office.

Every time John was promoted he had fallen into the habit of telephoning Jo Johnson, one of his group of close friends in the constituency, who like Emily Blatch and Olive Baddley had known him since his adoption. She would invariably hold a small dinner party for him by way of congratulation. He telephoned after his first day, when he had been met at the Foreign Office by a bank of press photographers and reporters.

I went to the office at my usual time of 7.45 and I had a good deal of difficulty getting in. Everywhere I went along these long corridors there was the noise of a scramble and people pushing things and moving things. There were very few bodies, Jo, but the place filled up by about 10 o'clock.

It was more than his early starts that took the Foreign Office by surprise. He set about bringing it into the modern age. He spurned the grand room he had been designated. It wasn't actually the

Foreign Secretary's room – that was being redecorated – it was the former Home Secretary's office, and they apologized. It was very large and hung with important paintings. Instead he chose to work in a little ante room next to it, where he felt far more comfortable. Nobody seemed to realize, he says, that it wasn't the days of Palmerston any more. He was closer to his private secretaries, so he could call to them, instead of buzzing imperiously, and there was a big table that he could spread his papers out on, which is how he likes to work. He also likes to work in shirtsleeves, which raised a few eyebrows from the mandarins.

On a personal level he got on very well with the mandarins. He was everything an official likes: courteous, decisive, clear and knew what he wanted to do; but there is no doubt they had some misgivings about the political weight of their new Foreign Secretary. Under Sir Geoffrey Howe the Foreign Office had been very well matched in the power play with Number Ten. Some would say the Foreign Office had the upper hand. They were dismayed to find a successor who didn't know his way around the world, didn't have a grip on the issues, who wasn't established as a key Whitehall player in terms of their own area, and who would therefore, they feared, either be reluctant to counter views coming out of Number Ten, or be out-manoeuvred by the combined experience and force of argument put forward by Mrs Thatcher and Charles Powell. He was not a recognized public figure, neither in Britain nor on the world stage. An *Economist* survey revealed that only 2 per cent of the population of Great Britain had heard of John Major.

The cards were certainly stacked against him, but he quickly won the respect of the officials he worked with, most notably Stephen Wall, whom he inherited as Principal Private Secretary from Sir Geoffrey Howe. Stephen, he says, is one of the most efficient working machines he has ever come across, with a sharp, radical brain. John admits he must have seemed a very strange fish at the Foreign Office, but Stephen absolutely approved of what he wanted to do there, and they became good friends almost from the moment they met. What first impressed Stephen about John, 'apart from thinking what a decent guy', was how methodical he was. 'I would go in and say this is the situation, I think we should do so and so, and he would say, "Hold on a minute." And he would draw a line down a piece of paper, with the Pros on one side and the Cons on the other and write them down.'

One of the first things he had to deal with, within days of taking office, concerned a bid to sell Hawk trainer aircraft to Iraq. In the wake of the Iran–Iraq war there had been an embargo on the sale of arms to Iraq. There could be no trade in the instruments of war, but these were trainer aircraft so the issue was not entirely clear-cut and views within the Foreign Office were divided. Some thought the deal should go ahead on the grounds that they were only trainer aircraft and it was big business for the UK. Others argued that the Iraqis could attach bombs to them. The debate had been going on within the Foreign Office for some time. John came in, looked at it systematically and decided very quickly indeed that this was something the British could not do – there was no question about it. He then took his recommendations to the relevant Cabinet committee for overseas and defence matters and they were agreed.

At the same time he was confronted with a difficult hostage problem. Videotape was released from Lebanon which allegedly showed the hanging of an American hostage, Lieutenant-Colonel William Higgins. He was executed, they said, in reprisal for Israel's kidnapping of a leading Hizbollah sheikh, Abdul Obeid, and threatened further executions. There were reports that Terry Waite, the Archbishop of Canterbury's special envoy who was kidnapped in Beirut in January 1987, would be one of them. There was very little that could be done, but it was a tense time.

Further East there was the problem of fifty thousand Vietnamese boat people being held in hideous conditions in refugee camps in Hong Kong. And then there was the matter of Hong Kong itself, and the fate of its British passport holders at the expiry of the colony's lease from China in 1997. The massacre in Tiananmen Square of hundreds of pro-democracy students by the Chinese authorities had not inspired confidence.

Soon afterwards, with Parliament in recess, John went off on holiday loaded down with a monumental pile of paperwork, which amounted to Britain's known foreign policies on every country around the world. The Major family holidays have usually been marred by one disaster or another. They've had an apartment in Spain with no water or electricity; in 1976, the year of the heatwave, they cut short a holiday in Cornwall because they had such terrible weather – and three days later the heatwave started. And the one time they stayed in a hotel – in Romania – Norma had food poisoning, and when she opened the window on their first evening the entire thing fell out on to the bed. On this occasion they went to Spain to stay in a villa belonging to Tristan Garel-Jones' wife,

150 kilometres from Madrid. Set in five thousand acres of its own land, it was ideal from the security point of view and they have holidayed there ever since. Although there was no disaster on this occasion, it was hardly a time for togetherness or relaxing in the sun. They went with the Atkinses once again, Robert and Dulcie and their two children, Victoria and James, and while the wives and children enjoyed themselves, John sat on the terrace, with Robert beside him for much of the time, and absorbed everything the Foreign Office could provide. He spent eighteen hours a day for an entire month – two weeks in Spain and two weeks at home – reading not just what the problems were but how they arose, who took which particular view of it, how much was historical, how much to do with direct commercial interests and what the options on each were.

By the end of August he felt more confident. He also had a better understanding of what had been going wrong in the relationship with Number Ten, and applied the same technique as he had used as Chief Secretary. Stephen Wall remembers him saying after a few weeks, 'I can see why the Foreign Office has had such a bad time with the Prime Minister. She thinks you're all trying to hoodwink her.' The system had always been that, when a problem arose, Stephen would write to his opposite number at Number Ten, Charles Powell, telling him what the problem was and how the Foreign Secretary thought it should be handled. John went on,

> He would see that you were trying to conceal some of the difficulties from her, you were pushing her in a certain direction and she saw through it. What you've got to do is say, 'Here are the problems and here are the counter arguments, and this is why we come to the conclusion we do.' There's a better chance of her agreeing if she doesn't think you're hoodwinking her.

The tactic certainly improved the relationship and Stephen admits they did have a better strike record in John Major's brief time than they had had previously. But he was never her poodle. That had been evident from the start. Walking back along the corridor to his office after his first Cabinet meeting, John turned to Stephen and said, 'So I can take my dog collar off now; I can be unleashed.' If Mrs Thatcher thought she had chosen a right-wing ideologue for the appointment she had misjudged him.

Their first brush came in September during a trip to address the United Nations General Assembly in New York. There had been some debate about the stance he should adopt on Europe. Mrs Thatcher wanted him to take her strongly sceptical line and was not pleased when he didn't. His own views on Europe had changed. Having at one time been ambivalent about Britain joining the ERM, during his time in the Treasury he had come round to Nigel Lawson's view that it was the only way to counter inflation and create prosperity; and he was certain that Britain's future lay in Europe. He was very much in tune with Mrs Thatcher over federalism, however, but his time at the Foreign Office taught him that Mrs Thatcher's bullying tactics in Europe were doing Britain no good. He says,

> I've never had any doubt that our economic interests mean we must take a leading role in the Community. The belief that we would benefit by cutting ourself off is fatuous.
>
> I don't like the bureaucracies of Europe but I do like its opportunities. We British don't lose all the arguments in Europe often, we win. Mrs Thatcher won on our rebate and on the single market. We won on enlargement and much else at Maastricht and Edinburgh.
>
> We can shape the future of the Community but not if we stand at its fringe. Not if we gripe and complain about everything. Not if we're hostile in every respect. We need to be at the heart of the EC to protect *our* interests. When I said 'I wanted to be at the heart of Europe' people misunderstood it. They thought I wanted a Federal Europe. Quite wrong. I wanted to be in a position to prevent it.

He departed from the hallowed line over the Falklands and sovereignty during his stay in New York too, which provoked another angry response from Number Ten. It was to do with how we described our claim to sovereignty. Stephen Wall had a letter from Charles Powell saying that the Prime Minister thought what he had said was quite wrong, and the Foreign Secretary should not use this phrase again. John immediately dictated a letter to be sent by return of fax, saying that the Foreign Secretary had said what he said advisedly, he thought it was right and he was going to stick to it. Answer from Number Ten came there none.

The other memorable event was the Commonwealth Heads of Government meeting in Kuala Lumpur, where John was seen to have been stabbed in the back and publicly humiliated by Mrs Thatcher over the question of sanctions against South Africa. Prior to this, the Commonwealth had set up a group, chaired by the Malaysian Prime Minister, to monitor its recommendations on sanctions. It consisted of the Zimbabweans, Malaysians, Canadians, Australians and Indians, but the British had refused to take part in the group because they didn't believe that mandatory sanctions were the best way of dealing with apartheid. However, at the CHOGM in Kuala Lumpur the British were invited to take part in drafting a communiqué on the matter.

Negotiations to agree the wording of this communiqué lasted all day and most of the night. John Major found himself alone in pitched battle against the rest of the Commonwealth, and in particular Gareth Evans, the garrulous and supremely difficult Australian Foreign Minister.

The British were as unhappy about the situation in South Africa as everyone else, and were keen for pressure to be brought to bear on the country, which was the whole point of the communiqué. Their argument was that the sole effect of mandatory sanctions would be to penalize those people who stood to lose most, namely the black community. All the evidence pointed in that direction, including opinion polls taken among black workers in South Africa, which showed the majority of people in work were against sanctions.

John objected to point after point, and as the night wore on tempers became a little frayed. At about 3.30 in the morning, when John asked for yet another change, Gareth Evans exploded, hurling his pen to the floor. 'For Jesus Christ's sake,' he said, 'this isn't the fucking Koran.' The multi-coloured faces around the table, the Malaysians and Nigerians, all Muslims to a man, turned quite white.

Before dawn they had agreed to differ. A communiqué was drafted, and where the British had failed to agree, on four or five points, the text simply said 'With one member excepting'. There was no further explanation. Mrs Thatcher saw the agreement and approved it and everyone went to bed.

By the time the text of the communiqué was released Mrs Thatcher and John had parted company. She and her Press Secretary, Bernard Ingham, had gone to the retreat at Langkawi.

Meantime all the other participants, including the Commonwealth secretariat, were briefing the diplomatic corps with the majority view, which clearly didn't reflect the British position. The British team, under the circumstances, felt they should explain why they had not agreed the four or five points and drew up a statement. It was drawn up by John Major, Stephen Wall and Charles Powell, and approved by Margaret Thatcher. They were all agreed on what should be said and all agreed that it should be released. Their mistake was in letting Bernard Ingham release it from Langkawi. The press immediately took this as a sign of division. It was Mrs Thatcher undermining another Foreign Secretary. No amount of telling could convince them that there was, in fact, no blood on the carpet. When John arrived home two days later the story had made banner headlines in every newspaper, and the back-stabbing theory is still widely held. So little was the dispute between them, he says, that two days later she made him Chancellor.

The strain these three months put upon John and the Major household is incalculable. There have been suggestions that he and Norma came close to divorce. That is untrue, but there is no denying that their marriage did go through a very difficult period, 'but not to a degree,' Norma insists, 'that was insupportable or insurmountable'. The real problem was that there was never any time to talk, so all their differences, problems and worries couldn't be aired. Even when John was physically with Norma and the children, his mind was elsewhere; and the house had become home to a band of strangers. Norma found the whole business a nightmare:

I have no doubt I would have got used to it, I'm an acceptavist. If something's going to happen it may be a struggle to begin with but you get on and do it, you don't back off. It was difficult to judge how it would have gone, because, although he was doing the job for three months, that was recess, so clearly it wasn't a guide. But by the end I was getting used to it. But it was a tremendous upheaval. There you were suddenly plunged into this job you perceive to be huge, from absolutely nowhere, with no qualifications, no training, and you're expected to put a smile on your face and say 'Well, this is absolutely great.' It wasn't because you've got to go through that period of adjustment, which you can't do in private. There are very few jobs, it strikes me, in any other sphere, where you're one thing one day and another the next. There's no rehabilitation in politics. You're up to your neck in it, and have to conduct yourself in public. I find it impossible to do that. I think I am a bit immature. I have been rather slow to grow up, I accept that. Here I am middle-aged, and I don't feel I have learned some of the things I should have done. I'm prepared to, but it doesn't mean things are necessarily easier. You have to find your own way of doing it. I would have lived with it if John had been Foreign Secretary for a couple of years – it wouldn't have been a problem in the long run.

Everyone who knew the Majors were worried, however, especially Norma's mother, Dee Johnson, who was very protective of her only daughter. Dee had moved up to Huntingdon to be near the family some five years earlier. She lived in a flat in St Ives and had been invaluable in looking after the children when Norma had to be away from home. She had settled in well, Elizabeth and James adored her, and she had a regular bridge four with Jo Johnson – although there was a golden rule that John would never be discussed at the bridge table. None the less she couldn't help worrying about Norma. 'They have an awful life,' she used to say; 'an awful life. There's no time for each other, no privacy.' It was affecting the children too. They grumbled about never seeing their father, and having no family life any more. Norma seemed to spend her entire time on the road, dashing between London and Huntingdon, trying to be all things to all men, and she looked perpetually tired out.

Looking back over it all, Norma says,

I hate the world 'traumatic', it sounds as though you need counselling or something, but it was. Everything he's ever done has been a bed of nails. But becoming Foreign Secretary the way he did – that really was ghastly – then three months later another new job, then, blow me, thirteen months later you're plunged into another new crisis. And it's all very exciting and all the rest of it, but it was traumatic.

On top of everything else Norma was still managing the house – cooking, cleaning, and doing the laundry and the garden – on her own. Friends had been trying to persuade her for some time to get some help but she had resisted. 'Why pay someone to do something

I enjoy?' she had always said, but she finally gave in and agreed to someone helping two hours a week. It wasn't so much because of a wild passion for housework; for Norma it's a therapy, and at that time, when her whole life was in turmoil, it was quite a comfort to come home and do something quite ordinary like the ironing. She became moody and depressed, and lost weight. It was clear to everyone around her that she was deeply unhappy. But John was too busy or too preoccupied to help. He has always been genuinely sympathetic to constituents who come to his surgery in trouble, and is quick to put a comforting arm around any friend or colleague who needs it, and can find the time to listen if they want to talk, but his sympathy has always been in rather short supply at home. In fact home has been the one place where he has felt he could relax and let out all his frustration and anger, and during those three months it showed.

He also relaxed with his brother and sister, particularly Pat. They have had some serious shouting matches over the telephone.

He's not as quiet as people think. He was under the impression as a younger man that I was cleverer than him. As a result he would sometimes listen to what I had to say, particularly about people – he listened to my instincts about people. Now he's got his own. I used to think sometimes he was looking for his mother's approval. If I said, 'no, I don't agree' he would defend himself and we would end up having a shouting row. He's as tough as old boots. Majors don't give in. My father was blind and he still wouldn't give in.

The families seldom saw one another after John and Norma moved to Huntingdon, except at Christmas. John and Norma always spent Christmas Day at home – and for the first three years of John's premiership they spent it at Chequers – but at some time during the holiday period they would go down to Terry's house in Wallington for an exchange of presents. It was a small, neat terraced house on the outskirts of Croydon, which Pat says was their natural meeting place, mid-way between their three lifestyles. It is not a demonstrably close family any more, which Terry, in particular, regrets. He sets great store by the family and turns up at Downing Street every so often to see his brother. If John is busy he chats to his staff, and was well known at Number Eleven, and now at Number Ten; but Pat has kept her distance. In the past he used to visit her in

Thornton Heath occasionally and they would pop across the road for an Indian meal. Nowadays they talk on the telephone. During the difficulties of autumn 1992, when so much seemed to be going wrong, John turned to her more than ever for moral support. But his career has taken him on to another social plain. He's still a Major, but he is not the John she used to know. Pat is philosophical about it:

> That woodenness of John's is John cutting out his theatricality and it makes him grey. He's cutting it out because that was what made him different and might have held him back. Ten years ago he couldn't have been Prime Minister with his background. It would have been unthinkable. He has had to look and sound and become somebody, so that his background is not reflected in him now. You're not seeing someone he's not because that's who he is. He has become what he wanted to be.

Another person he had good healthy rows with was Barbara Wallis, his constituency secretary, who has seen him in all lights and has no illusions about the man:

> He can be very thoughtless and very demanding, but on the other hand he can be terribly kind. The thoughtlessness is the mind concentrating on something else. Not turning up on time for a meal, or suddenly ringing up to say he's not coming home on time when there are people coming in. There's always a good reason for it – someone has said 'you must do this', and his assessment of the situation demands that he should do that.

She and John had known each other from Lambeth days, when they were both councillors – they had gone out collecting rubbish together during the dustmen's strike – so they were both as political as each other, and often discussed political issues.

> We don't agree on a number of things, and we could always have a jolly good argument. There was never any nastiness about it. We could have a real fight at 4 o'clock and we'd both go off in a huff, but next morning we'd be back where we started. Sometimes he would come back and say, 'I've been

thinking about what you said, and while I still think you're wrong about x and z, I think you might just be right about y.' It was very gratifying, and indicative of how he works. He doesn't dismiss other people's arguments, even if he doesn't agree with them, but he will think about them, and if three or four people put the same point to him he will then start saying, 'Now, is there something in this? I should look at this.'

But he does have some human frailties. 'He's a great one if he's got a cold for thinking it's pneumonia,' she says. 'One day in Number Ten he wanted an inhaler, but in no way would he go and look for this inhaler, he just accused everyone of having taken it.' Finally the message came to Barbara. Could she help? Muttering quietly, she went up to look in the flat upstairs. She found the inhaler, took it down to the study where he was in a meeting with his political team, and put it down on the table in front of him.

'You're marvellous, where did you find it?' he asked.

'Where you left it,' said Barbara. 'In your pocket.' There was an audible gasp from everyone in the room, but Barbara has known John a long time.

'Thank you,' he said. Then, as she reached the door, 'Oh, Barbara?'

'Yes.'

'You're fired.'

'I wish I thought you meant it!' she said.

One of the perks of being Foreign Secretary was the use of Chevening, a large Regency-style country house in Kent, which had been left to the nation by the last Earl of Stanhope in the 1960s. The Howes had been very fond of the place and used it constantly. John and Norma never went there. Norma had wanted to visit, but the occasion never arose. Events moved too quickly and by October Chevening had a new tenant.

Nigel Lawson's relationship with Mrs Thatcher had been deteriorating for some time as their differences over the ERM had become more entrenched, but it came to a head during John's period as Foreign Secretary. It was not so much the differences in themselves, which, as Nigel Lawson says, he had been living with for most of his six years as Chancellor. 'What made my job impossible was Number Ten constantly giving the impression that it was indifferent to the depreciation of sterling. I cannot recall any precedent for a Chancellor being systematically undermined in this way.' The real cause of the problem was Alan Walters, who had returned for a second spell as Mrs Thatcher's personal economic adviser in May. He had a high profile and it was no secret that he was firmly against most of the Government's economic policy, including Britain's entry to the ERM – and it was obvious to all that she preferred his advice to that of her Chancellor. The Shadow Chancellor, John Smith, took every opportunity of exploiting the situation in the House, and Lawson's position became increasingly difficult. The final straw came the day after John and Margaret left for Kuala Lumpur, when extracts from an article written by Alan Walters for an American journal appeared in the *Financial Times*. He reiterated his familiar view that the ERM was 'half-baked' and that the case for sterling joining the ERM had never 'attained even a minimum level of plausibility', adding that 'my advice has been for Britain to retain its system of flexible exchange rates and stay out . . . So far, Mrs Thatcher has concurred.'

The morning after her return to London he went to see Mrs Thatcher and told her bluntly that he couldn't carry on as Chancellor if Alan Walters continued to be her adviser. His authority was being almost daily undermined, and it was not only giving aid and comfort to the Opposition, but doing great damage to the economy. 'I had gone to Margaret not to tell her I wished to resign, but to ask her to wave goodbye to Walters,' he says in his book, 'making clear to her, however, what the consequences would be were she not to do so. She had made it clear to me she would not do so.' She begged him to reconsider, but was not prepared to sacrifice Walters. So Nigel Lawson went away and wrote a letter of resignation which he delivered to her at shortly after 2 o'clock that afternoon. She put the letter unopened into her handbag, and asked him once more to think again, but it was obvious the die was cast. She left to prepare for Prime Minister's Question Time and arranged to meet him again afterwards. He said he would make the letter public on the 6 o'clock news.

It was Thursday 26 October. That afternoon Mrs Thatcher made a statement in the Commons about the Commonwealth Conference. When she had finished she asked John Major to go to her room in the House, where she told him about the events of the morning and Nigel Lawson's resignation and said she wanted him to be her new Chancellor. John said, 'Let me go and talk to him. I know him very well. Can I persuade him?' She said, 'It's too late, you won't be able to persuade him.' John told her to try again, she should do everything she could to keep Nigel, and went back to the Foreign Office to wait for news.

Stephen Wall met him as he arrived and said how well the statement in the House had gone. 'Never mind that,' said John. 'You may have a new Foreign Secretary by 6 o'clock this evening.'

An hour-and-a-half later Mrs Thatcher called him over to Downing Street and the 6 o'clock news carried the announcement that John Major was the new Chancellor of the Exchequer.

10

CHANCELLOR

CHANCELLOR was the job John Major had always wanted. From the moment he first came into the House it had been his ambition, as he had declared at the first meeting of the Guy Fawkes Club. What took the edge off his pleasure when it fell into his lap so suddenly that Thursday afternoon almost ten years later, was the way in which it had come about. He felt bad about inheriting Nigel's job under such circumstances and rang him almost immediately to say so. John also knew that, because he had been at the Foreign Office for three months only, and because of all the adverse publicity when he had arrived, his time there was likely to be misunderstood.

It has, he says, been much misunderstood. He was perfectly happy there and he was really beginning to get to grips with the job and enjoy it when the move came. The first three months of every new job have been the hardest, and none more so than at the Foreign Office, but he did feel things actually went rather well and he was succeeding in making it a much less stuffy place – the mandarins were in retreat.

Among other things, he was in the process of changing the reporting structure, which he thought ludicrous. Under the existing system everything came to the Foreign Secretary for a decision, leaving the junior ministers with no discretion at all. He had two very able junior ministers, William Waldegrave and Francis Maude, both Ministers of State, and left a number of issues to them. The relationship between John Major and William Waldegrave was never likely to have been easy under the circumstances, given that they came into the House at the same time, and William was the one tipped to go far. But he says he had realized some time ago that the Prime Ministership wasn't a realistic ambition, and speaks generously about John:

> It was a hell of a learning curve to be thrown into that job without any background; an incredible test for him, and he did it effectively by selecting rigorously what he was going to do. Various things he left entirely to me, quite rightly. By the end he was well in control of it, but I don't think even he would say it was anything other than one hell of a task. I am sure if he had gone on he would have become extremely effective, a dominant Foreign Secretary.

Nevertheless there were audible sighs of relief all round when John was removed and Douglas Hurd put into the Foreign Office in his place. John had gone down very well, everyone liked him, and their relief at seeing him go was not remotely personal, it was political. The mandarins felt that John's had been an ideological appointment, an attempt to shift the Foreign Office to the right, and that in appointing an inexperienced minister to the post Mrs Thatcher had effectively disabled the Foreign Office in its power play with Number Ten. They knew that in Douglas Hurd they would have someone who could play their game very effectively, who would be a street-fighter in the Whitehall system, who knew the ways and byways of the Foreign Office, and who they thought was less likely to be kicked around by the Prime Minister.

John hadn't been kicked around by the Prime Minister, he had stood up to her and fought his corner, but inevitably the brevity of his time at the Foreign Office, followed by a second move into a position where she had fallen out with the previous occupant, confirmed commentators in their belief that he was Mrs Thatcher's poodle. As Alan Watkins writes in *A Conservative Coup*, John Major 'was in danger of becoming the utility half-back of the government team'. It is unlikely Mrs Thatcher thought he was her poodle, given the tempestuous nature of their relationship, but it is quite probable she still thought he was more right-wing than he was.

What she had failed to see was that John was seriously worried about the divisions that the Thatcher years had wrought in society, and although he was still a loyal supporter, he was beginning to fall profoundly out of step. He felt that the country was becoming sharply divided into the 'haves' and the 'have-nots'. There were divisions between North and South, and feelings of alienation in Scotland and in Wales, and he was certain that these divisions were immensely dangerous. The Government, he felt, had grown too big for its boots, and what better position to be in to do something about it than the Treasury?

The new appointment elicited some audible sighs of relief at home too. The Chancellor is not considered to pose so much of a security risk as the Foreign Secretary and instantaneously all the round-the-clock rota of armed guards that had descended on the Finings ninety-three days before, hitched up their caravan and left the shattered household in peace. By this time, having resisted at first, Norma had become quite fond of the policemen. The children had helped ease the situation by befriending the men and swapping jokes. None the less it was a relief for everyone to see them go and know that they could wander into the garden or sit in the sun and come and go into their own house without constantly being watched. John was still tremendously busy, but there were not so many foreign trips, not so many functions to attend, and Norma was not required to parade so regularly. The family could once again enjoy the pretence of a weekend together, even if John did arrive home with four or five red boxes and a diary full of constituency engagements. Life generally returned to a much more even keel.

The Treasury was the place he had felt most at home before, and it was a welcome return. Officials, while brilliant, tend to be self-made in the Treasury, and less prone to tossing Greek or Latin quotations into the conversation than their counterparts in the Foreign Office. But any ease in his surroundings was immediately offset by the difficulty of the job that awaited him. The boom years of the late 1980s, and falling unemployment, which had made his task as Chief Secretary comparatively trouble-free, had given way to galloping inflation, massive wage demands, rising unemployment and a country on the brink of recession. His inheritance could hardly have been worse, and it was not helped by the dramatic events that surrounded it. When the news of Nigel Lawson's resignation broke, sterling plunged on the financial markets. And while Nigel Lawson set about finding himself somewhere to live, being now homeless as well as jobless, John Major was left to pick up the pieces, in the knowledge that an election would not be too far off. Mrs Thatcher had surprised her Cabinet after the departure of Sir Geoffrey Howe by saying that she now had the Cabinet with which she planned to fight the next election. Little did anyone guess that of all the people around that table, with the exception of Nigel Lawson, she was the one who would not be fighting any more elections.

John's entire experience within the Treasury, as Treasury Whip and Chief Secretary, had been under the Chancellorship of Nigel Lawson, and his economic thinking was very much in tune with that of his predecessor. He believed strongly in the evils of inflation, and he had come to believe that the ERM was the means by which inflation could be countered. What characterized his reign as Chancellor was a determination to get inflation down, which he shared with Mrs Thatcher, and an equal determination to take Britain into the ERM, which he finally achieved in October 1990, despite Mrs Thatcher. At the beginning of October 1989, three weeks before John took over, Nigel Lawson had been forced to put interest rates up to 15 per cent, following a one point increase in German interest rates, and when John arrived at the Treasury there was talk of putting them up still further. John refused to put them up, but equally resisted bringing them down, on the grounds that any premature reduction would be very badly received on the foreign exchange markets and might jeopardize the struggle to bring down inflation.

Everyone at the Treasury liked their new boss. It was a joy to them to have someone who read ten pages of briefing notes if they were presented to him, instead of asking for the salient points. He was relaxed in the office, neither pompous nor arrogant, and once again adopted the habit of wandering out to talk to people in the outer office. He brought some humour and fun into the place, and at the end of a hard day he would take people off for a meal, as he had done in previous years. He enjoyed having the freedom to travel about London anonymously once more, to go and eat in the curry house in Kennington where he used to go as Chief Secretary.

He inherited several officials from Nigel Lawson, including Sir Peter Middleton, as Head of the Treasury, Sir Terence Burns, who was Chief Economic Adviser, and John Gieve, who was Principal Private Secretary. He also met up again with Andrew Tyrie, who had been a special adviser to Lawson when John was Chief Secretary. He stayed in the job until the following September, and subsequently came back to help with John's leadership campaign in November. Andrew was a frequent curry companion. Another special adviser was Judith Chaplin, whom he took to

Number Ten, and who subsequently stood for Parliament in the 1992 elections. She was MP for Newbury but to everyone's shock died suddenly a year later after an operation. John has become very close to the people he has worked with in every job, and this was no exception. Gus O'Donnell, Lawson's Press Secretary also became a close friend, and has been a key figure in John's team ever since. He had been a senior economist whom Lawson had wanted as Principal Private Secretary in 1988, but Gus and his wife were planning to have a baby, and he didn't want to work such long hours. He said he would like to be Press Secretary instead. So Lawson did a switch and made John Gieve, who had been Press Secretary, his PPS, and gave Gus the job he wanted. The only new member to the team was Tony Favell, who John appointed as his Parliamentary Private Secretary, but who didn't stay the course. He resigned over Europe shortly after John had secured Mrs Thatcher's agreement to join the ERM.

Her agreement involved a considerable amount of horse-trading, and a great many high-voltage rows. But pragmatism and political skill have been the hallmarks of John Major's success in every job he has held. As Judith Chaplin said before she died,

John was no ideologue. Nigel Lawson knew what he wanted to achieve, and how he was going to get it was bound up with his philosophy of life. John Major knew what he wanted as well but he approached it in a quite different way. He would let the discussion range widely and take everyone's view. He would then say, 'This is a difficult decision, it's not at all easy to decide.' He would then sum up as he had intended to in the first place, but there were no bruises.

Comparing the two men, Andrew Tyrie implies that Lawson wasn't a complete politician.

Perhaps occasionally he erred in thinking that to be right was enough. He was right about a hell of a lot of things – more than almost anybody. There are people who say he got the economy wrong and to some extent he did, and he acknowledges mistakes. None the less, his hit rate for getting things right, including highly political judgements like why the Poll Tax could scupper the Government, for rigorous analysis, getting to the heart of a problem was outstanding.

John Major is a more complete politician in that he has enormous skills in handling people, which could be mistaken for manipulation, but is not. On the whole it is the stuff of politics which is all about people.

John has plenty of critics of his period as Chancellor, particularly to the right of the Party. They say that it is impossible for a Chancellor – or indeed a Chief Secretary – to be successful and be liked, because the nature of the job militates against it. And they argue that his refusal to put interest rates down as Chancellor prolonged the recession. They would argue that many of the problems of public expenditure control suffered in the last two or three years date back to John's time as Chief Secretary. The economy was booming and he didn't take the opportunity of reining in public expenditure, but opted for the easier route of amicable settlements which let things slip.

They also point to his decision to take Britain into the ERM as a pragmatic decision. Sir Geoffrey Howe and Nigel Lawson had seen the ERM as a means of creating a framework of monetary discipline which would be a reference point for future economic policy. John, they argue, saw that there was a feeling in the financial markets that the current level of the pound was unsustainable unless it was going to lead to entry into the ERM: that if we weren't going in, the pound would fall. So Britain's entry was dependent on the politics of the moment, and what John thought he could get past Mrs Thatcher.

She had resisted for five years during Nigel Lawson's term, and finally agreed in time for the start of the Party Conference in October, just seven weeks before she was ousted from office. The trade-off was a one percentage point cut in interest rates. To quote Alan Watkins once again, 'Mrs Thatcher had by now been converted, much as an infidel might have embraced Christianity under a threat of painful death.' Sterling entered the ERM at a central parity of DM 2.95. Economists have said that was too high. Mrs Thatcher has subsequently agreed with this, although it is said at the time she wanted the pound to go in at a higher rate because she liked the notion of a strong pound.

John was himself a convert to Europe and the ERM. It would have been hard to have been otherwise among the resolutely pro-ERM mandarins he inherited from Nigel Lawson at the Treasury. Douglas Hurd was also an enthusiast, and his own time at the

Foreign Office had removed any lingering doubts about the importance of Europe. But in 1990 it was the circumstances that dictated the need.

Mrs Thatcher had said after the Madrid Summit that one of the conditions that needed to be met before joining the ERM was a significant reduction in inflation. When Britain joined in October 1990 inflation was high and rising, and it was specifically because it was high and rising that membership seemed appropriate. A strong and fixed exchange rate would put a downward pressure on prices, slow the economy down and squeeze inflation out of the system, thus allowing interest rates to come down. By October the recession was seriously beginning to bite, and businesses and mortgage holders, struggling to keep their heads above water, were clamouring for lower borrowing costs. The other advantage of the ERM, from the economists' point of view, was that it prevented the politicians from reducing interest rates too quickly to gain easy popularity as they approached an election.

John is very sorry that he didn't stay in the job longer but he is proud of having taken sterling into the ERM, and thinks that it did its job admirably. It delivered lower inflation and it slowed the economy down. It subsequently became a straight-jacket and inhibited recovery, but he is in no doubt that at the time it was the right decision to have taken:

> The case for or against the ERM is nearly always put in black and white. In truth, it was never as clear as that.
>
> On balance, I prefer stable exchange rates. More important, so does industry. I felt the ERM would provide these, and remaining outside was causing constant market difficulties. These daily turbulences are the hourly concern of the Chancellor of the Exchequer. Every recent Chancellor – Barber, Healey, Callaghan, Howe, Lawson, myself and Lamont – all favoured entry. They did so because of their experience at the Exchequer.
>
> So I wanted to go in. It was nothing to do with the political debate. It was all about the economic advantage.
>
> Looking back, we couldn't have gone in at a much different rate. It wouldn't have been negotiable and, in any event, we thought the rate was right. And so did the Confederation of British Industry and most others. It's quite untrue that the Bundesbank suggested a lower rate.

John Major is also proud of some of the reforms he introduced in his one and only Budget, including the abolition of the Composite Rate of Tax, and the introduction of TESSAs – Tax Exempt Special Savings Accounts. Nigel Lawson had been the architect of the Composite Rate of Tax: it had created a level playing field between the banks and the building societies, whereby savers in both would be taxed at source, which had previously only applied to building societies. By abolishing it, John kept the level playing field, but taxed the interest paid on deposits instead of at source, helping savers who didn't pay income tax.

He also helped small business by increasing the VAT threshold, and introducing tax relief on bad debts. He put £100 million into football over five years to improve ground safety in the wake of the Hillsborough disaster, where ninety-four supporters were crushed to death in the FA Cup semi-final. And for poorer people he raised the level of income support, and Poll Tax benefit, prior to the introduction of the tax in April. But since people had been paying Poll Tax in Scotland for the past year, with no such assistance, there was some angry protest north of the border. John presented his Budget on 20 March – it was the first Budget ever to be televised and he was extremely tense about how it would look. He knew it would be very high profile, and knew it was a difficult year for a Budget, but he also knew he had some original ideas. The question was, given the cameras, would the Opposition misbehave, would there be demonstrations? And while he pondered the prospect, he walked around the garden at Number Eleven with Gus for an hour before going across to the House to deliver his speech.

The day had begun with the usual Budget-day photocall. John and Norma have never had a dog, a traditional prop for Chancellors in the past, and despite suggestions that they might pose with the family guinea pig instead, John decided to present some British Empire medals, which he has since abolished in his overhaul of the honours system. It was this that brought the unfairness of it all home to him: working-class people, who had been doing unglamorous jobs, in the normal course of events were given their medals by a Lord Lieutenant or someone similar with no great ceremony and no publicity. On this occasion, at least, three ladies found themselves on television with the Chancellor of the Exchequer on Budget day and were thrilled to bits.

Then there was the traditional picture of the Chancellor and his wife standing outside the door to Number Eleven, holding the famous battered red box. Looking back, Norma can laugh about it, but at the time she found it a terrible ordeal. There was no rehearsal but every move they made once the door was opened had been choreographed to the last step, and Norma and John had their orders. As the door opened, they were to walk to the edge of the step then stop side by side, the door would be closed behind them, and the bank of waiting cameras would begin to roll. Norma remembers stepping out and realizing there was no step outside Number Eleven, just pavement – 'crazy the things you remember,' she says, but the real trial was standing still for two minutes, which seemed an eternity, trying to compose her face. She hated it.

That afternoon Norma sat in the Strangers' Gallery with Elizabeth and James and watched John present his Budget. It was only the second time she had heard him speak in the House of Commons; the first had been when he was Chief Secretary, and it was an equally rare event for the children too. It has never been a noticeably political household, and James is the only one who has inherited any interest. Even when he was quite a small boy he would recognize political voices on the radio, as they would listen to the *Today* programme in the car on the way to school; he took Politics for A level. Elizabeth has never shown the slightest interest; nothing has rubbed off on her over the years. She has adhered to her love of music and animals, and is now working as a veterinary nurse at the Animal Health Trust in Newbury. She and her father are very alike and have a fairly turbulent relationship at times. James is more like Norma, much more easy going; he is a good judge of John's moods and knows just how to treat his father to get the right response. Elizabeth, on the other hand, says Norma, 'Is like a bull in a china shop', but she's quite likely to have been given some provocation. 'John could practise his politics on her rather more than he does,' she says wryly.

Norma had brought the children down for the day. She didn't move into Number Eleven with John. She was once again driving back and forth from Huntingdon whenever she was needed. She still felt that her place was at home with her children. James was only fourteen when John became Chancellor, Elizabeth was seventeen, and it was a critical time in their education. Elizabeth had A levels coming up, James had GCSEs. Nevertheless, it gave rise to all sorts of stories about their marriage, and it allowed rumours to circulate about other women in John's life, but there was no significance in her decision to live at home rather than in Downing Street. Nothing had changed. It was the routine they had adopted from the very beginning and both John and Norma were happy it was the right one. He felt bad enough about being an absent father, but he would have felt infinitely worse if he had taken their mother away from the children too. The alternative, as colleagues' wives have never been slow to point out to Norma, would have been to send Elizabeth and James to boarding school. John and Norma didn't want their children to go to boarding school; they could not have afforded it either. And to have dragged them back and forth between two homes was another non-starter. Both Elizabeth and James have always had active social lives, they have a lot of friends; Elizabeth plays the clarinet in a local orchestra, James plays a tremendous amount of sport; it would have been unfair to disrupt them.

It would no doubt have been comforting for John at the end of a difficult day to have had Norma to relax with over a beer or a gin and tonic in the flat upstairs, but to have brought her to London simply to keep him company for the hour or so at the end of the day when he emerged from his boxes would have been supremely selfish. She would have seen precious little of him, and her life, her interests and her friends were in Huntingdon. John has always respected Norma's individuality, and he has always respected her desire to stay in the background. Indeed, his only regret about his life in politics is that she, and to a lesser extent the children, have been dragged into the limelight and had their privacy invaded. She had devoted her energies to making a solid, secure family base in Huntingdon. In the long run it was more of a comfort for him to know she was happily installed there, and not sitting in the flat at the top of Number Eleven Downing Street, wondering when he was coming up for dinner.

But John loves to be with people. There are moments when he likes to be alone, when he might amble round the garden rapt in concentration, but on the whole he seeks out company wherever he is and whatever he is doing. He even likes people around him when he is working. He never shuts himself away for a couple of hours, as other ministers do, so he can concentrate on a brief or paperwork. He likes to have people with him to chat things through. And in the evenings he would always prefer to find a companion to eat with or have a drink with than be on his own. Companions were usually in plentiful supply, most of them from the Private Office.

He also loves the company of women, and he is good at talking to women. He doesn't patronize them, as so many politicians do, particularly the wives of colleagues who are not necessarily political. He is thoroughly charming; he looks at them when he talks to them, listens to them, touches an arm or a shoulder – as he does with men – and if he is greeting someone who is a particular friend, be she seventeen or seventy, he is quite likely to throw his arms around her waist and sweep her up, with genuine affection. It is a familial trait. The Majors are very demonstrative, gregarious people with more than a hint of theatricality in their blood.

It is impossible to know who started tongues wagging in Whitehall, but the Palace of Westminster is a notorious incubator of gossip, and once the name of Clare Latimer was linked to John's there it stayed. Clare Latimer runs a catering company in Primrose Hill called Clare's Kitchen, which has catered for political parties from select Cabinet lunches to large cocktail parties, for many years. John had known her slightly since she was catering parties for the Whips, and when he arrived at Number Eleven, when he needed a caterer he automatically chose Clare. The daughter of actor Hugh Latimer, she was charming, bright, professional, rising forty, pretty and unmarried. To the mischievous eye, given John's single status during the week, his tactile manner, and the fairly common knowledge that his marriage had been under some strain while he was at the Foreign Office, the rumours sounded only too plausible. It was only finally scotched in 1993 when John issued a writ for libel against two magazines which had linked their names in print, *New Statesman and Society*, and a satirical magazine, *Scallywag*. But that was not before Clare's life had been made a misery, with newspaper men camped on her doorstep for months on end.

Anyone who knew John's schedule during that year at Number Eleven has always found the idea that he had either time or energy for a mistress quite laughable. Three or four people from his Private Office were with him day in, day out, people like Andrew Tyrie, Gus O'Donnell and John Gieve. They usually joined him for breakfast, which he would cook himself, and one or all of them would be by his side until quite late in the evening. He would quite often send out for a Fray Bentos pie and chips with lots of salt, which he would eat at his desk early on, and then later, if someone suggested going to 'that ghastly Indian place' to have dinner, he would jump at it.

John likes women but he also recognizes their potential. He has been surrounded by intelligent women in his life – his mother, his sister, his wife, and so many of his friends and colleagues – and when Angela Rumbold approached him as Chancellor, wanting tax relief on child care, in her capacity as Chairman of the Women's National Committee, he was more than ready to listen. The stumbling block to their plans was Mrs Thatcher, who, despite her sex, did very little for women during her time in office. Angela says John was sympathetic, and did give tax relief for workplace nurseries in his Budget, but wouldn't give any relief to working mothers who had to pay for independent nurseries, largely because he just couldn't afford the lost revenue. Mrs Thatcher had set her heart against it on ideological grounds. Her attitude was that, if a woman had a husband who was earning enough to be able to afford a nanny, then a woman could pursue her own career. If not, then she should stay at home and look after her children herself. She had no concept of the two-income family, no understanding that families might need two incomes to survive, nor of the plight of the single parent, and she was not interested in learning about them. She had brought up two children with the benefit of a rich husband, she had employed nannies and had been free to pursue her career. Her daughter, Carol, tried hard to convince her about the realities of modern life, but she was bolstered in her conviction by the head of her policy unit at Number Ten, Brian Griffiths. He was a pro Christian, pro family right-winger on such matters who did nothing to change her mind. John, on the other hand, had seen both sides of the coin, and knew from his own life experience that women who want or need to work while their children are young have a tough time, but he is equally certain that there can be no rigid view of what is absolutely right and wrong in the matter of child care.

Another colleague who appreciated John's support at much the same time, albeit in a very different way, was Kenneth Clarke, the embattled Health Secretary. On top of the difficulties arising from the introduction of the health reforms, he had become embroiled in a prolonged and bitter ambulance strike, which lasted six anguished months. It was, he says,

> my own personal lowest moment – the nearest I have got, so far, to political catastrophe.

The ambulance strike proved what is true in all walks of

life, but certainly in politics, that you don't half discover who your friends are when you're in trouble. Nameless colleagues, who I've never had any time for since, distanced themselves rapidly from this difficulty and were really not at all helpful. One character in particular used to cheerfully brief journalists that it was being handled so badly, he could have sorted it out. John was quite the reverse. He and Margaret Thatcher were the two most stalwart supporters I had at a time when I certainly needed support. If it had gone wrong I could certainly have been made a scapegoat for the Government, and I suppose I would have been turfed out. John, I have to say, just was all the way through quite unflappably, unshake-ably supportive, and when you're in politics, when you're in trouble, you never mind the opposition in front of you, it's the itchy feeling between your shoulder blades and the enemies behind you you've got to keep your eye on, and John was extremely, extremely stalwart, extremely useful, as, to be fair, was Margaret. In fact, it is one of the reasons I still feel as loyal to John as I do.

Nineteen ninety was not a happy year for Mrs Thatcher's Govern-ment. Not only the ambulance strike and the on-going battle over Europe, but the introduction of the dreaded Poll Tax, or Com-munity Charge, as it was officially called, was accompanied by riots and demonstrations, including a massive protest rally in London, which stopped just short of a bloodbath. The Conservatives had been in bad odour for much of 1989 too, and in June had suffered a salutary defeat in the European elections. Mrs Thatcher's style had become more and more dictatorial, the country seemed to be motivated by greed, with very little compassion, and Labour's star was in the ascendant. Labour had been ahead in the opinion polls during the autumn, and in February their lead was 15 per cent. By April it was over 20 per cent and Mrs Thatcher's personal popu-larity had plummeted.

The Poll Tax was an issue that had been simmering quietly for some time. Like many Tories, John had thought it was a disaster from the start, but he kept quiet about his reservations. As a member of the Government he had an obligation to support Govern-ment policies, and when Nicholas Ridley presented it to the House, as the Local Government Finance Bill, John's name was among those backing the Bill. It was brought in to replace the domestic rating system, which was assessed on the value of property, and which for years Tories had thought unfair. A poor widow living alone could have found herself paying the same amount as a family of four wage-earners living in an identical house next door. Ted Heath had promised to abolish the system as early as 1974, but it was not until 1987 that an alternative proposal found approval. Even then, approval was limited; but the Prime Minister was keen, plans for the new tax were set out in the 1987 election manifesto, and she proclaimed it as the 'flagship' of her third term of office. The manifesto promised:

> We will reform local government finance to strengthen local democracy and accountability. We will legislate in the first session of the new Parliament to abolish the unfair domestic rating system and replace rates with a fairer community charge. This will be a fixed-rate charge for local services paid by those over the age of eighteen, except the mentally ill and elderly people living in homes and hospitals. The less well-off and students will not have to pay the new charge – but everyone will be aware of the costs as well as the benefits of the local services ... Business ratepayers will pay a unified business rate at a standard rate pegged to inflation.

Many back benchers had seen the writing on the wall from the start. When Michael Mates proposed an amendment in April 1988 that the Poll Tax should be related to income, thirty-seven Conservatives supported him, with eleven abstentions. But it was only when local councils starting sending out their bills, which in many districts were three or four times higher than the Government had predicted, that the disaster really hit home. It was patently unfair. Voters in Wandsworth, for example, were paying a Poll Tax of £148 – the lowest in the country, whereas in Haringey each adult was being sent a bill of £573. It was also a nightmare from an administrative point of view and fiendishly difficult to collect. Many people simply didn't pay and had to be chased in lengthy and expensive proceedings through the courts. In its first year of operation £2 billion in Poll Tax went uncollected.

Nigel Lawson says that 'The Poll Tax was without doubt Margaret Thatcher's greatest political blunder throughout her eleven years as Prime Minister.' It certainly played a very significant part in her downfall. She had failed to persuade the country of its merits. Tim Bell had told her she needed £1,500,000 to mount a campaign, but the Party was in debt and she wouldn't let him spend the money. Whether it would have made any difference is debateable. As it was, she was seriously out of tune with the people, and colleagues were convinced that the issue of the Poll Tax alone would lose the Conservatives the next election, yet she stubbornly refused to listen. But there were other factors. Her public disagreement with Nigel Lawson was one, contradicting her Chancellor had not pleased the knights of the shires. When he resigned, an article in the *Economist* ended with the words, 'The day Nigel Lawson said "enough" may be the day that Mrs Thatcher's term of office started to draw to its close.' It was prophetic, but it was her treatment of Sir Geoffrey Howe that probably had the more devastating effect in the end. Quiet, mild, gentlemanly Sir Geoffrey, who had put up with humiliating treatment at her hands in Cabinet week after week, who had been ridiculed and abused and was the butt of endless jokes, finally took his revenge.

Mrs Thatcher had been to a European summit in Rome in October, where she had applied the brakes on economic and monetary union, as well as offending most of the assembled gathering. And she gave a strident performance in the House on her return.

Two days later Sir Geoffrey wrote her a letter of resignation. The mood she had struck, he said, 'most notably in Rome last weekend and in the House of Commons this Thursday – will make it more difficult for Britain to hold and retain a position of influence.' But it was his resignation speech in the House ten days after that which wreaked the damage. It was calm, humorous and completely and utterly devastating. He talked about his own 'commitment to government by persuasion', but said,

> I realize now that the task has become futile, trying to stretch the meaning of words beyond what was credible, and trying to pretend that there was a common policy when every step forward risked being subverted by some casual comment or impulsive answer.

And concluded,

> I have done what I believe to be right for my Party and my

country. The time has come for others to consider their own response to the tragic conflict of loyalties with which I myself have wrestled for perhaps too long.

The next day Michael Heseltine announced his intention to stand against Mrs Thatcher as Leader of the Conservative Party. Under the latest rules for election, amended in 1974, the very rules under which Mrs Thatcher had ousted Ted Heath, an election could be held annually, if requested, and could take place when Parliament reassembled in November. It had been requested just once since then, in 1989 when Sir Anthony Meyer challenged Mrs Thatcher, and won 33 votes to her 314. Not enough to win but quite enough to dent her standing, and more than enough to prove that a Conservative Prime Minister could be challenged constitutionally. He had not been a serious contender. He had been a 'stalking horse' to test the mood of the Party. Election was a two-ballot affair. In order to win outright in the first ballot, a candidate had to win more than half the votes of those entitled to vote, and his or her majority over the nearest rival had to be at least 15 per cent of the total number of Tory MPs. If the Leader failed to secure sufficient votes, the way was open in the second ballot for others to enter the contest. Some say one of the biggest mistakes Mrs Thatcher made in the whole sequence of events that led up to her fall was to have let Sir Anthony get so far. She should have sent him to the House of Lords and been rid of him, but she couldn't resist a fight. It had demonstrated the extent of hostility that was growing towards her within the Party and opened the door to speculation about a new challenge; and whenever there was speculation, Michael Heseltine was the name that immediately came to mind.

Michael Heseltine was a flamboyant figure within the Party; appropriately nicknamed 'Tarzan' by *Private Eye*, he was tall, charismatic and an inspiring speaker. And he had had a colourful career in Government, up to and including his dramatic resignation in 1986 when he walked out of a Cabinet meeting over the Westland affair – a dispute involving the rescue of a West Country helicopter firm. He was pro Europe, anti Poll Tax and deeply ambitious, a fact which had not been lost on Mrs Thatcher, who had come to loathe him; and he had been biding his time with patience. When Sir Geoffrey resigned, Michael Heseltine wrote an open letter to his Henley constituency chairman which was widely seen as a challenge to Mrs Thatcher.

'There is only one way to preside over a democratic political party,' he wrote, 'and that is to pay proper regard to the myriad of opinions and, indeed, prejudices that go to make up its support.'

It opened up the debate. The tabloids asked whether he had the courage to take her on, and the reaction from Downing Street via Bernard Ingham in the *Daily Mail* was that Heseltine should 'put up or shut up.' It was a red rag to a bull. Ideally he would have liked to put his name forward for election if and when Mrs Thatcher stepped down. That way he would almost certainly have had the majority support of the Party. He had been working hard during his years on the back benches to win support, and he knew that by challenging her mid-term he would lose a lot of that goodwill. He knew he could get no more than 156 votes this way, but the challenge had gone out to 'put up or shut up' and put up he did.

The first ballot took place on 20 November. Mrs Thatcher, proposed by Douglas Hurd and seconded by John Major, won 204 votes; Michael Heseltine, 152, and there were sixteen abstentions. She was four votes short of the majority she needed for an outright victory. The contest would go to a second ballot. All that remained uncertain was who the contestants would be.

11

LEADERSHIP CONTEST

WHEN the results of the first leadership ballot were announced, Mrs Thatcher was in Paris for a Conference on Security and Co-operation in Europe. 'Jasus,' the Canadian Prime Minister, Brian Mulroney, had remarked to Bernard Ingham earlier in the day, 'in Canada we erect a monument to a chap who loses three elections. In Britain you threaten to get rid of your Prime Minister when she wins three.'

The news came as a shock. Supporters say her campaign, run by Peter Morrison, her PPS, and George Younger, had been half-hearted and inefficient and none of the people around her had told her the truth. Tim Bell, knighted in 1990, says they were all

wish-fulfilment merchants. She was very badly advised before the end. Close friends found it more and more difficult to get in to see her, and it became more difficult to help. Our calls were monitored and we were attacked. Terrible things went on. Our calls were monitored and then a civil servant would go in to her and say, 'He's wrong. That isn't what happened.' The purpose of monitoring is so that if you say you'll do something they write it down in their book. It's not about saying what he said is wrong. They lied to her, they would all create this illusion. And Peter Morrison . . . Ken Baker and I went through his list of who was going to vote for Margaret and found forty-six Heseltineies there the first time we glanced through it. He just rang people up and said, 'Are you going to vote for Margaret?', and they said 'Yes', so he wrote them down. We knew we'd done our homework. He didn't have a clue.

As a result she hadn't realized the danger she was in. She had believed the 'wish-fulfilment merchants' and not the friends who had tried to warn her. Had she known the real situation, she would never have gone to Paris. It was not essential, and instead she could have been talking to Party members, walking about the House of Commons, and visibly making an effort. As it was, she was seen to assume their support when they would like to have been asked for it.

So the news was a shock. She was in the British Embassy when the call came from London; Peter Morrison had an open line to the Deputy Chief Whip, Alastair Goodlad. He wrote the results on a piece of paper and handed it to her, with the line, 'Not, I am afraid, as good as we had hoped.' She took it well, remained very calm, and, without pausing for thought, went straight out to the awaiting press to announce her intention to let her name go forward for the second ballot. Her statement was intended to rally the faithful, to sound steadfast and strong. Instead it sounded boastful and bossy and made many of those who had supported her out of loyalty in the first ballot conclude that her time was up.

John Major says it had been clear for some weeks that she was in serious trouble, but it was not clear to him that she would be defeated, even after the first ballot. On balance, he thought she could have won, but he agrees her campaign was badly handled and she didn't realize the danger she was in. If she had had better advice the results might have been quite different. She had made some fundamental errors of judgement in recent times, however. Her public disagreement with Nigel Lawson and flat contradictions to him did her no good at all. The knights of the shires didn't like it. Then her treatment of Sir Geoffrey Howe was very bad. Whether he or she was right or wrong on different issues was not the point. In Cabinet she went out of her way to be beastly to him and to humiliate him, time after time. Cabinet didn't like that. She had also been growing further and further away from the Party on Europe. The Conservative Party doesn't want a federal Europe, but neither does it want to be isolated on Europe. Europe has created a great schism in both major political parties, which will be there for some years to come. She totally misjudged it and allied herself to a minority part of the Party, which inevitably meant that her stance on Europe was driving a larger part of the Party against her. They also thought she was completely out of touch over the community charge, which they were certain would lose the Tories the election. John Major also believed it would.

None the less, when Peter Morrison had asked John to second her nomination he had no reservations about doing so – she had been Prime Minister for a long time, she had done a good job, she still had a towering international reputation, and he didn't believe it was a good idea to ditch a Prime Minister mid-term.

> I wanted her to stay. She had achieved a lot. She had a right to contest the next election. But, apart from that, I thought replacing her was wrong as we faced up to a war in the Gulf. I also thought it would lead to long-term bitterness.

Although some of John's colleagues couldn't wait to see Mrs Thatcher deposed, others agreed with him and campaigned enthusiastically for her in the lead up to the first ballot; but when the result was so poor, they felt they could, with a clear conscience, abandon ship and line themselves up behind someone else. The most obvious candidate to stand against Michael Heseltine was Douglas Hurd, but there was a growing support for John Major to stand too.

John was at home on the day of the ballot and was quite out of touch with the manoeuvrings of his colleagues. He was recovering from an operation to remove a wisdom tooth that had been performed on the previous Saturday. It was another example of his extraordinary luck to have been out of harm's way when the knives were out for Mrs Thatcher. People have suggested it was a convenient ploy. Far from it, he had been waiting six months for the operation – the family have no private medical insurance – and had been living on antibiotics and in a great deal of pain for much of the summer and autumn.

The day of the operation clashed with the Mencap Christmas Fair, so Norma was unable to drive John to hospital. He was having it done in Bishop's Stortford, but he was also due to open the Fair, so he did that mid-morning and Peter Brown then drove him to the hospital.

'What are you going to do if she loses?' he asked. 'Are you going to put your name forward?' He was afraid that it was too early, that people would think he needed to spend more time holding senior office before taking on the leadership. John replied:

> I've been asked. I won't oppose Mrs Thatcher, but I've been asked, and if there is the chance there I shall let my name go forward. It may not happen again.

Norma and Elizabeth visited him in hospital that evening, and the following morning Norma brought him home and he went straight to bed. He had had a general anaesthetic and slept for most of the day. He was due to be at home for a week. On Sunday afternoon Roger Juggins phoned to see how he was. Norma explained that he was still quite heavily drugged, then said,

'I've had "Mother" on the phone,' which was her name for Mrs Thatcher. 'She was just about to leave for Paris. She asked how he was. "No, don't disturb him," she said, "don't do that. He's my favourite son; give him my best wishes."'

By Tuesday night Mrs Thatcher's tone had changed. The results were scarcely through when the telephone rang and she was there, making sure that John would nominate her in the second round. He would no doubt have done it, he says, but he didn't take kindly to the automatic assumption. It might have been nice if she had asked for his support, if she had said that it had been a pretty bad result but she still thought she was the best person for the job. Douglas Hurd was in Paris with her and he had been approached in exactly the same way, and was also somewhat indignant.

That night, while Mrs Thatcher was inextricably caught in the ballet and dinner laid on by her hosts at the Palace of Versailles, back in the Palace of Westminster John's PPS, Graham Bright, found himself on the receiving end of a constant stream of people who came into his office asking whether John would stand if Mrs Thatcher went. Graham, who was John's friend from local council days in the late 1960s, had taken over from Tony Favell in September. John had telephoned him at some unearthly hour in the morning in America, where he was working for Lord Caithness, and said, 'I know you've done it for a long time, and you're probably fed up with being a PPS, but would you consider coming with me?'

'You?' said Graham. 'My goodness, how can I say no?'

His ambition at that first meeting of the Guy Fawkes Club had been to be PPS to the Prime Minister. He knew his friend would one day be in the running, but when he came to work for him as Chancellor, he had no idea that just six weeks later his dream would come true. But that Tuesday night there was no mistaking the number of people wanting John to stand. Graham was reporting back to John every hour, on the hour.

'You've got lots of support,' he said.

'Oh, no I haven't, not to that degree.' By 8 o'clock on Thursday morning, however, John realized he had been wrong, and once Mrs Thatcher had announced her decision to stand down, he agreed to let his name go forward.

Meanwhile, on that Tuesday evening there was another gathering at Tristan Garel-Jones' house in Catherine Place, and more conspiring there. Alan Clark describes the scene in his *Diaries* as 'Blue Chips wall to wall,' including five Cabinet ministers. 'Waldegrave was the only person to say what a personal tragedy it was for her, how she was still of a different dimension to all the others.' A number of names were thrown up as possible candidates to counter Heseltine, some even said they felt they could work with Heseltine, but the majority favoured Douglas Hurd as the most likely challenger. The other name to come out of the evening was John Major.

The notion didn't come entirely out of the blue. John says that eighteen months before he had been approached by two senior members of the Party, neither of whom are currently in the House, who told him that when Mrs Thatcher went he was the most likely replacement and he should prepare for that. He batted it aside, he says, and didn't take much notice.

Mrs Thatcher had returned to London on the Wednesday morning and met her supporters over lunch. Most of them believed it was futile for her to go on. If the second ballot was a straight fight between her and Heseltine, the result would split the Party down the middle, whoever won; but no one had the courage to tell her this, and so, as she left for the Commons to report on the Paris Summit, she told reporters, 'I fight on, I fight to win.'

That evening she saw her Cabinet ministers one by one, to sound them out. Kenneth Clarke was the first to see her, and told her bluntly that, although he had fought vigorously for her up to this point, the Party didn't want her to carry on. If she did, Heseltine would win, it would split the Party and shatter the Government's authority. She should leave the field, he said, and open it up – release Douglas and John.

Her mistake, he says, was getting the Cabinet together while they waited for their five-minute interviews. They discovered they were in agreement with one another, and therefore became much more united in their stance. By the end of the evening, Kenneth and Alastair Goodlad, the Deputy Chief Whip, had been to find Douglas Hurd to tell him he must stand, and Kenneth had telephoned John in Huntingdon. Even as he spoke, Jeffrey Archer's

19. At Massey Ferguson Tractors in 1992. Later, his support for manufacturing industry, though welcomed by many, was made controversial by the media.

20. The Edinburgh Council in December 1992, with EC President Jacques Delors. Yet again he won the arguments for Britain that no one thought he could. His officials were so impressed they cheered him.

21. Welcoming Chancellor Kohl to the Birmingham summit in October 1992. Still friends despite the traumas of Black Wednesday.

EUROPEAN
COUNCIL
BIRMINGHAM

22. Putting on a brave face at the Party Conference in Brighton in October 1992. The recession was hurting the Tory faithful, his economic policy had fallen apart, his personal rating had hit rock bottom and the Government was more unpopular than it had been in over ten years.

23. British success: The PM with Sir Ranulph Fiennes and Dr Michael Stroud after their successful crossing of Antarctica on foot.

24. On board the Queen's Flight on the way to Rome for a bilateral
meeting with Prime Minister Amato in the run up to the Edinburgh
Council. In two weeks he flew to all eleven countries in the Community
for similar talks. The plane is a travelling office, with satellite phone,
lap-top computers and fax, and a staff of ten so he is in constant
touch with government.

25. With Sarah Hogg and Alex Allan at Number 10. 'He has an uncanny way,' says Sarah, 'for seeing and thinking his way round difficulties. He's a man for whom ideas and instincts are very closely linked.'

26. Preparing for Prime Minister's Question Time with William Chapman (left), former Private Secretary for Parliamentary Affairs, and former Press Secretary, Gus O'Donnell, in the study at Number 10. He didn't use the study to begin with because he didn't like the soft chairs – he worked in the Cabinet room instead. They have now changed the furniture.

27. During a visit to the Mission Hi-Fi factory in Huntingdon. As well as the bouquet, he was given a stereo, which he has in the flat at Number 10, but, like all gifts, it is not his to keep – it will be passed on to his successor.

28. Seated at the Cabinet table with John Wakeham, Leader of the House of Lords. Gus O'Donnell behind. A natural chairman, he enjoys teasing people round to an agreement that looked unreachable.

29. Could he have done it without her? His marriage is pivotal. There wouldn't be much point in any of the other things, he says, without Norma.

driver was on his way with Mrs Thatcher's nomination papers for John to sign, although she had told everyone he had already signed. 'John sounded bloody ill and distinctly out of touch with events,' says Kenneth Clarke. 'He said he had promised Margaret and couldn't run himself.'

By late evening she had made up her mind to quit. John was aware of this. He had had a series of calls from Number Ten, from Peter Morrison, which had kept him in touch with her mood, and he had sent her a message of support. One Cabinet minister also got through to him, and said he thought she should go, but John had given him short shrift and refused to speak to anyone else. He didn't want to be any part of a Cabinet rebellion, and he is glad he took no part in it. It is not the way the Tory Party should behave.

At 11.15 Mrs Thatcher rang Tim Bell, who was having dinner with some friends in Hampstead. She said, 'I've decided to go. Can you come and see me?' and put the phone down. He had taken the call in the dining room, where the party was still seated at table, and as the tears began to roll down his cheeks, wondered how on earth he was going to escape without giving the game away. Everyone knew what was going on and, to make matters worse, there were two journalists at the table. He stood for some time listening to the dialling tone, with his back to the party, while he tried to compose himself. In the end he called his wife, Virginia, over, told her where he was going, and asked her to say his goodbyes after he had gone.

Before going to Downing Street, he went to collect Gordon Reece, the man credited for changing her image in the early days and still, like Tim, a much trusted adviser. Gordon happened to be having dinner with Nick Lloyd, editor of the *Daily Express*, at his home in Belsize Park. His wife, Eve Pollard, was editor of the *Sunday Express* and the house was stiff with journalists. Tim had 'blubbed hopelessly' in the car; when he arrived at the Lloyds' house his face was streaked with tears, and, although everyone immediately asked what had happened, he couldn't say a word, knowing that if he did, it would be banner headlines the next day.

The two of them drove to Downing Street and sat up with Margaret until 2 o'clock in the morning working on her resignation speech. Michael Portillo was there too, also Andrew Turnbull, her Principal Private Secretary, who in a matter-of-fact way sat telephoning the news to everyone who needed to know. 'Governor, I thought you ought to know for the markets that the Prime

Minister will be resigning at 7.30 tomorrow morning. If you would keep it to yourself until then.' Tim Bell was appalled. The machine was preparing to take control until such time as there was a replacement. 'It really was "The King is dead, long live the King."'

At 9 o'clock the next morning she broke down in tears as she told a Cabinet meeting of her decision. The Lord Chancellor had to finish reading her prepared text. But she then recovered herself sufficiently to get on with business, which included the decision to send more troops to the Gulf. In August Saddam Hussein of Iraq had provoked international outrage by invading Kuwait, and the forces of twenty-four nations were being assembled in Saudi Arabia in preparation, if necessary, for war. That afternoon at Prime Minister's Question Time in the House she gave a brave and memorable performance. She was asked whether she intended to continue her personal fight against a single currency and an independent central bank when she left office.

'No,' interjected Dennis Skinner, The Beast of Bolsover, 'she's going to be the governor.'

To which Mrs Thatcher replied, 'What a good idea! I hadn't thought of that.' Then after a spirited attack on the single currency being 'about a federal Europe by the back door,' said, 'So I'll consider the honourable gentleman's proposal. Now, where were we? I'm enjoying this! I'm enjoying this!'

At one point in the exchange Michael Carttiss shouted, 'You could wipe the floor with the lot of 'em.' A lot of people felt the same way. Defence Minister, Alan Clark, summed it up in his *Diaries*, 'What a way to go! Unbeaten in three elections, never rejected by the people. Brought down by nonentities!'

After eleven years as Prime Minister, fifteen years as Leader of the Conservative Party, she was gone, a phenomenon whose miracles had turned sour, the victim of her own arrogance. And she was bitter. She was bitter towards Michael Heseltine, whom she had never liked, but she had to admit he had attacked head on. It was the treachery of others that hurt more, like that of his proposer, Sir Neil Macfarlane, who was one of Denis Thatcher's golfing chums and closest friends. That hurt Margaret almost more than anything else. Towards John she held no grievance. He had been loyal to the end. When he put his name forward she let it be known that he was her preferred choice.

As soon as her resignation was official, so many supporters piled into Graham Bright's office that he could scarcely move. 'The good and the great, everybody, all saying "You must speak to him", "Tell him I said he must stand".' Others telephoned John at home. Norman Lamont said he would like to be campaign manager, Richard Ryder and David Mellor would handle the media and Francis Maude would be in charge of counting heads. Others wanted to help – Peter Lilley, John Gummer, Michael Howard, Gillian Shephard. Terence Higgins, a senior member of the back-bench 1922 Committee, had already been to visit John. The response was quite overwhelming; but they had to move quickly. Nominations had to be in by 11.30 and John was still on his sickbed in Huntingdon, quite taken aback by the warmth of the support and huge number of people who were keen to work for him.

He had asked Norma if she would mind if he stood, and, although she wasn't very enthusiastic, she said she didn't think he could avoid it. He came to the conclusion she was right. There was no way of avoiding it. He had looked for ways. He had said he was reluctant and told Graham he wanted to nominate Douglas Hurd, but Alastair Goodlad and Richard Ryder had said they needed a third candidate, and it should be him. He was told Douglas Hurd himself thought the same. John had also told Graham he wouldn't stand unless he was sure he would get eighty votes. Graham said he was certain to get more. There were no more objections he could put up, and with so many people wanting to support him, he felt he couldn't let them down. He would have looked wimpish, he says, if he had refused; but it was with no great enthusiasm that he agreed to let his name go forward. He told Judith Chaplin,

Too early, it's too early. I like the job I've got, it's the one I always wanted.

Having made the decision, however, he set off for London, to determine who would nominate and second him. His office at the Treasury was full of people and there were others waiting in a room outside. He liked the idea of a senior back bencher being proposer. He suggested Terence Higgins, who had been the first senior member of the Party to suggest he let his name go forward for the election, but the consensus was that it should be two Cabinet ministers, and in the end he settled on Michael Howard as proposer and John Gummer as seconder. The deed was done and, with time rapidly running out, Graham whisked the nomination over to Cranley Onslow, Chairman of the 1922 Committee, very nearly dropping it down the lift shaft en route, and handed it in with five minutes to spare. The third nomination came as a complete surprise to Cranley Onslow.

Battle was commenced, but John was feeling edgy about his decision. He was still in pain and unwell, and he was not at all certain he was going to get a credible amount of support.

By 7 o'clock that evening, however, Graham told him he had over one hundred pledges of support, and from that moment on John Major was convinced he was going to win. What is more, he thought he would win on the first ballot, which no one else believed. Throughout the five days of the campaign, he says he was consistently fed figures which understated his support. It was clear they had two sets of figures, and they were insistent that no one would win outright in the first ballot. But John knew. From walking around the House of Commons, absorbing the atmosphere, watching the reaction when he walked into a room, watching people's body language, seeing who was keen to talk, he knew. Norman Lamont insisted John spend the weekend ringing people – grandees of the Tory Party – to see what they proposed to do. Everyone thought he was getting over confident, and the phoney figures kept coming, but the game was up when John knew he had picked up an extra six votes at least after talking to some senior back benchers, and only four were added to his total. A fatal mistake, he says. It proved his case.

At the beginning of the contest Douglas Hurd was seen by most people, both in the media and in the Party, as the man who would stop Heseltine. It would be a straight contest between the two, with John Major as an also-ran, who was essentially putting down a marker for a future contest. In explaining the ballot system on the news that Thursday night, the BBC and ITV news broadcasts all showed, for illustrative purposes, what would happen to the votes of the candidate who came third: they would be distributed on a single transferable basis, i.e. shared between the other two. On all the news bulletins, it was John Major's face crossed out, and his votes distributed to the other two.

The general public didn't know John Major at all. When he became Foreign Secretary only 2 per cent of the population had heard of him, and although he had been Chancellor for thirteen months, he was still not widely recognized. Mrs Thatcher had been similarly unknown when she became Leader in 1976.

Douglas Hurd was not a glamorous figure, nor was he in any way inspirational, but he was very well liked, and a safe bet. He was also the man whom the public at large, if asked some time before, would have named as Mrs Thatcher's natural successor. Educated at Eton and Cambridge, he was the last real gentleman of the Party, a good, solid citizen, with middle of the road views on most issues, and although pro Europe, no fanatic. He seemed an obvious candidate to heal the Party, and at sixty he had a wealth of experience behind him, including more than five years in the Cabinet. The drawback was that an election would not be far off and many felt Douglas Hurd lacked the charisma to lead the Tories to victory. Michael Heseltine had plenty of charisma – some felt that was all – but he had put a few backs up over the years. There was also tremendous anger among many MPs and grass-root Tories alike at the way Mrs Thatcher had been treated, and Heseltine was seen as the man responsible. Many felt guilty for having played a part in her downfall, and they were happy to expiate it by voting for her chosen successor.

The fact that she made it so clear that she supported John, gave people the impression that John Major was the right-wing candidate of the bunch. He never set out to deceive anyone. In fact, David Mellor, in handling the media, was told to make it absolutely clear that John was liberal on social policies. The truth of the matter is that no one knew very much about John Major at all. He had made a lot of friends in Westminster during his eleven years there, but he had always played his cards very close to his chest, and even those who thought they knew him well were uncertain of his views. This is still true today, and it has led to the misguided belief that he has no views. He had taken Britain into the ERM, but no one really knew where he stood on Europe, or indeed anything else. They assumed. Mrs Thatcher assumed, even Norman Tebbit, who led the Praetorian Guard in supporting him at that time, assumed that John Major was going to carry on where she left off. As Kenneth Clarke says,

> One of his skills is that everybody thinks he agrees with them. It's not because he says one thing to one person and another to another. It's the way he expresses his views. It's one of his most successful qualities – everyone is confident and convinced they have John as their ally.

His campaign was good, but he was also helped enormously by 'the dog who didn't bark', Norman Tebbit. He was someone who really did share Mrs Thatcher's right-wing views, who was as Eurosceptic as they come, and would have taken a substantial section of the Party with him, making it very difficult for any of the other candidates to emerge as a clear opponent to Heseltine in the third ballot. The right wing had been pressing him to stand. They were even harassing him in the corridors of the House of Commons up to half an hour before nominations closed, but he didn't want to. He would only have stood if there had been no one else capable of stopping Heseltine. He believed John Major could.

This gave a tremendous boost to John's campaign, and once the momentum had built up it was difficult for anyone to stop it. But it wasn't just the Thatcher inheritance that brought John into the lead. A crucial part was also played by his decision to talk about class at the launch of his campaign. It was an inspired idea. The concept of a society of opportunity, a classless society, of which John Major, the boy from Brixton, was a shining example, caught the mood of the moment. It explained the rationale of his candidacy, and was in a curious way an antidote to some of the worst excesses of Thatcherism in the 1980s. It also demonstrated to the back benchers that he was a man who could have a lot of popular appeal – Honest John, John the Straight Man. The media loved it, and the spotlight immediately fell on the other two in terms of class. Heseltine was unashamedly and ostentatiously rich, money he had made himself in the best Thatcherite tradition, and was forever being filmed posing beside the entrance gates to his country house. Hurd was an old Etonian and found himself on the defensive about it, explaining that there would have been no question of his father, a tenant farmer, sending him to Eton had he not won a scholarship. His protestations were met with a certain amount of derision.

John Major didn't invent the idea of the classless society. The phrase had been doing the rounds in the Conservative Party for many years. On the Thursday night when Andrew Tyrie and John Major were sitting at Number Eleven discussing what John should say at the opening press conference on the Friday morning, Andrew suggested the theme of the classless society. John liked it and it proved very effective. Another idea included in the statement was the need to raise the morale of the teaching profession. When they had thrown around a few more ideas, the need to rethink the Poll

Tax, the need to heal the wounds over Europe and the fact that the next election would be fought on the economy, Andrew went away and wrote the statement, John made some alterations, and at 10 o'clock the next morning it became his credo.

The press conference was held in the largest room in the Treasury overlooking Parliament Street; it was packed, and showed every likelihood of being a disaster. There were so many stills-photographers with blinding flashbulbs at the front of the room that it was impossible to see the reporters, whom he wanted to address, sitting behind them. It was a complete shambles, 'But this shambles,' says Andrew Tyrie, 'which had threatened to destroy the conference, had the effect of creating a considerable buzz. Here was something tremendously exciting. A sense of energy was injected into that conference which really launched the campaign.' And they never looked back. 'I think by about Saturday afternoon he had already won, and I think he knew that, whatever the numbers – and everyone told him to keep working, to keep ringing people, to keep pressing – the truth was he probably already had it in the bag.'

Douglas Hurd never really recovered from the assault on his background, although it was a weak campaign from the start. He had a good team; among his supporters were Kenneth Clarke, William Waldegrave, Chris Patten, John Patten, Malcolm Rifkind and Virginia Bottomley, but he had no imaginative policy to unveil at his press conference and he struggled thereafter. John told his campaign strategist to lay off Douglas because he wanted to have him as his Foreign Secretary, and it was important he maintained his credibility, and had a reasonable number of votes.

What he didn't tell any of his own team, not Norman Lamont, not Francis Maude, no one, was that he and Douglas Hurd spoke daily during the campaign and compared notes, so John knew who had pledged themselves to both of them. He also knew who of his friends had pledged themselves to Douglas Hurd. One was Tristan Garel-Jones, whose wife's house in Spain the Majors stayed in, who was once so close that he offered to lend John money to help him out of the clutches of a bridging loan. He says he found himself in a very anguished position, because he knew John better than Douglas, but Douglas was his boss at the Foreign Office and he had committed himself to him long ago.

For all kinds of reasons in the end I supported Hurd and not

Major and I doubt if there was anyone in the Party for whom that would have been a more difficult decision. I don't regret it or apologize for it, but I found it really difficult. It was a black cloud hanging over me. In the middle of the campaign one rainy night, late, I was trudging off home in the rain from the House, it was eleven or midnight, and J. Major pulled up in his car. This was the middle of the election, in two days' time he may or may not be Prime Minister. He gets out of the car and says something like, 'I hear you're very upset.'

'Well this is not an easy decision for me,' I said. We'd spoken several times in the run up to it all, and he just said, 'You're not to worry about it for one minute. We spoke last week. I understand what you're doing better than you think, and if I was in your position I would probably vote for Douglas Hurd.' Then he got into his car and drove off.

That weekend was frantic, and while everyone was pushing John to keep working, Barbara Wallis and her husband, Derek, moved into Number Eleven in order to feed the hungry hordes. The campaigners were divided between Downing Street and a little house they had requisitioned in Gayfere Street on the other side of Parliament Square, known to its inmates for the five-day campaign as 'the bunker'. They had moved in all sorts of sophisticated equipment and had twelve telephone lines, which were constantly busy. It was a chaotic time, but enormous fun. There was plenty to gain, but they all knew they had nothing to lose. At 6 o'clock on Saturday, when the shops were closing, John had said there would be eight for dinner. Derek cooked a chicken fricassee. At 6.30 it went up to nine, at 7 o'clock, ten, then eleven. The shops were closed and there was nothing for it but to find whatever they could in the kitchen to make it stretch. What turned up was a giant tin of baked beans which they tipped into a silver salver and took into the dining room, whereupon David Mellor looked up and said, 'Baked beans, oh, boy, my favourite food.'

That night, as Derek was trying to get to sleep, Norman Lamont was bouncing angrily up and down on the end of his bed, on the telephone. It was the only extension that seemed to be working that night. The telephones took on a mind of their own after a certain time. Calls came into the most bizarre places and there was no means of transferring them for love or money. On the Tuesday night, when the results were announced, President

Bush telephoned to congratulate John. He was calling from Air Force One, and John had to take the call leaning against the wall in the kitchen, only to be cut off. It was, says John, a complete carnival.

On Monday night Norma had arrived from Huntingdon with her car full of food, including the most enormous lasagne. She had spent the whole day cooking because she figured that, win or lose, there would be an awful lot of clearing up to be done the following day and people would need to be fed.

On the afternoon of the ballot, John took himself off to bed. He was feeling pretty ropey, and he was still in some pain, and having worked flat-out all weekend he was exhausted. There was nothing more to be done – the results of the ballot would be announced at 6.00. He was still confident he would win that afternoon, but his team were not and John Gummer insisted on producing three statements in preparation for all eventualities – outright victory, a second ballot and total defeat. John slept soundly from 2.00 to 5.30, when he got up, wandered about the flat, had a bath, and took himself downstairs, arriving in the drawing room where all his friends and supporters were gathered at about two minutes to six. He needed 187 votes for an outright victory. He guessed he would have 193. The room was abuzz with nervous chatter. Suddenly there was a call for silence, as Cranley Onslow's face appeared on the television screen at one end of the room to announce the results. John had his arm around Norma as they listened. 'Michael Heseltine, 131.' His vote had gone down from 156; that was it, John knew the job was his. 'Douglas Hurd, 56. John Major, 185.' There was a great gasp on television from the back benchers who were hearing the results live in the 1922 Committee, and everyone in the room began jumping up and down. He was two votes short of an outright win, but he knew that it was over, and within five minutes Michael Heseltine was out in front of his Belgravia House, with his wife beside him, gracefully conceding defeat. A moment later Douglas Hurd did likewise. Mrs Thatcher came bursting through from the connecting door with Number Ten to be the first with her congratulations. She hugged Norma. 'It's everything I've dreamt of for such a long time,' she said. 'The future is assured.' She would go to the Palace in the morning to tender her resignation to the Queen.

Shortly afterwards John went out into Downing Street with Norma by his side to address the nation.

It's been a very clean election ... I'd like to offer my very grateful thanks to Douglas Hurd and to Michael Heseltine both for the way they conducted the election and also for the very gracious way they have conceded that they will not stand on the third ballot. It is a very exciting thing to become Leader of the Conservative Party and particularly exciting, I think, to follow one of the most remarkable leaders the Party has ever had.

In the background, a head was momentarily seen at the window as Mrs Thatcher watched the scene outside. It was a poignant moment; the end of an extraordinary era.

It was an evening of very mixed emotions. Away from the excitement and the hubbub, and on his own for a brief moment, John paced the kitchen floor at Number Eleven, saying over to himself, 'What have I done to my family? What have I done?'

There was no great feeling of exhilaration when he heard the results. No desire to punch the air and say 'At last, I've got it.' His thoughts at the precise moment he heard were about the Cabinet changes ahead – how to do them, where to put people. He didn't have time, he says, to contemplate what was happening. His mind was on what was going to happen; as it usually is:

I was under no illusions about what the future would hold. There isn't a single Prime Minister who has followed a long-serving, powerful Prime Minister who hasn't run into trouble with his party, and I knew that. I knew the Conservatives were fifteen, maybe seventeen, points behind in the opinion polls, I knew I had an election in not less than eighteen months, and I knew the expectation was that the Tories could lose that election.

He also knew two other things. One that the public really didn't know him at all, he'd been in the Cabinet for a little over three years. For two of those he had been Chief Secretary, whose job was to be anonymous, three months in the Foreign Office, which had, he says, been dreadfully perverted, a year as Chancellor, which had gone rather well, although he had been trapped by international circumstances. He knew just how bloody and difficult it would be.

Ideally he would have liked Douglas Hurd to have become Prime Minister. John Major wanted the job himself one day, certainly, but not at that time. It was too soon.

I was forty-seven. I had the job I had wanted all my life, I'd only had it for a year; I had plenty of time. From my perspective: suppose I'm Prime Minister for ten years, which is longer than anyone should be Prime Minister, my political career will be over at fifty-seven. I could have spent four or five years as Chancellor, then gone on to do this job, and gone for a longer political career.

It was also bad timing from the family point of view. Elizabeth and James both had exams ahead of them and he knew that life would become very difficult for them. The three months of security and attention when he had been Foreign Secretary had been a foretaste and he knew none of the family would enjoy it.

But at the end of the day he doesn't think he had any choice. If he had refused to stand and the Party had lost the election, would he have been blamed for not standing at a time when people were telling him he was more likely to win the election than anyone else? Would they have taken different economic decisions if he had been someone else's Chancellor? By and large, he says, politics are constrained by events. He doesn't think things would have been done very differently – even if Mrs Thatcher had remained Prime Minister.

12

PRIME MINISTER

THE morning after he became Prime Minister John Major rang Barbara Wallis, his constituency secretary.

'Good morning Prime Minister,' she said, and there was a slight pause.

'You've called me John for the last twenty-four years,' he said, 'it would do very nicely for the next twenty-four.'

The same day he put in his customary call to Josephine Johnson, his friend and Association worker in Huntingdon, whom he had rung after every promotion. She wasn't expecting a call this time, he would be far too busy. 'Hello, Jo,' he said.

'Prime Minister . . .'

'Stop that,' he said quickly, 'don't let's have any of that. I'm still John.'

It was that attitude which appealed so much to everyone as John Major settled in to Number Ten. That and his sense of humour, his ability even in the midst of a crisis to make some funny remark which immediately took the tension out of the moment and made everyone feel relaxed. His style as Prime Minister could not have been more different from Mrs Thatcher's. Where she had been strident and bossy, he was quietly spoken and considerate; where she had dominated Cabinet meetings and dared anyone to speak, he encouraged discussion and brought in everyone round the table. It was evident from the very beginning that this was the antidote everyone had been looking for. He had said during his campaign that he wanted 'a nation at ease with itself', and after the divisiveness of Mrs Thatcher, it had struck a chord.

Sir Charles Powell, her Private Secretary for seven years, says:

She was tensed up all the time, highly strung, very active. She would be up at 5 a.m. telephoning all hours of the day and night, meeting this person and that, get this done, that done, never stopping for a moment. John Major has quite a placid temperament. He functions much better with a nice regular life. He needs seven hours' sleep a night and it's far better to let him have it than create a myth that he's up half the night dealing with international crises, because if he were to do that he wouldn't be operating effectively during the day. She, for some reason I never understood – an extra gland or something – could cope with three hours a night for weeks at a time and it didn't affect her performance.

But the most significant difference between them was the way in which they handled their Cabinet. As Sir Charles says,

John Major was more disposed to listen to his Cabinet colleagues than Mrs Thatcher was. Mrs Thatcher was an instinctive leader and felt, as a woman, that, unless she got her voice in loudly first, it wouldn't be heard. Her idea of chairing a meeting – most people will sit down and say, 'Now this is what we're going to discuss, will the Foreign Secretary explain his point of view, then the Chancellor explain his point of view,' and so on, then you sum up at the end with some conclusions – Mrs Thatcher's idea of chairing a meeting was to sit down, announce what the conclusions were going to be and challenge anyone to fight her. John Major is quite different, he's a natural chairman. He likes to hear points of view and then he will draw his conclusions. That's why, on the whole, officials love him because he chairs an orderly meeting and you can write the minutes quite simply. I used to have to invent the minutes of Mrs Thatcher's meetings because otherwise government couldn't have got on.

Norman Tebbit believes that a great myth has been created about the fall of Margaret Thatcher. It was not so much about Europe, he maintains, it was about how she handled her Cabinet. If it had been because she was anti Europe, which is the general assumption, because of the disastrous European election results in 1989, the beneficiaries of the disaster would have been the most pro European party, the Liberal Alliance. They weren't. The Green Party did better. The dispute with Nigel Lawson over the ERM and the resignation of Sir Geoffrey Howe reinforced this view that Europe was Mrs Thatcher's mistake. He thinks the real reason she came unstuck was because she had lost control of her Cabinet. She had also lost control of the economy, but that was because she had lost control of her Cabinet.

John Major himself says that if he has one gift it is a capacity to produce an agreement out of a lot of colleagues who have sharply differing views, and an agreement they will all be able to live with. That is what he finds so exhilarating about politics. Mrs Thatcher, he says, regarded a majority of one as sufficient, and fine, you can run a Government like that for a long time, but you get a lot of disloyalty, a lot of carping in the background. He prefers to get agreement if he can, and enjoys teasing people round to an agreement that seemed quite out of reach at the beginning.

John Major likes to keep senior ministers in their posts long enough to allow them to get fully on top of the job, so that they will be not only responsible for managing their departments, and carrying out existing policy, but also be responsible for formulating future policy. Below senior level, he thinks it is a good idea to give people a much broader experience than they have had sometimes in the past. The tendency to label people right, left, interested in economics, interested in social affairs, sometimes goes too far, he thinks. Better to spray junior ministers around, give them as much experience of the different departments around Whitehall as possible.

He chose his Cabinet carefully, with all the cunning of a Whip, balancing all the different factions and interests within the Party. Of all the tasks that faced him when he became Prime Minister, harnessing these various talents must have been one of the most daunting. There were the constitutionalists, who were arguing for fundamental constitutional reform; another sizeable group who believed that Government could and should play a more active role in the restructuring of industry and in creating industrial policy; the pro-Europeans, who thought all that should happen in a much wider European grouping; anti-Europeans, who thought Britain's industrial condition should be sorted out on her own and independently of Europe; and a group of free-marketeers, who favoured no intervention of any sort. All of life was there, and it was John Major's lot to carry them all with him into the next general election – to ensure that each section of the Party was satisfied.

Mrs Thatcher never thought in those terms. She had simply

filled her Cabinet with as many of her own supporters as possible. As one of them says, 'Ideally she would have liked a Cabinet of clones.' But many of the most able people within the Party were not Thatcherites, and so it was never a strong Cabinet.

John Major has approached every Cabinet reshuffle with the same shrewdness. His general view is that annual reshuffles for the sake of pandering to the public's appetite for change are a mistake. If you don't give people time to become thoroughly acquainted with the job, to think through policy, and look at it long-term, then policy ends up being determined by events and civil service briefings. If a minister has been in position for a while, he knows the background to events, can recall what happened in the past, having lived through an event like this before. He knows what the snags are and can see where he wants to push policy. As he says, that needs time. It doesn't matter how clever you are, how brilliant you may be, how fast your lawyer's capacity to pick up a brief, nothing can compensate for the experience of knowing immediately something comes up that you've seen it before, you've done it before, you know what the background is, you know how it can be seen, you know what the special interests of a whole competing series of groups of people may be, and you know how to push policy forward. That needs time.

In that first Cabinet he had less room for manoeuvre than subsequently, when he made certain no serious malcontents were left unoccupied – although the reshuffle in May 1993, when Norman Lamont returned to the back benches, proved more difficult to manage. In that first Cabinet he brought Kenneth Baker into the Home Office, and replaced him as Chairman of the Conservative Party with Chris Patten, who had been viewed for many years as John's chief rival. Chris Patten was one of the original Blue Chips, marked out for stardom from the moment he arrived in the House in 1979. But where John had quarrelled with Mrs Thatcher, then basked and prospered in her good esteem, Chris had quarrelled and been cast into the wilderness, where he languished for five years. Their quarrel was over Margaret's decision to move the Conservative Research Department, where Chris had been Director of Research before becoming MP for Bath, from Old Queen Street to Central Office in Smith Square. He believed fervently that the CRD should be separate. Central Office was a political machine and the CRD was a great think tank which created philosophy on the dreams of the future. It shouldn't be tainted. Mrs Thatcher felt no such emotion. The Party was broke and couldn't afford to pay the rent on Old Queen Street any longer. It was a simple matter of prudent housekeeping. Matters came to a head when Chris wrote her a long letter on the subject, which he made public, in which he accused her of having no belief in anything, no ideals, and no interest beyond balancing the books.

Underlying the argument, however, was a fundamental difference in their political philosophy. Chris Patten was thoroughly 'wet' and against everything that Thatcherism stood for. He believed in social intervention and the Welfare State. Mrs Thatcher, of course, believed the very opposite. Her entire *raison d'être* was to get government out of the way as much as possible and leave people to get on with their own lives. Its only role, in her view, being to create some rules by which the free market could operate.

She was finally persuaded to bring him in from the cold by her husband, Denis, Tim Bell and others who couldn't bear to see his talents wasted any longer. They liked him, he was very clever, and was obviously quite capable of presenting their philosophy – it was he, after all, who had written the manifesto for the 1979 election. But, although she finally agreed and did bring him in as a junior minister first, then Secretary of State at the Environment, the damage was never entirely mended.

John Major had never really known Chris Patten. However, when he became Prime Minister – thus robbing Chris Patten of any immediate chance himself – and made him Party Chairman, they formed a friendship which was a tribute to them both. It wasn't just a political convenience; there was real generosity of feeling on both sides, a genuine friendship, which had a significant bearing on the general election when it finally came.

One person John Major had no option but to bring into the Cabinet was Michael Heseltine. Having brought about Mrs Thatcher's fall, he could hardly have been left out, but John gave none of his supporters Cabinet jobs. To Michael he gave the task of sorting out the Poll Tax, one of the issues Heseltine had concentrated on during his leadership challenge of Mrs Thatcher, acknowledging that if anyone could present a new tax to the nation, Heseltine could. He is nothing if not a superb showman. It was also the single issue which everyone knew would lose the Party the election unless something radical was done. John rewarded his own supporters – Norman Lamont, for example, became Chancellor, David Mellor, Chief Secretary, Ian Lang went to the Scottish

Office, and there were more appointments at junior ministerial levels, like Gillian Shephard, but he also brought in some of Douglas Hurd's supporters too, like Tim Yeo and Ann Widdecombe. The only noticeable absence was a woman in the Cabinet. Perhaps after Mrs Thatcher the men felt they needed a rest.

But although Mrs Thatcher had made enemies in Cabinet, she had some very loyal admirers within Number Ten. Her staff adored her. As John himself says, this was her one great virtue. He never saw her be unpleasant or rude to people who were serving her in any way. Other politicians, heads of nationalized industries, senior ministers, top members of the armed forces, she could be brutally rude and obnoxious to, but never to anyone who was not in a position to answer back. That, he says, was one of the qualities he liked most about her. But it also made the transition very difficult. They were Thatcherite to a man, and although they worked extremely hard for their new boss, it was inevitable that after eleven years they should find it difficult to adjust. Some felt so attached to her they preferred to leave than work for her successor.

Bernard Ingham, who had identified himself so closely with Mrs Thatcher as her Press Secretary, was one. As he says in his memoirs, *Kill the Messenger*, he had already said he would do his best to ease her successor into Number Ten

> but I was determined that neither Mr Major nor Mr Hurd should be tainted by my entirely undeserved reputation for Ministerial assassination and leaks. Unprofessional though it may seem, if Mr Heseltine walked in the door, I would walk out. There were limits.

So John Major was able to bring Gus O'Donnell with him from the Treasury to be his Press Secretary, who was friendly and good humoured where Bernard Ingham had been bluff and blunt. He also brought Judith Chaplin as a special adviser. In place of Brian Griffiths, who had been the head of Mrs Thatcher's policy unit, he brought in Sarah Hogg, the formidably bright financial journalist, who ten years before had been invited to the Blue Chips, in the words of Tristan Garel-Jones, 'To give us all a tutorial on how public finances are run.'

Sarah Hogg was at the theatre when she was found and asked to see the Prime Minister. She went to Downing Street in the interval in evening dress and was offered the job.

'She took a long time to make up her mind,' says the Prime Minister. 'About half a minute.'

Married to Lord Hailsham's son, Douglas Hogg, and the daughter of Lord Boyd-Carpenter, a former Tory Cabinet minister, she was the only member of his team with an Establishment background.

Charles Powell, Mrs Thatcher's Foreign Affairs Private Secretary, agreed to stay on in view of the impending Gulf War, although he had been wanting to leave Number Ten and return to the Foreign Office for a long time. He had already been with Mrs Thatcher for seven years, and during that time he had been posted as Ambassador to various places three times, but on each occasion Mrs Thatcher had cancelled it and said he must stay. He was indispensable to her, and provided enormous support to John Major in his first eight months too.

'Yes,' says Sir Charles, 'I think he was insecure about his ability. But what you might call insecure, I might call becoming modesty – one of the more effective traits of his character. He's certainly not boastful, he's not arrogant, he's anxious to do well and is concerned in case he doesn't do well.'

Well might he have been anxious. For a man who had no military experience whatsoever, he stepped straight into a major national emergency, with the Gulf War. It occupied his waking hours almost solidly from the day he walked into Number Ten in November until well into the following year; first the preparations, well advanced when he came into office with more than 14,000 troops already in the Middle East; the war itself, which involved more than 45,000 British servicemen and women; and then the aftermath. Immediately he was plunged into an entirely new area of expertise. He was the first of all his immediate predecessors to have no wartime experience. Born in 1943, most of his growing up was done in the 1950s, a generation that didn't even do military service. Leading the country at war was a pretty daunting task, but one which, according to Sir Charles, he did 'with great fortitude and great composure'.

But if he was anxious, so too were Britain's allies in the proposed action to remove Saddam Hussein from Kuwait. Mrs Thatcher had been a key mover in the Coalition, and they were stunned by her sudden removal from the scene. As General Sir Peter de la Billière, Commander of the British Forces in the Middle East, says in his memoirs, *Storm Command*, 'Her fall was a shattering blow for Arabs and Americans alike . . . For us Britons, her demise was extremely unsettling. It distracted us from the business of facing up to Saddam Hussein and created a damaging sense of uncertainty.' They all knew precious little about Mr Major – like much of Britain – but to the allies, his soon became a very familiar and firm voice on the telephone. There were calls to President Bush in America, which was providing most of the muscle, to President Mitterrand in France, and to President Kohl in Germany; visits here and there; and letters to people like King Fahd, the Saudi Arabian ruler, assuring them that, notwithstanding the change of Prime Minister, the British Government remained fully committed to the cause.

But while John Major was busy managing events in the Persian Gulf, as well as trying to pacify the Party at home and deal with the day-to-day job of government, Europe, the recession, and the Poll Tax, the press were busy with a thorough investigation of the new Prime Minister. They looked into everything from his style of dress to his haircut, including the vexing question of whether he tucked his shirt into his underpants. 'He does not,' says Norma, settling the matter for once and for all. 'That was a typical piece of nastiness. We've had a lot of that.' They also delved into his background and became foxed by the number of O levels he did or did not have. The records had disappeared from Rutlish and no one was prepared to say what academic qualifications he had, least of all John, who claimed he couldn't remember. The records had in fact been placed in the Surrey archives at John's request back in 1989, and he had asked their contents to be kept private. In retrospect he now realizes he should have checked earlier and the whole business would have gone away, but he was intensely irritated by their obsession with something so petty, and against all advice, stubbornly refused to be cooperative. This raking through his past, and present, was inevitable, and it was pretty standard fare – pseudo-psychological analysis with passing swipes at anything slightly out of the ordinary, and innuendo aplenty at the discovery that Norma would not be moving into Number Ten. Norma came in for the same treatment too, as did his sister, Pat, and brother, Terry.

John hated it. He hated the intrusion into their privacy, hated the snobbish tone of the writers, who were snide and patronizing by turns, and hated total strangers talking with authority on things they knew nothing about. He had experienced something of the sort when he became Foreign Secretary, but apart from that brief period, he had enjoyed a favourable press for the most part, and had built up no immunity. Abuse in the House was water off a duck's back, and he could give as good as he got, he was as thick-skinned as the next man, but attack in the newspapers was another matter entirely. He couldn't shrug it off any more than he could stop reading it. In the early days he was obsessed by it, he read everything first thing in the morning. He became angry at the inaccuracies, hurt by the unkindness, worried about the effect it was having on his family, whom he didn't consider fair game. But most wounding of all were the quotes from nameless colleagues. They were to go on.

Norma also fretted. Her life was once again turned upside down. Being Chancellor's wife, even being the wife of the Foreign Secretary, had been bad, but nothing had prepared her for this. Her home became a prison once again, the security forces moved back into the Finings, and instead of the caravan they had brought before, built a semi-permanent hut in the garden. The press camped at the gate, they followed Elizabeth and James, and they followed Norma. She couldn't do the weekly grocery shopping without someone commenting on where she went, what she bought and how much she spent. And once again there was the ubiquitous put-down.

The nightmare began on the evening of the election. She had had very few clothes at Number Eleven; after all, she didn't live there, and only ever used to bring what she was going to need with her on each trip. Her smart things were in Huntingdon, and when she had packed the car with the lasagne to feed the troops in the aftermath of the campaign, she hadn't thought much further. When she saw how the week was evolving she told Barbara Wallis, John's secretary, that she really ought to go shopping, but they both agreed she couldn't be seen buying a new outfit. So she was left with a choice of two blue suits that she had with her, neither of which was new. John disliked one of them, and so on the evening of his victory, when she stood in Downing Street beside him facing the world's press, mesmerized by flash guns, and television cameras, she was wearing the other.

The next day when she accompanied John to Buckingham Palace she wore it again, little imagining what an opportunity it would provide for the tabloids. Fashion writers had a field day. They took her apart limb from limb, criticizing everything – her hair, her make-up and, of course, what she now calls, 'that ghastly suit'.

Analysts burst into print about the 'message' implicit in her choice of outfit, columnists made cheap cracks, and pundits pontificated on the ways in which she could smarten up her act and start looking like the wife of a Prime Minister instead of a mousey member of some country branch of the WI.

Ten days later one of the newspapers presented its readers with the 'new-look' Norma. There was a photograph of her 'before' in the old blue suit, and 'after', dressed with the sort of elegant sophistication you would expect in the wife of a British Prime Minister. Little did they know the 'transformation' they detected was simply Norma dressed in the other blue suit, the one that John had not let her wear the previous week, and it was at least two years old. The irony was not lost on her but it was slim satisfaction. She had been wholly unprepared for such an assault and the hurt went very deep.

The first fifteen months were very difficult for everyone – John, Norma and all the staff who were new to Number Ten. They were all on the most tremendous learning curve and events moved so quickly that there was simply no time for anyone to adjust or even stop and talk about their problems. Norma was greatly helped through this period by Barbara Wallis, who for the first year ran Norma's office as well as continuing with John's constituency work. She was so much a friend to them all that she was virtually one of the family. But even she, with all her experience as a parliamentary secretary, found the transition to Number Ten extremely difficult. Where before John had given her a free rein in replying to constituency letters, at Number Ten she needed a Government briefing for virtually every one. The reason was obvious enough – the MP for Huntingdon couldn't give a view on any matter that wasn't exactly the same as the Government's, if he was also Prime Minister. Nevertheless it made her job very much more time consuming because of all the referrals she had to make; and she had to be constantly on her guard not to commit him to anything as an MP that he couldn't pursue as Prime Minister. Previously she had fixed all his constituency engagements. Now those had to be juggled with Prime Ministerial engagements and a very much fuller diary, not to mention the massive security arrangements that had to be considered. Any decision involved reams of paperwork. It was all part of the system dictated by the civil service at Number Ten, and certain procedures had to be followed, whether they liked it or not.

John Major hates the security. He hates being unable to walk round St James's Park on a sunny day, or go shopping for a birthday present without two armed detectives by his side. He has personal protection twenty-four hours a day, seven days a week, and every excursion is elaborately planned. He can do nothing on the spur of the moment. He can't pop in to visit a friend, or even take Norma and the children to a restaurant or the theatre without sniffer dogs having been ahead and checked out the premises first. He can't even drive in his own car. He travels in a specially reinforced Jaguar which weighs three tons, with a driver and a bodyguard, and a police car on its tail, which travels so close behind that they almost touch bumpers.

Sadly it is necessary. He would like to be able to address open meetings, to answer questions off-the-cuff, to keep him in touch with ordinary people. The security services tell him he would survive safely no more than three meetings. He can't argue. The threat of terrorism is very real. Not only was there the tragedy of the Brighton bomb in 1984, Airey Neave was blown up driving out of the underground car park at the House of Commons in 1979; Sir Ian Gow was murdered in a similar fashion outside his own home in East Sussex in 1990; and in February 1991, John and most members of his War Cabinet had a lucky escape when the IRA had a go at Number Ten. They launched a mortar rocket from a transit van parked in Whitehall which landed, by the grace of God, in the garden at the back of the house. John was chairing a War Cabinet when suddenly there was the most almighty explosion and all the windows blew in. Some of them dived under the table. 'Gentlemen,' said the Prime Minister, with astonishing cool, when the last of the glass had fallen, 'I think we should restart this meeting somewhere else.' They did, in the Cobra Room, deep in the bowels of Whitehall.

Barbara Wallis was on the telephone to Norma in Huntingdon when the bomb went off.

'What on earth was that?' she said on hearing the blast.

'I think it's a bomb,' said Barbara. 'I'll go and find out and ring you back.'

By the time she rang back ten minutes later, Norma had already discovered what had happened from the television. She knew John was unhurt and knew there was no point in rushing down to Downing Street; better to carry on as normal and make sure Elizabeth and James were not unduly upset.

Norma's workload multiplied when John became Prime Minister, as charities and special interest groups jostled to get her name on their letterhead. She was also inundated with mail, many of the letters asking her to intercede on the writer's behalf with her husband – something as a private citizen she couldn't do even if she wanted to. The initial flood of thousands, subsided to its current rate – a steady sixty to eighty letters a week – many of them wanting a favourite recipe to include in a charity cookery book, or something similar, and many more requests for engagements.

She took on many of the charities that approached her, although Mencap still remained her favourite, but she tried hard to be more than just a name to them. She likes to feel she could contribute something more positive. She has certainly helped a number of charities raise a great deal of money during her time at Number Ten. But at the same time she has been determined to keep some time for herself and her family. She has always been a very organized person, and she and Barbara managed a very efficient system which had letters answered within three days, and all her engagements slotted into two days a week which she routinely spent in London. The rest of the time she was at home in Huntingdon so that she could keep a degree of normality going with the children, as well as keep a piece of herself intact.

Critics – even friends – have said that Norma should have lived at Number Ten, as Denis Thatcher did, so that when the Prime Minister climbed the stairs at the end of the day, tired and battered from the daily round, he had someone to unwind with, someone to listen while he let off steam about incompetent colleagues or cursed at the iniquities of the press. Denis was certainly Mrs Thatcher's saving grace. He would pour her a large Scotch, put in his two-cent's worth on whatever the issue of the moment, and provide some release from the job. But John and Norma's relationship has never been like that. He has never brought his worries home. Norma sometimes wishes he would. She knows when he is under stress, because he's miserable and distracted and it's impossible for her to get close. She can talk but she knows he's not listening. She frequently receives letters telling her to look after him, and says he would be a very difficult man to look after in the fullest sense.

He's pretty much in control of what he does. When he's had enough he knows it. I've never felt I could say, 'Look, you've done enough work, come and watch television or go and have an early night,' because he knows what he's got to do. If he's not prepared the next day, I don't want to feel responsible. I worry when I think he is getting tired, but I'm not sure there's a great deal I can do about it. I don't think I've ever been able to say, 'Come on, that's enough.' He's got a job to do. I don't like getting in the way, to be honest. He has to do it his way, and he doesn't need me to nag him. That's what it amounts to. I've always felt like that.

Besides, Downing Street is hardly a home from home. Norma has made the flat upstairs very comfortable and pretty, John has brought some of his favourite books from the Finings, including a much-treasured first edition of *The Small House at Allington* by Anthony Trollope, and there are family photographs and cricketing mementoes scattered about, but Number Ten is first and foremost an office, and even in the flat John is never free from interruptions. There is always someone needing a decision, or a signature or a quick word.

Graham Bright, his Parliamentary Private Secretary for the first four years, like Barbara Wallis, also found the procedures inside Number Ten something of a shock. It was, as he says, 'A day of wonderment when I went in there and discovered I had secretaries and staff and goodness knows what.' So covered in wonderment was he that within days of John becoming Prime Minister he managed to lose a speech John was due to deliver in Altrincham. It had all been a tremendous rush, the speech was written and released to the press, and 'with all the fiddling around, the speech was lost'; the Prime Minister had nothing to deliver.

'I thought, "well that's it",' says Graham, '"I've spent a day at Number Ten and that's the end of my career." But even a thing like that, he made a huge joke of it. He wound me up in public, he told the truth, and had everyone in fits of laughter. It was the feature of the whole evening – but he did it in a very nice way.'

John Major's popularity rating with the public was high in those early days. People didn't know him but they liked the honest image he projected, and they liked his calm and courteous style at Question Time in the House of Commons. After Mrs Thatcher's school-mistressly finger-wagging, his relaxed, plain-speaking manner was a pleasant change, and his handling of the Gulf situation only served to reinforce that view. By the end of January 1991, after just two months in office, with the Gulf War in full swing, he had become the most popular Prime Minister for thirty years. Mrs Thatcher had never been good at communicating with the public. Her brilliance lay in communicating with the Party faithful, who were on her side, the rousing call-to-arms at Party conferences. But what John Major lacked in that situation he made up for when there was a more gentle message to be got across, just by explaining things calmly, patiently, reasonably. And he is always at his best without a text. With a text he is wooden and he knows it. He hates having one.

The broadcast he made before the Gulf War, explaining to the nation why it was necessary to send our boys out to the Gulf, was a case in point. Ending with the words, 'God bless', it was perfectly judged for the mood of the people, and the effect was extraordinary. So too were the off-the-cuff press conferences he gave during the hostilities, when he stepped out of Number Ten into Downing Street and appeared happy to answer questions openly and honestly as they came.

Allied bombing of Iraqi targets began at one minute past midnight, Greenwich Mean Time, on Thursday 17 January, six weeks after his arrival at Number Ten. John Major had known when and how it would start since just before Christmas. George Bush had invited him to Camp David, the President's country retreat in Maryland, and the plan was that he would fly into Washington, meet the President and then they would all travel up to Camp David by helicopter. However, when the Prime Minister arrived in America it was foggy and impossible to make the journey by helicopter. Instead they took a car. Four people were in the back of the car – President Bush, General Brent Scowcroft, John Major and Charles Powell – and during the course of that two-hour drive they agreed the date for Desert Storm to start, they agreed how it would start – with sustained air attack for some weeks – and they agreed that they wouldn't send in ground troops and tanks until they were sure that the Iraqis were weak enough for them to be able to resist with the minimum loss of life. They had already both done a great deal of work, but it was in those two hours that they went through all the details, agreed what the timescale for it would be, and worked out how they would run the campaign. And that two-hour conversation absolutely described what happened in the Gulf War. The planning by the generals had been impeccable. Never was planning on paper put into practice so effectively.

The only difference between the planning and the reality was the number of casualties. They had dramatically overestimated the number of British and American servicemen who would die, for two reasons. One, they underestimated the capacity of the American Air Force and the RAF to target their bombs; the precision in this first high-tech, fully computerized war, with laser-guided missiles, was incredible. Two, they overestimated the capacity of the Iraqi ground troops, particularly the Republican Guard, whom they had been led to believe were exceptional. They also had no indication at that stage that the Iraqis would put their inferior tank troops at the front. Other than that, in those two hours, as they drove through the freezing fog, with snow lying on the ground outside, the four in that limousine effectively decided how to conduct the Gulf War.

So when John Major went to visit the troops in the Gulf in January he was under no illusion about what he was going to be asking them to do and the idea appalled him. He telephoned his sister, Pat, soon after his return,

> He said it was one of the hardest things he had ever done in his life, to face them and tell them they would have to fight. He said he felt absolutely terrible. How could he, who had never been involved in a war, stand there and tell them they would possibly have to give their lives? He thought he would feel a wave of their hatred. Instead they were so relieved to be told they could get on with it.

The trip was a great success. He flew into King Khalid International Airport in Saudi Arabia to a hero's welcome – a band, a guard of honour and all the Saudi Council Ministers from the Crown Prince and the Prince Sultan downwards were lined up on the tarmac to greet him. An audience with King Fahd came later. Word suddenly arrived while he was addressing a group of servicemen and women that the King would see him at once, and he was bundled into a car and swept off in a cavalcade to the palace, where he was shown straight into the Royal presence without the usual interminable wait.

During the course of the audience the Prime Minister raised the matter of the Host Nation Agreement, whereby the Saudis would pay for the fuel, water, vehicles, food and accommodation which the British forces were using in their country. 'So well did the exchange of views go,' records General Sir Peter de la Billière, 'that the King promised to sign our agreement.'

The exchange of views with the soldiers went even better. As Sir Peter says,

Nothing better epitomized his touch with ordinary servicemen than an incident in the port at Jubail. Because his schedule was so tight, he sent word ahead asking if he could be excused any formal lunch and have a sandwich instead. Martin White made suitable arrangements and in due course one of the cooks produced a large platter, covered by greaseproof paper. Just as the Prime Minister was about to arrive, Martin's Chief of Staff removed the greaseproof paper and to his horror saw a letter stuffed down among the sandwiches.

'By God!' he said. 'The cook's had the nerve to complain direct to the Prime Minister. What shall we do?'

'Open the envelope,' said Martin, expecting that he would have to destroy the note and reprimand the writer. However, the note turned out not to be a complaint, but a *cri de coeur* from one Chelsea supporter to another, begging John Major, now that he was at Number Ten, to sort out the chaos at the team's ground, Stamford Bridge.

'What do we do now?' asked the Chief of Staff.

'Give it to the Prime Minister,' Martin told him. So they did and the Prime Minister, though in the middle of the most hectic tour and beset by new faces on every side, sat down and wrote the cook a full-page answer in his own hand, not only thanking him for his delicious sandwiches, but promising to do what he could to put matters right at the Chelsea ground.

Writing home to his wife, Bridget, after the incident, Sir Peter said,

This was one of JM's first visits to any military formation and he crammed a year's worth of visits into a day. He spoke very well and sincerely to the servicemen, with no prevarication, and said we go to war if Saddam does not get out. He realized that what they wanted was a straight answer and there's nobody better at giving one. That's what he gave people and it pleased them. Having started the day uncertain of what sort of reception he would get, he soon found he was among friends and gained confidence by the minute. I believe it's been of great value to him, as well as to us.

But the final accolade came from the men. To quote Sir Peter de la Billière again,

> With good, plain talk, rather than high rhetoric, he put across the message that in the United Kingdom fifty million people were behind them and he fired them up to do the job of evicting Saddam as best they could. Not many official visitors provoke the members of a REME workshop to throw their caps in the air and cheer. John Major did and nobody forgot it.

John Major certainly didn't forget it. He remembers his first visit to the Gulf with great affection, and with a few laughs, especially the occasion when he climbed out of a helicopter in the desert, and a young man came up and grabbed his briefcase and walked off with it. He turned out to be one of the generals, one of the fighting generals right in the front line, but all he knew was that a perfect stranger had disappeared with his briefcase. He went deep into the desert, he visited dug-outs, he drove a Challenger tank, he went out in the Gulf on board the destroyer, HMS *London*, and wherever he stopped during the tour, he addressed great masses of troops who gathered round, most of whom, as he says, were probably wondering who on earth he was. They had had ten years of Mrs Thatcher, they had been sent out there by Mrs Thatcher, and they wanted to know who this character was who had appeared from absolutely nowhere to talk to them.

The reception they gave him was immensely warm everywhere, but there was one gathering he will never forget. It was evening at Dhahran, dusk was gathering, and he went to talk to the RAF base. Everyone on the base was there – men, women, technicians, pilots, navigators – all gathered in a huge semi-circle around him. John was standing on a soapbox with a microphone, there were placards, he remembers, saying 'Hello, Mum'. He spoke for some time, then answered their questions. They asked him whether they were going to have to fight, and he said they probably would be invited to fight, to which their response was that they hadn't expected to be invited. It was a very warm evening and perfectly clear. When he had finished speaking and come down from his soapbox he could hear them talking. They hadn't expected to get a straight answer, to be told that they probably would have to fight. They had thought he would bat it away.

He received letters from them subsequently saying how pleased they were that he had told them the truth. About a week or so later the fighting did begin, and they did start combat flights from Dhahran. But it was a magical evening, he says, because it was getting dusky, the sun was setting in the distance, it was warm, and there was that magical spontaneous atmosphere that sometimes you get and sometimes you don't. It was a meeting he will never forget. It was the last time he saw the troops before the war started.

John Major's personal success in the Gulf did a great deal to boost his confidence, just as the success of the Coalition action as a whole gave a kick start to his authority as Prime Minister. But it was a wearing and worrying time. Not only was it a war of unparalleled sophistication, it was the first televised war. Events in all their horror were beamed into people's homes as they happened. He had had many many meetings in Downing Street before the start about the likely scale of casualties and how they would cope, given the effect that seeing them on television would have on the public. They envisaged a lot of bodies, some of them British. Saddam Hussein was a ruthless dictator; he had placed hostages as human shields to protect his military installations, and the threat of chemical warfare was with them daily. When he took prisoners, such as the two Tornado pilots shot down on the first day of the hostilities, Flight Lieutenants John Peters and John Nichol, he paraded them on Iraqi television for all the world to see. The situation was highly volatile, and the Iraqi propaganda machine thoroughly distressing. It was also effective.

The ground war began on 24 February. Saddam Hussein had been given until midday of the day before to start pulling his troops out of Kuwait and he had failed to do so. That evening John Major telephoned Sir Peter to wish his Division luck in battle.

The Prime Minister told me that he had been receiving large numbers of blueys from servicemen and their wives. The letters, he said, taught him much about the quality of the people in the Services: some had demanded higher pay, and one author had had the nerve to say that he did not join the Army in order to fight a war, but most correspondents were constructive and enthusiastic about what they were doing. As before [a call on the eve of the first air strike] the call from Number Ten left me with the comfortable feeling that we had an exceptionally human and sympathetic champion in Whitehall.

John Major's role in the war was considerable. As Graham Bright says,

> What a lot of people don't realize, is that he was very much the anchor man for the allies. He spent night after night, sometimes all through the night, talking to all the leaders, updating them, making sure they stayed on-side; the European leaders, Mr Mulroney in Canada, Mr Bush, the Australians and the New Zealanders. He played a very significant part.

The ground war lasted just four days. By 28 February it was all over. Saddam Hussein had surrendered, but he was still alive, and there were many who thought at the time, or subsequently, including Mrs Thatcher, that the Allies should not have stopped when they did. They should have gone on to capture Baghdad, and should never have left Saddam Hussein alive.

John Major is in no doubt about it. They were absolutely right to stop when they did. They had reached a stage which the media were rightly beginning to call a 'turkey shoot', that is to say, the allied troops were unstoppable, and facing them were untrained eighteen-, nineteen- and twenty-year-olds – conscripts with poor equipment, who were in no position to defend themselves. You couldn't have asked our boys to fight against such youngsters, John says. They were boys as well. They didn't want to kill unarmed soldiers, or soldiers who couldn't fight back. That's not what the generals wanted their soldiers to do, and it's not what he wanted them to do.

They were a day-and-a-half from Baghdad. They could have killed lots of those youngsters and fought their way through to Baghdad. If they had done that and dragged Saddam Hussein out by the heels, he argues, what would they have achieved? An Arab martyr. And they couldn't be certain he would have been replaced by anyone better. They had clipped his wings.

There was another point, a legal point. They went to war under international law. The mandate was a United Nations resolution. It emphatically did not say go on fighting when you have won the war, go right into Baghdad and bring out Saddam Hussein and kill him. It said liberate Kuwait. The Coalition had run out of its legal mandate and John Major thinks they had run out of their moral one too, because they would have been killing people no longer able to defend themselves, in the hope of getting a man whose whereabouts they didn't know. They did all they could to kill Saddam Hussein during the war but they couldn't find him. If they could have killed him they would have killed him, because, as Mr Major says, he's a monster and it would have stopped the war. But the fact was they couldn't find him, and there was no certainty they would ever find him.

The Prime Minister had not a shred of doubt that they were right to stop. That was the advice he was given by his generals, it was the advice President Bush was given by his generals, despite what people might have said subsequently. It was later suggested that General Norman Schwarzkopf, Commander-in-Chief of the American Forces, wanted to push on to Baghdad, but John Major says this was not the case. He spoke to Bush on the day, at the time, and they compared advice. They had both had the same advice and reached the same conclusion, and he is certain they were right to stop. He regrets, he says, that they didn't kill Saddam Hussein, but that's life, they didn't.

John Major flew to Dhahran for his second visit to the Gulf, to thank the troops, on 6 March, on his way back from Moscow, where he had met President Gorbachev. Defence Secretary Tom King had already been out, but John Major was the first of the Western leaders to see the devastation that the Iraqis had left behind them in Kuwait, both human and physical. Almost everything in the city had been destroyed, people and animals were starving, and outside the city it looked as though there had been a nuclear attack – an impenetrable black cloud of smoke hung over a desolate landscape as oil fires burned furiously.

Standing on the roof of a jeep in the desert, with hundreds of men in a huge semi-circle around him, the Prime Minister said his thank yous. The men were very buoyant, and presented him with a captured AK-47 rifle, but their prime concern was how quickly he could get them home. At the RAF base, where the airmen lined up on the wings of a Tornado, they had erected a large banner behind them. 'THE MAJOR ISSUE TODAY IS, WHEN ARE WE GOING HOME?' He promised it would be soon, and by the end of the week a token batch had been sent on their way.

Iraq was a country deeply divided by factions at the best of times, with the Shi'ites in the south, the Kurds in the north, the Baathists in government, and the Sunnis on the periphery, but as the Allied forces began to move out of the region, Saddam Hussein turned his murderous attention to the Shi'ites and the Kurds. Emboldened by the Allied action, possibly even encouraged by President Bush who said he hoped that the Iraqi people would rid themselves of Saddam, the Kurds took to arms against the dictator, no doubt in the belief that the Americans, if not the Coalition, would help them. Alas no shining cavalry came to their aid. They were pitilessly crushed, and those that were able – men, women, children, the elderly, an entire people – were left to flee for their lives into the mountains in the very north of Iraq, where they faced almost certain death in the bitter cold, with no shelter, no food, and only those clothes and blankets that they had been able to carry with them.

The situation was clearly unacceptable to anyone with an ounce of humanity, but much as he tried, John Major was unable to get anyone to take any action. A special meeting of the European Council was convened to discuss the matter, and during the flight there, John and his travelling companions came up with a solution. His companions were Stephen Wall, who had recently left the Foreign Office to join the Private Office at Number Ten, Gus O'Donnell, and another adviser, John Weston, and they were all wracking their brains when John Weston suddenly suggested having enclaves for the Kurds. John Major immediately seized on the idea and, within a matter of hours, it had developed into 'safe havens'.

He decided to float the idea at the meeting. He knew if he could get the backing of the European Community he would have strong enough support at the United Nations to be able to compel the Americans to take action which he knew they were unwilling to take. They formed the major part of NATO and without them, even with Europe, Britain could do little. It was, he says, a huge risk. He could have looked very naive. He could have been turned down by the Community, the UN or the Americans, and, within the first couple of days of floating the idea, the press were savage. They said he had stuck his neck out and had it chopped off. In the event, he won the argument with the Americans, but it took a lot of telephone calls to President Bush, a lot of diplomatic pressure from the British Ambassador, a lot of pressure from the Foreign Office, and a lot of public support, but its strength was the fact that it came through the European Community.

Before addressing the meeting he had squared President Mitterrand and Chancellor Kohl, who lent their support, as John says, most generously, and in a far far more effective way than he had imagined they would. At the same time he tried to set up an arms register at the UN, to determine who was selling arms to whom, to ensure that no ruler would again be able to build up a disproportionate stock of arms for offensive purposes, as Saddam Hussein had done. When the Gulf War started, Saddam Hussein had, numerically, the fourth largest army in the world.

It was the first occasion on which Britain had used the Community to back up British foreign policy. If it had just been the British, the Americans would never have taken action, but with the rest of the Community lined up behind her, plus the Commonwealth, which John Major had been at pains to bring back on board during the previous three years, she had sufficient clout, and 'safe havens' came into being.

John Major had a lot of bridge-building to do with people like Mitterrand and Kohl when he became Prime Minister. Mrs Thatcher had successfully antagonized almost all of her European partners, and John was left to pick up the pieces, and build up individual relationships one by one. He did so with a varying amount of success, given the mix of personalities and party politics, but the friendships he made in Europe have paid dividends. Helmut Kohl he describes as one of the warmest personalities he has ever met, a supreme optimist, a great lover of the next generation, a man who is always planning ahead. He is very concerned about Germany's past, he wants to sink Germany firmly in the middle of the European family of nations for the future, and, according to Mr Major, is prepared to take a lot of domestic pain in Germany for the policies that he thinks are appropriate for Germany in the middle future. He's a very warm character, very pro British – he works closely with the French but his gut instinct is pro British. He could never understand why Mrs Thatcher was so beastly to him all the time.

François Mitterrand, who died in January 1996, he described as a fascinating man, immensely imbued with the pride of France. As John Major said,

It isn't the pride of Mitterrand, it's the pride of France – indeed it is difficult to imagine that any of the great French kings were any more proud of France than Mitterrand is. He is a great historian, with an understanding of the history of

Europe as a whole, and a fascination for the history of individual nations. Show Mitterrand a problem and he will go back to its historical roots first and find out how the problem built up. Show him the Yugoslavian problem, for example, and he will go back to a 1916 map of Serbia and surrounding countries to see how it looked in the past. Show Chancellor Kohl a problem, on the other hand, and he will look forward and wonder what things will look like in the future and how he should deal with it.

It was not just the personal friendships that John Major forged with these European leaders that helped still the waters in the wake of his predecessor, and extract the concessions he went on to win for Britain in summits at Maastricht and Edinburgh. It was also his positive attitude to Europe, and his commitment to the completion of the Single Market. Speaking in Bonn in March 1991, he declared that he wanted to see Britain 'where we belong. At the very heart of Europe.' But it was a double-edged sword, as well he knew. He had to reassure the Community on the one hand while reassuring the Euro-sceptics in the Conservative Party that he was no fanatic. It was a balancing act he performed with considerable skill, with this knack, once again, of giving everyone the impression that he is in sympathy with their views without ever betraying his own.

Some people say he has no views of his own, no ideology, no philosophy, that he is a pragmatist who licks his finger to see which way the wind is blowing before embarking on any policy. There is no doubt he takes the course of least resistance in pursuit of any given objective, but he denies vehemently that he has no clear objectives. On Europe, for example, he is very precise about what he wants. He wants to see a Community that stretches from one end of the Continent to the other, that incorporates the EFTA countries in the north (Austria, Finland, Iceland, Norway, Sweden and Switzerland), now all-but achieved, and the newly emerged democracies in the east (Bulgaria, Czechoslovakia, Hungary, Poland and Romania), thereby extending the area of free trade and common purpose right up to the Russian border, because, as he said when he first suggested this widening of the Community at a conference in Paris in September 1991,

We should remember that trade is a peacemaker – one of the most powerful and persuasive. Countries locked together in trade have mutual interests that prevent them being locked together in conflict.

Twice this century we have had world wars that started in Western Europe. It won't come in his political lifetime, he says, but if those boundaries could be extended within the life of his children or grandchildren, man would have created a war-free zone right across Europe. That, he says, would be the biggest gift that any politician has ever given Europe at any stage in its history. That's what he wants to do. And not only would such a Community provide a wider area of free trade, it would be impossible to turn it into a centrally administered federation. It would be too wide and too diverse – each country would have to maintain its national identity.

He doesn't want federalism any more than Mrs Thatcher, who has been waging a war on Europe and John Major's policy towards Europe ever since she left office. But what he finds so frustrating about her activities, he says, is that she and her supporters are going about it in such a way as to ensure the rest of Europe does go federalist. What he is trying to do is wean the rest of Europe off federalism, to make the Community so vast that the idea is absolutely impossible.

Europe is the single most damaging issue to have hit the Conservative Party since it was torn asunder by the Corn Laws in the last century. But it wasn't the only divisive problem he inherited when he came to power. The Poll Tax was every bit as explosive, and had already been the cause of mass rioting. It had to be changed; on the other hand, the Poll Tax had been the flagship policy in Mrs Thatcher's last election manifesto, and a large section of the Party supported it. In bringing about change, he had to take this section with him or risk a potentially lethal split. His critics say he should have taken a much stronger line with the Poll Tax and announced that he was going to abolish it the moment he came into office. It would have been a sign of firm leadership, and although he would have faced a revolt on the back benches, he could have brazened it out, and would have established his authority from the very beginning.

However, the other problem that came with the job in November 1990 was the knowledge that he would have to call a general election in the not too distant future, and the only certainty about elections is that people do not vote for divided parties. If the

Tories were to have any hope of winning the forthcoming election they would have to present a united front. That was his overriding concern during his first year-and-a-half as Prime Minister. People forget, he says, but the election campaign started almost as soon as he took over. People expected him to have a spring election, capitalizing on the success of the Gulf War in 1991. Then they said he wouldn't wait beyond the summer, then speculation fell upon the autumn. When he missed the opportunity to go to the country in the autumn, the prophets of doom moved in and said he had left it too late, he would never win. So for eighteen months, until he finally named the day in April 1992, he was restricted by the need to keep the Party together and electable.

In retrospect, he wishes he had been able to hold the election in June 1991. If the Council Tax, which replaced the Poll Tax, had been ready three weeks earlier, he could have done so, but it wasn't. Michael Heseltine announced the new tax to the House on 23 April – a tax levied on each household, like the old rates, but based on the number of adults living in the house as well as the value of the property – which left insufficient time to mount a campaign for early June. A June election would have enabled him to get the Maastricht Bill through the House more quickly, before the Danish referendum in June 1992, which effectively threw the whole issue into turmoil. He knew there would be problems whenever he presented it to Parliament because Europe is the one issue on which ideological beliefs run high, which is why he wanted to have the election behind him before he began. As a result of the delay, and the Danes voting against ratification, Maastricht, a Bill which few people ever seemed to understand but which aroused furious passions none the less, dominated politics and the media, and turned John Major from one of the most popular into one of the most unpopular Prime Ministers ever.

13

ELECTION

JOHN MAJOR came back from the meeting of the European Council at Maastricht in December 1991 a hero. He had wrested from the Community three major concessions, which before the negotiations had seemed impossible. Everyone had told him he would have to surrender on the matter of a single currency, he would have to surrender on federalism and he would have to accept the Social Chapter, governing working conditions. He didn't. He won an opt-out for Britain on all the essential points, which brought praise from even the most ardent sceptics. At the time, even Mrs Thatcher congratulated him.

It was a tremendous feat by any standards, achieved entirely because of his ability to digest detail; and, furthermore, to know the details that the other European leaders didn't. Tristan Garel-Jones, who as Foreign Office minister spent his whole time working on the subject, was astonished by his ability, and says, despite his knowledge, he could never have done what John Major did, because there is no back-up in a summit. Negotiations are between the leaders – their advisers take a back seat – and Maastricht was a long and deeply complex treaty, amounting to 312 pages. There were mounds of briefing notes to be read and retained, and he was up against some formidable opponents. He had spent the past six months in preparation, and he had had a series of bi-lateral meetings with most of the other leaders in advance to prepare the ground, but however friendly and cooperative they were in principle, he knew as well as anyone that, at the end of the day, good relations would count for nothing if they stood in the way of national or political interests. It was a stormy debate, which lasted two days. When he reported back to the Commons he was cheered and order papers were waved. Few imagined what lay ahead.

Speaking about the negotiations three months later, during the election campaign, he said,

> Those negotiations were tough. They were gruelling. Let me tell you something. When you are negotiating in Europe with your fellow Presidents and fellow Prime Ministers, there is nobody else with you. You are on your own. You have got to have your wits about you. You have got to be clear about what you want to achieve. You have to understand the detail. One mistake, one slip of the tongue, one careless word, one moment of indecision, one gaffe – and you have sold Britain down the river.

There was much celebrating among the British contingent in Maastricht when the negotiations came to a close. John Major's hotel suite the next morning bore all the signs, and when Tristan came into John's room to tell him his car had arrived to take him to the airport, he found John busily tidying up.

'What on earth are you doing?' he said.

'We can't leave the room like this,' said the Prime Minister, gathering up empty beer cans.

'But it's a hotel,' said Tristan in disbelief. 'They clear up.'

But it was only by promising to do the clearing up himself that he managed to get the Prime Minister to leave.

Tristan's wife had once again lent John and Norma her house in Spain for a fortnight in August, but this time their family holiday had involved rather more than the family. They were accompanied by detectives, secretaries, a complete office, and communications equipment which would have done any multi-national corporation proud. They were thirteen in all, and not surprisingly, having brought the team out to Spain, John Major spent most of his time working.

By good chance, however, he was back in London when the news of a military coup in Moscow, mounted by hard-line communists opposed to *perestroika*, began to filter through. President Gorbachev, the architect of reform, had been taken captive, but it was unclear whether any of his colleagues were still at large. Because of the time differences, John Major was the first world leader to react to the news. He was also one of the few who was not away on holiday, and stole a march on everyone, not least on Neil

Kinnock, who had the psychological disadvantage of being a voice on the end of a telephone – the perception, unfairly, being that he was not there when important things were happening. John Major was. By the time the Americans had woken up, the Prime Minister had already been on CNN television with a robust reaction which was finely judged. He said events in Moscow were clearly a return to an unacceptable pattern and the world would not accept that democracy and freedom were at an end. President Mitterrand, by contrast, indicated that France would do business with the new regime. President Bush reiterated the British line, telling John Major on the telephone that he was absolutely right and he would say the same. It was then a question of waiting and watching events as they unfolded, but as soon as it became clear that the coup was far from absolute, and that Boris Yeltsin, his deputy, was holding out in the Moscow White House, the Prime Minister immediately started telephoning with support and encouragement to as many people as he could get hold of in Moscow, including Yeltsin himself, whom he spoke to at a critical time when the tanks were beginning to roll in the streets outside.

Whatever success John Major had on the world stage, the picture at home was one of intense gloom. Britain had sunk deep into recession, but it was unlike previous recessions, which had primarily hit the manufacturing regions in the north, and left the south relatively unscathed. This recession had hit the south of England, the Tory heartlands; it had hit not just manufacturing, but service industries as well. Professional men and women, and skilled and unskilled workers alike, found themselves out of a job, unable to pay their rent, unable to pay their mortgages, unable to sell their houses. House prices plummeted, leaving many people with negative equity, paying mortgage repayments on a house that was no longer worth the value of the mortgage. Old established businesses collapsed no less than new ventures, homes were repossessed, and bankruptcy abounded. Uncertainty touched every family, and most had at least one relative who was out of work in the south of England. No one was immune, whatever their status.

Recession was not confined to Britain. Economically no government is an island, and not even the United States, the most powerful economy in the world, was immune from what was happening elsewhere. This recession was a world-wide phenomenon, and remarkably similar the world over, although varying in intensity, but it was the English-speaking countries that were the most severely hit – Britain, the United States and Canada, where the role of credit in the economy was greatest and the effect of financial deregulation the most pronounced. Britain was the first into this particular recession, almost off the top of the boom in 1986, 1987 and 1988.

According to John Major,

> It happened because the Government lost control of the housing market, which grew too fast, and lost control of financial deregulation after 'Big Bang' in October 1986, when credit became more readily available. Ten years of deregulation were done in three. It moved too quickly and distorted the statistics so that the Government couldn't see what was happening, and by the time they could, Britain was in the grip of an uncontrollable housing boom.

According to Nigel Lawson, 'net advances for house purchase rose from £19 billion in 1985–86 to £27 billion in 1986–87, a jump of almost 50 per cent.' Neither he, as Chancellor, nor his advisers saw the danger. He writes in *The View From Number 11*,

> This was unfortunate, since it turned out that, during this period, rising house prices were an important part of the transmission mechanism from credit creation to inflation – namely the effect of a sharp rise in house prices in increasing perceived personal wealth, and the increase in personal wealth in leading to an upsurge in consumer spending.

Inflation was the inevitable outcome.

John Major knew all this when he became Prime Minister. What he didn't know was how deep it would be or how long it would go on for, and it turned out to be both deeper and longer-lasting than he or anyone else, in or outside the Treasury, imagined. The problems faced in Britain were mirrored to a lesser extent right the way across Europe and on two occasions, just as Britain started coming out of recession, it was dragged back by other countries that were going into recession.

One of the factors which undoubtedly made the recession worse than it might otherwise have been was the collapse of the Berlin Wall and reunification of Germany in November 1989. To ward off problems in West Germany, which was suddenly being flooded by cheap labour from the East, Chancellor Kohl began subsidizing employment in the East on a vast scale, and paying out high levels of social security provision to the former East Germans. But rather than find the money for this new expenditure by raising taxes, or cutting back public spending in the West, Kohl borrowed the money, with the result that the German Budget swung from a surplus in 1990 of $48 billion, to a deficit in 1991 of $21 billion. Inflation rose and the Bundesbank responded by pushing up interest rates.

No government is popular in recession and John Major knew after Christmas in 1991 that he was likely to have to call an election, in almost unprecedented circumstances, with the Government behind in the opinion polls. Between Christmas and New Year he had a series of private meetings with the Party Chairman, Chris Patten, to discuss strategy. The economic news wasn't good, they knew that January, February and March would be difficult months. The Prime Minister favoured 9 April for the election. It would give them time to present the Budget. If they went to the country before the Budget, he knew they would be accused of bringing the election before the Budget because they were planning to do x, y and z. In fact Labour did attempt to say that the Tories were planning to put VAT up to 22 per cent. Better, he felt, to go after the Budget, but their fear was that, during that time, Labour might pull too far ahead in the opinion polls for them ever to recover. Whatever happened, they both knew they would be behind when they went to the country, and they also knew that they were holding the reins of a runaway horse, and if they were to stop the opinion polls running away entirely, they would effectively have to start the general election campaign immediately. The election, the Prime Minister says, was really won between January and the middle of March.

John and Norma had spent Christmas at Chequers – as they had the year before too. Norma's mother, Dee, had come up from Beckenham. She had surprised everyone by moving back to Kent nearly two years before, shortly after John became Chancellor. She had originally moved up to Huntingdon to see more of Norma and her grandchildren, but the situation had changed. There was no longer any babysitting to do, where she had been so invaluable in the past, the children were now largely independent and out with their friends; and she seldom saw Norma either. Norma had become increasingly busy, and was looking more and more exhausted. Friends suspect Dee was beginning to feel a bit redundant and a little out of place in Huntingdon. The final push was the offer of a job. The company she had worked for in Beckenham, as an accountant, before she ever moved to Huntingdon, wanted her back. She had a lot of friends in Beckenham – in Huntingdon she was just the MP's mother-in-law – and so she decided to go back.

Robert Atkins and his family were other guests over the Christmas holiday. Also friends from Huntingdon with their families – Olive Baddley, at whose recent wedding John had been best man, Peter Brown, John's agent, Emily Blatch, Jo Johnson. Most of his real friends come from Huntingdon, but real friends are few and far between, and not many penetrate his hard protective shell. Less initimate friends abound, many of them believing, or leading others to believe, they are closer than they really are.

Norma loves Chequers and has spent a lot of time there, particularly in the last couple of years, researching a book she has been writing about the history of the house. Her publishers had wanted her to write another biography after the Joan Sutherland book, but she had turned it down because she didn't think she could cope. She had even wondered about the wisdom of agreeing to this book on Chequers, because she had so little time, and with so many other demands on her, the pressure of a deadline for completion added one more worry to everything else. But she loves the house and it's been fascinating to write about. Her husband has never really shared her enthusiasm for Chequers. It is a magnificent house, with beautiful grounds, a heated swimming pool – in which James swam eighty lengths a day that Christmas – and there are staff to look after his every need. The staff, all service men and women, couldn't be friendlier, nor less intrusive, but John Major can't relax there. He is infinitely happier in his own home, where he and his family are entirely alone, where he is surrounded by his own books, his own records, where he can go and make a cup of coffee for himself, or potter in the garden, and unwind.

John Major is an enthusiastic and tireless host. About a year after he became Prime Minister he gave a party for the House of Commons secretaries at Number Ten. Every secretary was invited, no matter what the political persuasion of their MP. It was the first time they had ever been to a party at Number Ten, and for most of them, even those who had been working in the House for twenty years, the first time they had been inside the Prime Minister's house. Barbara Wallis had mentioned the idea in passing one day and John had immediately said, 'We'll have a party. Organize it.' It happened to fall on a day when he was particularly busy, and the civil servants had said he couldn't spend more than half an hour at the party. 'No, these are the people who do the work,' he said. 'I am going to concentrate on them for an hour.' The party was scheduled to finish at 7.30 p.m., but was still going strong at 8.50. John stayed two hours, and had to stay up half the night afterwards, making up for lost time. Typically, the moment he arrived, he noticed one of the girls was crippled and sitting on a sofa, and went straight over and sat down beside her, realizing she would be unable to circulate herself.

The secretaries had presented him with a gift, so he made a quick off-the-cuff speech, then told them to divide themselves into two groups and he would take them down to the Cabinet room. He said,

> Now, you all sit in round the table, and I'll tell you whose chairs you're sitting in. Then you can all go back and tell your MPs that they might never make it to the Cabinet table, but at least you've sat there.

They had a night to remember – he charmed the lot of them, and the next day one leading Socialist's secretary was heard to remark, 'Well, if we've got to have a Tory Prime Minister, thank God it's John Major.'

During the three-month lead up to the general election, the Prime Minister introduced some populist measures, which helped slow the runaway horses of the opinion polls. One was to reverse the freeze on Child Benefit that he had implemented as Chief Secretary, which many economists think was a mistake. It was a sop, they say, to the middle-class lobby.

John Major defends the decision on the grounds that the freezing of Child Benefit had been harsh. Back in 1987, John Moore, the Secretary of State, had agreed to freeze Child Benefit when the Government was seeking public expenditure savings. As Chief Secretary, John Major had accepted it. But Child Benefit had been introduced to replace the old child tax allowances, as a targeted cash benefit payable to mothers, and in freezing it, the Tories had, in practice, broken their word. In retrospect John Major freely admits that, had he known at the time how big a fiscal deficit the Government would incur – which at the time was unapparent – he would never have lifted the freeze.

There were other changes he introduced which pushed public spending up that critics say he should have avoided – enhanced pensions for the widows of World War Two soldiers, for example, and compensation for haemophiliacs who contracted the HIV virus from AIDS infected blood.

John Major denies that he spent badly. The one or two areas where he raised expenditure accounted for perhaps £1 billion, out of a projected deficit in 1993 of £50 billion. The rest is a result of the recession that he inherited and some very worrying longer-term trends in spending on benefits. The deficit rose, he says, because Government income fell away. With nobody buying houses there was no Stamp Duty, with fewer people employed there was less income tax, with reduced spending on consumer goods there was less VAT. At the same time expenditure was going up, with more people becoming unemployed, more money was being spent on benefits, and money was being injected into the construction industry to prevent still more unemployment. The deficit was the gap between what was coming in and what was going out.

John Major knew it would mean difficult decisions ahead, and unpopular cuts. The day after he won the election, Jeffrey Archer was saying what a wonderful result it had been over a drink at Number Ten. John had said,

> It's all right today, Jeffrey, but in six months' time I'll be the most unpopular man in Britain.

He had meant because of the difficult decisions that lay ahead. In the event he was right – dramatic problems conspired to fulfil his prediction in spades.

Jeffrey Archer is a complete one-off. The day John became Prime Minister he called Jeffrey.

'Good evening Prime Minister,' said Jeffrey.

'That isn't going to last more than two minutes, Jeffrey.'

'I beg your pardon, Sir?'

'J-O-H-N, try it.'

'Thank you, Sir.'

He hasn't called him John since. 'He doesn't like it,' says Jeffrey, 'and he gets quite cross with me, but he's leader of my country, end of story. How can he believe he's the boss if scruffs like me call him John?'

Jeffrey was to play a full part in the election campaign. Planning had started in early January when Chris Patten and John Major discussed possible dates. They sat in the flat at Number Ten in the early days of the year, and tentatively fixed on 9 April. They fully expected to be behind in the opinion polls when they began, but they expected to win. They were right on both counts, although the campaign they and others devised was roundly criticized by the press, and shortly abandoned.

The original idea was that John should tackle a theme a day – twenty Government departments, therefore twenty themes. On Transport day, for example, the Prime Minister would go off and visit an airport and a railway marshalling yard; but they soon realized that the election was not going to be won by talking about transport one day, overseas aid the next, and the environment the day after. It swiftly became apparent that this election was about one subject, and one alone – tax – and the difference between Labour and Conservative tax policies. Just a week before, Norman Lamont had taken the Labour Party by surprise by introducing a reduced rate band of 20 pence in the pound on the first £2,000 of taxable income in the Budget. John Smith's 'shadow Budget', by contrast, showed Labour to be the Party of high taxes.

However, there was a technical problem in changing the nature of the campaign. Having mapped out his twenty days' worth of departmental locations, the elaborate security measures that had been set in motion for the Prime Minister's visit to each one meant that it was practically impossible to change their plans. And Tim Collins, from Central Office, who handled the press during the campaign, had his work cut out trying to explain to journalists why taking them to a railway marshalling yard was a particularly apposite way of demonstrating the evils of Labour's plans to increase National Insurance.

The message was that Labour would impose the biggest increase in tax since the war. The spending programme proposed in their manifesto would cost an extra £31 billion – that is to say, on average every person would have to fork out an extra £1,250 every year to pay for it.

John Major told an audience in Sheffield on 23 March,

Labour invoke the great themes of fairness and justice, while denying their substance at every important point. What is fair about a society that denies those with ability the means to advance? What is just about a society that confiscates from the hard-working the fruits of their labours? Where is the fairness in undermining the value of the shares, the pensions or the houses which people bought to give their children a better start than they had themselves? Where is the justice in hitting those who do extra work or who earn promotion, with penal tax?

Speaking in Manchester on 19 March, he said,

> I know the Labour Party. I grew up with it. I know the envy – and, yes, the spite – that so often motivates it. I know the way it thinks. The determination to treat people as blocks and groups – as pensioners, trade unionists or council tenants – never as individuals.
>
> Labour's 'vision' for the 1990s is now clear. It goes as follows. If it is successful – tax it, penalize it, control it, nationalize it – and never offer hope or encouragement. Nothing shows more clearly that Labour don't trust the people – with their own money, with their own choices, with their own future.

John Major would not have gone into a terrible decline if he had lost the election on 9 April. He says,

> Losing power doesn't particularly worry me, it's in the nature of politics, you win some you lose some.

But he was not prepared to lose to a Labour Party which he thought was deeply unprepared for office, which was still living in the 1960s, and which he felt would have had no method of coping with the economic whirlwind which was undoubtedly coming around the world. That was why he wanted to win so badly in April 1992, and he knew that, to win, he had to hold the Conservative Party together.

But what won him the election was not tax, not bettering Labour; it was his personal style, which was in no way enhanced by the media for most of the campaign. John Major doesn't believe in media plots, but there is no doubt that television, and even the Tory press, were singularly unhelpful. It had been the same for months, a constant drip of bad news, with any good news that happened on the way, tucked away on an inside page, or run at the end of a news broadcast. Labour's story that the Government planned to privatize the Health Service found particular prominence, did grave damage to the Tories, and won Labour the Monmouth by-election. That, says John Major, was a straightforward political lie. There is no other way of putting it. It was a lie. But how do you counter a lie? One of the wisest things Harold Wilson said, he says, was that 'A lie can be halfway round the world before Truth gets its boots on.' John says,

> If you are in opposition, you can say something that may be wildly inaccurate. If it is wildly inaccurate and if it's picked up – if – it is a one-day wonder. If you're in Government and you say something that is partly inaccurate, then you're deceiving, you're misleading, you're politically corrupt and the story runs. So Governments, when faced with a straight political lie, often find it difficult to respond because it can be misinterpreted and twisted in some way or other that causes them great difficulty. The result is often a delay, by which time the speed and immediacy of publicity has fixed the misconception, the lie, in the people's minds. It's a great disadvantage for Governments, very great.

Even once they were into the election campaign, the newspapers that the Tories had traditionally looked to for support carried damaging stories, and for at least a week the election was eclipsed entirely from the front pages by the separation of the Duke and Duchess of York. They said the campaign was a shambles, so badly run, the Tories didn't deserve to win. And it was only in the closing stages that the newspapers gave the Tories any serious help.

By then John Major was well on the way to winning without them. His campaign managers had realized early on that his brilliance lay in meeting the people, and they entirely altered the nature of the campaign to get him doing just that. The team at Central Office used to say that if they could get John Major to meet fourteen million people they would be home and dry: every person he met, with very few exceptions, would be won over by him. And it suits him; he likes nothing more than old-fashioned campaigning, the sort he used to do in Brixton High Street, with hecklers shouting the odds from the crowd. What he likes is the feeling of talking one to one, even if it is one of a crowd. He had originally wanted to hold a series of open meetings where he would sit on a stool with the audience in a horseshoe around him and have the public fire questions at him. He was not allowed entirely open meetings – security wouldn't wear it. But because they thought it would look good on television, they decided to keep the concept, known as Ask John Major, but to do it with tamer audiences. He had used the format twice before the election campaign with stunning success, but the campaign was a different matter. Although he had no idea what the questions would be, no guarantee they wouldn't be hostile, and no certainty that he would have the necessary facts at his fingertips, the press smelt a fix, and panned them.

They also panned his decision halfway through the campaign to bring out a soapbox. It was not Prime Ministerial, they said – disgraceful. Neil Kinnock was more Prime Ministerial, as indeed he was. Neil Kinnock was positively Presidential in style, while John Major came across as a man of the people; and the difference between the two leaders was not lost on the public.

John Major toured the country in a converted coach, known as the 'Battle Bus'. It was a refurbished, updated version of the one Mrs Thatcher had used in the 1987 election – armour plated with about a dozen seats, and the rest given over to office machinery – telephones, fax machines, photocopiers and computers. An entire mobile command post, where speeches could be written, where he could change out of egg-spattered suits, relax, eat – mostly fish and chips – and cat-nap. Most of the way, regular coaches filled with journalists followed in convoy, although sometimes for security and other reasons they travelled a separate route.

Rather than drive the buses back to London every night, particularly when they were in the north of England or Scotland, he would often fly back and forth, using a British Aerospace 146, which they fondly christened Death Airways. According to one terrified passenger, 'the pilots seemed to think that the way to land an aircraft was to fly over the end of the runway and turn the engines off.' On one landing, captured for posterity by ITN, one wing-tip very nearly touched the ground, and landing in Gloucester one day they bounced down the runway.

One evening the Battle Bus arrived at the airport about half an hour ahead of the journalists. The Prime Minister said he felt like some fish and chips, so one of the party went in search of some, and when he returned they all sat in the bus, parked on the edge of the tarmac, and started to eat. It was dark but the lights were on. A little later they saw the reporters arrive, climb out of their bus and up the steps into the aeroplane; then the photographers, and all the while the fish-eating party were waiting to see who would be the first to spot this wonderful photo opportunity. Finally one head turned, then another and another, and they all came rushing over, pulling off lens caps as they came for a picture of the Prime Minister eating fish and chips out of a newspaper.

There were light moments, but there were some alarming moments too. The Battle of Bolton Square was the first. There were a couple of marginal seats in Bolton and the Prime Minister had been due to walk round the town square. Word of his plans was leaked to the Opposition, and when they arrived in the town they were met by a howling mob of Labour Party supporters and Socialist Workers. John was not going to let them alter his plans. Much to the discomfort of the security people and the local police, who endeavoured to keep a cordon around him, he and Norma set forth into the howling mob. It was a rough ride, with a lot of pushing and shoving, but they both remained remarkably cool. John did manage to shake a few hands, but most of the people who had come to see him were too far away to even catch a glimpse.

That was when he decided to use a soapbox, so that if meetings were disrupted again, at least he would be able to stand higher than the mob and say something to the people who had come to listen. He also, quite rightly, thought it might irritate the agitators. The first time he used it was in Luton one Saturday, where once again he found himself surrounded by Labour supporters and Socialist Workers. The scene turned quite ugly. People in the crowd were shouting 'Stab him! Stab him!' and a number of eggs were thrown, but Mr Major calmly stood up on his soapbox and started speaking over the shouting hordes.

Eggs were thrown all through the campaign. They were nasty moments but, as Tim Collins says,

moments when those people who were there with him really saw the strength of John Major. You saw someone bringing back traditional campaigning, moving aside from the artificial photo opportunity, not doing what Kinnock was doing – going from one well-organized photo opportunity to another, never meeting a genuine voter. He was going and talking to real people, even though he was the Prime Minister, with all the well known security threats against him, from the IRA, the PLO and the rest. He was prepared to get on a soapbox, pick up a microphone and talk to people without giving it a second thought.

John Major talked to his supporters, and much to their amusement, often made references to the agitators too. Like the occasion in Cheltenham, where it was pouring with rain, but at least seven thousand people had turned out to listen to him in the market square, including a number of Liberals, who heckled him. 'Oh, there's a Liberal,' he said to the crowd. 'What a great pleasure to see a Liberal still around. I thought they were all extinct.'

After the criticism he had had for the sessions in the round, that it was stage managed, too organized, too artificial, the media were beginning to say he was vibrant, real, bringing back traditional campaigning. He looked like someone who was prepared to fight for the job, who wasn't taking anything for granted. 'He was an ordinary bloke,' says Tim, 'talking ordinary language, not being pompous about anything, and he displayed real courage – because of course from the security point of view, the eggs that hit him could have been something else.'

Eggs were bad enough. At Southampton, visiting a new shopping centre, one hit him in the face, on the cheekbone, and drew blood. It was also extremely sore. The rest of the team told him eggs were good politically – he would get a lot of mileage out of an egg, but he never quite shared their enthusiasm. But although he was always the target, he was not always the recipient. Edward Llewellyn from the Conservative Research Department, was hit by so many eggs that John dubbed him Eggward.

Both were wryly amused some weeks after the election when the man who had thrown the egg in Southampton was charged with a minor public order offence, fined, and ordered to pay the Prime Minister £10 towards his cleaning costs. 'If they think you can get a suit cleaned with that much damage for £10 they must be joking,' said the two in unison. Every egg meant several visits to several different dry cleaners, and the suit was out of service for at least a week. The Prime Minister was becoming quite worried that he was going to run out of suits.

He had gone into the election campaign down in the opinion polls, as he had expected, but nevertheless confident of victory. Everyone was forecasting defeat. Every Government since the war which had gone into an election behind in the polls, had come out behind. The other accepted wisdom was that the governing party always did slightly worse in the general election than the first opinon poll of the campaign indicated. Facts like this cast a shadow over the campaign for most of the people involved in it, but John Major himself was supremely confident from the start. He went into it believing he would win, and according to those who were with him every day, he didn't waver once. Routinely they would find that when they went about the country, talking to the local candidates or area agents, talking to people in the streets, they would find time and again that what they were hearing from the grass roots was quite different from what the opinion polls were indicating. The opinion poll results would come through mid-afternoon, and John's reaction was always, 'Oh, God, we're still behind. That's going to upset the morale of the troops.' He was afraid that the ordinary constituency workers, out canvassing in filthy weather for the most part, might get disheartened.

John Major didn't even waver when the matter of 'Jennifer's Ear' blew up. The Labour Party found themselves with a gift from the gods, a little girl whose sad story of medical neglect proved everything they had been saying about the Government's running down of the NHS. Jennifer had 'glue ear', a condition suffered by hundreds of children, which requires a simple operation to fix. Jennifer had been kept waiting for nearly a year because of hospital cuts, and this pretty little girl was a picture of misery. The Labour Party used her in a Party Political Broadcast, without giving her surname, but the next day she was all over the front page of every newspaper and causing intense embarrassment to the Government. It turned out, however, that the story was less than the whole truth, and the pretty little girl's father was a Labour Party activist. Her furious mother, on the other hand, was a Tory, who had been unaware that their daughter was being used in this way. It no doubt led to many a happy family discussion.

John Major was in Scotland the night the Jennifer's Ear broadcast was shown, and didn't see it because Labour showed a film about devolution in Scotland instead. 'Quite frankly,' says Tim Collins, 'the Prime Minister's primary concern the next day was nothing to do with Jennifer's Ear, it was to do with the cricket World Cup – England against Pakistan – and I had the singular honour – or lack of it – of telling him we had lost.'

However, that night, speaking in Edinburgh, John Major said,

They [the Labour Party] have no regard for the truth. No

regard for the feelings and emotions of the families they use. Nothing but concern for their own self-seeking propaganda. None of that simple decency which the British people expect. I tell you this. This attitude tells you more about the people who lead the Labour Party than it does about the Health Service.

He knew a lot of the players in the Test and had thought long and hard about sending them a message of support. At any other time he would have had no hesitation, but he decided against.

People will only say it's a political gesture, and because we're in the middle of a general election campaign that I'm trying to exploit the England cricket team for the Conservative Party. I wouldn't want any of the cricketers to think that that was what I was doing.

He has always been scrupulous in keeping sport and politics apart. Tim Bell once received a cheque from a client for £100,000 which they had raised for a charity, and which they wanted to present to John and Graham Gooch at the Test match. John said,

No, I won't do it. Not because I don't want the cheque or don't like your client, but I have always promised the cricketers and footballers that I will never ever let them get involved in politics.

When he goes to a match he is a cricket fan or a football fan, never a Prime Minister. He gets quite anxious none the less, if they lose, that people will think of him as an albatross. 'I wouldn't have dared come again if they hadn't got that goal,' he said to David Mellor when Chelsea had been one nil down until the eighty-ninth minute on Boxing Day. The previous season he had seen them lose three matches in succession and was beginning to take it personally. And when sportsmen come to Downing Street, or to Chequers, as they do quite frequently to receptions and lunches, they never talk politics. During the election, stories started to appear saying that Ian Botham and others were going to vote Tory. John Major was furious. He would never ask for their help, and reject it if it were offered.

One of the policies which played a significant part in his election success was Scotland and the question of the Union. The other parties were moving towards an eventual break up of the United Kingdom. The Prime Minister felt strongly that national-ism would cripple Scotland and weaken the remaining Union, and felt strongly that he would have support in Scotland if he championed the Union. His advisers were against the idea, but he was adamant, and backed his judgement against 90 per cent of the advice that was coming in. He had made an important speech on the subject in Scotland earlier in March, and came back to it at every available opportunity during the campaign. It was largely ignored by the media, until the last few days before the election. Speaking in Edinburgh he said,

> I want to see our Kingdom stay a United Kingdom ... together, across nearly three centuries of our history, the peoples of these islands have shaped the destiny of the world.
>
> No one asked in those years whether the statesmen, the administrators, the men and women of industry and the arts, the writers and the law-givers who came from these shores were Scottish, English, Irish or Welsh. It was enough that they came from this United Kingdom. It was enough that they carried our language, our law, our principles, our civiliza-tion. Together our nations have been far, far greater than the sum of their parts. Separate, we could never have changed the face of half the world.
>
> Labour policy would weaken us all. It would mean a Disunited Kingdom in a United States of Europe. And this Party will have none of it.

Norma was with her husband throughout the campaign, but couldn't share his confidence. 'I'd never say to John, "What if we might lose?"' she confided to Jo Johnson, '"because he's so sure, and so determined that we won't, but what would we do for a job?"

'I said, "Norma, John is made for life now, whatever happens."'

Norma says,

> I did worry about John losing this job, for all kinds of personal reasons, never mind the good of the nation. I'd have been devastated if he had lost because of what it might have done to him. In spite of what he said, and the reassurances, it would have been ghastly. Having got beyond that, I've stopped fretting about how permanent this is now. For eighteen

months from the time he got the job to the election, it did seem terribly uncertain, unsettled, it was hanging over us, you didn't feel you could think about tomorrow or next month or whatever. Now I've stopped worrying. I now say 'We're going to spend next Christmas at Chequers', instead of saying, 'If we've still got it'.

Although John Major was entirely confident about how he would do nationally – which he says was pure instinct – he was less certain about his own constituency. He was anxious that he was not going to be able to spend much time in Huntingdon, for the first general election ever. The first Ask John Major session had been in Huntingdon and had been a wash-out because he knows the issues so well in Huntingdon, and has such a good rapport with the people there that there was no bite to the evening, no edge to the questions and no opportunity for him to display any quick sharp responses that he had done so well in the rehearsals. As Tim Collins says,

As far as he's concerned that constituency is his home, those people are his local people, he knows them instinctively, that association is composed of his friends, and he cares about it. We always say the Westminster system's greatest virtue is that it does require even the grandest minister to have a link with his constituency and have a foot on the ground. That is his, but he attaches huge value to it – sentimental and historical value – and if everything else fell apart or went away he always knows he could go back there and be among friends. It is a great strength in any MP, particularly so in a Prime Minister.

Throughout the campaign he was asking Mike Harford, Constituency Chairman, how many votes he thought he would get, whether he thought he could increase his majority. Mike promised him a majority of 30,000 and even put it in writing. His previous majority had been 27,500.

Election day was very tense for everyone except John Major. He spent the day out in the constituency with Peter Brown. Norma went with Mike Harford and they met for lunch at the Finings. Norma was worried, so was everyone else. The opinion polls were still showing a Labour lead yet 'John was happy and confident,' says

Mike, 'laid back, full of jokes. I couldn't understand how on probably the most important day of his life he was in that mood. He said, "I'm going to win, I'm confident."'

As the results began to come through, John and Norma were at home at the Finings with friends. Sarah Hogg was there with notes on what to do if the Tories lost and the Prime Minister had to leave Number Ten. They weren't needed. When the Basildon result came through, John got up.

'That's it,' he said, 'we've won. We've done the buggers.' He meant the pollsters, not the Labour Party.

The count took place in the St Ivo Centre sports hall. The exit polls predicted a hung Parliament, but by the time John Major arrived, by which time the results were in from Basildon and some of the Scottish constituencies, the pollsters were predicting a Conservative majority of six. He arrived with Norma, Elizabeth, James and Dee, knowing by that time that he was assured some kind of victory – there was a bet on, Peter thought they would have a majority of eighteen. When later in the evening his own result came through he was, in the words of Mike Harford, 'gobsmacked'. He had a majority of 36,000, one of the largest majorities in parliamentary history.

The relief was incredible, but he was still under a lot of pressure, he was tired and there was still a lot to do.

He had to go to London, to Central Office, and as he left the St Ivo Centre he suddenly realized he had forgotten to thank Norma, from the platform at the count, for her support. Neil Kinnock had thanked Glenys, Paddy Ashdown had thanked his wife, all seen on television. 'Oh, my God,' said John to Peter Brown, almost in tears. 'I've forgotten to thank Norma.' In the few minutes before he climbed into the car, Peter did his best to sort him out. There would be another speech at Central Office, and a chance then to thank Norma. John had thought of that, but was still mortified to have forgotten at the count.

Norma had made the supreme sacrifice during the election campaign. She had made a speech. She and Tessa Sanderson, the Olympic athlete, had opened the new Huntingdon Sports Centre. Peter Brown says,

Only I know the trauma she went through before she did it, and I would never wish to put her through that trauma again unless it was absolutely necessary. No one would have known.

You see her as a very competent, polished person, which she is, but she did have a great deal of trouble in bringing herself to get to that point. She can be physically sick, she can be very ill. It's not worth it from her point of view, and I don't believe it's necessary any more.

When the polls closed on the 1992 election the Conservatives had a majority of twenty-one. John Major had achieved one of the most astonishing political victories of this century. His election triumph was at least as great, and arguably more so, than any of Margaret Thatcher's. He won against a less divided opposition, with more votes than ever before, in economic circumstances as difficult as they have been for any incumbent Government.

The constitutional historian Vernon Bogdanor, in *The Conservative Party 1900–1990*, wrote that the task of a leader of the Conservative Party is fourfold.

First, he must display competence and efficiency at his task; second, he must be perceived as an electoral asset, and have a reasonable prospect of carrying the country in a general election; third, he must retain the allegiance of Conservative backbenchers; and fourth, he must retain the support of the party in the country. Above all, a Conservative leader must not split the party.

The avoidance of a formal split is an over-riding consideration in the Conservative Party. It has been split only once – by Sir Robert Peel, following the repeal of the Corn Laws in 1846, and, following the split, it did not form another majority government again for 28 years, by far the longest period that the Conservatives have ever been in opposition in modern times. The example of Peel, therefore, is one to be avoided at all costs. It is for this reason that it could be said that the founder of the modern Conservative Party is not, as Norman Gash would have it Sir Robert Peel, but rather the ghost of Peel.

John Major is nothing if not an assiduous student of history.

14

BLACK WEDNESDAY

B Y any standards John Major pulled off an extraordinary feat at the General Election. Fourteen and a half million people had voted Conservative – more than any party had ever polled in any election ever. He was the toast of the Party, he had done what no one thought he could do, what all the opinion polls had shown was impossible. The benches were full of MPs who were beholden to him for their seats, and beholden to him personally. He keeps a small statue of a cricketer in the flat at Number Ten, given to him by Terry Dicks, who won his seat by a majority of fifty-seven, and knew just whom he had to thank for it. There was confidence in the Party and a new-found optimism in the country. John Major had promised that recovery was set to begin – 'vote for me on Thursday and recovery will start on Friday' – he had promised sweeping reforms in education, in the Health Service, in Law and Order, he had promised the Citizen's Charter to improve service in the public sector, he had promised low taxes and renewed prosperity, and people believed in him. He had said,

> I want a Britain, where there is a helping hand for those who need it; where people can get a hand up, not just a hand out. A country that is fair and free from prejudice – a classless society, at ease with itself.

This was not electioneering rhetoric, it was what he did want, and what he had come into politics to try and achieve. If you get locked out of things, he says, because you don't fit, you're apt to want to change them. He wanted to change them, he disliked doors being closed to him.

But the kind of classless society he wants for Britain has been grossly misunderstood. As with so many of his policies and ideals, personal experience is at the root of it – experience of the sort of attitudes that pervade society on the wrong side of the tracks. He loathes prejudice and snobbery, can't bear to see people treat waiters as though they are not there, bus conductors as though they don't matter, cleaning ladies as though they don't have feelings. He detests the artificial distinctions between blue and white collar workers.

What he wants is to remove the barriers that prevent people who start from a poor beginning from going wherever they want to go. He wants a society where people are just as happy for their sons and daughters to go into industry and commerce when they leave university as they are for them to go into the City. Where people can go as far as their talent, their ambition and their effort can take them. Where people no longer regard the plumber as 'the little man who comes round to fix the leak'. It is not – emphatically not, he says – an attempt to break down the vivid tapestry of distinctions that exist in Britain. It's not an attempt to axe the honours system. It's not an attempt to seek a greyer quality for everybody. Far from it. It is an attempt to make sure that a Permanent Secretary can start at somewhere like Stoneygate Secondary School and still get to the top. He despises the attitude that still prevails in many quarters, that someone who went to a good school is intrinsically more able than someone who didn't.

He has met this himself time and again, but more in the last three years than at any time in his life – largely at the hands of the high Tory press. He can no longer remember who it was, which of what he calls his highly educated friends, Chris Patten he thinks, who spoke such prophetic words after the election:

> They'll never forgive you for not going to university, or for not going to the right school, or for winning the election when they said you were going to lose.

Sure enough it was not long after the election when things began to turn sour. The recovery that he had promised didn't start – at least not so that anyone noticed. A year on the statistics showed that growth in the economy had actually begun again in June, albeit gradually, but as far as the public were concerned, nothing had changed, the despondency and uncertainty continued, jobs and houses continued to be lost, crime continued to make the streets unsafe, young offenders continued to put two fingers up to the law, beggars continued to roam the cities, the homeless continued to bed down under cardboard in the doorways. Meanwhile the Prime Minister, who had sounded so concerned and committed to improving life in Britain, who appeared to be so in tune with the way ordinary people thought and felt, whom they had believed and trusted, vanished into Europe. As one domestic incident followed another, John Major was nowhere to be seen, apparently more interested in Brussels than the worsening situation at home.

What had happened was that in July, three months after the election, John Major took over the European Presidency, which is a six-month term of office that rotates between the twelve member countries. It was Britain's turn and he was stuck with it, but it was, he says, a poisoned chalice, which he could well have done without during those particular six months. Even without the presidency, Europe now takes up a sizeable part of the week, for those six months it took up even more, and it inevitably did take his attention away from domestic matters. But as he points out, like it or not, European policy is domestic policy, Britain is a part of Europe – that was established more than twenty years ago – therefore what happens in Europe is material to people losing their jobs and having their houses repossessed. He appreciates that it looks like foreign policy to the man in the street, but it is not. What do people complain about? he asks. European directives and interest rates. The way to make both work for Britain is to go in there and make sure that when policies are made, they are right for Britain, and have Britain's interests at heart.

John Major knew he had trouble ahead. He knew that the first nine months after the election would be difficult, although the difficulties that did beset him were not quite the ones he had foreseen. He knew it would be painful coming out of recession, and that it must be slow. If we came out too sharply it would recreate the very circumstances that had thrown Britain into recession in the first place. He knew that there would be problems abroad, that the rest of Europe, a large part of the British market, would go into recession – what surprised him was that it took so long to take grip elsewhere. He also knew that the problems over Russia, Yugoslavia and Iraq would intensify. In every respect it would be a critical period. The one difficulty he foresaw, which in the event proved surprisingly trouble-free, was the introduction of the new Council

Tax. But of all the problems ahead, he knew that Europe would be the biggest, because there he had an internal problem – and a very small majority.

It was essential he choose his Cabinet carefully. He had his own mandate to govern now, he had time on his side, it was the start of a new Parliament, he had five years to do the work that had to be done; but Maastricht loomed large and he knew that, no sooner had the polls closed on 9 April, than the Party would split apart again over Europe. If he was to get the Treaty through the Commons, his choice of Cabinet was crucial. He needed to bring in each faction of the Party, as he had done in his first Cabinet, while easing out some of those he was less enamoured of and prepare himself for a prolonged and difficult time ahead.

One of the great sadnesses of the election was that Chris Patten had lost his seat in Bath. On the night of the election the Prime Minister brought him into Number Ten and made it abundantly clear to all the staff that Chris had been the architect of his victory, as he did again at Central Office, and found the largest bottle of champagne that had been sent and gave it to Chris. Cynics saw his appointment as Governor of Hong Kong as a clever way of ensuring that the ambitious Mr Patten would be well out of harm's way until the handover to the Chinese in 1997. Others said it was inspired to put a heavyweight politician like Chris Patten up against the Chinese instead of the usual diplomats.

John Major brought Kenneth Clarke into the Home Office in place of Kenneth Baker, who was offered an alternative job, but chose to leave for the back benches and the pursuit of poetry. Peter Brooke took much the same route, but such was the skill of his removal, that when John asked him to return as Heritage Secretary following David Mellor's sudden departure six months later, he returned with alacrity. Michael Heseltine was given Trade and Industry, which he had hankered after for years, and William Waldegrave was put in charge of the Citizen's Charter and the Department of Science. He kept the two Thatcherites, Peter Lilley and Michael Howard in the Cabinet, putting them in charge of Social Services and the Environment respectively, and brought in another of Mrs Thatcher's staunchest supporters, Michael Portillo, a former special adviser at the Treasury, as Chief Secretary. He also brought in two women, Gillian Shephard at Employment and Virginia Bottomley at the Department of Health. He thought carefully about the lower level of appointments too, to be sure that all the factions were satisfied, bringing in people like Jonathan Aitken who had spent years in the wilderness, and Nicholas Soames, who represented the artistocratic wing of the Party.

Alan Clark says that guile is a prerequisite for any Prime Minister, and John's choice of Cabinet was full of it:

> The principal concern of every Prime Minister the moment he walks into Number Ten and is greeted by the staff, is to defend the succession, because he's there at the top, and everybody is out to get him and take his job. So the first thing you must do is isolate your closest threats, and the two who are most likely to threaten Major are Heseltine and Clarke. He gave Heseltine the DTI, which was very clever because Heseltine has been spouting hot air for years about how the DTI ought to be the powerhouse for British industry, but of course powerhouse means spewing out money. You can't do it by spewing out hot air which is his speciality. Clarke he gave the Home Office to. All fine and everyone says what a wonderful man you are, but the fact is no leader of the Tory Party has ever come from the Home Office because the sheer weight of the department, and the direction it is inexorably taken in by officials and traditions, makes you unacceptable to a large mass of your parliamentary and constituency party. The Home Secretary is suspect. He quarrels with the police, he's involved in scandals, he always ends up not putting down a prison riot and letting someone out who's strangled a lot of children. It all piles up and of course Clarke is a wet, a liberal. So that was quick of Major, ingenious. That's his Whips' office training.

However, all the guile known to man could not have warded off the disasters that awaited the Government in the coming months, and Kenneth Clarke turned out to be the only member of the Cabinet prepared to put his head above the parapet in John Major's defence. Kenneth Clarke, he believes, is as loyal as any member of the Cabinet, despite the speculation after his remarks that the Government was in a 'black hole', that he was after the top job. He's an original, says the Prime Minister, a lawyer, so he's paid by the yard for words, and doesn't always have the sensory device that tells him when there's trouble coming. He's so buoyant, slings and arrows bounce off him. But if he had to go into a jungle with anyone, he would go into it with Ken Clarke and have no worries.

The first disaster and the most cataclysmic struck on 16 September, the day Britain was forced out of the Exchange Rate Mechanism and the Government's entire economic policy was turned on its head. It didn't come entirely out of the blue, there had been some strains on the mechanism in early part of summer, but when it blew apart, it did so with astonishing speed. The real problem was high interest rates in Germany, which had been causing great problems, not just in Britain, but in a number of countries within the ERM. Germany wouldn't reduce her interest rates, and the Bundesbank went so far as to say that its prime duty was to ensure German inflation was contained and it was not responsible for what happened elsewhere. This remark threw the markets, already in turmoil due to the approach of the French referendum on Maastricht on 20 September, and pressure immediately increased on sterling. The pressure was manageable, but John Major and the Chancellor, Norman Lamont, did have several discussions at that stage about what they would do if the pressure on sterling became impossible. Other countries in the same situation were putting up interest rates, including the Italians. They concluded Britain would probably have to do the same.

The weekend before Black Wednesday John and Norma were going to Balmoral as guests of the Queen – who had been particularly pleased by Mr Major's championing of the Union during the election. It cemented an already warm relationship. On the way up, they spent the Friday in Glasgow, where the Prime Minister made a speech to the Scottish CBI, in which he promised 'There will be no devaluation, no realignment.'

He said he had been under no illusions when he took Britain into the ERM that it was a soft option. The soft option, the devaluer's option, the inflationary option, 'would be a betrayal of our future at this moment,' he said, 'and I tell you categorically that is not the Government's policy.'

Five days later, he had been forced to eat his words. He had agonized over these paragraphs because he knew the strains on sterling. Sarah Hogg advised him to tone them down. 'Be softer,' she said, 'less definite.' He declined.

'If I equivocate the market will smell it,' he said.

So he was definite – and the words came back to haunt him.

The Majors went on to Balmoral. Alex Allan, who had taken over from Andrew Turnbull shortly after the election as John's Principal Private Secretary, was also with them, and while they stayed in the castle with a number of other guests, Alex stayed with Sir Robert Fellowes, the Queen's Private Secretary, in a house in the grounds. It was a very relaxed weekend. As Norma later said to Judith Chaplin, 'It couldn't have been easier. Prince Philip cooks the barbecue, the Queen lays the table and does the washing up and everyone else mucks in.' One of the greatest pleasures was being able to walk in the grounds at Balmoral, in open countryside, without protection officers two paces behind. It was a rare treat to have such privacy.

Shortly before the party left for church on the Sunday morning, John Major had a telephone call from Giuliano Amato, the Italian Prime Minister. He was going to devalue, what would Britain do? The Prime Minister made it clear Britain would be sticking to her parity, which meant the Italians would be on their own. Amato sounded slightly wistful, but there was no particular pressure, and no approach from any other country.

They left Balmoral on the Monday and drove to Glamis Castle for lunch with Lord Strathmore, the Deputy Chief Whip in the House of Lords, then flew back to London. By the time they reached Downing Street that evening the pound had risen slightly and the pressure had come off – the situation seemed to have improved, but the Prime Minister had so much work to do that he decided to drop his plans to visit Expo in Seville later in the week.

The next day the pound suddenly came under quite a lot of pressure on the foreign exchange markets. In other respects it was a normal sort of day. There was a Cabinet committee meeting about Hong Kong, lunch with the Country Landowners Association, King Hussein came in, and he had a meeting with the European TUC, but all the while pressure on the pound continued. That evening he and the Chancellor agreed, on a contingency basis, that if the pressure did not let up, then interest rates would have to go up the next morning.

At the time John Major was based at Admiralty House, which he didn't enjoy, while work was being done at Number Ten to replace the windows with bomb-proof glass. He had temporarily taken over Malcolm Rifkind, the Defence Secretary's, flat there – 'far grander than Downing Street' he didn't hesitate to point out – and a lot of the meetings that took place over the next couple of days happened there. His staff were still at Number Ten but everybody was displaced from their rooms; all the state rooms were covered over, including the Cabinet room, the furnishings had been removed, the floorboards covered over, the chandeliers, curtains and pictures had all been taken down and everything was rather strange and out of the ordinary, and people had to keep trekking back and forwards to Admiralty House.

Great problems blew up overnight on the Tuesday. Helmut Schlesinger, President of the Bundesbank, had made some comments in an interview to the effect that realignment of the European Monetary System was inevitable. He denied this was the authorized version, but the implication was clear: he thought the pound should be devalued, and that the Germans would not help sterling. The governor of the Bank of England, Robin Leigh-Pemberton, spoke to Schlesinger several times, to get him to set the record straight, which he did eventually, but by then the damage had been done. By Wednesday morning it became clear that British interest rates would have to go up.

As it happened, on Wednesday morning John Major had a meeting with Douglas Hurd, Michael Heseltine, and Kenneth Clarke to discuss the French referendum on Maastricht being held the following Sunday, and plan what to do in the event of a yes or a no vote. Norman Lamont should also have been present, but he was delayed with the Governor of the Bank of England back in the Treasury, and arrived late, with the recommendation that interest rates should go up by 2 per cent. The Bank of England had started pouring billions of pounds into the market very early that morning to try and shore up the pound, but it was too late, the speculators had scented blood and the value was falling fast. Everyone present agreed that there was no alternative but to put up interest rates, and it was duly announced at 11 o'clock.

Everyone waited to see if this action would stem the tide. Meanwhile John went ahead with other meetings at Admiralty House. He met David Howell, and three back-bench MPs, John Watts, Stephen Milligan and Geoffrey Johnson Smith, also came in to see him. There was a great deal of toing and froing throughout, with people passing him messages – the pound was still under pressure; the interest rate rise hadn't been well taken, hadn't stopped the pressure, the pound was still right at the bottom of the ERM band. He took these messages during his meetings with back benchers.

He has been criticized for calmly chatting to back benchers while the Government's entire economic policy was in the process of collapsing, but throughout it all he was in minute to minute contact with events, and while this remained so, saw no reason to cancel other meetings and possibly create unnecessary panic. It also gave him the opportunity to consult senior back benchers and explain to them what was going on so that the message could be transmitted to the rest of the Party that it was necessary to put interest rates up.

During the course of the morning, however, it became clear that the medicine wasn't working. Business and industry had been aghast at the rise in interest rates, which could only make the recession worse, and speculation against the pound had increased sharply. The Chancellor and the Governor returned for further meetings with the Prime Minister. It was clear to all three of them that one of the options was going to be to suspend Britain's membership of the ERM. Douglas Hurd, Ken Clarke and Michael Heseltine, also Richard Ryder, the Chief Whip, joined these meetings, so did Eddie George, Deputy Governor, and senior Treasury officials, including Terry Burns. They arrived at about 12.30 and went through the options, and the general feeling was that, having put up interest rates 2 per cent, it would be wrong after waiting just two hours to say 'Oh, well, that's it, goodbye,' and temporarily leave the ERM. They all felt strongly that they should do all that was possible to stay within the ERM, and decided to try putting interest rates up further to see if that had any effect. They agreed to announce an increase to 15 per cent the next day. In the meantime John said he would speak to Chancellor Kohl and to Pierre Bérégovoy, the French Prime Minister.

The ministerial meeting broke up, the Prime Minister went off to the flat, spoke to the various members of his staff who were around – people like Sarah Hogg, Alex Allan, Stephen Wall, Gus O'Donnell – then telephoned Kohl and Beregovoy and spoke to them both at some length. He wasn't asking them to do anything very explicit, it was more a case of keeping them in touch, warning them, and asking if they had any views or advice because it did look as if Britain would have to suspend her membership and this would cause big problems in the ERM. Kohl was supportive in principle, but said the German Government didn't control the Bundesbank. He was rather surprised, however, to hear the effect that Schlesinger's remarks had had, because they obviously hadn't made much news in Germany.

The Prime Minister then thought he had better have a word with Marcus Fox, Chairman of the 1922 Committee, who came over at about 3.00 p.m. Meantime it was becoming apparent that the position was untenable. So the senior ministers were summoned back, but the meeting couldn't start until Norman Lamont arrived, and he was clearly still deep in discussion with Robin Leigh-Pemberton in the Treasury. The Prime Minister came down to chat to them where they were all sitting waiting in a room downstairs, but had to keep going back up again to make phone calls, and Alex Allan remembers being acutely aware that they were keeping the Home Secretary, the Foreign Secretary and the President of the Board of Trade all hanging around doing nothing – a quite bizarre situation. He went down to apologize and suggested calling them back when he had the meeting set up, but they wouldn't hear of it.

Eventually the Chancellor and the Governor arrived and it was obvious there was no alternative: Britain would have to suspend membership of the ERM. The full meeting was assembled and they agreed that nothing else could be done. But there was a further worry. They didn't want to suspend Britain's membership and put up interest rates – to have had both would have been very, very damaging to confidence. So they decided immediately to cancel the increase to 15 per cent that was to have taken effect the following day. A day or so later it was agreed that the increase from 10 to 12 per cent should be rescinded too. A week later, interest rates were reduced still more, to 9 per cent.

After that final meeting, as Black Wednesday drew to a close, Norman Lamont went out into King Charles Street to announce to the waiting cameras that he had suspended Britain's membership of the ERM. Britain would rejoin 'as soon as circumstances allow.' Sterling had effectively devalued by 10 per cent. It was 7.40 p.m. Since 9 o'clock that morning, according to some newspaper reports, £10 billion pounds had been spent in the effort to save sterling, and speculators and currency dealers had had the most frenetic, exciting and profitable day ever. It later transpired that one individual speculator, George Soros, had made nearly £1 billion in forty-eight hours.

As the day wound down there were still phone calls being made. Stephen Wall, John Major's Foreign Affairs secretary, spoke to Kohl and Beregovoy's staff to explain what was going on. A Cabinet meeting had to be set up for the next day – which lasted three hours and was held in a rather cramped room in the bowels of the Cabinet Office – and arrangements made for Parliament to be recalled early, so there could be an emergency debate the following week.

The Prime Minister made various phone calls to people he felt ought to know. And at the end of it all he was handed a large box filled with all the other issues that had been stacking up during the day and settled down to work. The next day his diary and the routine of his day was back to normal, but his reputation and that of his Chancellor was in serious question.

There were calls for Lamont's resignation. After the reshuffle at the end of May 1993, in his resignation speech Mr Lamont said that he had not resigned because 'that was not what the Prime Minister wanted'.

That was certainly true. John Major felt he had carried out Government policy loyally and effectively and the events of 16 September had been market-driven. No Chancellor could have prevented what happened that day. Sterling had been unsettled in the markets for some weeks. This was partly due to domestic circumstances and partly the impact of external events. Among the latter was the Danish referendum on Maastricht which was narrowly lost. Then there was the French referendum which was narrowly won, although fears of the result in the days before voting caused great market disturbances. And there were also the problems created by reports that the Bundesbank was not confident about the future exchange rate of sterling. All these events added to the difficulties on the Exchange Markets.

There was a lot of bad luck in all this. The Danish referendum was a constitutional necessity, but there had been no reason for the French to hold one and the reports from Germany about sterling – allegedly whisperings from the Bundesbank – caused great difficulty. Against this background, John Major obviously felt that it would be unfair to replace the Chancellor, and publicly and privately, he gave Norman Lamont his full backing.

Privately both Major and Lamont were furious about the Bundesbank's behaviour – incandescent with rage – as Schlesinger knew perfectly well. Kohl also knew. For months and months and months before Black Wednesday Norman Lamont and John Major had been telephoning to press the Germans over monetary policy. They felt the Germans should have reduced their interest rates or realigned upwards – but the French opposed the latter course. German interest rates may have been right for their domestic purposes but they were not right as the benchmark of the ERM.

Not surprisingly the Germans weren't keen to take any of the blame for the catastrophe of Black Wednesday, and immediately issued statements saying that criticism was 'not appropriate', it was 'unfair' and 'Everyone would be better advised to analyse what should be done in their own homes to improve the situation.' The Bundesbank said, 'Those pointing the finger would do better to clean their own doorsteps first.'

The Prime Minister was not short of criticism on his own doorstep. He was criticized for almost every aspect of Black Wednesday, and there is no escaping the fact that it was a disaster, but he did not come close to nervous collapse, as journalists later said; he did not 'suffer a nervous setback of some sort' or 'wobble in a nervous sense'. He was perfectly calm throughout the crisis, as the people who were with him all testify. Sarah Hogg is one:

> All that nonsense that is talked about Black Wednesday. I was there the whole way through, and I have never seen anyone in such seriously difficult circumstances and a very, very fast-moving situation, so calm, so in control, so organized with his colleagues. He was very, very impressive, very cool, he is someone who gets cooler under heated circumstances. He has a quiet personality anyway. He doesn't shout and yell and bang the table, or make a tremendous performance about being in control and taking decisions.

As he himself says of that day, of course he recognized the implications of dropping out of the ERM and it wasn't welcome, but you have to be dispassionate about politics. If you sit there and think 'God, this is the worst thing that's ever happened to me', you've got the wrong focus. The focus should be 'What does it mean? What is the impact of this event likely to be? How can we maximize the good things in this and minimize the bad? How can we use this in the interests of the United Kingdom?' If you think 'Oh, God, this is frightful', you might as well give up and go away because you're in the wrong job. That was his attitude on Black Wednesday, and it is his attitude today.

Black Wednesday was a colossal failure of Government policy, but worse still, it provided a focus for all those members of the Party who had lined up behind Lady Thatcher against Europe. She had been an irritation from early on. At her farewell party she had said she was a 'good backseat driver', and although she was not supposed to have been referring to John Major's driving, she certainly lost no time in complaining about his navigation. She let it be known that she was disappointed in her successor, and that he didn't appear to believe in anything; and all those people who had voted for him thinking he was Mrs Thatcher's clone, and would carry on exactly where she left off, felt as betrayed and bitter as she did.

John Major never retaliated. He might have been better advised to have done so, but it went against the grain. Out of loyalty and good manners he said nothing, but apart from a rogue call from Lady Thatcher in the middle of June 1993 to support him, the attack was almost incessant. If she had thought she was going to have carried on running the Government through him, she had made a bad mistake. In the long run her antics may have done more harm to her than him, but in the short term they were intensely damaging.

Black Wednesday was a gift for her and she lost no time in exploiting the Government's misfortune. While Norman Lamont was talking to European finance ministers at a G7 meeting in Washington that Friday about restructuring the ERM to guarantee better support for currencies under pressure, Lady Thatcher was busy in the same city telling another economics conference that she congratulated John Major and Norman Lamont 'for taking off this economic straitjacket.'

Immediately the old sores over Europe and Maastricht opened up, all the old fears about monetary union, and all the old opponents of the ERM, like Sir Alan Walters, burst into print to say, 'I told you so'.

John Major was publicly and privately unrepentant about joining the ERM. He says,

People forget the circumstances of the time. Day after day the speculators were circling, day after day the markets, business, commerce and the politicians were all urging entry. The Exchange Markets work on confidence. There was none. Britain was the nation that wouldn't go in. People have forgotten these pressures. They've also forgotten the inflationary pressure we needed to damp down. Whatever people may say about the ERM, it helped bring inflation down more rapidly than at any time in the last half a century, to its lowest rate for thirty years.

Another charge is that Britain went in at the wrong rate, that DM 2.95 was too high. There was certainly not much talk of it at the time, in the general euphoria that greeted Britain's entry. And although Lady Thatcher was on the phone from Washington on Black Wednesday to all her friends saying at last she had been vindicated – she had been right all along – at the time she had endorsed the DM 2.95 rate. She had clearly wanted a firm parity as part of a counter-inflation policy.

John Major is conscious of the criticism that sterling could have either left the ERM or devalued within it before Black Wednesday, but neither he nor Norman Lamont ever regarded leaving the ERM as a practical proposition. They both believed in disinflationary bias. As for devaluation, he replies, 'By how much? How often?' The purchasing power parity of the pound showed no cause for devaluation. Other members of the ERM would probably have opposed any such devaluation. But even if sterling had been devalued by a small amount – say 5 per cent – it would probably have been followed by a further devaluation, driven by a market belief that sterling could be forced further down – which is, indeed, exactly what happened to Spain.

That Sunday the French went to the polls on Maastricht. A No vote would have entirely destroyed the Treaty, a narrow Yes would have boosted the Euro-sceptics in the Party; it could have gone either way. In the event, it was a result that unleashed mayhem in the Conservative Party. The French voted Yes by just over one per cent: 51.5 per cent were in favour of ratification, 48.5 per cent were against. It was the worst possible outcome for the Government. There were immediate calls for a referendum in Britain, which Lady Thatcher soon added her voice to, the rebels re-grouped, the following week seventy of them tabled a motion welcoming the Government's decision to leave the ERM and demanding that it stayed out and made 'a fresh start to economic policy'. Norman Tebbit said on the BBC *Panorama* programme that, if Mr Major sought to force Tory MPs to vote for ratification against their consciences, it would 'tear the Conservative Party apart'; while Ted Heath attacked the Prime Minister for 'a vacuum of leadership'. The nightmare of Maastricht, and years of personal attack, had begun.

15

AUTUMN OF PROBLEMS

WHEN the Conservative Party met in Brighton for its annual conference in October 1992, John Major's personal standing, according to a Gallup poll, had fallen to its lowest level since he became Prime Minister. The Government was the most unpopular it had been for over ten years. The 'feel good factor', which had been plus 4.7 shortly after the General Election, had sunk to minus 23. The months ahead did nothing to improve matters. Every week, if not day, some new drama broke, some new embarrassment, some new spanner was thrown into the works. And the press feasted on a diet of disaster.

John Major had led a relatively charmed life in politics. Promotion had come quickly and easily, and although he had always had to work hard at every job and put abnormal hours into each, he had been successful, and for the most part he had basked in universal approbation. He had not been a senior minister long enough to have experienced a major crisis. Even if he had, nothing could have prepared him for the events that engulfed the Government during the autumn of 1992.

The David Mellor affair had been one. Back in the summer, in July, the *People* newspaper had published details of a three-month affair between David Mellor, the Heritage Minister, and a thirty-year-old actress, Antonia de Sancha. The story was backed up by a recorded telephone conversation, in which Mellor told the actress that he was 'seriously knackered' after spending the night with her, and having problems writing two ministerial speeches. The seedy room in Earl's Court where they had met had apparently been bugged. The Prime Minister publicly demonstrated his support by attending a reception David was holding in his Department.

'He did so,' says Norma, 'because he is quixotic. Also he was contemptuous of the way the press played the story.'

Over the coming weeks photographs emerged, and details were given to the press of steamy sex sessions. Mr Mellor was said to have made love in a Chelsea strip (later said to be untrue) which he wore under his suit, he sucked Miss de Sancha's toes, and recited Shakespeare in the nude. The Heritage Secretary was rapidly becoming an object of ridicule, but he exacerbated the problem by a display of extraordinary arrogance. He showed not a hint of remorse or sensitivity about the feelings of his wife and two sons, and even paraded them for the cameras at his in-laws' house in the country.

John Major continued to give him his full support. He says,

> I didn't believe David should be driven out of office because of a sexual peccadillo – not in the 1990s. Most people would have thought it rather strange if I had accepted his resignation on that account.

He also thoroughly disliked the methods that had been used to get the story. What he didn't know, at that time, was that further revelations were round the corner. These emerged in court during a libel action brought by Mellor's friend Mona Bauwens against the *People*. Mrs Bauwens, daughter of a PLO executive, had paid for David, his wife, Judith, and their two sons, Freddie and Anthony, to fly to Marbella for a month's holiday in a villa she rented for $20,000 for the occasion. And all this during the Gulf crisis. Indeed her father, Jaweed al-Ghussein, at that time Chairman of the Palestine National Fund, was due to have joined them in Spain but didn't because of the Iraqi invasion of Kuwait. David Mellor, said George Carmen QC, had behaved like an ostrich who has buried his head in the Marbella sand 'and exposed his thinking parts'.

Still John Major stood by his minister. In a letter to Bryan Gould, Mellor's Labour shadow, he said,

> The guidance to Ministers about the acceptance of gifts or hospitality is clear and published. In this case David Mellor took the view that the holiday which he and his family took with Mrs Bauwens at her expense was a purely personal

matter and did not touch on his ministerial responsibilities or place him under any obligation in respect of his ministerial duties.

Privately he thought David Mellor had been very foolish, but that was all. More important, he was an excellent Heritage Secretary and the Arts Lobby bombarded Number Ten with support for him. Moreover, John Major had established the new Heritage Department with David Mellor in mind. He didn't want to lose him.

There was growing discomfort all round, however. The 1922 Committee even sat in judgement. Finally on 24 September, the day after details of a second free family holiday had been revealed – in Abu Dhabi with all expenses paid by the ruling Sheikh – David Mellor realized he couldn't go on. He tendered his resignation for a second time, and this time the Prime Minister accepted it.

There is no doubt that the whole business damaged him at a time when he could have done without it. He was immediately accused of weakness, of not having the courage to sack a friend, of allowing his judgement to be clouded by personal considerations. Friends say his closeness to David Mellor has been overrated. Certainly they went to football matches together, and had known one another for many years, but that was the strength of it. No Prime Minister enjoys sacking a colleague. Mrs Thatcher hated it. Harold Macmillan used to burst into tears. But John Major is quite capable, friend or not, when he thinks it is justified. A number of people have gone since he first formed his Cabinet, not all because of a desire to spend more time with their families. But John Major doesn't believe that people have to be humiliated before they go. He feels that's unnecessary and unjust.

He may not earn the media praise for being tough and ruthless and a leader to reckon with by this attitude, but he seldom makes unwelcome enemies either. If he had sacked David Mellor, or for that matter Michael Mates, who was forced to resign as Northern Ireland Minister after his association with Asil Nadir, either of them might have gone away to the back benches nursing a grudge. David Mellor in particular is an articulate man with friends in the media and he could have turned his talent, his pen and his bitterness against John Major and a Government that was already in deep trouble. As it was, he retained a valuable ally.

As David Mellor now says,

He is a man of strong principle and strong friendship. In relation to my own problem during the summer, his total commitment to keeping me on board, which some would say went beyond what he should have done, was a sign of how strong his personal loyalties are, his sense that these things didn't undermine my ability to be effective in my job. It was a job he had created for me and wanted me to do, in truth I think one has to concede that quite a lot of people outside felt that I was well placed to do it. Even on the day I resigned he didn't really want me to go, but I couldn't go on. Never did he let me think that what had happened was anything other than just one of those things that happen. There was no recrimination, no judgement. He's very good at that. He does run these things through his mind.

He has an interesting balance in his character. He's not an insipid person, not a grey person, anyone who knows him knows that; he's a man of strong passions and energies and convictions, but somehow he manages to keep those within the framework of a very stable personality in a way that most people don't. Most people who are that steady either don't have those passions, or are incapable of remaining steady. He has that balance, which still makes him, in my judgement, a formidable person, who I hope will soon be able to re-establish that.

The next hurdle was the Party Conference, which began with a furious debate on Europe. Four days earlier John Major had risen from the ashes of Black Wednesday to announce that his intentions on Europe were unchanged. The Maastricht Bill had been approved by a majority of 244 when it had been introduced in May, before either the Danish or French referenda. He planned to press ahead with it, 'during this session of Parliament', without waiting for a second Danish referendum. He said,

I don't believe, on reflection, the Commons will think it proper for a British Prime Minister to negotiate a Bill, agree it and then abandon it, and I don't propose to do so.

As a prelude, he would hold a Commons debate shortly after Parliament resumed on 19 October, with a vote on the principle of the treaty. He had promised Neil Kinnock before the recess to hold such a debate.

Ninety-two hardline MPs, twenty-two of them Tory, had opposed the Maastricht Bill in May, and, immediately, leading Tory opponents like Bill Cash and Sir Teddy Taylor declared war.

Thus the Conference which should have been a celebration for a stunning fourth Conservative election victory, which brought the Tories fourteen-and-a-half million votes – more votes than ever before in any election in the whole of British history – turned into a battleground. It was one of the most divisive, combative and entertaining Conferences ever, and the issue of the week was Europe. Norman Tebbit, among others, made a blistering speech; young right-wing extremists disrupted debates; and on the final day, when John was due to make his keynote speech in the afternoon, a poisonously timed article written by Lady Thatcher denouncing the ERM and Maastricht appeared in the *European*. She appeared briefly on the platform beside him, but there was none of the adulation which had greeted her appearance the previous year.

It was just before that Conference the previous year in 1991 that Sir Ronald Millar, the playwright turned speech writer, had had a telephone call from Number Ten. He had just been putting the finishing touches to his memoirs, secure in the belief that nearly twenty years of writing speeches for Tory Prime Ministers were at an end. John Major wanted help with the Conference speech, his first since taking over from Mrs Thatcher, and critical, not just for what it said, but how it would be received.

The Prime Minister had begun by saying he knew I was used to all-night sessions at Party Conferences but he was in favour of a good night's sleep and he hoped I wouldn't find the idea too eccentric. I said I would do my best to adjust to this bizarre caprice and he gave the smile and seemed relieved.

The smile, he says, 'which is like being hit by a follow-spot at twenty paces'.

Ronnie has been part of the speech writing team ever since. He calls John 'the Clark Kent of the democratic West', and was involved in all his major speeches throughout the election and was in the thick of it that year at Brighton too. Delivering speeches has been a serious weakness in John's political repertoire. He is happiest when he feels he is talking one-to-one, which is why he was so effective when he brought out his soapbox during the election. He sounds genuine and witty and, above all, like a normal human being. After Mrs Thatcher's curious voice and Ted Heath's plummy tones, it was enormously refreshing. But the minute he gets on to a platform to make a formal speech he loses all character and becomes entirely wooden. He recognizes the problem, and has now decided that, whenever possible, he will do away with a text and speak from notes, and steer clear of autocues.

He began his address to the Conference of 1992 by reflecting on the election, thanking Party workers and thanking individuals, including Norma. As he said,

> Her role was even bigger than you may think. If I hadn't met her on 9 April 1970, I might never have picked 9 April 1992. All those oceans of ink guessing the election date! Wasted! If only they'd asked Norma!

John had been worried about thanking Norma so publicly, afraid that he would become too emotional and might not be able to get through it, but the effect was extraordinary. The audience in the Winter Gardens spontaneously leapt to their feet, clapping and cheering in a show of enormous affection.

It had been a difficult day for Norma. She had wanted a new outfit for the last day but she hadn't had time to go shopping in London. Norma gets no allowance for clothes, and normally has to manage within a tight budget, but she had just had a cheque from the *Sunday Express* for an article she had written, and was feeling flush.

The following morning, thanks to the *Daily Mirror*, the whole country knew about her shopping trip and how much she had spent: £570. And to complete her embarrassment, they revealed she had bought a German make, Escada. What the *Mirror* didn't know in their haste to brand the Prime Minister's wife unpatriotic, was that the fabric was British. She says,

> Somebody must have rung the *Daily Mirror*. I thought it was such a spiteful thing to do, I wasn't going to give the shop the satisfaction of seeing me wearing it, and I didn't want the newspapers to get photographs to go with their story, so I didn't wear it. I've worn it a couple of times since, and I still think it looks quite nice, but I don't like it. It's soured for me.

John went on to talk about Maastricht, discounting popular fears about the Treaty one by one:

> If I believed what some people said about the Treaty, I would vote against it. But I don't. So I'm going to put the real Treaty – the one I negotiated – back to the House of Commons.

He spoke for fifty-nine minutes and was given a standing ovation of seven. It had gone well, not least of all his announcement to wage war on Government regulations:

> It isn't just Brussels that rolls out the red tape, it's Whitehall. And town hall.
>
> Of course we want to have confidence in the safety of the food we eat; the homes we buy; the places we work in; the people who take charge of our children. But when this reaches the point where you may need twenty-eight separate licences, certificates and registrations just to start a business, then I say again: this sort of thing must stop.
>
> I have asked Michael Heseltine to take responsibility for cutting through this burgeoning maze of regulations. Who better for hacking back the jungle? Come on, Michael. Out with your club. On with your loin cloth. Swing into action!

Tarzan had scarcely left the cheering and stamping of the Conference centre behind before his club had taken a mighty hack not at red tape, but at Britain's coal industry. As he calmly announced that British Coal would be closing thirty-one pits – more than half the entire industry – with the loss of thirty thousand jobs, the Government was plunged into crisis on an unprecedented scale. It was the most insensitive, inept and quite incomprehensible bungle, from which the Government very swiftly had to do a complete and embarrassing U-turn, but what surprised people most of all was that John Major should have allowed this to happen. It seemed to betray everything they thought they knew about him. They could have believed it of his predecessor, but John Major was a man who looked as though he cared about ordinary people, who would understand what this would mean to communities that had relied upon the coal mines as the only source of employment for generations. They had thought he was a man they could trust.

Telephone calls and letters of outrage began to flood into Number Ten. The Prime Minister normally receives about four thousand letters a week. That week over twenty thousand arrived. The Confederation of British Industry accused the Government of making 'a monumental cock-up', industrialists said they would be 'out on their ears' if they had run their companies in the way the Government had handled the pits issue. It was not just the public. Scores of back-bench MPs, even those most loyal to the Government, expressed equal disgust. Labour called for a debate on the closures the following Wednesday, after Parliament returned from the summer recess, and it was clear that the Government might face a serious revolt from its own number, some of whom were demanding Michael Heseltine's head.

To cap it all, on the Friday that the first closures were due to take place, John Major spent the day in Birmingham, talking about 'subsidiarity' at a meeting of the European Council, and reaffirming commitment to Maastricht. In a news conference at the end of the day he said he wasn't going to alter the timetable or the closures.

We did it because it was necessary and economically unavoidable, [but] no one could be anything but anguished and concerned about this decision and the impact on the families. The important thing is to get on with helping the miners and their families, and to get on with beating this recession.

The message the general public picked up was none the less clear: the Prime Minister cared more about Maastricht than about the fate of thirty thousand miners and their families. The following week the miners descended on London and marched through the streets towards Westminster, carrying placards which said, 'Sack Major, not the Miners', or more simply, 'Major or Miner?' Norman Tebbit happened to be passing as they were climbing back into their buses to go home. Several of them stopped to speak to him.

'You're right, mate,' they said.

'Of course,' said Lord Tebbit, 'but about what?'

'The trouble with this bloody Government is they don't care what we think. They only care what f . . . ing bloody foreigners think.'

Of all the disasters that hit John Major in that year – and they were several – coal was the one which upsets him most. It could and should have been avoided. He made a mistake, and he was cross with himself for doing so. British Coal had been routinely shutting uneconomic pits for some time without any great resistance. It was no secret, and leaked reports had indicated that many more would have to be shut down. Coal's main customers, electricity companies and generators, were no longer using coal as their principal source of power. As they built new power stations, they were shifting to gas, which, among other things, didn't require the expensive anti-pollution equipment to clean up carbon and sulphur emissions. Where they still used coal, it was cheaper to import it mostly from the United States, Australia and Colombia, where opencast mining, and in some places child labour, cut production costs.

On strictly economic grounds, it was clear that a sizeable number of pits had to go. No doubt the forthcoming privatization had a part to play in which particular pits fell under the axe. Heseltine had come away from the Treasury with a very generous settlement, and at the end of the day the focus of everyone who had been closely involved was on the redundancy terms. They had lost sight of the central issue, which was putting thirty thousand miners on the dole, and overlooked the fact that the outside world would be hearing of this proposition for the first time.

John Major first became involved in the details of the whole business the week before the Party Conference, and didn't like the sound of it. Norma remembers him pacing up and down the garden at the Finings the weekend after the Conference, before they had to take final decisions, worrying about what it would actually mean to the miners. People wouldn't understand why they were doing it. Even if it was economically unavoidable, he didn't know how you could suddenly say to thirty thousand people who had spent half their lives working in the mines that they were no longer needed. He was genuinely very worried about that, but the economics seemed to be indisputable and he didn't have a solution.

Two things were compelling: it was clear no one would buy the coal, and it had been known for a long time in some of the pits that their pit was becoming defunct. But he made the mistaken judgement from that, that the miners were prepared for the closures. He thought that there was an expectation and a readiness for closure and that what was hanging over the miners' heads was the uncertainty.

John Major had accepted the economic case that was presented to him, but wasn't happy with the provisions for the families. He had wanted to put some kind of scheme in place which would regenerate hope in the condemned areas, along the lines of one which had worked very successfully in Shotton on Deeside. There a large steelworks had been closed in 1982, with a loss of ten thousand jobs in one day, but the Government put in an enterprise zone, and ten thousand people had been re-employed in modern factories, medium and high-tech industry, and export – high-income work – and were no longer dependent on a single industry which was dying. He had seen Shotton and this is what he wanted to do with coal.

But during the weekend immediately after the Conference, while he was pacing up and down the garden, plans for the closures were leaked and Michael Heseltine was bounced into making an announcement the following Tuesday, a week earlier than they had intended, and before the plans for a rescue package were complete. The news that six thousand of the miners would be losing their jobs on the Friday came from British Coal, in fact, not Heseltine, but the distinction was lost in the clamour. It offended the British people's instincts for fairness. They have always had a soft spot for the miners, but it is not fair for anyone in any job to suddenly come in to work and be told you're out of a job this Friday. John Major says,

> People were mortally offended by it. They thought it was brutally unfair, and if we had been doing what they thought we were doing, it would have been brutally unfair.

As it was, they spent hours agonizing over the help – they were the most generous redundancy payments that have ever been made by the Government, and there was a whole series of other measures too. One of the points about doing it all together was that you could put in things like enterprise zones, which would be a real help to the whole area. Closing them down in little penny packets meant they would never get that sort of help, and would then be unemployed much longer.

All this became academic. The bald facts were out, the public had reacted and the Prime Minister was thrown on to the defensive. He called a meeting at Admiralty House on the Sunday evening of all the relevant ministers to decide upon a way out of the mess. Michael Heseltine was in no mood to grumble about more cold chicken and sandwiches – that morning he had had three tons of coal dumped across the entrance to his Oxfordshire house, with the message 'Coal Not Dole. Frickley NUM. Up Yours.' John Major very clearly took charge of that meeting and it was agreed that they would make an early statement suspending closure for most of the pits until there had been proper consultation over a three-month period. Ten pits, which were loss-making and had no hope of becoming anything but in the foreseeable future, would be given ninety days. The next day the Prime Minister called an emergency Cabinet meeting to endorse the conclusions reached the previous evening, and Michael Heseltine announced the turn around to a reconvened House that afternoon. As well as announcing a moratorium on redundancies while the future of the twenty-one pits was reviewed, he promised £165 million for the range of rescue measures, including enterprise zones, which had been planned all along.

It was a humiliating climb-down. Michael Heseltine had come to the House to apologize and for two long hours he was shown little mercy. There was a chorus of 'resign' from the moment he took his seat – some was aimed at John Major, who sat silently beside him throughout. Labour's Dennis Skinner shouted 'For God's sake, go!' Others taunted 'Tarzan the chimp.'

'Stop being so plain bloody stupid!' bellowed the President of the Board of Trade, his patience at an end.

But the last word went to Skinner, The Beast of Bolsover, who had been sent a pit uniform by the wife of a miner from his constituency.

'Here, take them,' he sneered, throwing the clothes at Heseltine's feet. 'She says, "PS I have washed them, but the socks need darning".'

Despite the barracking, the speed with which the Government moved did ward off the further humiliation of defeat in the debate that Wednesday. Labour set down a motion calling for a stay of execution for all thirty-one pits until a review of the future of the coal industry had been completed. It was a rowdy and impassioned debate – Michael Heseltine had to abandon his speech halfway through because of the uproar – and some of the Party's back benchers were still profoundly unhappy, but when it came to the vote only six rebelled, five abstained and the Government won by a majority of thirteen.

Disaster had been narrowly averted, but public confidence in John Major as a leader had been severely shaken. He may have taken a firm lead with his ministers in digging them all out of the hole, but there was no evidence of this leadership, no expression of regret or sympathy for the miners and their families, which the public was looking for. There had been no real sign of him since Black Wednesday. This man who had strode so confidently out of Number Ten to talk to the cameras during the Gulf War, who had been happy to take any question that was thrown at him, no longer seemed to have the appetite for it. People had been suffering under the intolerable burden of high interest rates – going out of business, losing homes – because we had been locked into the ERM, which all, it seemed in the aftermath of Black Wednesday, had been for no good reason. And without so much as an apology from either John Major or Norman Lamont – not even at the Party Conference – interest rates had been cut and the country was off on some other course, as yet unspecified. It was beginning to feel as though there was something wrong, that the top seat had been vacated.

It was not until 20 October, the night before the debate on the pit closures, a whole week after the original announcement, that the Prime Minister made his first serious television appearance on the matter. He gave live interviews to the *Nine O'Clock News* and *News at Ten*, in which he defended the Government's new position on coal, and explained that ministers had become so involved in the detail of the closures beforehand that they had failed to see the wood for the trees. He then announced an unexpected shift in economic policy, saying a new strategy for growth would be unveiled in the Chancellor's autumn statement. It went down well, and brought the first glimmer of praise for many a week. 'At last, it seems, the Government is listening,' said the *Daily Telegraph*. 'Mr Major has emerged from the bunker.'

The Prime Minister felt cross with himself over the whole sorry affair because his instincts had told him something was wrong right at the beginning. But because the economic arguments were irrefutable, he had ignored his instincts and followed the economics. He also, inevitably, felt bruised, downcast and depressed. In all the other political disasters, both before this and since he has felt he has been a casualty of events. Coal was the one that he knew could have been avoided – and would have been if he had listened to his instincts. According to Alan Clark, Whitehall advice needs to be routinely questioned 'because civil servants don't give strategic advice, they give tactical advice on how to cope with a particular problem that may be impeding the advancement of a policy.'

Kenneth Clarke, who seemed to have become the Government's

official apologist since Black Wednesday, and had been robustly ducking and diving on radio and television thereafter, says John Major was clearly getting conflicting advice.

> If you're in trouble in politics, the only way out of the mess is to win the argument, and it was essential that the Government was seen to be out there – that we avoided the allegation of bunker mentality, which was being hurled in our direction, and the idea that every minister was invisible, and no one prepared to put their head above the parapet and go out and argue the case. Given politics is a team effort, if you don't hang together, you will undoubtedly hang separately. Somebody had to go out and seek to defend us.

In the absence of anyone else, he did, and enjoyed what his critics called 'defending the indefensible'. Apart from Michael Heseltine, no one else seemed to be out there.

Kenneth Clarke says,

> You cannot sit inside the walls of Downing Street or Admiralty House, hoping things will go away. Politics is like falling off a bicycle. If you fall off, particularly if you're surrounded by people who are laughing at you, it's doubly important you get back on the bloody bicycle and pedal again. It doesn't matter if you fall over again. Otherwise you lose the self-confidence to go out and face the enemy. John hesitated a bit.

When he gave his first big interview after the coal announcements, the situation improved somewhat, but there was no respite. While the coal issue rumbled on, the Maastricht paving debate was upon him. What was intended originally as a general discussion about the Maastricht Bill before it went into the committee stage, turned into a fight for John Major's political life. There are strongly differing views about the debate. Some say it was John Major being petulant and bloody minded and choosing the wrong issue on which to try and assert his authority. There was never any need to have held it, they say, and it was folly to have brought the Government so close to the brink of destruction in this way. Norman Tebbit says,

If he had thought, he would have concluded that the Treaty shouldn't be brought back until after the second Danish referendum, and he would have had no problem. Most people would have been content. And that's what he had to concede in the end to get himself a majority of three, with the support of the Liberal Democrats, so it was silly.

In many ways Norman Tebbit is quite right. But John Major had committed himself to the debate, effectively a second reading before the Bill was taken into committee, in the summer. He and Douglas Hurd had talked about it and agreed, and been backed up by the Cabinet, that in the light of the Danish referendum results, Parliament should be given time to reflect on the changed circumstances. Technically they needn't have done so. The Bill could have gone straight into committee stage, but there was alarm among some MPs that the Government would rush through legislation, and they wanted to reassure Parliament.

There was another reason for his decision to press ahead, and it wasn't one he took lightly. He knew it would be difficult, and the Government had difficulties enough, but he came to the conclusion that you have to be prepared to take a stand in politics, or there will be no issue on which you could not be knocked off course. This happened to be an issue on which he felt very strongly, and if he was perceived to have no principles, what was he in business for? Stephen Wall, his Foreign Affairs Secretary, wondered at the wisdom of it. 'You won the election,' he said, 'it would be stupid to be pushed out by this kind of thing.' To which John Major replied,

Life isn't worth living if you are just going to be pushed from one expedient to the other, if you were knocked off your perch on that one, you'll be knocked off your perch on something else.

Whether he was right or wrong to up the ante over Maastricht, it was a conscious decision and one he had thought through.

The debate was scheduled for 4 November and, as the day drew nearer, the rebels grew more trenchant, and Labour, led by John Smith since the General Election, made it plain that they would vote against the Government. Labour had voted for Maastricht in May, as had the Liberal Democrats, the parties were broadly united in their pro-European policy, but they claimed that the paving debate had turned into a vote of confidence in the Prime Minister, and they would therefore vote against. They would be voting not against the substance of the Bill but its timing.

John Major's critics say that his timing over the whole Maastricht process was wrong and strengthened the anti-European's case. By not nailing his colours clearly to the pro European mast in advance of the Maastricht negotiations, he lost the advantage. The Treaty was finalized in February but not introduced into Parliament until just before the Danish referendum – four months were lost. Then the decision to postpone ratification after the Danish result – all this, they say, allowed the anti Europeans to get some wind into their sails.

Hindsight makes so many things apparent. At the time they would have had him nailing his colours to the mast, the Prime Minister still had a general election ahead, and had to keep both the pros and the antis happy for the sake of Party unity. It was precisely the same argument as his softly softly approach to the Poll Tax. It was a matter of simple political pragmatism. And as for starting the ratification process before the Danish referendum, no one thought for a moment that the Danes would vote no, so there was no particular urgency. It was just another item of parliamentary business.

By late October it was far from just another item. As the tension grew, stories appeared that John Major had said if the Party didn't trust him over Europe they should find themselves another leader. Norman Tebbit said in a radio interview that if Mr Major wanted to resign then the Party would find someone else. If it had come to that, he says, he would have stood himself. Next thing, the Prime Minister was supposedly briefing journalists on the flight to Cairo for the El Alamein celebrations that, if he were defeated on the Bill, it might not be a matter of resignation, but of a dissolution of Parliament: he would call a general election.

John Major says he never actually threatened either to resign or to call a general election, but Number Ten didn't deny the reports immediately because they didn't want to provoke any more U-turn stories. It would have been totally counterproductive to threaten either. As it was, the story that he had was enough to encourage some people to vote against the Government quite simply because it had been made so much of an issue, and looked like a tactic to force people into line, which they didn't like.

The executive of the back-bench 1922 Committee had pressed for a noncommittal motion, but John Major was determined to see it through, although it was increasingly obvious there was a very serious risk he might be defeated. In the build-up to the debate he was under obvious strain. The night before, five members of the executive went to see him – Sir George Gardiner, Bob Dunn, James Pawsey, John Townend and Sir Rhodes Boyson. They all intended either to abstain or vote against the motion, but being in a slightly awkward position as members of the executive, felt they should see the Prime Minister first to let him know. They saw him at 5 p.m., and he had had a gruelling day; as well as the worry about the debate, 2,400 British troops had just arrived in war-torn Bosnia to escort humanitarian relief convoys. He was in the midst of trying to prevent the GATT (General Agreement on Tariffs and Trade) talks from collapsing and had two telephone calls from President Bush on the subject that day, plus a meeting with some European head of state.

The five back benchers were shocked by the state they found him in. George Gardiner says,

> We were amazed by the way the stuffing seemed to have been knocked out of him. There was no threat to resign, as the Whips had been saying he would. He was exhausted, and gave us the impression that he was not far from throwing in the towel. The look in his eyes was very unsettling. We argued our case, explained why we were abstaining. He asked us not to, but there was no guff about 'we must be part of Europe'. We went away and discussed it and concluded that if he were defeated and didn't resign he would be so undermined that he wouldn't stand up to the next challenge, which would be the Autumn Statement. So we typed a note, which we gave to Graham Bright, saying we had decided to support him, but this must be seen as personal support and not support for the Maastricht Treaty.

Throughout the day of the vote the Whips and Party officials, who had already been working overtime, employed every tactic in a very extensive repertoire to bring the last of the rebels into line. Their methods caused a lot of ill-feeling amongst those most brutally coerced. Sir Teddy Taylor said afterwards, 'It is very sad to see such arm-twisting. It would not have been necessary if only the Government had agreed to a referendum.' But a referendum was never on the cards. He had all the authority he needed from the original vote earlier in the year.

It was a six-hour debate, with two votes. The first, for a Labour amendment calling for the Government to delay the Maastricht Bill until after the Edinburgh Summit in December, the Tories won by six votes. The second, on the Government motion to begin the ratification process before Edinburgh, was even tighter. An hour before, the final divisions defeat seemed inevitable. They had done the arithmetic and they were still short of four votes. During the divisions the rebels were surrounded by senior ministers and cajoled, threatened and pleaded with. The drama and suspense went on until 10.30, when John Major was saved by three rebels changing tack and voting with the Government after a last-minute pledge that the third reading of the Bill would not take place until after the second Danish referendum. Five others abstained and the Government scraped home with a majority of three.

Matthew Parris, former MP of the 1979 vintage and Blue Chip, now political sketch writer, described the scene in *The Times* the next day.

> The last half hour before the 10 o'clock vote captured the flavour, as it so often does, better than the whole of the preceding day. The chamber was packed, tense. A sprinkling of dinner jackets on the Tory side. A Rolls-Royce of a speech from Douglas Hurd, the Foreign Secretary. Euro-sceptical interruptions hissed by the multitude, then the vote . . .
>
> Tense faces on the government front bench. Next to me sat a previous private secretary to Mr Major. We looked down. Tristan Garel-Jones whispered something to him. The Prime Minister pulled up his socks. 'He's won,' said the man beside me. 'He's pulled up his socks. He only ever does that when he's won.'

Actually John Major pulls his left ear-lobe when he has won, but why spoil a good story?

There was no champagne. The fridge in John's room in the House is stocked with beer, whisky and Coca-Cola, and maybe the odd bottle of wine. The relief none the less was tremendous, and all sorts of people arrived to offer their congratulations and join the celebrations. But first the Prime Minister went to thank the Whips. Because of them he had survived the most difficult day thus far of his political career. He had gambled and he had won. He had established his authority within the Party, won respect from the commentators. What would have happened if four people had voted the other way didn't bear thinking about. It hadn't happened, and as with everything else in his fast-moving life, there was no time to reflect on what might have been. He could start the ratification process, and go to Edinburgh to negotiate for Britain's interests with a strong suit.

He had come through some dark hours in the preceding weeks – and there was more to come. He had been tired and tense and clearly under tremendous strain. The disasters and difficulties and the degree of hostility had taken him by surprise, but John Major was a tougher proposition than his critics gave him credit for. He had met disaster and difficulty as a child, and if there is one thing a street fighter brought up in the slums of Brixton has, it is an instinct for survival.

16

PAYING THE PRICE

THE next challenge that Sir George Gardiner had foreseen was the Chancellor's Autumn Statement, just a week after the Maastricht paving debate. A quite reasonable assumption, but as Harold Wilson observed, 'a week is a long time in politics'. And to imagine there was no time for any other disaster to descend upon the Government, was to seriously underestimate the horrors that have accompanied John Major's premiership.

Events were queuing up to keep him and his colleagues in a perpetual state of embarrassment. And at every turn the newspapers were there to ensure they were spared nothing.

John Major has had a turbulent relationship with the press since he first took office and, although he tries to play it down and now has a considerably thicker skin than he had in the early years, there is no doubt he has been extremely hurt by some of the things journalists have written. With few exceptions they have talked of incompetence, policy failures, blunders, U-turns, intellectual bankruptcy and lack of leadership, and allowed his successes to pass largely unnoticed. And time and again the authors reveal themselves motivated by nothing but snobbery. No previous Prime Minister has had to put up with such an onslaught from those papers which they have traditionally looked to for support.

There have been several reasons for the seemingly remorseless attack. At the height of the recession newspapers suffered as acutely as any other business or individual and, like their readers, wanted someone to blame. Rational explanations about why times were tough were not what people wanted. They wanted things to get better right away, and if the Prime Minister couldn't do that then he was clearly no good.

John Major is philosophical about it. He realizes that most people don't understand why he couldn't bring interest rates down earlier, or why Britain fell out of the ERM.

'We're an apolitical nation,' he says, 'all people have seen is a politician buffeted by events who couldn't stop them. Politicians are either heroes or villains, they are either the person who got it right or the person who got it wrong.'

What he is less philosophical about is the personal abuse on behalf of a number of individuals writing in arch Tory publications, motivated as much by snobbery as anything else. Some of his harshest critics are loyal Thatcherites still angry she was deposed, or editors who have felt let down by Mr Major when they have backed a policy that failed. Others are rabid anti-Europeans who have been determined to destroy Maastricht, and if it meant destroying a Prime Minister who refused to give up, so be it. Two newspaper editors actually went to Denmark in June 1992 to canvass against Maastricht before the second referendum.

Had John Major been prepared to woo the newspaper editors as Mrs Thatcher had done before him, he may have found them more sympathetic. She entertained them at Downing Street and Chequers, accepted lunch invitations from them, graced their parties, called them in to discuss issues, confided in them, flirted with them, asked their advice, and generally made them feel as though they were playing an important part in Government. When they came up with the goods and supported her and her policies, she repaid them with knighthoods. John Major has done much less of this, and most of those that do know him don't understand him. The editors, whatever their origins might have been, are now Establishment figures. They are uneasy with someone like John Major who doesn't appear to want to join the club. And his initiatives, particularly the Citizen's Charter, have been easy to mock.

The cynics can sit there and criticize the Citizen's Charter because the cynics don't use public services: they don't care whether the trains run on time, because they don't use them; whether their GPs will see them, because they go private; whether they can get into a hospital quickly, because they're on BUPA; whether they can get their child into the right school, because their child goes to a private school. For 90 per cent of the people out there these things matter, and that's what the Charter is about.

It is all part of making sure the little man, who isn't sophisticated, is treated fairly by the system and by the central and regional bureaucracy of this country. No longer do they have to wait until it's convenient for the consultant to see them, convenient for the person in the unemployment office to see them. They now have timed appointments, they're treated like human beings and so they should be because it is their taxes, compulsorily extracted from their purses, that actually pay for these services.

It's knocked and scoffed at by the clever people who know how to play the system, but our Citizen's Charter is now being copied by the French, the Americans and by countries up and down Latin America. There is a great list of people who have been over here to copy what we have done.

Looking back he says he can see the things he might have done in the early years to get the media off his back, and some things that he should have done, but he was contemptuous of doing them. His sister Pat knows him almost better than anyone. She says,

If people attack him, he won't respond, and he won't go out of his way to mend fences with them either. He would regard that as demeaning. That's him. He can see the harm it has done. If you read day after day, in article after article, in paper after paper that Bloggs is a scoundrel who couldn't lead you from here to the washroom, you're apt to believe it. We live in a cynical age.

He will have no truck with image-makers either. For better or worse, politics has become a glorified branch of show-business, there are cameras in the Chamber of the House of Commons, at Party Conferences, and waiting outside Number Ten each day – presentation is all – and the cunning politician is the one who uses the camera. Mrs Thatcher for all her faults, understood that. When she became Prime Minister in 1979 she was a wholly unremarkable-looking woman with a rather shrill voice. Professional image-makers gave her a new wardrobe, new make-up, a new hair style, new teeth, and they trained her voice and taught her how to handle television. Gradually she was transformed into a woman of stature, a leader.

John Major has refused to do that. His old Huntingdon friends have given him ties for Christmas, and several people have suggested bringing in a professional adviser, but they have been given short shrift. This is the way he is, and if people want him they can take him the way he is. What you see is what you get.

The sentiment is refreshing and admirable, but he is doing himself, and by association his policies, no favours. He is not a good orator, as he is the first to admit, and seldom comes across well on television unless he is speaking off-the-cuff. His voice is flat, his speech lacks poetry, and the result is a rather down-beat performance, which confirms the grey label. His strength is one-to-one when there's not a hint of grey. He has charisma in the flesh which disappears on television. He has a good sense of humour, he is fun, relaxed, easy to talk to, and above all interested in people and what they have to say – from the chairman of the board to the person who cleans the lavatories. He speaks in the same manner to both and gives both equal time to say what they think.

He is the original classless man, a man who is truly at ease with himself, and it shows. As Chris Patten was the first, but by no means last to say, if the 20 million voters in Britain could only meet John Major face to face his majority in the House would be over three hundred.

But the fact is they can't. He has to rely on television – and using television is a skill that can be learnt like any other. During the 1992 election he knew that he was getting through to people, since then he knows he has not been. People blame him for their woes, because he said he could make things better and he didn't. The fact that no one else probably could have done any better – and may have done a lot worse – is immaterial. A great many things have gone right in the last three years but they have been masked by the things that have gone wrong, by the obsession with Maastricht and the divisions within the Conservative Party.

John Major has done exactly as his father instructed, he has refused to 'bang his chest' and has sat back and allowed others to comment on what he has done. It may make for a decent human being but it is not the way to be recognized as a decisive Prime Minister in the 1990s.

Andrew Tyrie says,

> I don't think one should underrate the extent to which John's background has given him a set of values and a clear sense of right and wrong. And something else which I think is greatly

underrated, and which I think is a crucial quality in a leader of a country, and which he has, is a sense of decency. It is plain as a pikestaff that this man is not corrupt, that he would never brook corruption, and would stamp it out immediately.

It's plain too to everybody that he has a sense of balance; that he's not likely to do anything wild, that he's not likely to indulge whims, that he's not going to pursue vendettas. You know the famous quote that power tends to corrupt and absolute power tends to corrupt absolutely. I would say John Major is not easily corruptible, and that's worth a hell of a lot – a hell of a lot. I don't mean corruptible just in the sense of taking pecuniary advantage: I mean corruptible in a sense of becoming carried away by the trappings of office.

It follows that John Major has tried very hard during his time as Prime Minister to make politics and the House of Commons less confrontational. He finds it frustrating that every issue has to be turned into a party political issue, often quite unnecessarily: he says,

There is actually quite a broad consensus across the majority of both parties on a large number of issues and how they're handled. Yet for partisan reasons, everything has to become an issue. Either the Government has got it spectacularly right, or they have got it spectacularly wrong. There's never anything in between, there's never any allowance for the force of external events, for the logic of dealing with things slowly, and working out what can actually be done.

This is the price we pay for our adversarial system of politics in Britain, where the need to play the game and answer questions in a politically correct way has driven at least one of the many Members of Parliament who have revealed their intention to leave politics, George Walden, to announce he is giving up his seat at the next election.

The alternative is coalition, but attractive though it might be in some respects, it is not a system John Major would favour.

The reason there's been no great European debate in the European countries by and large is because most of them have coalition governments or because there is an agreed line across parties, and that has meant the debate has been very poor. For all our frustrations during the debate on Europe it has been a real debate about issues that matter and that is actually a strength of the British political system. What George Walden aches for is a system where adversarial politics is subordinated to intellectual discussion. Very attractive in theory but I'm not actually convinced it delivers better policies, because in such a political environment the accepted wisdom is not challenged. It is healthy in our politics that we say 'That is wrong and we oppose it flatly'.

During John Major's premiership he has faced opposition and abuse not just from across the Dispatch Box in the House of Commons but from his own side as well, never more swingeingly than when his former Chancellor unexpectedly rose to his feet in June 1993.

It had all begun more than seven months before. Norman Lamont's Autumn Statement in November had been scarcely announced when a series of stories about his personal life hit the headlines – a mixture of fact, fiction and innuendo – which grew ever more grisly. It began with the revelation that he had used £4,000 of taxpayers' money in the course of ejecting a sex therapist known as Miss Whiplash from his basement flat in Notting Hill. Then came the news that he had failed to settle a hotel bill of several hundred pounds after his stay in Brighton during the Party Conference. Next it transpired he had failed to pay his Access bill; and as the obvious cracks were made about what chance was there for the nation's finances in the hands of someone who couldn't even manage his own, a story appeared that he had bought a bottle of cheap Champagne and cigarettes, of the sort favoured by women, with his credit card at a Threshers wine shop in Paddington. The latter, which was instantly dubbed 'Threshergate', turned out to be a hoax, but protest as he might, the damage was done.

The Prime Minister recognized that his Chancellor was losing his credibility and by May 1993 he realized that he had no choice but to let him go. The clamour in the wake of the Newbury by-election disaster, following the death of Judith Chaplin, grew too loud to ignore. The Tories had hit rock bottom. The swing to the Liberal Democrats in Newbury had been an incredible 28.4 per cent. In the local elections on the same day the Tories lost control of fifteen councils and lost a total of 473 seats – most of them to the Liberal Democrats. The Government, as the Prime Minister immediately conceded, had been given 'a bloody nose'.

Many senior Tories felt Lamont should have gone after Black Wednesday, but John Major had resisted and given him a chance to put things right. By May, by and large he had done so, but he had predicted 'green shoots' too often. Now that the green shoots of recovery were actually beginning to appear, no one was listening. The City had lost its faith in the Chancellor, and it was time for a change.

John Major moved Norman Lamont in a reshuffle at the end of May. Kenneth Clarke became the new Chancellor, with Michael Howard taking his place at the Home Office. John had offered Lamont another Cabinet position, but he had turned it down and elected to return to the backbenches.

It was clear from the start that Norman Lamont had not taken the move well. There had been no row at his meeting with the Prime Minister, but he had not sent the customary reply to the Prime Minister's farewell letter. Lamont was hurt and cross, as was apparent when he stood up before a packed House of Commons two weeks later and savaged the Prime Minister, just as Sir Geoffrey Howe had done to his predecessor with devastating effect some years before.

After giving his version of the events leading up to Black Wednesday he said, 'there is something wrong with the way we make our decisions. The Government listens too much to the pollsters and the party managers,' with the result there is 'too much short-termism, too much reacting to events, not enough shaping of events. We give the impression of being in office but not in power.'

Lamont's attack had come out of the blue. Although there was immediate speculation after the reshuffle that he would 'do a Geoffrey Howe', he had said he would remain silent. The first anyone in Number Ten knew he had changed his mind was at one o'clock on the day of his speech. The Speaker's Office rang to say that Mr Lamont would be speaking at 3.30 that afternoon. It was a vicious assault but John Major refused to retaliate. He and Norman Lamont had known each other a long time, they had worked very closely together for two and a half years, been through some major traumas together, and he felt that by and large Lamont's financial judgement had been sound. They had never been close personal friends, but he had no desire to get into a slanging match, and was hurt and disappointed that Lamont had felt the need to do so.

John Major has no difficulty with people disagreeing with him.

He can sit through furious debates in the House of Commons with colleagues and members of the Opposition and walk out and have a drink with them afterwards, still friends, because he respects their views and their convictions. That's politics, the argument is water off a duck's back; but if someone is disloyal or hits below the belt, as he feels so many journalists have done, they are seldom given a second chance. He has been advised time and again to approach people who have written poisonous articles, but he won't hear of it. He is reluctant to butter-up people who have been rude and offensive.

As if to confirm Norman Lamont's bitter accusations, the Government had and continued to suffer an embarrassing number of U-turns at that time, and at each turn John Major was accused of having no clear objectives and of being buffeted by events.

In some cases, such as coming out of the ERM, he undoubtedly was buffeted by events. In others the Government changed tack, he claims, because something proved to be unworkable, such as an absurd fining system in the Criminal Justice Act, and ridiculously bureaucratic national tests for 14-year-olds. Or, in the case of the Army cuts, the situation had simply changed. When the Government planned to reduce the number of troops from 150,000 to 116,000 Europe had seemed a benign place. A year later when they changed it to 119,000, the Bosnian war had broken out and the continent was no longer so benign.

But other U-turns, particularly those made during the anguished months when the Maastricht Bill was making its way through the Commons, were what he calls 'tactical necessities'. They were not U-turns on policy objectives, they were U-turns on how to get to those objectives. There is a clear distinction between the two. He wanted the Maastricht Treaty. If he couldn't get it through one way he would get it another way. He was prepared to tack and trim, to manoeuvre. 'If I lose a vote,' he says, 'I have to accept it, that is democracy. Britain is not a dictatorship, I can't dictate to the House of Commons. I can state what I want and fight hard to get it, but if I lose I have to accept that defeat.'

Maastricht had dominated the year. It had alienated the public and made him the most unpopular Prime Minister ever, but he kept on with a dogged determination. He felt and still feels that nothing is more important for the future prosperity of Britain than being a central figure in Europe – and he cares more about Britain's future than his own popularity.

'I could have played to the gallery, and thrown the Maastricht Bill away, and donned a John Bull shirt, and five years from now when we had lost the inward investment, when we were excluded from the decisions in Europe, when we were still in the Community but other people were making decisions for us, when we were seen as irrelevant, people would say, "Why on earth did he do that, why did he do it?"' He clearly believes the Maastricht Bill is essential to retain Britain's influence in Europe.

Before he negotiated the Maastricht Treaty he set out in detail in the House of Commons what he would accept, and he had the endorsement of the House. He went to Maastricht. He sat there for hour after hour late into the night with no one else in the Community on his side, refusing to accept things until others shifted their position, until they were offering something he was prepared to accept within the remit that Parliament had given him. He came back and Parliament overwhelmingly endorsed the treaty he had negotiated. He set it out clearly in the Conservative manifesto in the General Election, spoke about it repeatedly, and won the election. In the second reading of the Bill he had a majority of 244. It was only after the Danish referendum in 1992, when the Danes said no, that everybody began to play what he describes as parliamentary games. He refused to bend. It was too big an issue. He believed it was essential for Britain to have a key role in European decision making; otherwise there was a fear that the Federalists would dominate the agenda and determine European policy. That was why he wanted Britain at the heart of Europe so that Britain could play a central role in shaping the future direction of the Community. He believed that if Britain failed to ratify the Maastricht Treaty it would lose that influence, and with it the chance of building a wider Europe based on free-market principles and with effective authority remaining with nation states.

He has made success after success at the negotiating table over Maastricht. Edinburgh, in December 1992, was a make or break summit, the agenda was 'a Rubik's cube' – enormously complex – but when the meeting at Holyroodhouse finally came to an end eight and a half hours behind schedule, the twelve leaders had found a way to make Maastricht more acceptable to the Danes, they had put the EC's financing on a 'sound, fair and affordable basis' for the rest of the century, they had agreed to start negotiations for Sweden, Austria, Finland and Norway to join the Community, and agreed to withdraw more than twenty of the most obnoxious EC directives. All the issues on the agenda were inter-locking. If they had reached deadlock on any one the rest might have been doomed, yet with negotiating skill that everyone involved acknowledged was brilliant, John Major found a way through the maze and came away with agreement on all six issues, and everything he wanted for Britain, including the clause on subsidiarity, which prevents the Community from doing what Member States can do better themselves. Once again he had done what no one had thought possible. The team of officials from Number Ten and the Foreign Office up in Edinburgh with him, a cynical bunch, were so impressed by his performance they clapped when he came into the room at the end of it all. Not many ministers can claim that accolade.

Kenneth Clarke says that before he saw these same extraordinary negotiating skills at Maastricht

> fan of him though I am, I could have been prepared to go along with the judgement, 'Nice guy, not quite up to the job' – but it's not true. Where he convinced me he was a nice guy and up to the job was negotiating Maastricht. The most striking feature of his premiership is the collective and inter-minable discussions he allows all his colleagues, as a way of hooking them all in so they are tied into a decision. This collective discussion produces a negotiating brief, which if you had asked me, I'd have said he was very much odds-against delivering, then he goes off and does deliver. That is nice guy suddenly delivering a hard act, and he's been winning that argument ever since.

The Prime Minister found Edinburgh immensely exhilarating. It had seemed impenetrable but he was convinced he could find a way through, and finding it was fun. It was hard work. But above all, it was a classic Major operation: infinite preparation, mastery of tedious detail, meeting after meeting, interminable travel to Europe to find out the demands and the weak spots in everybody's case, an evaluation of every country's priority and everyone's bottom line – then spread it out like a jigsaw and put the pieces together. When it came to Edinburgh he knew the detail that other people didn't, and when it came to the negotiations he delivered the agreement that others thought wasn't there. Colleagues say he uses the same technique to run his Cabinet.

The drawback to this collegiate style, however, is public perception. Because he operates this way people think he doesn't have a view of what he wants, they think he has no vision, and regard him as chairman of the board, who accepts what the consensus is. John Major has a very clear idea of what he wants when he goes into meetings. The question he wrestles with is how to get it with maximum agreement. That is what he enjoys – teasing people round to an agreement that looked in the first place as though it was unreachable.

When asked about his style of leadership, John Major points to passages from Rudyard Kipling's poem 'If'. 'I regard that as leadership by example,' he says.

> If you can keep your head when all about you
>   Are losing theirs and blaming it on you,
> If you can trust yourself when all men doubt you,
>   But make allowance for their doubting too;
> If you can wait and not be tired by waiting,
>   Or being lied about, don't deal in lies,
> Or being hated, don't give way to hating,
>   And yet don't look too good, nor talk too wise:
>
> If you can dream – and not make dreams your master;
>   If you can think – and not make thoughts your aim;
> If you can meet with Triumph and Disaster
>   And treat those two impostors just the same;
> If you can bear to hear the truth you've spoken
>   Twisted by knaves to make a trap for fools,
> Or watch the things you gave your life to, broken,
>   And stoop and build 'em up with worn-out tools:
>
> If you can talk with crowds and keep your virtue,
>   Or walk with Kings – nor lose the common touch,
> If neither foes nor loving friends can hurt you,
>   If all men count with you, but none too much;
> If you can fill the unforgiving minute
>   With sixty seconds' worth of distance run,
> Yours is the Earth and everything that's in it,
>   And – which is more – you'll be a Man, my son!

His Cabinet colleagues applaud his style of leadership. 'If you want people in your team to give of their best they need to feel that their views will be heard,' says Virginia Bottomley. 'John Major is courteous, he does listen, but there is also a steeliness behind that, and in many ways it's more intimidating to present a case to someone who knows an enormous amount of the detail and is listening to the arguments and how they are presented, than it is if you're instantly involved in a heated debate.'

William Waldegrave says

What makes people follow other people is that strange mixture of respect and affection. You can't do it just from fear, and that in the end is what brought Mrs Thatcher down. You can't just terrorize people into following you, they've got to feel affection, otherwise they won't help you out when you fall in a hole, they'll just laugh at you. He started with immense affection, he's now added to it with a bit of fear as well. You need the capacity to instil fear in your followers and more importantly in the enemy, but you can't do that without having the bedrock of affection.

Virginia Bottomley again,

I recall the virulence of feeling about Mrs Thatcher in 1980 because at bad times of economic difficulty, people feel upset, distressed, angry and the easiest people to feel angry with are the leaders. I also remember the tremendous divisiveness of the Cabinet at that time and the sense of different factions. That is not something I feel at all in John Major's Cabinet. Yes people have strong views, we're not all clones, but I think there's a very strong commitment to his leadership and very strong determination that the issues of the economy and our relationship with Europe are interrelated and we have to take those forward.

Europe, he knows, is a subject on which some of his opponents have very strong principles and he respects those principles. There are others whose motives are less honourable, but none of them has come up with any convincing alternative. There are three possibilities. To leave the EC, which no one has seriously suggested because of the impact it would have on jobs; to form some sort of North Atlantic arrangement with the Americans and Canadians, but there has been no offer from the Americans and Canadians to that effect; or to stay in the Community but become sidelined. Start excluding Europe and you not only sideline Britain in Europe and damage our jobs, you upset our relationship with the US and others. They want to know that Britain has got influence in the Community. He cannot understand how people fail to see that.

To John Major Europe is not foreign affairs. Maastricht is not abroad. A hundred billion pounds' worth of investment has come into Britain in the last five years, which he claims would not have come here had we not been prominent in the EC – there would have been no Nissan, no Toyota, no great motor factories up in Washington, none of the investment in Wales, none of the investment in Scotland, and we would have been hundreds and hundreds of thousands of jobs short.

He has paid a high price for his convictions, however, and never more so than over the issue of the Social Chapter, which brought the last session of Parliament to a dramatic close before the summer recess of 1993. Tory rebels, voting with Labour in order to try and block ratification of the Maastricht Treaty, brought the Government to the brink of collapse. In the face of humiliating defeat, the Prime Minister played his final card, and immediately tabled a motion 'That this House has confidence in the policy of the Government on the adoption of the protocol on social policy'. Had he lost he would have called a general election, which the Conservatives would certainly have lost.

He was prepared to commit political suicide rather than give in because he believed the protocol would mean fewer jobs here and more in Japan, the Pacific Basin and America.

In Europe unemployment goes inexorably up. Why? Because we're uncompetitive. Our EC unit labour costs in manufacturing rose by 4 per cent a year throughout the 1980s, in the US the increase was 1 per cent a year. In Japan there was no increase at all. As a result, in 1992 average labour costs in manufacturing were 20 per cent higher than in the USA and Japan. It's no coincidence that our share of OECD countries' exports fell by 10 per cent in the 1980s – I think not. I fear we are pricing ourselves out of world markets, and our workers out of jobs.

We need a labour force which is highly educated and trained, well-equipped and well-motivated, but also flexible and mobile. It is not a solution to drive down wages to the levels which exist in Eastern Europe, still less in Latin America or China; nor to return to the industrial conditions of the nineteenth century. That would be ludicrous. But none of us can afford to continue to go on piling additional costs and restrictions on our employers. It's the economics of a madhouse.

Epilogue

NEARLY two years later John Major put his political life on the line for a second time. In the most dramatic, dangerous but perhaps shrewdest gesture of his career he resigned as Leader of the Conservative Party telling his rebellious backbenchers it was time to 'put up or shut up'. They had two weeks to decide whether they wanted him to lead the Party or not.

He had won the day over Maastricht two years before but the carping and the sniping, and outright rebellion in the case of a handful of malcontents, had continued. Determined to follow their own agenda at the cost of the Government's they had become more effective than the Opposition and it was doing the Party a great deal of harm in the country. At the local elections in May 1995 the Conservative defeat had been utterly humiliating, the European elections had been similarly disastrous, and they had lost every by-election since John Major came into office. His fragile majority in the House had dwindled to such an extent that his authority was in serious doubt. He was presiding over a party engaged in civil war that seemed hellbent on self destruction.

Commenting on the Prime Minister's position after the local elections, in which many of the safest seats had fallen to Labour, Tony Blair said the Conservative Party's problem was not John Major. John Major was the one with the problem, and his problem was the Conservative Party.

For not only did the Prime Minister have the poisonous antics of the Euro-sceptics to contend with, the Tory Party itself seemed to have turned into a hotbed of sleaze, corruption and scandal. While the Prime Minister espoused family values and decency in public life, the behaviour of ministers and backbenchers alike provided the newspapers with a regular diet of sensational stories of deceit, sex, greed, bribery and abuse of parliamentary privilege. Two ministers resigned as a result of allegations, and with inquiries under way – the Nolan Committee reporting on moral standards in public life, and Scott on the Arms to Iraq affair – it looked increasingly as though the Conservative Party was doomed to a thoroughly well-deserved fall.

John Major is sceptical about the sleaze. He says,

> I may just be an innocent abroad, but I find it hard to believe these things are just in the province of Conservative Members of Parliament.
>
> The reality of some of the stories was sharply different from what was said. Many were heavily overdone. You can hold things up to the light or the dark, and a great many of those stories were held up to the dark. I am not saying there was nothing in them, but the way they were subsequently developed was a masterpiece of news reporting.

Having been the victim of some highly creative news reporting himself on many occasions, John Major may be allowed a degree of cynicism. Besides, two of the MPs caught accepting bribes were set up by a newspaper; another MP caught in an unusual sexual arrangement also appeared to have been set up. And there were undoubtedly a number of newspaper editors out to inflict maximum damage on the Government and the Prime Minister. When there was no scandal to feast on within Parliament, there was plenty outside it in the newly privatized utilities where chairmen, like Cedric Brown of British Gas, were being awarded embarrassingly high salary increases.

With every shocking story there followed opinion polls which found the Conservative Party at a record low and editorial speculation about whether John Major could carry on as Leader, whether a challenge in November would be inevitable and who might stand as a stalking horse. It was a theme that had surfaced year after year and thus far he had survived the threat. He had performed well at the Conservative Party Conference in October, calmed nerves, and the challenge had not materialized.

In 1995, however, there was a greater chance of a challenge actually being mounted because it would be the last opportunity before the next general election. John Major knew this would mean that the speculation about who would stand, what chance they had of success, how many votes they might expect, whether it would be enough to win and so on would fill the newspapers throughout July, August and September and obliterate the Party Conference, the Queen's Speech and the Budget. He explains,

> It would have dominated the next five months and wrecked some of the biggest shots that were still left. It would have been very debilitating for the Party in the country, very debilitating for the Party at Westminster. That sort of talk had done us great harm in the local elections and great harm in the European elections. I frankly wasn't prepared to let it go on for another five months, I didn't think it was in the Party's interests. I began thinking I guess in May that it might be feasible to bring an election forward, although there were some obvious difficulties.

But it wasn't the first time the Prime Minister had thought of forcing an election. 'I flirted with the idea a year before and for several reasons put it to one side, so it wasn't a wholly novel concept – but it was novel to everyone else.'

He had discussed it the year before with Sarah Hogg and Douglas Hurd, both of whom were against the idea. Sarah Hogg, although no longer Head of the Policy Unit, was one of the first people to be consulted in 1995 when he wanted to do it again. But she was not the first. The first person he talked it through with was Norma.

> I talked to Norma about it – and Elizabeth and James – then I went to the G7 Conference in Halifax. What nobody knew, and we made a great effort to stop anyone finding out, was that I had a terrible pain in the neck at that conference! It was the second vertebra in my neck and extremely painful. I had a physiotherapist coming in two, sometimes three, times a day in order to manipulate it. So I didn't get much sleep which gave me a lot of time to think about this idea really seriously. I discussed it in broad terms with Douglas Hurd on the plane coming back and I talked to Norma again on the Sunday when I got back. By then I had pretty much made up my mind that it was time to decide one way of the other, to put up or shut up if you like.
> When I have made up my mind I don't agonize over it. I

don't lie awake worrying. I just do it. It was the right decision.

Norma was enthusiastically in favour of it. Her view was why didn't I do it before? We don't normally sit down and have serious political discussions, we're not like that, we have far more important things to discuss, but we did discuss this because there was no certainty to the outcome at all, and I thought Norma had a right to have a shout in that decision. We mentioned it to James and Elizabeth too because they have had a great deal of harassment, James particularly, from the media. And if something like that is happening it's awkward for them if they don't know, so we told them. They were both unequivocally in favour. As Elizabeth put, quite succinctly, 'Go for it, Dad'.

I didn't tell anyone at Number Ten. I saw Sarah Hogg and showed her two different sets of statements, one for the press conference and the outline of what I might say to the 1922 Committee. Sarah's a very old friend and I knew she'd give me a frank, non-Number Ten point of view. I also knew she was as safe as the Bank of England to talk to, so I took her mind on it. She didn't say 'yes' and she didn't say 'no', she simply discussed some of the things one would have to consider: What was the likely outcome? How was one going to do it? How would people take it? What would be the cut-off point that made it an unacceptable result and so forth? But Sarah didn't know whether I was going to do it or not.

On the Wednesday night the Prime Minister told one or two members of the Cabinet and after the Cabinet meeting on Thursday morning, at which he said nothing of his plans, he told a few more, but individually, and only a few of them. At 4.15 p.m., after Prime Minister's Questions in the House, he saw the 1922 Committee alone in his room and told them. With the exception of Marcus Fox, the Chairman, with whom he had discussed logistics the day before, his proposed resignation was news to them all.

The journalists had meanwhile been sent over to Number Ten, so that none were hanging around in the lobby of the House of Commons to discover what he had said. After talking to the 1922 Committee he went straight back to Number Ten and into the garden where he made a statement at 5 o'clock which took everyone entirely by surprise. He says,

It was very exhilarating. I knew I would catch them by surprise, the intention was to catch them by surprise and I did, it worked spectacularly well. I was very relaxed about it. There was no certainty about the outcome of the election, but I have never yet gone into an election where my position didn't improve during the course of it. I was looking forward to the election campaign and it was a great deal of fun.

The Prime Minister set up his campaign headquarters in 13 Cowley Street, a house lent for the occasion, where Viscount Cranborne, the Leader of the House of Lords acted as chief of staff. Others in the team included Ian Lang, Scottish Secretary; Tony Newton, Leader of the Commons; Brian Mawhinney, Transport Secretary; and Michael Howard, Home Secretary. Within hours of his resignation offers of help and money were pouring in from both inside and outside Westminster.

I had a good team and the campaign got off to quite a good start. But I wasn't certain I would win with sufficient votes. The argument that I needed to have 165 votes and a 15 per cent lead was technically true but not politically true. I knew it had to be a good deal better than that. Before I announced that I was going to resign the leadership I had set a number that I thought was good enough. Norma and I know what that number was but no one else does, not even my campaign team. If I got the number of votes I had set, I would stay and I would fight on. If I didn't, I wouldn't.

What the Prime Minister also didn't know when he announced his resignation of the leadership was who would stand against him. In the end a surprise challenger came from within the Cabinet in the shape of John Redwood, Secretary of State for Wales, and generally acknowledged as one of the 'bastards' to whom John Major had referred in a leaked off-the-record conversation with ITN's political editor, Michael Brunson, some two years earlier, which was on the day he won the confidence vote on the Social Chapter.

The size of his majority in the House has been a critical factor throughout his premiership, particularly during the entire European debate, and one that has not always been fully appreciated. When Lady Thatcher introduced the Single European Act there was the same strength of feeling about Europe within the

Conservative Party as there is today, but she had such a large majority she was able to guillotine the debate. Without that luxury, John Major has had to tease through every piece of legislation on Europe clause by clause, and make concessions which he would rather not have made. As he said to Michael Brunson,

> The real problem is one of a tiny majority. Don't overlook that I could have done all these clever, decisive things which people wanted me to do – but I would have split the Conservative Party into smithereens. And you would have said I had acted like a ham-fisted leader.

Once the interview was over, but before John Major's microphone had been removed, Brunson asked why he had not sacked the three 'rebel' Cabinet ministers.

> Just think it through from my perspective. You are the Prime Minister with a majority of eighteen, a party that is still harking back to a golden age that never was, and is now invented.
>
> You have three Right-wing members of the Cabinet who actually resign. What happens in the parliamentary party?
>
> I could bring in other people. But where do you think most of this poison is coming from? From the dispossessed and the never-possessed. You can think of ex-ministers who are going round causing all sorts of trouble.
>
> We don't want another three more of the bastards out there.

Perhaps it should have been no surprise, therefore, that John Redwood, an anti-European right-winger, should have opposed him in July 1995, but surprise him it did.

> I was 85 per cent certain there would be a challenge. I didn't think it would come from John, but I wasn't shocked. It wasn't a blow, and in many ways I thought it might be quite a good thing because it would make it a real contest. And so it turned out. I think the fact that he stood was good for the Party as a whole.

John Redwood's campaign was not helped by the ostentatious support of the lunatic fringe of the Party, people like Tony Marlow,

Theresa Gorman and Bill Cash, who by their very presence at Redwood's first press conference immediately cast a shadow over his whole agenda. But there were those who voted for Redwood, not because they liked what he stood for, but because they wanted to force a second ballot which would put John Major out of the running, and open up the field to allow their choice of either Michael Heseltine or Michael Portillo to stand.

In the event it didn't happen. Despite newspaper headlines, such as the *Daily Mail*'s on the morning of the election, 4 July, which declared 'Time To Ditch The Captain', the Captain won a decisive 218 votes over John Redwood's 89. There were 22 abstentions or spoilt ballot papers.

The Major magic that had worked such miracles on the electorate and dumbfounded the pollsters in the 1992 general election returned. It was the boy from Brixton fighting for survival, his whole being suffused with political energy, demonstrating yet again that he is a lot tougher than anyone imagines. Alongside John Redwood he looked confident and positively statesmanlike.

As one of his close advisers says, 'When he is firing on all cylinders he is possibly one of the most formidable politicians in this country.'

The tragedy for John Major is that he can't produce this performance until and unless his back is against the wall.

When he is electioneering he speaks from the heart. He is not constrained by the knowledge that civil servants will be sieving through every statement, and both the media and the Opposition looking for inconsistencies in what he says in an unguarded moment or opportunities to trip him up.

Recalling those two weeks he says, ·

I enjoyed it. Elections are fun. I was relaxed, I wasn't having to be defensive. I could be proactive, I was proactive, I was able to get out. It cleared the air and the response from the Party in the country was remarkable. When we started polling in the constituencies, 96 per cent were rock solid. That's a good deal better than has ever occurred at any other time and indeed the share of the vote I got was higher than in any serious leadership election of either party at any time. So that was a pretty satisfactory outcome as well.

Perhaps more remarkable than the transformation that came over

John Major during the campaign was the transformation in Norma. Gone was all trace of the shy wife thrust into the limelight, reluctantly on parade. It has taken her the full five years to acquire the self-confidence, but acquired it she has and she now is much more relaxed in the role of Britain's First Lady. And she certainly wasn't prepared to stand by and let the Conservative Party walk all over her husband. He says with obvious pride,

> She likes winning. She thought it was time to smack some heads and she enjoyed the sound. 'It's always nice to win' she said afterwards, but it would not have broken her heart if we hadn't. She really would not find her life devastated if I gave up politics, but when I am in politics she expects me to play to win and she enjoys winning.
>
> I think her principal worry was that I might have been a great big sulk for fifteen years if I had lost. There was never any chance of that, but she wasn't convinced. So she was pleased with the result!

Norma has grown with the job and undoubtedly now dresses, looks and plays the part. She has taken on so much political work that she was more than 18 months late in completing her book about Chequers; and in the five years has raised between £3 million and £4 million for charity, mostly Mencap. None the less she still jealously guards a portion of her life for herself and her family and is not prepared to live on a regular basis, as he must, in the impersonal surroundings at Number Ten.

Had John Major lost the gamble and been evicted from Number Ten last July she would not have grieved.

> Norma's not like that. She rolls up her sleeves and gets on with life. She wouldn't have broken up in tears, that is for sure. She doesn't look back. Neither do the children and neither do I.

His tenure of Downing Street was secure, however. The Conservative Party had not chosen 'to jump into the abyss' as the Prime Minister had put it; and with the election over, the gamble won and his authority reaffirmed, John Major reshuffled his Cabinet. But for the loss of Douglas Hurd as Foreign Secretary, who had announced his intention to go long before, he came as close as he had come in five years to the Cabinet of his choice. He moved the weaker elements, distracted the more dangerous elements, and made Michael Heseltine First Secretary of State and Deputy Prime Minister. The newspapers meanwhile, sore at having been ignored, and having yet again misjudged John Major's talent for winning elections, talked of secret deals with Michael Heseltine to secure his loyalty.

John Major denies there were any deals.

I first discussed the concept of Michael as First Secretary of State about a month before I decided to have a leadership election. The concept was a deputy prime minister who would look across the scene and take with him some areas of responsibility and look at presentation and use the particular skills that Michael has, to best community, parliamentary and government advantage. I had thought about it intermittently throughout the previous year. In the end it was my decision to do it and it was done in the reshuffle; there was no hidden deal, no secret demands, no promises of votes, that's all tabloid nonsense.

He protests he is no longer obsessed by what the newspapers write, he has become as he says, 'case hardened', but seeing so many of them proved wrong on 4 July must have been almost as satisfying as winning the leadership election.

Having won he is now determined to move on to another phase of Conservatism, having exhausted, as he says, the old 1979 Thatcherite agenda. The problem of Europe, however, will not go away, but the Prime Minister does feel that at last he is beginning to win the argument and people are starting to see the sense in the line he has been pursuing.

Europe will only survive if it is real and if people in the European countries can see what it means. What they want to know is, 'Are we going to have jobs? Are we going to have peace? Are we going to extend the free market right across central Europe?' If we had done that twenty years ago we wouldn't have had a Bosnia today.

Those are questions that the European politicians ought to be addressing; not wouldn't it be nice to have a single currency and tear up the traditions of fifteen mature nation states that have their own currencies for years. They have been addressing the wrong points. They haven't forgotten the single currency, but the other issues are now beginning to be addressed and I think those will predominate.

To the majority of ordinary people in Britain John Major seems like a man possessed about Europe. The controversy has eclipsed many of the other areas which he holds dear, and which if he had lost the leadership election he would have been sorry not to have been able to carry through.

The peace initiative in Northern Ireland is clearly one. Until a massive bomb in London's Docklands brought the IRA ceasefire to an end, killing two men, there had been no significant violence for over seventeen months – something no other Prime Minister had achieved in the last fifty years.

Nobody thought we would do it. When it started the sceptics were out in force saying, 'It can't happen, it won't happen. He may have got the Joint Declaration but it will go no further.' We had nearly eighteen months of peace, raising everyone's hopes and transforming the position. The IRA's decision to end the ceasefire was disgraceful. But the terrorists will not be allowed to stop the peace process. The people will not let them. The churches, the Americans, the Irish Government are all working with us to try to see the peace process through.

I don't know whether we'll be able to carry it through, but I do know we have got a better chance of bringing peace to Northern Ireland than we have had for generations, literally for generations. I've never let myself be optimistic about Northern Ireland. It isn't all over, there are a lot of hurdles to overcome, but I think they can be overcome and frankly I would rather see it through myself than leave it to someone else.

The relationship with America, a major source of funds for the IRA, is vital, and there was welcome solidarity from President Clinton when the ceasefire came to an end. He refused to see Gerry Adams, president of Sinn Fein, once famously fêted at the White House, and banned him from fundraising during a St Patrick's Day visit.

The Lottery, launched towards the end 1994, is another achievement of which he is proud.

Within a year or two when the Lottery is in full flood it will raise over £300 million in perpetuity for sport, a separate £300 million for charity, a separate £300 million for heritage and a separate £300 million for the millennium fund. Instead of having £30 or £40 million from public expenditure and taxpayers' money they will have ten times as much and can plan to improve provision over a very long period. It will materially improve the quality of life for lots of people. I don't think anyone has realized that yet.

The other achievement I'm very proud of which I think history will give us credit for although nobody else does: we have broken the inflationary psychology of this country in a way not seen since the war. It's been painful and we have borne the scars of unpopularity for doing it, but three years after the recession ended we've got inflation running at an underlying rate of around 3 per cent and wages at around 3 per cent. Even at the height of the recession in the early 1980s wages never fell below 7 and a half per cent – with all the inflationary impact that had.

Not only have we got inflation down and protected savings, we have made British industry competitive in a way it hasn't been for forty years. We are now more competitive than the French and the Germans. We are taking their markets. We've had export records for nine months out of the last fourteen.

Now that doesn't win votes out in the Dog and Bill in the sticks because people would rather have more money jingling in their pockets, but my God it's changing the economic prospects for this country and I don't want to let that slip. Those things matter and I would have missed that if I hadn't been able to see things through.

The prospect of the next general election, however, in May 1997 at the latest, is undoubtedly the most important challenge ahead. Labour under Tony Blair is a very different prospect from the Labour Party which John Major defeated in 1992. He has turned it, on the face of it at least, into a very attractive proposition and one which many an instinctive Tory voter, disillusioned with the bickering and the sleaze within the Conservative Party, might be easily persuaded to vote for.

No one is more aware of the danger than the Prime Minister.

The next general election is crucial to the country because the winner is going to inherit the best economy that any incoming Prime Minister, whether new or previous, has inherited since the Second World War. They will be in a better position to carry out their social ambitions than any incoming government in living memory, so it is very crucial, and I will argue that case very strongly when we get there. I intend to win.

Mr Blair is an attractive political figure to the country as a whole. But what jobs are people like John Prescott, Margaret Beckett, Jack Cunningham and Robin Cook going to have in the Cabinet? What is to be the relationship with the trade unions? Of course you can be tough with the trade unions if privately you give them all they ask for like the Social Chapter and the minimum wage before they ask, but this is all public relations. If you actually ask what is their fiscal or their monetary policy? They don't have one. What is their foreign policy? It is to tack as close to the Government as they possibly can and be slightly pale-blue Tories, pale-pink social-ists and therefore responsible. Look at the way they have had to run away from regional assemblies, to reverse their women-only short list, and change their education and European policy. These are matters that will come into much greater focus as the election looms nearer.

They were matters which were predictably on the agenda last October at the Conservative party conference in Blackpool. The Labour leader had given a dazzling performance to his party faithful at Brighton the previous week, and the Labour conference had been widely deemed a resounding success.

John Major was not to be outdone. Everything Tony Blair promised, he topped. As the *Daily Telegraph* sketch writer, Robert Hardman, observed,

> Labour would scrap the assisted places scheme. Mr Major would double it. Mr Blair promised 3,000 new policemen in five years. Mr Major would do 5,000 in three. If Mr Blair had promised free vanilla ice cream, Mr Major would have pledged raspberry ripple and a wafer on top.

It was one of the best speeches he had ever made: in seventy minutes he managed to claim back conservative policies for the

Conservatives, while establishing his credentials as the ordinary man who was qualified to speak for ordinary people at the bottom of the social pile. The distinction between his own humble origins and Tony Blair's public school education and the irony of the situation were not lost on his audience.

'He exuded a confidence which demonstrated his renewed grip on the Conservatives,' proclaimed the *Daily Telegraph* the following day, not often noted for its support. 'A controlled anger – aimed not just at Labour but at all those who, on personal or political grounds, have belittled him in the past – seemed to give his words an edge that the other conference speeches lacked.'

Speaking with no clever devices, but a simple collection of notes on a rostrum, which gave his speech particular intimacy, he said,

> When I was a small boy my bread and butter was paid for by my father's small business. He made garden ornaments forty years ago and some fashionable people find that very funny.
>
> I don't. I see the proud, stubborn, independent old man who ran that firm and taught me to love my country, fight for my own and spit in the eye of malign fate.
>
> I know the knockers and sneerers who may never have taken a risk in their comfortable lives aren't fit to wipe the boots of the risk-takers of Britain.

It was a touching moment. The Prime Minister looked emotional and quickly put a finger up to his eye. This was a glimpse of the real Mr Major, a glimpse of the passion that drove him, despite the obstacles, from the slums of Brixton to Downing Street.

He now has a number of new people in the team working at Number Ten. Gus O'Donnell, his Press Secretary and friend, left in early 1994 to return to the Treasury. 'He had a career and a young family and I think his wife was quite keen on seeing Gus occasionally!' he explains. His replacement for two years was Christopher Meyer, a career diplomat, then in January 1996 Jonathan Haslam, formerly deputy to both O'Donnell and Meyer, took over as Press Secretary.

Another loss has been Sarah Hogg, Head of the Policy Unit, who now sits on the Government benches in the House of Lords. She was another close friend, but again the Prime Minister is entirely understanding about her desire for a change.

Sarah took a huge amount of often very unfair criticism and flack on my behalf and she had done the job for four years. If she had decided to stay she would have had to go on right through the election and beyond, effectively committing herself to the same job for another three years. That's a long time in somebody's life and she thought it was right to move on and do other things and bring in someone fresh for the next election with fresh ideas and a new look.

The architect of that new look is Norman Blackwell, a former senior executive of McKinsey & Company, an international firm of management consultants, who impressed John Major over all the other candidates because he talked in five- and ten-year spans rather than tactics for the next six months or strategy to win the next election.

I wanted someone who would plan long-term, who would think the unthinkable, have original thoughts and be prepared to think laterally, who had a first class mind but who lived in the real world and knew what it was like. He does all of those things. He's a very impressive man.

The Prime Minister's own input into the development of policy is far greater today than it has been in the past, and Conservative policy is undergoing a more comprehensive overhaul than it has had·in twenty-five years.

I'm concerned about where the next phase of conservativism goes. I'm not prepared to see the Conservative Party turn itself into a right wing rump with no chance of getting elected. That way is folly. We're a centre-right party and we must have our roots in every part of the country, in every income group or we can pack up and go home. That's my sort of conservativism and I'm not going to be shifted from it now.

When the nation at large comes to the next general election it will not tear its soul apart over Europe or any other issue like that. It will ask 'What is going to be best for the education of my children, the employment prospects of my family, the living standards and security of my family and the security of the nation?' just as it always has done.

I am supremely unmoved by opinion polls and predictions.

They are unreal and I dare say they will go on being grisly. But during the leadership election the opinion polls turned round 14 per cent within a week. That tells you a lot about the looseness of opinion and the capacity of the British nation to say 'A plague on all their houses but particularly upon the house of those who happen to be in government for the time being'. It is a different set of questions when they are faced with a hard choice.

Although Labour were able to make some capital out of the Scott Report, published in February 1996, and another Conservative deserted the cause in its wake, followed by a by-election defeat in April; reducing the Government's majority in the House of Commons to one, John Major is confident that he will win the next election. But if he doesn't it won't be the end of his world. The power to get things done that comes with the position he relishes, but the trappings that accompany it are another matter.

Living in Downing Street, having a car, having security, being restrained from doing all the things I like best in the world, I do not enjoy. And anyone who thinks I'm so bound up that life can't possibly go on unless I've got Red Boxes and the Prime Ministership doesn't know me.

On the day I give up politics the one thing you can be absolutely certain about is I will not spend the next ten years wandering around talking to people about when I was Prime Minister. I will be more concerned about tomorrow than yesterday. I will not spend my life looking back either with pleasure or with anger about politics. There will be other things to do.

BIBLIOGRAPHY

Anderson, Bruce, *John Major*, Headline, 1992
Billière, General Sir Peter de la, *Storm Command*, HarperCollins, 1992
Bogdanor, Vernon, *The Ghost of Peel and the Legacy of Disraeli: Conservative Leadership Selection 1902–1990*, taken from *Conservative Party, 1900–1990*, Oxford University Press, 1993
Clark, Alan, *Diaries*, Weidenfeld & Nicolson, 1993
Ingham, Bernard, *Kill the Messenger*, HarperCollins, 1991
Kissinger, Henry, *The White House Years*, Weidenfeld & Nicolson and Michael Joseph, 1979
Lawson, Nigel, *The View From Number 11*, Bantam Press, 1992
Lucas, Jean, *The Wandsworth Story*, WTCA, 1990
Major, Rt Hon John, MP, *Trust the People* (Keynote Speeches of the 1992 General Election Campaign), Conservative Political Centre, 1992
Major, Norma, *Joan Sutherland*, Queen Anne Press/Futura, 1987
Pearce, Edward, *The Quiet Rise of John Major*, Weidenfeld & Nicolson, 1991
Shepherd, Robert, *The Power Brokers*, Hutchinson, 1991
Walker, Tim, *Norma*, Fourth Estate, 1993
Watkins, Alan, *A Conservative Coup*, Duckworth, 1992
Wyn Ellis, Nesta, *John Major*, Futura, 1991

INDEX

Aitken, Jonathan 257
Alison, Michael 118
Allan, Alex 258–9, 262
Amato, Guiliano 259
Archer, Jeffrey 196, 240
Atkins, Robert 3, 97, 112,
   136–7, 165, 238

Baddley, Olive 156, 158,
   238
Baker, Kenneth 133, 211,
   256
Banks, Tony 111
Barber, Anthony 78
Bauwens, Mona 268
Bell, Tim 91, 129, 189,
   192, 197, 198, 212,
   248
Benyon, Tom 99, 107
Bérégovoy, Pierre 261
Black, Bernard 56
Black Wednesday 3, 260–3,
   264, 265
Blackwell, Norman 312
Blair, Tony 299, 309–11
Blatch, Baroness 122, 154,
   156, 238
Blue Chips dining club 97,
   99, 100, 106, 112
Bogdanor, Vernon 252
Boscawen, Robert 118
Bottomley, Virginia 203,
   256, 295–6

Boyson, Sir Rhodes 282
Bright, Graham 100–1,
   195, 199, 220, 226
Bronhill, June 65, 67–8
Brooke, Peter 120, 138,
   256
Brown, Peter 53, 115–16,
   121, 157–8, 194, 238,
   250, 251–2
Bruce-Gardyne, Jock 83, 84
Brunson, Michael 303, 304
Bundesbank 258, 261, 263,
   264
Burns, Sir Terence 178,
   261
Bush, George 205, 215,
   221, 227, 228, 235, 282
Butcher, John 99, 100

Callaghan, James 91, 92
Care in the Community
   150–1
Carey, Peter 54, 57
Carlisle, John 99, 106–7
Carr, Robert 81
Cash, Bill 271
Chaplin, Judith 178–9,
   199, 213
Chequers 108, 237, 238
Chevening 172
Chief Secretary to the
   Treasury 134–5, 139–
   40, 146

Child Benefit 142, 143,
   239
Citizens' Charter 53, 146,
   253, 286–7
Clark, Alan 196, 198, 257,
   278
Clarke, Kenneth 120, 124,
   142, 260, 261, 291
   ambulance strike, 186–7
   apologist for
     Government policies
     257, 278–9
   Chancellor 291
   Health Secretary 126,
     142, 144–6
   Home Secretary 256,
     257
   on JM 121, 144–5, 187,
     201, 203, 294
   and leadership contest
     196, 197
coal pits crisis 273–8
Cockram, Richard 44, 45,
   46
Collins, Tim 241, 245–6,
   247, 250
Composite Rate of Tax
   182
Conservative Party
   current unpopularity
     299
   on Europe 193
   post-war Party 60

Conservative Party
    Conference (1992)
    267, 270, 271, 272
Conservative Party
    leadership contest
    192–3
Conservative Research
    Department 97, 211–
    12
Cope, John 117
Council Tax 232, 256–7
crime 304–5
Crosland, Anthony 56

de la Billière, General Sir
    Peter 214–15, 222,
    223, 224, 225–6
Delors, Jacques 161
Dessoy, Pat (JM's sister)
    8, 12–13, 15, 16, 18,
    19, 21, 22, 24, 34, 36,
    42–3, 47, 67
    on JM 13, 155, 170, 171,
    222
    on JM's political career
    75
    relationship with JM 67,
    170–71
Dey, Tony 72, 76
Dicks, Terry 253
Douro, Charles, Marquess
    of 82, 83, 84
Drew, John 89, 137
Dunn, Bob 282

educational reforms 306
Elizabeth II 258, 259
Elphick, Mary-Jo 84–5
European Monetary
    System 160
Evans, Carys 145, 147,
    148, 150, 151–2
Evans, Gareth 167
Exchange Rate Mechanism
    (ERM) 160, 161, 180,
    181, 258, 260, 261,
    262, 265–6, 292

Fahd, King 215, 222
Falklands War 108–9
Favell, Tony 179
Finings, the 122, 159, 177,
    216
Forman, Nigel 81
Fowler, Norman 121, 123–
    4, 141
Fox, Marcus 261, 302
Fullbrook, Julian 93

Gardiner, Sir George 282,

285
Garel-Jones, Tristan 97,
    112, 119, 203–4, 213,
    233, 234
Geddes, Diana 59, 62
General Election
    (February 1974) 75–6
General Election (October
    1974) 76, 77, 79
General Election (1979) 90,
    92, 93, 94
General Election (1983)
    113
General Election (1987)
    127, 129–30
General Election (1992)
    231–2, 237, 240–53
George, Eddie 261
German, Clifford 89
Germany 236–7, 258, 263–4
Gieve, John 178, 179, 185
Gladstone, William Ewart
    58
Golds, Peter 48, 57, 58, 61,
    62, 70, 72, 75, 81
Goodlad, Alastair 193, 196,
    199
Gorbachev, Mikhail 227,
    234
Gould, Bryan 268
Gow, Sir Ian 218
Graham, Sir Peter 101–2
Griffiths, Brian 186, 213
Gulf War 198, 214–15,
    220, 221–7
Gummer, John 199, 205
Guy Fawkes dining club
    100, 195

Harford, Mike 86, 250–1
Haselhurst, Alan 83, 84
Haslam, Jonathan 311
Hayhoe, Barney 120
Healey, Denis 78, 91
Heath, Edward 2, 5, 75–6,
    90, 99–100, 188, 266
Heseltine, Michael 260,
    261, 305, 307
    coal pit closures 273,
    275, 276–7
    leadership challenge
    190–91, 196, 198, 200,
    201, 202, 205, 206
    Poll Tax and Council
    Tax 212, 232
    Trade and Industry
    Secretary 256, 257
Higgins, Terence 199
Hogg, Sarah 213–14, 251,

258, 264, 301, 311–12
Home Office 105
Hong Kong 164, 256
Howard, Michael 82, 199,
    256, 291
Howe, Sir Geoffrey 91, 97,
    159, 160, 161–2, 163,
    180, 189–90, 193
Huntingdon constituency
    81–2
Hurd, Douglas 139, 158,
    180, 260, 261, 301,
    306
    Foreign Secretary 176
    Home Secretary 162
    and leadership contest
    194, 195, 196, 199, 200,
    201, 202, 203, 205, 206
    and Maastricht Bill 280,
    283
Hussein, Saddam 214, 225,
    226, 227, 228, 229

inflation 178, 181, 236, 309
Ingham, Bernard 142, 167,
    168, 191, 213
interest rates 178, 258, 260,
    262
Iraq, sale of arms to 164,
    300

'Jennifer's Ear' incident
    247–8
Johnson, Dee (JM's
    mother-in-law) 63–4,
    70, 72, 169, 237–8
Johnson, Jo 85, 115, 162,
    169, 208, 238, 249
Jones, Clive 48, 49, 57, 58,
    63, 67, 68–9, 75
Jopling, Michael 109, 110
Juggins, Roger 84, 87, 95,
    113, 114, 129, 135,
    156–7, 195

King, Tom 154, 227
Kinnock, Neil 129, 130,
    234–5, 244, 245, 270
Kissinger, Henry 314
Knight, Dame Jill 72
Kohl, Helmut 215, 229,
    230, 237, 261

Lambeth Borough Council
    49, 50, 52, 53, 54–6,
    59, 71–2
Lamont, Norman 212, 265
    Black Wednesday 260,
    262, 291

criticizes JM's
  leadership 291
and the ERM 266
and interest rates 258,
  260
and leadership contest
  199, 200, 204
personal life 290
returns to back benches
  211, 263, 291
tax cuts 241
Lang, Ian 97, 212
Latimer, Clare 185
Lawson, Nigel 129, 130,
  131–2, 138, 140, 142,
  156
and Child Benefit 143
conflict with Margaret
  Thatcher 172–3, 189,
  193
and the ERM 160, 161,
  172–3, 180
on inflation 236
and interest rates 178
on JM 119–20, 131, 132,
  137
political judgement 179
on the Poll Tax 188
resignation 173, 177
Leigh-Pemberton, Robin
  260, 262
Liberal Democrats 290
Lilley, Peter 82, 138, 199,
  256
Lipton, Marcus 32–3, 54,
  56
Livingstone, Ken 56, 77,
  111, 135
Llewellyn, Edward 246
Lloyd, Nick 197
Lucas, Jean 49, 57–8, 72,
  80
Lyall, Sir Nicholas 97

Maastricht, Treaty of
  calls for British
    referendum 266
  concessions obtained
    139, 233–4, 293
  Danish referendum 232,
    263, 280, 281, 293
  Edinburgh Summit 139,
    293–4
  effect on JM's
    popularity 292
  French referendum 3,
    258, 263, 266
  Labour Party position
    280–81

Liberal Democrat
    position 280–81
Maastricht Bill 232,
  270–71, 273, 279–84,
  292–4
Social Chapter 233,
  297–8
Macfarlane, Sir Neil 198
MacGregor, John 126, 131
Macleod, Iain 33, 58–60
Macmillan, Harold 33, 134
Major, Elizabeth (JM's
  daughter) 73, 90, 122,
  148–9, 183, 184
Major, Gwen (JM's
  mother)
  character 10, 15, 23
  children 11, 13
  death 66–7
  ill health 19, 36, 39, 43,
    66
  marriage 10
  protective attitude
    towards JM 42, 47–8
  theatrical career 9
Major, James (JM's son)
  90, 122, 148–50, 183,
  184
Major, John
  academic qualifications
    31–2, 215
  appetite for work 152
  argument, openness to
    171–2
  at the DHSS 121, 123–7
  attitude to disloyalty
    292
  attitude towards the
    Establishment 114, 153
  banking career 41, 43–4,
    52, 75, 78, 88, 101–2
  birth 13
  Black Wednesday 3,
    260–63, 264, 265, 266
  in Brixton Conservative
    Association 56
  broken leg 46–7, 48, 68–
    9, 70
  Cabinet, choice of 210,
    211, 212–13, 256–7,
    306
  Cabinet, relations with
    209
  Cabinet reshuffles 211,
    306–7
  campaigning style 93,
    94, 243–4, 245–6
  candidate for
    Huntingdon 80, 81,

82–5, 90
  candidate for St Pancras
    72–3, 76–7, 79
  on Care in the
    Community 150–51
  Chancellor 173, 174–5,
    177, 178–83
  charitable work 89
  Chief Secretary 130,
    133–4, 135, 137, 138–
    9, 140–41, 142–8, 150,
    151–3, 154–5
  and Child Benefit 142,
    239
  childhood 7, 15–16, 17–
    19, 90, 183, 184
  children 73, 122, 148–50,
    169, 207
  Citizens' Charter 53,
    146, 253, 286–7
  clashes with Margaret
    Thatcher 118–19,
    154–5, 166
  classless society concept
    202, 253–4
  and the coal industry pit
    closures 273–8
  concern for Norma
    Major 109
  constituency MP 94–5,
    156–7, 217, 250
  conviviality 184, 238–9
  on council house
    privatisation 151
  criticisms of his
    leadership 291, 292
  debating skills 53
  diffidence 116
  dislike of security
    measures 218
  domestic ineptness 70–71
  early interest in politics
    32, 33–4, 86
  on educational reforms
    306
  and the ERM 166, 178,
    180, 181, 265, 266
  and Europe 166, 230–31,
    255, 292, 296–8,
    307–8
  European Presidency
    255
  family holidays 164–5,
    234
  first employment job 35,
    37, 39, 40
  food preferences 88
  footballing interests 17,
    26, 30

Foreign Secretary 158–
60, 162–4, 165–9, 172,
175, 176
future priorities 312
'grey' image 3, 288
Gulf War 214, 215, 220,
221–7
importance of family life
61, 149, 238
inverted snobbery 153
Iraq, sale of arms to 164,
300
Junior Whip 109, 110–
11, 112
on the Labour Party
241–2
leadership challenge
300–304
leadership contest 193–7,
198–206
leadership style 208, 210,
295–6
libel action 185
maiden speech 98–9
marriage 61, 63, 67–8,
70
married life, stresses in
168
mastery of detail 2, 13,
124, 131, 139
Member of Parliament,
elected 94
and Moscow military
coup 234–5
and National Lottery
308–9
on the need for
consensus 289–90
negotiating skills 2, 134,
294
Nigeria, works in 43–6
and Northern Ireland
308
'ordinariness' 112
passion for cricket 16–
17, 26, 30, 45, 88–9,
112, 120–21
personal image,
disregard for 77–8,
287–8
political ambitions 40,
58, 72, 86, 206–7
political heroes 58
political philosophy 53–
4, 121, 312
and the Poll Tax 231
popularity ratings 220–
21, 232, 267
PPS at the Home Office

105
press criticism 2, 3, 160,
215–16, 243, 244,
285–6
Prime Minister, elected
206–7
probity 1
and public expenditure
136, 240
public speaking 38, 57,
271, 272
on racism 52–3
rapport with others 4,
93, 95, 101, 243
on the recession 236
relations with staff 147,
148, 152, 178
relationship with
Margaret Thatcher
153, 165, 176
relationship with women
115, 185, 186
resignation as Leader 299
and safe havens for
Kurds 228
schooldays 7–8, 16, 19,
24–8, 29, 31, 32, 34
and Scottish nationalism
248–9
serves on Lambeth
Housing Committee
52, 53, 54–6, 57, 69,
71
soapbox (1992 election)
244, 245
on social divisions 176–7
stamina 151
supports David Mellor
267–9
supports Norman
Lamont 263
temper 155
thanks Norma Major
publicly 272
Treasury Whip 117–18,
119–20
understanding of social
security system 126–7,
131
working day, ministerial
148, 151
working day as PM 5
in the Young
Conservatives 38–9,
40, 48
see also General
Elections; Maastricht,
Treaty of
Major, Kitty (Tom

Major's first wife) 8,
9–10
Major, Norma (JM's wife)
at Downing Street 108,
220
Budget day (1990) 183
campaigning 76
charitable work 103, 127,
219, 306
children 73, 90, 122, 148–
50, 169, 183, 184, 207
and Downing Street
terrorist attack 218
dread of diplomatic
circuit 159
family background 63–4,
87.
home-making skills 70,
71, 103, 169–70
house moves 73–4, 87,
89–90, 122
on JM as Foreign
Secretary 168–9
letter-writing 74
life in Huntingdon 103,
184, 219
love of opera 62, 65,
103–4
marriage 61, 63, 67–8,
70
married life, stresses in
168
meets JM 61, 62
and politics 79, 108
and press criticism 215,
216–17, 272
on the prospect of JM
losing office 249–50
public speaking 251–2
self-sufficient character
74
teaching career 62, 64,
68, 71
unassuming manner 148
workload as PM's wife
219
writes Joan Sutherland's
biography 104, 127–8,
131
writing history of
Chequers 238
Major, Terry (JM's
brother) 12, 13–14, 16,
18–19, 20, 21, 22, 24,
34, 35–6, 37, 43, 67,
170
Major, Tom (JM's father)
7, 14, 16, 19, 20, 23,
33

American childhood 8
blindness 22, 30–31,
    34
circus career 8
death 39–40
garden ornament
    business 11, 12, 14,
    19–20, 21, 22, 35
high standards 1, 12, 16
ill health 15, 20–21, 34,
    39
Mates, Michael 188, 269
Mather, Carol 118
Maude, Francis 175, 199
Mayhew, Patrick 105
Mellor, David 81, 100,
    199, 201, 204, 212,
    267–70
Meyer, Sir Anthony 190
Meyer, Christopher 311
Middleton, Sir Peter 178
Millar, Sir Ronald 65, 92,
    271
Mitterrand, François 215,
    229–30, 235
Monmouth by-election
    243
Moore, John 120, 140,
    141–2, 143–4, 239
Morrison, Peter 192, 193,
    194, 197
Mulroney, Brian 192
Murphy, Sheila 115

Neave, Airey 91, 93, 218
Needham, Richard 97
Newbury by-election 290
Newton, Tony 124, 126,
    142
Nolan Committee 300
Number Ten Downing
    Street 108, 218, 220,
    259–60

O'Donnell, Gus 152, 179,
    185, 213, 228, 311
Onslow, Cranley 200, 205
Orsich, Alan 52, 75

Parkinson, Cecil 125, 142
Parliamentary Private
    Secretaries 105
Parris, Matthew 97, 283
Patten, Chris 82, 97, 106,
    203, 211, 212, 237,
    241, 254, 256,
    288
Patten, John 97, 100, 203
Pawsey, James 282

Payne, Ken 38–9
Perkins, Bernard 50, 52,
    53, 54, 55, 56, 57
Poll Tax 129, 182, 187–9,
    212, 231
Portillo, Michael 135, 197,
    256
Powell, Charles 165, 166,
    168, 208–9, 214, 221
Powell, Enoch 49
Prime Ministerial role 5

Raison, Timothy 105
recession 235–7, 255
Redwood, John 303–5
Reece, Gordon 91, 197
Renton, Sir David 80, 81,
    82, 83, 84, 86–7, 89,
    94, 127
Ridley, Nicholas 111, 187
Rifkind, Malcolm 203, 259
Robson, Steve 146
Royal Family 107
Rumbold, Angela 106, 107,
    109, 111–12, 125,
    133–4, 186
Rutlish Boys School 19,
    25, 26–7, 28–9, 31, 32,
    34
Rutter, Jill 147–8, 150
Ryder, Richard 199, 261

Saatchi & Saatchi 91, 129
Sandys, Duncan 54, 72
Schlesinger, Helmut 260,
    261, 263
Scotland 248–9
Scott Report 300, 313
Shephard, Gillian 199,
    213, 256
Short Brothers 153–4
Shotton 276
Simpson, Gladys 4, 51, 66,
    71, 88, 107
Simpson, Harry 50–51, 54,
    55, 66, 107
Single European Act 160,
    161
Skinner, Dennis 198, 277
Smith, John 173, 241, 280
Soames, Nicholas 257
South Africa 167–8
Stallard, Jock 73, 77
Strauss, George 57
Sutherland, Dame Joan 62,
    65, 103–4, 128

Taylor, Sir Teddy 101,
    271, 282

Tebbit, Norman 117, 129,
    138, 202, 274, 281
on Europe and the
    Maastricht Treaty
    266, 271, 280
leadership contest 201,
    202
and Margaret Thatcher
    125
on Margaret Thatcher's
    defeat 209–10
Thatcher, Denis 119, 212,
    219
Thatcher, Margaret
alienation of the Party
    193
announces Health
    Service review 142
attacks JM's leadership
    265
attitude to working
    mothers 186
background 2, 100
bullying manner 117,
    154, 161
Cabinet reshuffles 157–8
choice of Cabinet 177–8,
    210–11
clashes with JM 118–19,
    154–5, 166
communicating skills
    221
conflict with Nigel
    Lawson 172–3, 189,
    193
considers JM her
    successor 125
and the ERM 172–3,
    179, 180, 181, 265,
    266, 271
and Europe 160–61, 193,
    271
and the Falklands War
    108–9
favouritism 125
image-conscious 287
leadership contest 190,
    191–7, 205
leadership style 5, 208,
    209
monetary policies 97, 98,
    106
Party leader (1975) 90–91,
    200
political philosophy 212
and the Poll Tax 188–9,
    193
popularity ratings 106,
    187

relations with her
  Cabinet 209, 210
relations with the press
  286
relations with staff 213
relationship with JM
  153, 165, 176
reliance on JM's
  judgement 144–5, 160,
  162
resignation 197–8
on Socialism 92
and South Africa 167–8
treatment of Geoffrey
  Howe 161–2, 189, 193
Thompson, Andrew 84,
  94, 114, 115
Townend, John 282
True, Nicholas 126

Turnbull, Andrew 154,
  197–8
Tyrie, Andrew 120, 130,
  137, 138–9, 178, 179–
  80, 185, 202, 203, 288

Waddington, David 132
Wakeham, John 110, 117,
  119, 131
Waldegrave, William 97,
  106, 110–11, 175–6,
  196, 203, 256, 296
Walker, Peter 54, 55
Wall, Stephen 163, 165,
  168, 174, 228, 262,
  280
Wallis, Barbara 57, 71, 96,
  171–2, 204, 208, 216,
  217, 218, 238

Walters, Alan 173, 265
Warden Housing
  Association 89
Watkins, Alan 176, 180
Weston, John 228
'wet' and 'dry' Tories 98
Whips 110
Whitelaw, Lord, 91, 105,
  109, 132, 142
Widdecombe, Ann 213
Wilson, Harold 76, 79, 91,
  92, 243
Winter, Susan 76–8, 79

Yeltsin Boris 235
Yeo, Tim 213
Young, Sir George 50, 53,
  57
Younger, George 139, 146,
  192